# A History of Monetary Unions

EMU may well be trumpeted as the great economic experiment in monetary union, but as John Chown shows in this superb book, there have been many other examples of monetary unions over the years – some successful, others not so.

In this comprehensive historical overview, the author writes about monetary unions with an admirable completeness and covers such themes as:

- the gold standard and the drama of bimetallism
- nineteenth-century monetary unions in Europe and the world
- EMU and its policy ramifications
- the collapse of the rouble zone and of Yugoslavia
- the sterling area as an accidental monetary union: the contrasting experience of the former French colonies

Written in a readable and often enjoyable prose, *A History of Monetary Unions* combines historical analysis with present-day context. The book will be of great interest to students and academics involved in the study of money, banking and finance. Moreover, it is essential reading for anyone working in the financial sector.

**John Chown** is a partner in Chown Dewhurst LLP, an independent UK and international tax adviser. Another of his books, *A History of Money*, is also available from Routledge.

# Routledge International Studies in Money and Banking

# A History of
# Monetary Unions

**John Chown**

Routledge
Taylor & Francis Group

LONDON AND NEW YORK

First published 2003
by Routledge
11 New Fetter Lane, London EC4P 4EE

Simultaneously published in the USA and Canada
by Routledge
29 West 35th Street, New York, NY 10001

*Routledge is an imprint of the Taylor & Francis Group*

Typeset in Times by Taylor & Francis Books Ltd
Printed and bound in Great Britain by The Cromwell Press,
Trowbridge, Wiltshire

*British Library Cataloguing in Publication Data*
A catalogue record for this book is available from the British Library

*Library of Congress Cataloging in Publication Data*
Chown, John F., 1929–
A history of monetary unions / John Chown.
(Routledge international studies in money and banking ; 21)
Includes bibliographical references and index.
1. Monetary unions–History. 2. Economic and Monetary Union.
I. Title. II. Series.

HG3894 .C46 2003
332.4'56–6dc21

2002031946

ISBN 0–415–27737–X

# Contents

# Tables

# Part I

# The economics of currency arrangements

The principles of monetary union

# 1  General introduction

## Introduction

The main theme of this book is monetary unions, how they are created, and how they fall apart. The first six chapters set out the main principles of various types of international monetary arrangements, briefly citing examples which are to be discussed in more detail. There is a range of economic literature discussing the principles in great depth. I have not attempted to compete with this, but rather to illustrate the great range of examples.

There are two main types of monetary union. 'Type 1' monetary unions are between countries on a gold (or silver) standard, with each currency defined in terms of gold (*or* silver) meaning that exchange rates are already fixed. The collapse of bimetallism, an early 'monetary disunion', confirms that even metallic currencies have their 'exchange rate' problems.

'Type 2' unions are more interesting, where the countries would otherwise have independent monetary policies based on inconvertible fiat currencies: these can be subdivided according to whether or not exchange controls restrict the free flow of capital.

Many 'monetary unions' were simply a reaction to political change, as countries were linked by marriage or conquest, or achieved independence. There are also many examples of countries adopting the trusted currency of a neighbour: what we would now call 'dollarisation'.

### *Monetary union after the Napoleonic Wars*

The concept of 'monetary union' becomes much more interesting when coins (or banknotes convertible into metal) of a particular value are precisely defined by a given weight and fineness of gold or silver.

After the Napoleonic Wars (which themselves included some of the more important early experiments with inconvertible paper currency) there were major type 1 monetary unions within Europe. There were also disunions, such as when the former Spanish empire in Latin America fell apart, and where other newly independent countries followed a wide variety of monetary policies.

By this time monetary arrangements had become more formalised with the concept of 'free minting', when anyone could take gold or silver, in the form of bullion or foreign coins, to be minted into domestic coins without charge, the cost being borne by the state. Given a gold standard *or* silver standard, the value of each currency was defined in terms of a weight of metal, exchange rates were fixed and there was, in general, no question of exchange risk. The traveller from, say, England armed with gold guineas or sovereigns suffered no 'exchange risk' when he travelled to France, but would simply suffer 'transaction costs' of changing his English coins into gold louis (or later 20 franc napoleons). Reminting, though typically by then free of charge, took time and trouble and it was more practical to exchange them with a money changer.

Although the percentage transaction costs were much lower than those imposed by late twentieth-century banks (when the electronic revolution might have been expected to reduce them) they were still worth avoiding. All that was needed was for nations to agree to standardise the weight and fineness of their coinage: there were none of the technical economic problems involved in type 2 unions between countries with fiat currencies, but as in the twentieth century, national politics made the process fearsomely difficult.

### The Latin Monetary Union

The classic example of a type 1 monetary union was the Latin Monetary Union, under which a number of countries agreed effectively to bring the weight and standard of their coins into line with those of France. There were at about the same time other unions: what is now Germany began to rationalise a number of regional coinages in 1837; considerable progress was made, but full monetary union was only really achieved in 1892 after Bismarck had imposed political union. Switzerland, a loose confederation, had long arguments about what national currency unit to adopt eventually resolved by joining the Latin Monetary Union. The various coinages in what is now Italy were again only united following political union.

The Latin Monetary Union could easily have become the basis of what would have amounted to a world money. The gold sovereign was worth 25.2 French francs and could, by a trivial debasement, be reduced to the same gold content as 25 francs. If the French had then replaced their standard 20 franc gold coin with one of 25 francs the two national coins would change hands at par. The Americans, who were returning to a metallic standard after the Civil War, would have been very willing to adjust their own standard so that a 5 dollar gold coin would have exactly the same value as one British pound and 25 French francs. The coinages would have been interchangeable and many other countries would surely have come into line. Why did this not happen? The answer of course is that, then as now, politics and national pride took precedence over economic common sense.

## *Bimetallism*

There was also another and more subtle factor which led to an interesting and complex form of monetary disunion. Although the British were on a gold standard, the French, and therefore the Latin Monetary Union, were on a bimetallic standard which assumed a fixed ratio between the price of gold and silver. Up to a point this ratio had been self-sustaining, but when it collapsed there were widespread repercussions, both in Europe and more specifically in the United States where the 'silver lobby' was strong, and in the Far East and Latin America, which were also wedded to silver. I have never been able to find the quote, but recall that someone once said that 'there are three roads to madness: love, ambition and the study of bimetallism'. It was Hegel who said that 'we learn from history only that men do not learn from history', and this obscure nineteenth-century topic is proving surprisingly relevant to the early twenty-first century.

## *Inconvertible paper money*

The 'golden age of the gold standard' was very short indeed, and even before 1914 there were many examples of countries abandoning gold and silver for inconvertible paper money. In the twentieth century this was to become the norm: during and after the two world wars, many countries abandoned convertibility into gold or silver, and apart from a brief return to gold in the 1920s, each country would have its own paper currency, which it could in principle print at will. Each could, or thought it could, control its own money supply and monetary policy, and exchange rates between such countries could not be fixed.

Paper money creates an obvious inflationary bias and although this temptation was often resisted by monetary authorities, there were many examples of currencies being totally wiped out by hyper-inflation. Many attempts were made to civilise international monetary arrangements, one key debate being between 'fixed' and 'floating' exchange rates, while hybrid versions such as 'crawling pegs', 'managed floats' and others were and are widely discussed.

We need to distinguish between independent inconvertible paper currencies which are partly insulated from each other by exchange controls (much of the world for much of the period from 1914), and those freely traded in free markets (the industrial world in the late twentieth century). The latter are often referred to as 'convertible' in the sense that there are no restrictions on exchanging them into other currencies, but they are 'inconvertible' in the more classic sense that they are not exchangeable into gold or silver at a fixed parity.

There are many examples of smaller countries voluntarily surrendering monetary sovereignty, accepting the policy of a 'big brother', pegging a currency to that of a larger country (the Caribbean islands are interesting examples, having switched their allegiance from the pound sterling to the US dollar). The most formal and convincing type of link involves a currency board, or simply 'dollarising', permitting the dollar (or another currency) to circulate either as legal tender or at least as the *de facto* currency of the country.

### Bretton Woods

The Bretton Woods system was effectively a type of monetary arrangement attempting fixed rates but leaving sovereign states to manage their domestic economies; and with the ultimate, if in principle restricted, right to change parities. During its heyday, when it worked well, most countries were (fairly) successful in protecting their currencies by exchange controls, of which a little more later. The Exchange Rate Mechanism and other earlier experiments with monetary union in the European Common Market had similar characteristics.

### European Monetary Union

European Monetary Union itself is arguably a unique experiment: the only near-precedent for independent countries pooling their control of monetary policy and their right to issue fiat money without first creating a political union is Austria-Hungary.

## Monetary disunion

One of the lessons of this book is that monetary unions can and do fall apart: both supporters and opponents of European Monetary Union will find it well worth studying why and how 'monetary disunions' happen.

Monetary disunion often follows the break-up of a political union, and history offers plenty of examples, painful to the participants but instructive for historians and policy makers alike. The three most instructive examples are the end of the Austro-Hungarian Empire in 1921, the collapse of the Soviet Union and the break-up of former Yugoslavia. In all these cases there was a remarkable variety of monetary experience amongst the successor states.

The American Civil War was caused by the federal government (its powers deliberately limited by the Founding Fathers, but certainly including the sole right to coin money) seeking to impose a social chapter on certain states which were very attached to labour practices to which others (in that case rightly – the parallel is imperfect) took exception. The Confederate states introduced their own currency, which subsequently collapsed (Chown 1994, ch. 27).[1] Post-Napoleon Latin America combined the end of empire and the widespread use of paper money, while the later gradual break-up of the British empire and the sterling area is a fascinating, if undramatic, example of the break-up of a monetary union.

### The collapse of bimetallism as a 'monetary disunion'

The Latin Monetary Union was based on a bimetallic standard, assuming a fixed ratio (15.5:1) between the price of gold and silver, and it broke apart (perhaps unnecessarily, but politics so often overrides economics) when the price of silver collapsed. This event also had its repercussions in the East and Latin America. Nordic Monetary Union began as a 'type 1' union, based on gold, continued formally after currencies became inconvertible in 1914, but again ultimately collapsed.

### The special case of Germany, 1990

German political reunification in 1990 is particularly interesting, being followed by a monetary union on inappropriate terms (the Bundesbank said disparagingly that 'it was a political decision') which had to be corrected by a very tight monetary policy in Germany. This policy being quite inappropriate for the European Monetary System partners who were shadowing the deutschmark, the event created an 'asymmetric shock' leading to the partial collapse of that experiment in monetary union – an example of a union producing a disunion, and a classic case of 'how not to' achieve monetary union!

# 2 The gold standard

An instructive example of a system of fixed exchange rates, and indeed arguably of a monetary union, is the classical gold standard. This had its heyday after the partial collapse of attempts to extend the Latin Monetary Union, and had a surprisingly short life. However, the principles underlying it also apply to fixed exchange rates and monetary unions in an age of paper money, and the analysis in this chapter leads naturally into the arguments about the relative merits of 'fixed' and 'floating' exchange rates, 'optimum currency areas' and monetary unions generally. The collapse of the gold standard is an important example of a 'disunion'.

As explained in Chown 1994, ch. 7,[1] the UK had officially been on a silver standard since Newton's recoinage of 1696, but with the growth of trade, gold became the more important circulating medium. A Committee on Coin, one of many during the century, was set up in 1787, but before it reached any conclusion, the Napoleonic Wars intervened, and the British adopted an inconvertible paper currency: reform of the coinage had to wait.

Action was taken in advance of the 1821 Resumption of Payments, and the UK introduced a formal gold standard in 1816. The sovereign was defined as 123.27447 grains of standard 22 carat (11 ounces or 91.67 per cent fine) gold, i.e. 113.0016 grains of fine gold: silver was given a subservient status. Silver coins, legal tender for no more than £2, were deliberately struck underweight. At market prices a pound of silver was worth 61 shillings (a ratio of 15.46) but was struck into coins worth 66 shillings, a deliberate action to prevent silver coinage leaving the country. This gave some margin against a *fall* in the ratio which was, in the event, enough, but only just, to survive a period of rising silver prices which lasted until about 1870.

Portugal adopted a gold standard in 1854 and Canada in 1867, but the international gold standard only really came into being when Germany adopted gold in 1873, incidentally sealing the fate of bimetallism, and bringing in other countries such as the USA (1879), Austria-Hungary (1892), Russia and Japan (1897). Many large countries were never members. The system broke down in 1914, with a short-lived revival between the wars.

Gold and silver currencies had of course a much longer history, but the history included many debasements, and it was only with the fairly general introduction of free minting in the nineteenth century that travellers and traders could safely assume fixed parities. Under the classic gold standard, each participating country's coinage was defined as a specific weight of gold, banknotes were convertible into gold, and there were no restrictions (and low, if any, costs) on converting bullion into coins and vice-versa. A sovereign, or a US gold eagle, was just a denomination of gold as, in 1999, the deutschmark and the French franc were technically denominations of the euro.

The 'automatic' mechanism was simple in concept, and had indeed been described by David Hume in 1752. Assume a participating country suffers an 'asymmetric shock' (often, in those days, a bad harvest) and for that, or any other reason, internal prices rise. Given that the exchange rate (gold specie parity) is fixed, the change in relative prices means that its exports fall, and its imports rise, causing a balance of trade deficit which results in an export of gold, which (given that gold is the monetary base) means that there is a decline in the quantity of money in circulation. Domestic demand falls, forcing down prices and (through unemployment) wages, until a new equilibrium is reached, albeit at a lower level to take account of the real economic loss from the shock.

This might seem brutal (and often was) but balance of trade deficits could also be financed, again automatically, by capital movements. In the above circumstances tight money would, as part of the process of reducing demand, force up interest rates, and these higher rates would attract capital from other, unaffected, countries – provided that market participants assumed that exchange rates would remain stable, and that the deficit country would not default. Short-term fluctuations could be financed in this way, but countries with deficits resulting from unsound or profligate internal policies would (in principle) be left to meet the problem by a sharp and salutory internal deflation.

There are plenty of examples to show that it did not always work like that (see for instance Panic 1992)[2] but in principle the effect of the gold standard was to maintain equilibrium, and purchasing power parity, by forcing internal prices down or up in response to changing circumstances.

### The gold standard mechanism and fiat currencies

In the more modern world fixed exchange rates, with inconvertible fiat money, can only be maintained if governments (or independent Central Banks) take deliberate action to stimulate or restrain internal demand in response to balance of payments surpluses or deficits. As this history shows, sometimes they did, and sometimes they didn't, but the key difference between the nineteenth and twentieth centuries is that, for whatever reason, it became very difficult actually to reduce money wages. An event which would in earlier times have caused a mild recession and a reduction in wage levels would, in the changed circumstances, cause massive unemployment and a depression on the 1930s scale. The old adjustment process had ceased to work efficiently, and a more flexible exchange rate regime began to look attractive. More of this in the next chapter, but it is first worth noting another feature of the gold standard.

A gold standard, or indeed any other commodity standard, does not, as its more enthusiastic advocates sometimes claim, guarantee stable prices. For prices to be stable, the effective money supply needs to grow in line with the size of the economy, neither more nor less. The stock of gold grows every year as new gold is mined, but the rate of growth depends on gold discoveries. The gold brought home from South America by the conquistadores sparked off an inflation in Spain, with grave long-term damage to that country's economy. During the last couple of centuries, the world's economy has been expanding, and if gold had remained the only available money, there would have been a strict and intolerable limit to economic expansion: a deflationary bias. During the nineteenth century there were important gold discoveries, but more significantly the growing use of banknotes and bank deposits meant that money, broadly defined, became a high and rising multiple of the gold stock.

On this point, Panic (1992, quoting Triffin 1964)[3] says that in 1815 gold and silver accounted for two thirds of the total money supply in the UK, US and France, but by 1913 the figure was down to 10 per cent – but what definition of 'money' was used? Similarly, Davis Dewey (quoted by Kemmerer[4]) says:

> Before the passage of the Sherman Act nine-tenths or more of the customs receipts at the New York custom house were paid in gold or gold certificates; in the summer of 1891 the proportion of gold and gold certificates fell as low as 12 per cent; and in September 1892, to less than 4 per cent. The use of United States notes and treasury notes of 1890 correspondingly increased.

It could be argued that only by a lucky accident did the effective supply of money grow more or less in line with the needs of trade, and there were many, from John Law on, who argued for some 'new form of money' (Chown 1994, chs 22, 23).

The gold standard therefore did not provide the perfect solution, either to the problem of stable prices or that of how trading nations adjust their economies to changing conditions, but had, in the eyes of many, one great advantage. It kept one set of economic decisions out of the hands of politicians.

Indeed, one of the great debates on money over the years has been 'rules versus discretion': a government which has the power to influence monetary conditions and to keep money supply adjusted to the changing needs of trade and commerce can achieve much, if it uses that power wisely. It can also cause great damage if it does not understand that power, or uses it merely to achieve short-term political advantage or to patch up an urgent problem, and history, including very recent history, has too many examples of both to give us much comfort. Even a benevolent and wise government (possibly only an abstract concept) may well find that the issues are too subtle, and the data needed too unreliable, for them to be sure of doing more good than harm.

# 3 Fixed versus floating exchange rates

## Floating exchange rates

Chapter 2 explained some of the advantages and disadvantages of the gold standard, and many (not all) of these apply to fixed rates more generally. The case for floating, or at least flexible, exchange rates, is simple enough, and is based on an adjustment process different from that of the gold standard. If there is a balance of payments deficit, whether caused by an adverse shock or by domestic overspending, the exchange rate will weaken, lowering the relative price of exports and increasing that of imports. This will correct the external trade balance while leaving the country free to use monetary policy to steer between the twin dangers of inflation and recession.

Since the end of the gold standard and the general adoption of inconvertible paper money, currency arrangements between countries have varied enormously. These can range from a completely free float to an exchange rate rigidly pegged to another currency or basket of currencies. There are many intermediate stages. For instance, under the Bretton Woods system (and the European Exchange Rate Mechanism), currency rates were fixed, but could be (and frequently were) varied by formal devaluations and revaluations. Another variant is the 'crawling peg', where exchange rates move regularly and generally fairly predictably in line with differential inflation rates. Although these intermediate approaches have been dismissed by critics as 'half baked', they have often worked surprisingly well. The Bretton Woods system lasted for many years but was then abandoned before the stresses built up within it became too intolerable. In recent years the abolition of exchange controls, and of other more subtle barriers to capital movements, has facilitated the globalisation of capital markets: it has been argued that a really permanent fixed rate (effectively, monetary union) is now the only stable alternative to floating rates. (These arguments, although very persuasive, have been challenged. Figures quoted by Wyplosz (ms)[1] suggest that 'European countries on a fixed-but-adjustable regime have achieved more stability than other countries ... the standard deviation of their effective exchange rate is about half of that observed in the main countries with floating rates.'

## The fixed-versus-floating arguments

The main issue is how an international monetary system adjusts to shocks, and changes in economic circumstances between countries. Studying monetary history puts one's prejudices and generalisations into perspective, but two have stood the test of time:

1 History shows that any long period of living with rigidly fixed exchange rates swings opinion in favour of the benefits of flexibility, while after a period of floating rates, the public starts to yearn for the certainty of fixed rates![2]
2 Whenever politicians and rulers, from Nero onwards, interfere in monetary arrangements for political ends, disaster follows.

### Problems with fixed rates

One example of a fixed rate system was the classical gold standard, and its adjustment mechanism was explained in the last chapter. An inflationary tendency was checked by an outflow of gold, reducing money supply, forcing down prices and (it was hoped) wages.

By the 1930s changing institutions made it more difficult to reduce money wages, slowing up the adjustment process and dramatically increasing the economic damage, notably unemployment. The scale of the 1930s shock was in any case unprecedented, and most of the world was forced off the gold standard. Maintaining fixed rates between the inconvertible paper currencies used today requires the same adjustment to be achieved by deliberate government policies, and can be just as brutal.

### Floating and flexible rates

Floating, or flexible, exchange rates imply a quite different adjustment process. A balance of payments deficit tends to weaken the exchange rate, lowering the relative price of exports and increasing that of imports, thus correcting the external trade balance. The country is then free to choose a monetary policy, steering between the twin dangers of inflation and recession to suit its domestic conditions, letting the exchange rate take the strain of changes in the external balance (in contrast, fixed exchange rates require all participating countries to pursue similar monetary policies regardless of domestic conditions).

Adjustment via exchange rate changes means that money wages do not have to be reduced, although they will fall in value in terms of foreign currency (it was this money wage stickiness which contributed to the 1930s depression). However, if there is a decline in exchange rate (or a formal devaluation under a 'Bretton Woods' type regime) real wages will eventually fall as the price of imports, and exportable goods, rises in line with external prices. If employees can successfully demand and obtain higher money wages to compensate, we are, with a time lag, back to where we started. The benefits of devaluation or depreciation will disappear with inflation, with the added danger that the inflation may require a further devaluation, creating a vicious circle characteristic of Latin American inflations, and to a lesser extent the experiences of many European countries in the 1970s. This phenomenon may be made worse when currencies are influenced by financial and speculative, as well as by trade, flows, and financial markets have a notorious tendency to overshoot.

Floating exchange rates in countries with weak and badly managed economies can create unstable and uncertain markets, and a chronic tendency to inflation. Devaluation (or floating) was never a soft option, and can never remove the need for a government to keep its domestic finances in order. Indeed, it is still sometimes said, as an argument against floating, that any benefit of a depreciating exchagne rate is quickly dissipated in higher inflation. This was (broadly) true in the 1970s, but later experience has been very different.

Devaluations and less formal exchange rate adjustments can work very well indeed in the right circumstances. A classic example is the 1992 UK departure from the ERM, when depreciation was not neutralised by inflation, but caused a healthy economic recovery. The Russian currency collapse of 1998 had a similar effect on real rates, and coupled with a high dollar oil price, created an export boom. Even more recently, the sharp decline in the value of the euro had little impact on the inflation pattern, and caused dramatic changes in relative competitiveness.

Flexible exchange rates combined with a soundly managed domestic economy which is large enough to absorb import price changes without domestic prices and wages following suit (and thus negating the stabilising effect on trade competitiveness) gives the extra dimension needed to enable a country to maintain both its internal and external balance. They work better if the country concerned pursues stable internal policies, controlling money supply while avoiding budget deficits, and such policies should probably be regarded as the desirable and acceptable norm between (but not necessarily within) the major trading blocs of the world.

Where a country has suffered a serious economic dislocation, a new, sound government may need time to establish credibility, and this will affect the choice between floating and fixed rates. Where markets do not believe that the monetary authorities are competent to maintain a stable currency (for instance, when the central bank is under political control), then 'floating' is presumed, only too often correctly, to mean 'sinking'. In such cases one of the two 'strong' forms of fixed rate regime may be more appropriate than floating, at least for a time.

In more advanced countries with a fairly stable currency, the discussion is between 'exchange rate' targeting and 'monetary' or 'inflation' targeting. This has some parallels in emerging economies; Estonia and Slovenia chose different solutions. Barry Eichengreen[3] refers to the Mundell–Fleming 'impossible triad' of exchange rate stability, monetary sovereignty and free movement of capital. A nation can have any two, but not all three.

Another problem with pegged, but potentially variable, exchange rates is the temptation for the country (and international organisations) to engage in 'support operations' which can be, and often have been, disastrously expensive. A successful support operation costs nothing: an unsuccessful one costs the amount of support multiplied by the extent of the effective devaluation. Speculators profit (or hedgers avoid losing) correspondingly. Bordo has suggested (see Wyplosz, ms, on Asia) that the real cost of meeting these crises averages about 10 per cent of GDP, a figure supported by the examples we give later. This does not of course mean a sharp decline in living standards: the cost generally falls on the public sector capital account. As the stakes rise the odds can change dramatically against the authorities as new speculators look for a share of the free ride profit which appears to be on offer. As support funds are exhausted, more funds are deployed in protecting positions against the currency, making disaster (and huge profits for the speculators) inevitable. There is no such danger with a currency board which is self-managing: the economic consequences of an imbalance may be painful, but that is another matter.

# 4 Types of 'fixed' monetary arrangement

## Introduction

The formal monetary arrangements of a country may matter a lot, or a little. Money, as the textbooks tell us, has three functions: as a medium of exchange, a unit of account and a store of value, but citizens do not necessarily use the 'legal' money of their country for all these purposes. There may well be an element of 'choice in currency'[1] and many may prefer to use a 'foreign' currency as a store of value, and indeed as a unit of account. (There are problems: there may be exchange control restrictions, legal tender laws may make foreign currency contracts unenforceable, and the tax authorities will normally require returns to be prepared in domestic currency.) These are individual choices, and it matters little whether the many or the few take advantage of them, but 'foreign' money (often dollars, but in future also the euro) can only become an effective medium of exchange if there is a critical mass in circulation.

Monetary unions apart, fixed exchange rate regimes can simply be a commitment (sometimes credible, sometimes not) by the country to intervene to maintain a rate, but there are two 'strong' forms: currency boards and dollarisation.

## Currency boards

A currency board in principle issues notes and coins against 100 per cent backing by a specific reserve asset, usually the currency of a larger country, such as the US dollar, the pound sterling or the euro. The local currency is sometimes at par with the reserve currency, but may (e.g. Hong Kong) simply keep its value at the time the system is introduced, or be deliberately kept different to minimise political objections to using a 'foreign' currency. The backing assets are normally interest bearing securities, most appropriately treasury bills in the anchor currency.

Currency boards, in their pure form (there are variants), have an obligation to exchange local currency against the anchor currency on demand at the fixed exchange rate, sometimes plus or minus a small margin. Their virtue, and their vice, is that they have no influence over money supply, interest rates or exchange rates, but they do offer a really convincing fixed exchange rate. The general advantages and disadvantages have been discussed by Anna Schwartz,[2] Alan Walters,[3] and others, while Kurt Schuler, Steve Hanke, Lars Jonung and others have been fervent advocates.[4]

There are variations in practice.[5] Some boards permit gold, and long-term bonds, to be included in the backing even though these involve a risk (and opportunity) compared with holding short-term government backed assets. Some only require a percentage backing: examples are the Eastern Caribbean (60 per cent) and Brunei (70 per cent).

The papers of a January 1992 World Bank conference[6] contain much information, particularly on Latin America. They suggest that for a high inflation economy a currency board (or dollarisation) should be compared, not with the effects of doing nothing, but with a potentially credible domestic (indexed?) store of value.

## Dollarisation

Official 'dollarisation' implies that a foreign currency, but not necessarily the US dollar, becomes the *de jure* currency of an otherwise independent country. This can be regarded as a way of cutting out the currency board as middleman, and has a similar economic effect, except for 'seigniorage', a key point discussed below. The best known example is Panama.

Unofficial dollarisation is rather more common: Liberia used the dollar officially from 1944 until 1986 when it adopted its own currency. This depreciated sharply, while the US dollar continued to be widely but unofficially used. Cuba used the US dollar exclusively from 1899 to 1914: from then until 1950 the dollar remained a parallel legal tender currency. Kurt Schuler (a valuable source of more detailed information) lists twenty-nine dollarised countries at the beginning of 1998: most are obvious quasi-colonies or dependencies, interesting exceptions being Eritrea (Ethiopian birr) Liechtenstein (Swiss franc) and Andorra (French franc and Spanish peseta – which presumably implies no legal tender law.) There are earlier precedents, discussed in Chapter 7, while dollars are widely used in Latin America, Israel and the former Soviet Union, with the deutschmark and its successor the euro, being popular in Eastern Europe.

Schuler[7] has suggested that dollarisation is appropriate when a country's central bank has performed poorly. He makes an intriguing though disputable point:

> In contrast to the way economists think about steel or shoes or sugar, when it comes to currency the first question they ask is how to achieve what the *producer* – the government – wants instead of how to provide what *consumers* want. Absent restrictions that force people to use bad currencies

such as the Russian ruble, the Indonesian rupiah, or the Mexican peso, most people would cease doing so.

The first sentence may be true of some economists but certainly not all – and how would he explain the frequently observed persistent use of weak local currencies even when there are no effective prohibitions? A similar argument can be made for currency boards, on which Schuler and others[8] had enthused earlier.

## Gresham's Law

At this point it is inevitable to ask 'what about Gresham's Law?' This is popularly expressed as 'bad money drives out good', whereas a currency board or dollarisation implies that good money is predominating over bad. This paradox is only apparent. No definitive statement by Gresham of his 'Law' seems to have survived, but the Law, properly understood, applies only if government succeeds in requiring its citizens to accept the 'bad money' at an *effective* fiat value. Economists use a more precise statement of Gresham's Law, for instance:

> Where by legal enactment a government assigns the same nominal value to two or more forms of circulatory medium whose intrinsic values differ, payment will always, as far as possible, be made in that medium of which the cost of production is least, and the more valuable medium will tend to disappear from circulation.[9]

If the 'bad money' becomes discredited, merchants and other citizens will cease to use it and will prefer a sound alternative, even if it is 'foreign'. In this case 'good money drives out bad'; as with unofficial dollarisation.

## Problems with currency boards

There are two main economic problems. First, there are difficulties with fixing the rate. Second, banknotes, backed by currency board assets, are only a small part of money supply. Bank deposits are only backed by fractional reserves: over-banking is in principle checked by prudential considerations. Estonian and Lithuanian currency boards have explicitly backed commercial bank deposits at the central bank, but in most cases there is no central bank and the commercial reserve asset is the board's note issues.

A currency board also needs sound administrative arrangements and credibility, particularly where confidence in the old currency has collapsed. A country also needs foreign currency reserves to initiate a currency board: although this was no problem with an old-fashioned 'colonial' currency board it could be a serious one for a country urgently needing to create a sound currency.

### Problems with rates

There is a risk of catching the 'diseases of the anchor currency', particularly serious if this is of a country with which there is no close trading relationship. It may not form part of an 'optimum currency area', as Hong Kong's break with a sterling link in 1974, followed by the introduction of a dollar-based currency board in 1983, illustrates.

It is also technically very difficult to fix an exchange rate at precisely the level which produces a purchasing power equilibrium. Indeed, given that the exercise will, in many cases, be undertaken at a time of low confidence in a currency, the mere fact of restoring confidence will often mean that the original rate will prove to have been too low. 'Inflation' may therefore appear to continue, but this may simply reflect a once for all adjustment to a new reality.

For instance, the Baltic states Estonia, Latvia and Lithuania were quick after the collapse of the Soviet Union to reassert their independence, and introduced their own currencies. All three chose, in different ways, a pegged currency approach, but their subsequent experiences were unexpected: prices continued to rise sharply for some years, and the interest rate structure remained substantially above Western levels.

Milton Friedman,[10] in a classic paper, compares Chile and Israel: 'identical policies, opposite outcomes' (the policies followed fell short of formal currency boards, but the same principles apply).

### Do banks create money, and if so, so what?

Another weakness of the currency board mentioned above is that it normally only guarantees 'high-powered money'. When Hong Kong joined China there was a perceived danger of a run on the currency. A holder of Hong Kong dollar notes had the undoubted right to convert these at the fixed rate into US dollars, and the board held reserves which were more than adequate to meet all claims. However, 'money supply' in an advanced economy is dominated by bank deposits, and bank deposits are backed only by a fraction, perhaps 10 per cent, of banknotes or deposits with the central bank. This was not a problem with early currency boards, but has become one in countries which need to restore both an acceptable currency and a recapitalisation of the banking system. In Hong Kong, in normal circumstances, a holder of local currency deposits could readily convert these into Hong Kong dollars, but in a crisis might have to exercise two separate claims, first demanding Hong Kong dollars from the bank and second, converting the notes into US dollars. Reserves being adequate, there was no problem with the second claim, but an attempt to hold the currency against a major run would have brought down the banking system. There was never any real danger of this in Hong Kong, although the problem was widely discussed in that context. It did become a problem in Argentina, which was forced to limit withdrawals from banks, creating a two-tier market.

### Exiting a currency board

Many countries have abandoned currency boards in favour of central banks with more discretionary powers, and countries considering a currency board solution certainly need to be assured that it can be terminated. An 'honest' exit would require the outstanding notes to be converted into the backing currency, but issues could cease and they could be replaced as legal tender by something else. Exit strategies are discussed in an IMF 1997 paper.[11]

In 1914 Argentina abandoned its gold-backed currency board following an economic recession, a decline in exports and a financial panic caused by the European war. Financial institutions were closed for eight days, and gold exports were prohibited. Backing was reduced to 40 per cent, liquidity was increased and the peso declined in value. A new board was set up in 1927, but was abandoned by presidential decree in 1929 to avoid a sharp deflation.[12]

The Malayan Currency Board was replaced in June 1967 by the Singapore Board of Commissioners of Currency, issuing notes and coin fully backed by sterling, and by the Bank Negara Malaysia, (established 1958), which began to issue gold-backed ringgits. Following the floating of the pound in 1972, both boards pegged their currencies to the US dollar with an IMF approved wide band of 4.43 per cent. In February 1973, when the US dollar devalued against gold, both currencies reverted to a gold parity, but in June 1973 they floated, ceased to be interchangeable, and initially strengthened against the dollar.

## Seigniorage

The difference between a currency board and a dollarisation is that a currency board country collects the seigniorage. Printing money which is accepted in general use generates a profit to the issuer. 'Seigniorage' historically meant the profit accruing from minting coins, which were generally valued in trade at a legal fiat value representing a small (convenience) premium over gold or silver bullion value,[13] but in the modern sense, is the profit the central bank makes from persuading the public to accept printed pieces of paper as money. In a stable Western type economy this profit is simply the interest, amounts to at most about 1–1.5 per cent of GDP, and was for many years little discussed as a source of revenue.[14]

In an inflationary economy the economics are far more complicated and the crucial issue, famously identified by Philip Cagan in his analysis of hyper-inflation, is that a government can always extract some extra seigniorage in the short term by inflation, although at the cost of making its currency less attractive and thus reducing its future seigniorage revenues. When a country has suffered hyper-inflation and lacks a proper monetary base there is an opportunity, in effect, for creating a new interest-free loan equal to the amount of currency needed.

In the late 1990s there were some $250 billion of US dollar bills in circulation outside the US, 70 per cent by value being in $100 bills, a denomination little used domestically. Holders were effectively making an interest-free loan to the US government which earned seigniorage (saved borrowing costs) at a 4.5 per cent treasury bill rate of about $11 billion per annum.

In contrast, a country which adopts a currency board backed (e.g.) by US treasury bills can capture the seigniorage. This is the main motive in small territories such as the British Channel Islands and many West Indian islands.

There is a disadvantage for the currency-issuing country: the more dollars there are circulating abroad, the more difficult it is accurately to monitor US domestic money supply.[15] The first currency boards were set up precisely to avoid this problem. At the beginning of the twentieth century the amount of British silver coins (which, unlike the gold, contained less silver than the face value would indicate) circulating in the West African and other colonies (where gold was little used) was on a scale such that it was feared any major return of them (e.g. because of a local recession following a bad cocoa harvest) could have an adverse effect on the UK monetary system. The West African Currency Board was therefore set up in 1912 to issue coins and notes which would only circulate locally. In 1997 the then new Bosnia Currency Board was described as 'de-dollarisation'.

# 5 Monetary unions

## Introduction

There are plenty of examples of countries choosing to adopt the currency of another, but true monetary unions between otherwise independent sovereign states are rare. A country with a currency board simply accepts the monetary policy of the reference country, and does not expect to have any influence on it.

A true monetary union has most of the advantages and disadvantages of the 'hard' forms of fixed rates discussed in the last chapter, but with important extra features.

The member states have to give up the right to issue money, and will no longer have control of their own monetary policy, this being delegated to a joint central bank or other issuing authority. How is this body to be controlled, will it be answerable to all of them and, if is to pursue policies in the interest of all members, how will it balance rival claims and needs?

How will seigniorage will be shared, and will the joint central bank be able to operate as a lender of last resort?

A full monetary union has many advantages, will achieve greater savings in transaction costs than the alternatives, and will stimulate trade, and hence prosperity. Against this, the political and constitutional problems are greater: specifically (as the Austria-Hungary example shows) there is the problem of monitoriting the debt policy of the individual members, and breaking up a formal union, while certainly not impossible, is more painful than opting out of a currency board.

The main disadvantages accrue from the loss of monetary sovereignty, and the key issue here is how individual countries within a union can adjust to economic changes and specifically to 'assymetric shocks'. Will the creation of a union make such shocks more, or less likely? Generally the benefits must be weighed against the costs on the facts of a particular case.

## Optimum currency areas

Throughout history much has been written arguing, often passionately, for or against particular monetary unions, and indeed on monetary disputes of all kinds. Studying these from a broad, historical perspective shows that while there is no general and universal answer to these questions, there are some underlying issues and principles.

There is now an enormous literature on 'optimal currency areas', and nearly all contributors refer back to Mundell's classic article.[1] The actual article reads as somewhat dated, and Mundell himself has had much more to say on the subject since it was written. For instance, in 1961 he asked 'Should the Ghanaian pound be freed to fluctuate against all currencies or ought the present sterling-area currencies remain pegged to the pound sterling?', a question long since answered, and he expressed his doubts about the Canadian 'experiment' with floating, which has so far survived the article by forty years. His main example makes the implicit assumption that there is a simple trade-off between inflation and unemployment, a view long since discredited as an over-simplification.

Against this, he was well ahead of his time in his comments on the Common Market, a subject on which he still expresses strong views. Although he cites James Meade as saying that the conditions for a common currency do not exist, i.e. that the then Six, now the core countries, were (in 1961) not an optimal currency area, he adds (this time citing Tibor Scitovsky) that a common currency could actually help create labour mobility and the other conditions needed for one to emerge. Not all the seven key factors he lists in his conclusions seem particularly relevant today.

Since his much cited 1961 article, Mundell has made many contributions to the debate. One I found particularly interesting (although I wasn't there) was a talk at a 'Conference on Optimum Currency Areas' at Tel Aviv University on 5 December 1997, in which he describes his career and the development of his thinking. He worked closely with two advocates of floating: Meade, 'a liberal socialist, who saw flexible exchange rates as a device for achieving external balance while freeing policy tools for ... national planning objectives', and Friedman, a 'libertarian conservative' who wanted to get rid of controls. In 1966, though, he 'crossed the Rubicon' and distanced himself from the 'floaters', and his writings since then have shown a strong bias towards 'fixing' and bigger and better monetary unions. Later in his lecture he asks, 'Why not a monetary system for each continent? Or civilisation?'

The key factors are:

- Wage and price flexibility
- Labour mobility
- Degree of inter-regional trade – is the group of countries fairly self-sufficient in both economic and financial terms?
- How big a role does government play in the economy?

## Practical economic benefits of monetary union

The most obvious direct benefits of membership of a monetary union are the saving in transaction costs and the elimination of one particular financial risk – that of exchange rate movements.

In the modern world at least, the larger component of what business accounts would record as 'foreign exchange losses' arise not from fluctuations but from transaction costs, including direct and explicit bank charges. There are other costs, such as dealing spreads in foreign exchange and the loss of interest arising from delays in money transmission, whether resulting from inefficiency or deliberate policy by the banks, who benefit by 'warming their hands' (i.e. earning interest) on money in transit. Such costs have actually increased over the past century in spite of the benefits potentially available from modern technology. It will be interesting to see whether, after the full introduction of the euro in 2002, banks will find a way of maintaining these high costs within the eurozone.

Lower payment costs have the indirect benefit of stimulating cross-border trade, while the elimination of currency risk (and the complications of accounting in more than one currency) will stimulate cross-border investment. Even if transaction costs could be substantially eliminated, the unified common currency has one important advantage over fixed rates in that price differentials between countries are transparent, enhancing competition. A paper by Frankel and Rose[2] (August 2000) comes up with some surprisingly optimistic conclusions on the beneficial effect of currency unions on the long-run level and rate of growth of economies, arguing that currency union stimulates trade which in turn stimulates output. Currency unions, they show, promote bilateral trade and open economies with, they say, no 'trade diversion' away from non-members.

## The adjustment process

The main relevant problem has already been discussed in the 'fixed versus floating' arguments. How likely are individual members to be subject to asymmetric shocks, and, given that the exchange rate adjustment mechanism will no longer be available, how effectively will the 'gold standard' type procedures work? A monetary union actually offers more scope than a less formal fixed exchange rate for a good adjustment mechanism, and the commitment to a union expected to be permanent will, of itself, encourage policies to converge.

Mundell's classic 1961 paper cites a (now rather dated) example of how equilibrium can be restored if, for whatever reason one country in a union is suffering from a depression while another partner in the union is overheated. What tools are left to member states: do they remain free to use fiscal policy, regulation and the level of social security benefits as a corrective mechanism?

If money wages are flexible, unemployed workers in the deficit countries will moderate wage claims, while such claims will be encouraged in surplus countries in excess demand. This will cause a relative deflation, restoring equilibrium albeit at a lower level. This of course is precisely what did not happen in the 1930s.

Can workers in a relatively depressed country cross frontiers in search of work, relieving labour pressures in 'boom' countries? Monetary union is obviously more likely to work if legal barriers or fiscal penalties have first been removed, but even if workers are free to move, will they be willing? The fact that wages are expressed in the same currency both sides of the border obviously helps transparency, but are there language or cultural barriers to movement?

If neither of these two mechanisms work, the countries suffering from the shock will have a depressed, and its neighbours an over-heated, economy. Exchange rates cannot by definition take the strain and there is no real equivalent to the specie flow mechanism of the classical gold standard. There is a single issuing authority for the union and no real weapon by which an individual member state can affect interest rates. Within a Bretton Woods type fixed 'arrangement', each country could to an extent pursue separate monetary policy inducing capital flows but as indeed the example shows, the adjustment actually becomes harder to achieve if the fixed rates become more credible and if transactions cease to be inhibited by exchange control or differential financial and prudential regulation. (There is a fourth mechanism, fiscal transfers between member states, which is important in the United States but which would require a substantial centralisation of taxing powers within the European Union.)

Another problem discussed in the literature stemming from Mundell is the effect of differential preferences for inflation. Moderate inflation can be a source of seigniorage revenue to a government and an alternative to taxation. Both inflation and taxation impose a cost on the private sector of the economy and this cost is inevitably higher than the yield of taxation. As discussed in the literature, a rational tax system (in my experience, as a tax practitioner and policy adviser, an abstract concept) pushes each revenue-generating technique to the point at which the marginal costs to the economy per unit of revenue raised are equal. The trade-offs are different in different countries, but if they are members of a monetary union the common monetary policy will mean that some, and possibly even more, will be working at a less than optimum trade-off. This is a cost of monetary union.

It is interesting that the recent advocates of unions between Canada and the United States, and between Australia and New Zealand, have explicitly stated that monetary union would not mean the harmonisation (still less the standardisation) of taxes and social security benefits, while some in the European Union argue that monetary union makes tax harmonisation inevitable, rather than dangerous (I have discussed this issue elsewhere from the point of view of a tax specialist).[3]

Chadha and Hudson (1999)[4] discuss thirteen unions meeting their definition, beginning with that between England and Scotland, of which six (now all unitary states) still survive, while Mica Panic[5] draws comparisions with the classical gold standard.

All these issues are really only relevant to type 2 monetary unions, of which possibly the only pure examples are Austria-Hungary and the European Monetary Union. I argue, though, that the collapse of bimetall-lism, creating major diversions in exchange rates between the 'gold' and 'silver' countries, has many lessons for us, and that the sterling area was an 'accidental monetary union' which was taken apart mainly, but not entirely, painlessly.

# 6  Exchange control and currency reconstructions

## Introduction

This chapter briefly discusses two subjects, which, while not central to the main theme, recur throughout the story.

Peace-time exchange controls were first introduced in the 1930s in Germany, Austria and Hungary, but inevitably spread more widely on the 1939 the outbreak of war, and persisted for a surprisingly long time after its end. They are relevant to our story mainly because the controls, by preventing the free movement of funds across borders, hindered the adjustment process so that exchange rates could remain out of line with market realities for a long time. In the absence of controls, Bretton Woods would have undoubtedly broken down much earlier that it did.

Also, during the postwar period, many currency reconstructions were undertaken for various reasons, sound and unsound, and these also prove relevant.

## Exchange control

Although by the end of the twentieth century exchange controls had virtually disappeared, at least in industrial countries, they have had a major influence on development of international monetary arrangements. Exchange controls limit the right to convert one currency into another, and in their extreme, totalitarian, form can create a siege economy, reducing the currency to mere coupons for domestic use. In this form they are obviously incompatible with monetary union or cooperation outside the area under political control.

For a long time after 1945, Bretton Woods dominated monetary arrangements, and during the long transition from wartime controls on all international transactions to free multinational payment arrangements, exchange controls of a more relaxed form played an important role in the industrial world. Their supporters believed that they protected national reserves while permitting reasonably free and flexible international markets, a feat of juggling at which the Bank of England was particularly adept.

More recently it has been argued that controls may be needed to check allegedly destabilising movements of 'hot money'.

Those of us who argued for the early abolition of controls pointed out that they increased the delay between politicians making a bad economic decision and its inevitable consequences to the point at which the electorate missed the connection between cause and effect – or the politicians had been moved on anyway by the electoral process!

Residual controls, so long as they continued, made it easier for various forms of quasi-fixed exchange rate arrangements, such as Bretton Woods, to continue, but when they were eventually abolished it soon became clear that 'soft' fixed but moveable exchange rates were almost impossible to sustain, and that 'hard' forms, including monetary unions, were the only real alternative to floating rates.

## A classic analysis of exchange controls

Much has been written about theory and practice of exchange control but possibly the best account is still the classic work by Howard Ellis,[1] substantially completed before the outbreak of war in 1939, and which discusses controls in Austria, Germany and Hungary. His analysis reads well even to a later generation with a far wider range of experiences to study.

Ellis divides exchange control measures into five major types, 'arranged in order of severity, that is according to their departure from the character of a "liberal" international system wherein payments are free':

1   controls aimed 'merely to eliminate speculative activity and sharp variations in rates'. He includes temporary measures taken at the time of the pound and dollar devaluations in 1931 and 1933 in this category, but later they became more common. Ireland, in 1992, used residual and dormant controls to postpone exit from the Exchange Rate Mechanism.
2   'protection against loss of value ... through capital flight' without any restrictions on trade or implication that the exchange rate was other than in equilibrium. This assumes, in effect, that citizens want to move their currency because of political fears rather than distrust of the currency as such. There are many examples in the early postwar period, and more recently in South Africa and the former communist states.
3   The 'country sets official prices upon the foreign exchange and tolerates no other quotations'. Ellis sees this as merely 'to reassure the popular mind which is prone to identify exchange depreciation ... with outright inflation'. 'Money illusion' still persisted in his day, but after the postwar inflations the 'pound in your pocket' argument became unconvincing.
4   Exchange controls imposed where the real equilibrium price is (because of differential inflation or other factors) already below the official parity. This is an alternative to devaluation, and a theoretically possible

response to asymmetric shocks within a quasi monetary union or other system of fixed exchange rates.

5   His fifth type is exchange control which is 'perverted to a weapon of commercial policy', deliberately favouring particular industries or activities (in his day often rearmament) and degenerating into 'shameless partisanship regarding particular vested interests at home'.

Ellis is least interested in his type 1 as being technical and transient, but it has been important in more modern times, and has been suggested and occasionally implemented, even in free market countries attempting to operate systems of fixed exchange rates and finding they are thwarted (as they think) by speculators.

The substance of Ellis' book consists of three chapters dealing respectively with Austria, Hungary and Germany, and there is much in these for those interested in war finance or reactions to the great depression.

## Currency reconstructions

Monetary unions are a form of currency reconstruction in that one currency is replaced by another. There are many other cases, particularly in the postwar period, where, for various reasons, one currency has been replaced by another.

On becoming independent, or after a political change, countries generally issue new banknotes and coins and sometimes change the name of the currency. There may, at least at first, be no change of substance, and the new currency remains at par with the old. Others are examples of 'disunions', associated with monetary as well as political independence. Former British colonies often began by simply issuing new notes and coins, retaining the sterling link, but later switched to an independent currency policy.

After a period of inflation countries often 'drop noughts' so that (for instance) one new unit replaces 1,000 old. This may or may not signal the end of inflation. Hyper-inflations require the issue of a competely new currency. The introduction of a decimal currency system in the United Kingdom and elsewhere required new notes and coins, but had no substantial effect on monetary arrangements of a country.

Sometimes a dramatic reconstruction is needed to deal with potential inflation which has been suppressed by wartime or other controls. At the end of the war in 1945, people in many European countries had cash, but there was little to buy and prices were controlled. Normal incentives needed to be restored, and simply to remove price controls would have led to a runaway and probably uncontrollable inflation. In Germany, Belgium and elsewhere it was decided to wipe out surplus purchasing power through an exchange of banknotes. The resulting confiscation was arbitrary rather than just, but the exceptional situation called for drastic surgical measures. Both were successful, as was the much later experience of Poland. Russia and some other ex-communist countries were less lucky.

### Non-monetary motives for a currency exchange

Currency exchanges give an opportunity for partial confiscation, or to check the activities of black market operators, tax evaders and money launderers. Sometimes, indeed, one of these may be the main but possibly unstated motive. Historians need to be aware of these side effects, lest they misinterpret what appear to be odd quirks in the data.

The exchange may result in, or contribute to, a capital levy, depriving note owners of a proportion of their wealth, or converting it into a forced state loan. The examples of Belgium and Germany are a special case of this, but there are many other examples, including Poland, Cuba, Romania, Israel, Indonesia and the USSR. As such a measure will only affect owners of a certain kind of wealth, corresponding action will generally be taken on bank accounts, private debts, government and other securities and insurance policies. Owners of land and other visible assets can be dealt with fairly easily, but owners of gold, and foreign assets (including currency and overseas bank accounts) and hoarders of foodstuffs or commodities may escape.

A currency exchange may be designed to bring 'black' money into the open. Notes are declared obsolete and no longer legal tender, and are called in to be replaced. Those wishing to exchange an amount defined as 'excessive' would be required to explain how they came by it. This is, to an extent, a by-product of any exchange, and owners of large hoards of DM and other EU currencies are said to be having to work hard on the run-up to the introduction euro notes. In that case they had plenty of notice, and for the technique to be effective it has to be very short-notice and unexpected. Even then, the haul will be limited in an exchange-control-free world, and although the tax net may be somewhat widened, it still leaves the more sophisticated untouched.

# 7    Some early history

Most of the cases of monetary unions and other international arrangements discussed in this book date from after 1800, but it is interesting to look briefly at some early examples. Some of what might be described as monetary unions (and disunions) were simply a reaction to political change, as countries were linked by marriage or conquest or achieved independence: coins were a potent symbol of sovereignty.

## Early 'dollarisation'

There are many examples of independent states deliberately copying or shadowing the currency of a neighbour: Charlemagne, the first to divide a pound of silver into 240 deniers or pennies, imposed this system on the countries he conquered, but this sound money did not long survive him. He never conquered the six kingdoms which were eventually to be united in 973 to form England, but they adopted the system voluntarily. Indeed, Offa of Mercia (757–96) may have introduced the 'penny' into England, copied by neighbouring kingdoms, even before Charlemange or his father Pepin. Æthelstan, king of Wessex 924–39, introduced the first law ('Statute of Greatley') standardising the production of coins,[1] and as he styled himself 'King of all Britons' may have attempted to achieve monetary union. This had to await political union: in 973 Eadgar, first king of a united England, introduced a currency reform, based on the principle of a recoinage every six years to remove worn coins from circulation. This survived the Norman Conquest, and the general principles were retained, with only minor reductions in value (leaving aside the debasement of Henry VIII), until relatively modern times.

During the late Anglo-Saxon period, this sound English coinage was widely copied in Scandinavia, Viking Ireland and Bohemia, with a few examples in Northern Germany.[2] Initially these imitations contained the full weight in silver, but once the public accepted that the 'English' style coins gave honest value, their trust was often abused and the coins were debased.

## England and Scotland

When Scotland introduced its own coinage in 1136, coins were struck to exactly the same weight and silver content as those of its English neighbour, borrowing credibility but retaining seigniorage. The coins had a distinctive design (king's head in profile instead of full face) stressing Scottish sovereignty. During the next few centuries the silver content of the Scottish coins fell relatively to the English, and after the Union of the Crowns of England and Scotland in 1603, a proclamation of 1605 'fixed' the shilling Scottish at par with the penny English, i.e. 12:1. The metallic content was in the ratio of about 13:1, so there was a slight 'subsidy' to holders of Scottish money (Chown 1994, ch. 3).[3] Full monetary (and political) union was only achieved in 1707, with the Act of Union. 'Fiscal policy' was then already an issue. In return for Scotland handing over its excise receipts, used to pay interest on the English national debt, the Act provided that England would pay Scotland the 'Equivalent' – a precise sum of £398,885.10s.0d, £100,000 in cash ('moving in twelve wagons with an armed guard') and the rest, to the disgust of the Scots, in exchequer bills.[4]

The history of metallic currency is in fact riddled with examples of cases where coins changed hands at a 'fiat' value in excess of the (often debased) intrinsic value of the metal, generating seigniorage for the issuer and, in many cases, an opportunity to cheat. During these earlier periods there was a common pattern of the continual debasement of a particular coinage. Eventually, when there was a ruler wise enough to recognise the needs of trade, this was corrected. Sometimes a new, sound, coinage such as the silver groat or the gold florin would be introduced, but more often (particularly if the initiative came from merchants rather than rulers) by adopting a sound foreign currency of a known and guaranteed weight of silver or gold. There are plenty of examples, such as the Maria Theresa dollar, the trade dollar, and indeed the gold sovereign, the Spanish peso and the Venetian zecchino, trusted coins used far beyond the issuing country, and of 'trade dollars' deliberately struck for this purpose. Some cases could be regarded as embryo 'monetary unions' in the sense that a number of states might have a common gold- or silver-based currency, but it might be better to regard them as early examples of dollarisation.

## The ancient world

My *History of Money* essentially began with Charlemagne, but included a short chapter with some anecdotes about earlier periods. Having 'small Latin and less Greek', I knew little of the monetary arrangements of the ancient world. However, Andrew Meadows, curator of Greek coins at the British Museum, sent me an interesting paper[5] which confirmed my hunch that probing even further back in time would turn up some interesting examples. Whereas I had suggested (1994, 107) that the history of money began with the invention of coinage, Meadows intriguingly suggests that the period before when transactions were settled in silver and occasionally gold by weight was 'an economic paradise': 'life for the comparatively few people with the disposable income and desire to travel with money was simple'. Paradise was lost 'when someone in Western Turkey in about 625 BC came up with a revolutionary new economic idea: coinage. From the moment that the idea of coinage first flickered in that genius's mind the simple straightforward world of monetary union was doomed'. The Greek city states did not have a common weight standard, and each minted its own coins which were fully accepted only in its own territory and distrusted by traders in other states. This 'offered lucrative opportunities for the new opportunities for the new profession of money changers', which charged commissions in the range 6–7 per cent.

Meadows goes on to describe some early monetary unions which he classifies into three types, 'top down', 'bottom up' and 'consenting' unions.

1   'Top down' implies the imposition of monetary union from above (a change in political control in my terminology), which Meadows says was surprisingly rare, citing only the example of king Mitriditis VI of ancient times, but also mentioning some medieval examples which I used in my earlier book.

2   'Bottom up' union is the voluntary adoption by one state of another's coinage, i.e. 'dollarisation'. These were often supplemented by honest imitations, sometimes indistinguishable, and sometimes with clear indications of the state of origin. The classical examples are the Athenian 'owls' and the tetradrams of Alexander the Great (Davies,[6] 79–86, suggests that there was a bimetallist angle).

3   'Consenting' union is monetary union proper, although before the invention of paper money this would be between countries having a silver, gold, or bimetallic system – i.e. my type 1. Meadows gives three interesting examples, all of which seem surprisingly modern in concept.

At the end of the fifth century BC two cities, Mytilene on Lesbos and Phocaea in what is now Turkey, agreed on a common coinage and to secure a roughly equal division of seigniorage, coins were exclusively struck in each of the cities in alternate years. Meadows quotes a translation of an inscription in stone. The law states that:

An annual audit shall take place which shall take no longer than six months to prepare. If anyone is convicted of deliberately mixing the gold too weakly, he is to be punished by death; if he is found guilty of doing it accidentally the court shall decide a fitting penalty for him to suffer or pay. In the latter case the city shall be free from guilt and penalty. The Mityleneans drew by lot the right to strike first.

Burns,[7] the classic (but now discredited) source on ancient money, refers to this case and to an inscription (preserved in stone and which he does not quote, but probably this one) which he says probably simply formalised the existing arrangement within the league and that the coins developed into the international currency of the western part of Asia Minor. He says that the coins were made of electrum (a naturally occuring alloy of silver and gold) to a fairly consistent ratio, perhaps thanks to the audit, of 40 per cent gold, 52 per cent silver and 8 per cent copper.

The second example dates from around 404 BC, when seven states on the western coast of what is now Turkey agreed to mint a common currency. The obverse of these coins was identical, 'an image of the baby Heracles strangling a snake, with the first three letters of the Greek word for alliance'. The reverses, though, had a distinctive national symbol, a rose at Rhodes, Aphrodite at Knidos, a lion scalp at Samos, a bee at Ephesus and a lion and tuna fish at Cyzicus (this precedent was followed in Austria-Hungary, and in the British colonies and with the euro coins – but not banknotes).

The third example is the Achaean League, the main power from the end of the third century BC until its defeat by the Romans in 146 BC. The historian Polybius describes this remarkable union as having been achieved by those working for general liberty rather than 'lust for power'. He points out that this 'allied and friendly community' had

> the same laws, weights, measures and coinage … the whole Pelopponese falls short of being a single city only in its failure to enclose its inhabitants within a single wall, all other things – at both federal and city level – being almost identical.

Again, the coins were struck with a common obverse with distinguishing national symbols on the reverse.

Burns (1928) also discusses several Ancient Greek monetary unions (90ff.). The Asia Minor union was involved with Persia's attempted domination, but he suggests that the actual currency measures were agreed with Athens, that city recognising that its 'owls', by then already widely circulating, were inappropriate and that 'instead, a currency suitable to local traditions was established'; but he also says that the Athenian merchants found problems with the electrum coins when they traded with the Black Sea, as 'electrum was looked upon as a kind of gold and was therefore a clear infringement of the Persian royal prerogative'. What Burns says is intriguing, and again suggests that variations in the gold/silver ratio (and the difficulty of achieving a stable composition for the electrum coins) may have had some influence, as did the question of who enjoyed seigniorage. Monetary unions in these areas also, of course, came and went with political and military changes.

# Part II

# Monetary union in post-Napoleonic Europe

The key issue of bimetallism

# 8 The Napoleonic wars and after
## Bimetallism

### Introduction

The Napoleonic Wars proved a turning point in European monetary history, and during the rest of the century there were three relevant, closely interacting, themes. The United Kingdom, having 'suspended payments' operated with inconvertible paper money (but without serious inflation) until cash payments were resumed, and a gold standard formalised, in 1821. This gold standard was to dominate world monetary arrangements by the end of the century.

France had also resorted to inconvertible paper money (the assignats) but after these had lost all their value a bimetallic system, following Calonne's ratio set in 1785, was introduced in 1803. This was to prove remarkably stable for many years, being adopted by neighbouring countries, and is the main topic of this chapter: the collapse of bimetallism was a major 'monetary disunion' which had consequences in the 'silver' countries of the Far East and Latin America. These are discussed in later chapters.

The third and most important concept was the Latin Monetary Union, which was born in response to one bimetallic problem: the 1848–70 fall in the ratio and the disappearance of small change. The LMU very nearly became the basis of a world monetary system, but collapsed, quite unnecessarily, as a reaction to the post-1870 rise in the bimetallic ratio and the fall in the price of silver. The United Kingdom, mainly by luck, escaped both problems, and the gold standard triumphed by the end of the nineteenth century.

### France and the UK compared

Why did the French, the losers, introduce a stable currency eighteen years before the victorious UK resumed convertibility, and how did the French system 'conquer' so much of Europe? Sometimes, during periods of monetary upheaval, things have to get worse before they get better, and this is an example. France's disastrous attempt to finance the war with paper money (the assignats) having collapsed, the only way out was to introduce a really credible monetary reform. Paper money had become worthless by about 1799: inflation, as a method of war finance, was burnt out, and in 1803 the

French had no alternative but to revert to a really credible honest money. This, arguably, as the result of an historical accident, was based on a bimetallic system.

The UK was different. There was no excessive issue of paper money, convertibility was eventually resumed with the pound at its old gold parity, and the gold standard was formalised. These differences were the driving force of monetary developments in Europe, with major and unexpected repercussions in the 'silver standard' countries of the Far East and Latin America. Bimetallism at that time did really seem to be a convenient arrangement, and only became an emotional issue later in the century. Another important distinction, overlooked by most contemporary commentators, was that the United Kingdom, unlike the French where the idea had become discredited, following experience with the assignats and the earlier machinations of John Law, made extensive use of paper money and of bank deposits. The USA, newly independent at the beginning of the century, was to suffer problems with both paper money and bimetallism, although there the main political driving force was not so much monetary theory as the commercial interests of the silver-producing states.

## Bimetallism

Bimetallism was to rival the growth of banking in dominating monetary events and disputes for much of the nineteenth century. It gave impetus to, and eventually caused the collapse of, one of the greatest and most exciting initiatives ever taken towards monetary union. This, once regarded as an obscure byway of economic history, again became topical and relevant in the late twentieth century.

The problem of bimetallism goes back a long way. For centuries gold and silver coins circulated side by side, at least in Europe, and governments tried to set a simple relationship between the two. It is obviously convenient if a gold sovereign of stated weight is exactly equal to 20 silver shillings, but the relative value of the two metals as bullion varied for place to place and time to time. If gold was valued eleven times as highly as silver in France and only ten times in England, a merchant could bring ten pounds of silver to England, convert it into a pound of gold, ship it over to France, convert it into eleven pounds of silver and repeat the operation at a 9 per cent profit – less what were, in earlier times, the very substantial costs and risks of the operation. Because of these costs, significant discrepancies between countries could persist without materially affecting domestic monetary arrangements.

### Gresham's Law

Sir Thomas Gresham, Queen Elizabeth's financial adviser and founder of the Royal Exchange, is said to have formulated Gresham's Law: 'Bad money drives out good'. The Law applies only if government succeeds in requiring its citizens to accept the 'bad money' at an *effective* fiat value. Economists use a more precise statement of Gresham's Law, for instance:

> Where by legal enactment a government assigns the same nominal value to two or more forms of circulatory medium whose intrinsic values differ, payment will always, as far as possible, be made in that medium of which the cost of production is least, and the more valuable medium will tend to disappear from circulation.[1]

Suppose that clipped or debased coins worth less than their bullion value (bad money) circulate alongside full weight ones (good money), and that both are accepted in trade. Anyone receiving a 'good' coin holds on to it and spends the 'bad' one. In the context of bimetallism if, for instance, the ratio undervalues gold (which is then 'good money'), gold coins will be withdrawn from circulation and melted down or sold abroad, leaving silver (in this case the 'bad money') in circulation.

In Queen Elizabeth's time, changes in the gold/silver ratio did not have a particularly dramatic effect, as gold coins were normally handled only by merchants and were likely to change hands in accordance with the value of the gold content and there could be, and were, frequent changes in the 'official' value of these coins. Gresham's Law in its precise form simply did not apply, although attempts by governments to impose a fiat value on coins which was out of line with international market rates could, and during the eighteenth century increasingly did, stimulate an outflow of the over-valued metal.

### Earlier history

The early history of the ratio was discussed in Chown 1994, ch. 2,[2] followed by more detail on the early history of the UK coinage, including the Henry VIII debasement. A more recent book, specifically on bimetallism, by Professor Angela Redish,[3] also covers this period and specifically includes more information than my own book on what had been happening in France. She explains that after some upheavals, the French coinage was stable from 1561 to 1701 but states 'the depreciation that occurred intermittently between 1690 and 1726 has generated less debate than the debasements of medieval France.' As I did not discuss these, they are worth a brief summary here by way of background to subsequent developments.

The French crown was virtually bankrupt towards the end of the seventeenth century and resorted to various expedients to raise funds. On four occasions between 1689 and 1704 existing coins were called down in value and replaced by over-struck (or newly minted) coins, each transaction yielding a substantial seigniorage profit to the Crown. Redish quotes Despaux (which I have sometimes found an unreliable source) as generating the equivalent of eighteen months normal revenues. There was, at this stage, no actual debasement of the coinage.

From 1693 if coins were brought to the mint for over-striking or otherwise re-issuing, the mint issued *billets* which were redeemable a few months later. These circulated as the equivalent of coins, and in 1701 the mint started to issue such *billets* unbacked by actual metal, so that by 1706 a substantial amount of paper money had in effect been paid into circulation without any formal backing, and these were eventually accepted only at a discount of 50 per cent.

There was a major recoinage in 1709, when all existing gold and silver coins were demonetised and replaced by a new coinage on terms which amounted to a depreciation of 16 per cent in the value of the currency. There were further reductions in the value of the gold louis and the silver ecu between 1713 and September 1715. All these events paralleled the dramatic and disastrous plan for paper money created by the Scotsman, John Law.[4] There were also various further depreciations, cryings down and renaming of the coins, culminating in the reform of May 1726.

This 1726 reform was on the basis of a bimetallic ratio of 14.45, which was below the English ratio of 15.2, the latter being too high. In the 1770s the price on the Hamburg market was about 14.7, meaning that gold in France was slightly under-valued. In 1785 Calonne, the minister of finance, undertook the reduction of the weight of the gold Louis by 6.7 per cent, from 8.1580 grams to 7.640, (.917 fine) bringing the ratio up to 15.5, well above market rates. (The 20 franc 'napoleon' introduced in 1803, was, at 6.45 grams, rather lighter than Calonne's louis: the 1803 reform and particularly the ratio was influenced by Calonne, but was *not*, as sometimes suggested, simply a revival of his law.) Calonne argued that this adjustment was necessary to bring the bimetallic ratio into line: his opponents said it 'was simply a fiscal manoeuvre to generate seigniorage revenue'.

### Bimetallism in the nineteenth century

With growing prosperity after the Napoleonic Wars, gold became the more appropriate metal for larger and more widespread transactions, and it became easier, cheaper and quicker for a trader to exchange gold for silver. There were no longer any material mercantilist restrictions ('exchange controls') to be evaded, mint charges had been reduced or abolished, transportation was cheaper and safer, and market information could be exchanged more rapidly. If the legal ratio was even only slightly out of line with international markets, the country would quickly lose either gold or silver, depending which was undervalued. If a country permits free minting of both gold and silver and affords both the gold and silver coins full legal tender status at pre-determined rates, there will inevitably be problems.

In this context, 'free minting' means that any citizen (and in many countries, foreigners as well) could bring metal to the mint and receive in exchange coins containing the same amount of the metal less a deduction ('seigniorage') for expenses. (This could sometimes include a substantial element of profit, although in later years 'free minting' often meant just what it said – the costs were borne by the state.) 'Full legal tender status' meant that the offer of coins of the appropriate value had to be accepted as good legal discharge of a debt of any amount: the creditor was not entitled to demand (although they could agree to accept) payment in any other form.

Calonne's pre-Revolutionary reform of 1785 had in fact been attacked and debated in 1790 mainly by opponents of the bimetallic concept (Redish 2000, 168) and in 1795 as part of the introduction of the metric system it was determined that a new basic coin, the franc, was to weigh exactly 5 grams of .900 fine silver. There were also provisions for a gold coin, but at this stage none were minted. There were further discussions in 1798 and 1801 when Gaudin, the minister of finance, proposed a compromise setting out what amounted to a silver standard based on the *franc germinale* but stating (Article 6) that 'the proportion of gold to silver will be 1:15.5. If circumstances force a change the gold coins will be reminted'.

The Act eventually passed in 1803 (English translation from Laughlin 1892, 236–7) states that 'five grammes of silver nine-tenths fine' constitutes the monetary unit which retains the name of 'franc' but otherwise treated silver and gold symmetrically. Article 11 states that 'The expense of coinage alone can be required of those who bring material of gold and silver to the mint', and fixed these changes at 9 francs per kilogram for gold, and 3 francs for silver. These minting charges meant that it was only profitable to bring gold to the mint for coining if it could be bought cheaper than 15.46 times the cost of silver, the corresponding ratio for bringing in silver being 15.74. Minting expenses were said to ensure that the ratio remained in the range 15.46 to 15.74, but this assumes, in effect, that the metal is at the door of the mint and ignores transport and other expenses, which were initially significant but fell sharply in the course of the century. The 1803 Act did not, as noted, merely confirm Calonne's law of 1785, and certainly at this stage France adopted bimetallism rather half-heartedly, and almost by accident: there was plenty of discussion of the fact that ratios could change.

## The United Kingdom and the gold standard

Britain had formally been on a silver standard since Newton's recoinage of 1696, but with the growth of trade in the eighteenth century, there was at some stage, about which economic historians can argue, a switch to a *de facto* gold standard, coupled with an extensive use of banknotes. There were discussions on the silver/gold ratio, and of the standard,[5] but before any action could be taken, the Napoleonic Wars intervened, and the suspension of payments left the country with an inconvertible paper currency.

Gold had certainly been over-valued in 1717, and the silver coinage was in a poor state at the end of the eighteenth century. There was a gold recoinage in 1774 and the problems of the silver coinage were partly addressed by closing the mint to private coinage of silver and declaring that silver coins were not to be legal tender for amounts in excess of £25. This was effectively abandoning or limiting the silver standard.

In 1787 a Committee of Coin was set up under the Privy Council mainly to address the problems arising from the shortage of silver coin and the poor state of those actually in circulation. Nothing happened, and a second committee was set up in 1797 chaired by Charles Jenkinson, First Earl of Liverpool. He made detailed proposals which were subsequently published in 1805. He proposed that only gold coins should be full legal tender, silver and copper being merely representative coins with limited legal tender. This led to the Act of 1816 ('Lord Liverpool's Act' – the second Earl, son of Charles Jenkinson), at which time it was of course irrelevant as payments were still suspended. Formal convertibility was restored in 1821 at the old parity, but there had been effective 'convergence' since 1819, when although there was no legal right to convert notes into gold, banknotes were effectively accepted at their gold parity.

A key point was that silver coins, legal tender for no more than £2, were deliberately struck underweight, initially 7.5 per cent below their legal tender value. This UK system gave some margin against a *fall* in the ratio (i.e. the price of gold in terms of silver) which proved, in the event, enough, but only just, to survive a period of rising silver prices which lasted until about 1870. There would in fact have been a problem had the value of silver risen *above* 66 shillings in relation to gold: i.e. if the market ratio had fallen below 14.29. As France would have already hit problems at 15.46, this was an adequate margin. The French system was more rigid, requiring equal treatment of gold and silver.

There could have been another solution. Before the war banknotes had only been legal in England in amounts of £5 and above. If smaller notes had been permitted, as they were in Scotland, it might have been possible to adopt a formal 'silver exchange' standard, leaving banknotes for everyday larger transactions and with gold coins trading at market value as they had often done in the past.

### Why was bimetallism a problem?

Bimetallism arguably became an issue because of the need for 'small change'. Before the commercial revolution of the fourteenth century England managed with the silver penny as the standard unit supplemented only by half-pennies and 'fourthings' and no larger coins at all. By the mid-nineteenth century the largest coin in circulation, the gold five pounds, was worth nearly 5,000 times as much as the smallest, the copper farthing. Silver coins would have been far too heavy for large but still everyday transactions, while even the smallest practical silver coins did not meet the need for small change. To us, an obvious solution would be the creation of low-value token coins in base metal, but some countries, including the UK, regarded it beneath their dignity to issue such coins, while the French populace had a deep and understandable distrust of any money not represented by full value metal.

The British solution, of issuing silver coins worth a modest premium (which at the end of the century was to become substantial) over the silver content and giving them a limited legal tender status, created its own problems. Were these coins to be regarded as an obligation of the state like state-issued paper money or not? In the event the Royal Mint had been creating them and putting them into circulation at a profit represented by the discount while the banks, notably the Bank of England, had been accepting them at fiat value and found themselves with large stocks which, if melted down, would have created a loss. There were disputes (see Redish 2000, 150–3) about whether the (privately owned) Bank should be allowed to sell these back to the 'government-owned' mint at face value, or at least to be permitted at a later stage to buy equivalent amounts of coins from the Mint at bullion value plus the cost of minting. Agreement was eventually reached in 1834, by which time

> the monetary authorities had finally learned that for the silver tokens to circulate at a value in excess of the market value of their silver would require not only limited legal tender and controlled supply but also an agency that would convert them on demand into a money form that was an unlimited legal tender.
>
> (Redish 2000, 153)

## The systems compared

The United Kingdom had introduced a gold standard by accident with a token silver coinage at a discount which, again by luck rather than judgment, proved adequate. France had introduced a rigid bimetallic system, but it was clear from the debates which preceded this measure that many people, but not all, understood that there could be future problems arising from variations in the ratio. The United States, a new country at the beginning of the century, also had a bimetallic system without monetary arrangements (then) being very developed. Much of the rest of the world, notably India, the Far East and Latin America, were on a silver standard.

Bimetallism initially worked fairly well partly because the large French monetary stocks acted as a buffer. Merchants needing to transfer funds to France could choose between delivering gold or silver: with the market ratio above the range 15.46–15.74 they could and did deliver silver, and vice-versa. The difference represents only the formal minting costs: because of transport and other costs and risks, the ratio could deviate even further before actual systematic arbitrage (which would quickly denude a bimetallic country of coins of one metal or the other) could take place. In the nature of things, this extra margin narrowed as the century progressed.

Problems inevitably soon hit – and were to change the monetary history of the world.

## The period of silver shortage

The history of the ratio is set out in Table 8.1 below.

*Table 8.1*    Bimetallic ratios, France 1815–95

| Year | Ratio | 5 year moving average | Year | Ratio | 5 year moving average |
|------|-------|-----------------------|------|-------|-----------------------|
| 1815 | 15.26 | – | 1856 | 15.27 | 15.34 |
| 1816 | 15.28 | – | 1857 | 15.38 | 15.35 |
| 1817 | 15.11 | – | 1858 | 15.19 | 15.32 |
| 1818 | 15.35 | – | 1859 | 15.29 | 15.30 |
| 1819 | 15.33 | 15.27 | 1860 | 15.5 | 15.33 |
| 1820 | 15.62 | 15.34 | 1861 | 15.35 | 15.34 |
| 1821 | 15.95 | 15.47 | 1862 | 15.37 | 15.34 |
| 1822 | 15.8 | 15.61 | 1863 | 15.37 | 15.38 |
| 1823 | 15.84 | 15.71 | 1864 | 15.44 | 15.41 |
| 1824 | 15.82 | 15.81 | 1865 | 15.43 | 15.39 |
| 1825 | 15.7 | 15.82 | 1866 | 15.57 | 15.44 |
| 1826 | 15.76 | 15.78 | 1867 | 15.59 | 15.48 |
| 1827 | 15.74 | 15.77 | 1868 | 15.6 | 15.53 |
| 1828 | 15.78 | 15.76 | 1869 | 15.57 | 15.55 |
| 1829 | 15.78 | 15.75 | 1870 | 15.57 | 15.58 |
| 1830 | 15.82 | 15.78 | 1871 | 15.63 | 15.59 |
| 1831 | 15.72 | 15.77 | 1872 | 15.92 | 15.66 |
| 1832 | 15.73 | 15.77 | 1873 | 16.17 | 15.77 |
| 1833 | 15.93 | 15.80 | 1874 | 16.59 | 15.98 |
| 1834 | 15.73 | 15.79 | 1875 | 17.88 | 16.44 |
| 1835 | 15.8 | 15.78 | 1876 | 17.22 | 16.76 |
| 1836 | 15.72 | 15.78 | 1877 | 17.94 | 17.16 |
| 1837 | 15.85 | 15.81 | 1878 | 18.4 | 17.61 |
| 1838 | 15.62 | 15.74 | 1879 | 18.05 | 17.90 |
| 1839 | 15.62 | 15.72 | 1880 | 18.16 | 17.95 |
| 1840 | 15.7 | 15.70 | 1881 | 18.19 | 18.15 |
| 1841 | 15.87 | 15.73 | 1882 | 18.64 | 18.29 |
| 1842 | 15.93 | 15.75 | 1883 | 18.57 | 18.32 |
| 1843 | 15.85 | 15.79 | 1884 | 19.41 | 18.59 |
| 1844 | 15.92 | 15.85 | 1885 | 20.78 | 19.12 |
| 1845 | 15.9 | 15.89 | 1886 | 21.13 | 19.71 |
| 1846 | 15.8 | 15.88 | 1887 | 21.99 | 20.38 |
| 1847 | 15.85 | 15.86 | 1888 | 22.1 | 21.08 |
| 1848 | 15.78 | 15.85 | 1889 | 19.76 | 21.15 |
| 1849 | 15.7 | 15.81 | 1890 | 20.92 | 21.18 |
| 1850 | 15.46 | 15.72 | 1891 | 23.72 | 21.70 |
| 1851 | 15.59 | 15.68 | 1892 | 26.49 | 22.60 |
| 1852 | 15.33 | 15.57 | 1893 | 32.56 | 24.69 |
| 1853 | 15.33 | 15.48 | 1894 | 31.6 | 27.06 |
| 1854 | 15.38 | 15.42 | 1895 | 30.66 | 29.01 |
| 1855 | 15.38 | 15.40 | – | – | – |

To begin with, the market ratio remained within the range of 15.46–15.74, and in any case France had 'buffer stocks' which could absorb quite substantial fluctuations. Between 1841 and 1847 the gold price rose, and France exported gold, but following the enormous gold discoveries in the 1840s, during the period 1848–60 the ratio was falling: silver was becoming relatively overvalued, and following Gresham's Law this resulted in silver coins disappearing from circulation and into the melting pot in France and the United States, and in other countries where their exchange value was fixed by statute. Britain was protected by its extra margin.

The first effects were felt in the United States, which had introduced a bimetallic system with a 15:1 ratio in 1792, and where bimetallism was to become a major political issue in the second half of the century. This was too low, and in 1834 had been changed to 16:1, too *high*. Within three months $50 million (nearly 40 million ounces) of silver disappeared from circulation, and was shipped across the Atlantic in exchange for gold, on a scale which caused some alarm at the Bank of England (Clapham 1970, ii, 151).[6] After the gold discoveries of the 1840s, the ratio fell still further and it became worthwhile to melt down the small silver coins: quarters and dimes, and to prevent this, silver was effectively demonetised in 1853 and the United States went on to a *de facto* gold standard. The silver dollar coin retained its full value and legal tender status, but as the value was about $1.04 in terms of gold, none were minted and it had disappeared from circulation years before. Soon after this the Civil War intervened and inconvertible paper 'greenbacks' became, for a time, the main circulating money.

A similar 'small change' problem hit France and those of its neighbours which had adopted the French monetary system. Because of the rigid bimetallic ratio, full value silver coins were being driven from circulation. Switzerland was the first country to respond by reducing the silver content of its smaller coins (two francs and less) from 0.900 to 0.800 fine silver, and other countries eventually followed. This created problems when these 'token' coins circulated in other countries. The 1865 conference, convened in response to these international aspects, was actually to lead to the Latin Monetary Union. However, bimetallism persisted under the influence of the French, which helped the project on its way but was to cause its downfall when the ratio rose sharply later in the century. These events are discussed in more detail below, when the main story continues, but meanwhile we have to examine the smaller 'monetary unions' taking place in Italy, Germany and Switzerland, and the case of Austria-Hungary, a particularly interesting and relevant example in both its rise and its fall.

# 9 Monetary union in Germany, Italy and Switzerland

## Introduction

At the end of the eighteenth century the territories which are now Germany and Italy comprised many separate states, some large, some small, with a range of different currencies. This chapter discusses their moves towards limited monetary unions. In both cases, a united single currency was achieved only after political union, but the development of the broader Latin Monetary Union influenced, and was affected by, the intermediate developments. Switzerland, already a federation, also had to take steps to achieve a single currency, which it did, after long debate, by linking with the Latin Monetary Union.

## Germany

In 1790, what is now Germany comprised some 300 separate states (there had at one stage been over 1,600) and the unsatisfactory Germanic Confederation of 1815 (replacing the 1806 Confederation of the Rhine) created a loose confederation of otherwise sovereign German states, of varying sizes. Germany was said to have had an 'alternative system' (introduced by Frederick the Great after the peace of Hubertsburg, 1763) by which gold and silver could be substituted for each other in making payments. This eventually became a *de facto* silver standard, with gold 'trade coins' circulating at market value.

Each of these states had levied its own customs duties, with great damage to trade. A move towards a *Zollverein* (customs union) began with Prussia in 1818. Other German states formed themselves into three separate groups in 1828, and the union was finalised in 1833. Monetary union came more slowly, and indeed was only completed after political union in 1871. Meanwhile the currency, after the Napoleonic Wars, was in a state of confusion.

Kindleberger (1984, 119)[1] comments that 'The German mini-states'' experience illustrates precisely Adam Smith's statement that small countries are obliged to use foreign monies. 'The Rhineland', he says, 'had at least 70 types of foreign coin in circulation in 1816'.

A group of southern members entered in a treaty in Munich in 1837, based on 24.5 gulden (or florin) to the Cologne mark (3608 English grains or 233.85 metric grams of fine silver). On 30 July 1838 a group of northern states adopted the Prussian thaler standard, defined as 14 to the Cologne mark, and the Dresden convention fixed the exchange rate at 4 Prussian thalers to 7 gulden.[2] This also provided for a new silver coin, the *Vereinsmünze*, worth 2 thalers or 3.5 gulden. This reduced the number of coinages to two from the previous seven. 'All ... had a silver standard with the single exception of the free city of Bremen, the monetary system of which rested on a gold basis'.[3] Paper money, the issue of which was regulated on a local basis, was an additional complication.

Del Mar (1895) summarises later developments, referring to a coinage treaty in Munich on 27 March 1845, a monetary 'cartel' at Carlsruhe on 27 October 1845, and another on 19 February 1853, by which the *Zollverein* members coordinated arrangements for punishing coinage offences. Attempts at further unification were complicated by Austria's wish to join the *Zollverein*. Austria had suspended specie payments in 1848, and had in 1859 suggested that it and the *Zollverein* states switch to gold.

### The Vienna Convention

In pursuance of a provision of the Treaty of Carlsruhe, 19 July 1853, the Vienna Convention united its members with the rival systems of Prussia and Austria on the basis of the 'pound' of 500 grams, with 30 thalers being struck from a pound of fine silver. This Convention thaler was made equal to 1.5 florins Austrian or 1.75 florins (gulden) South German, leaving three currency systems.

The Vienna Convention conferred the right of coinage of full legal tender silver and of gold coins on private individuals – gold coins were forbidden to be made legal tender in any of the states. The silver coins were to be legal tender coins in all the states in the appropriate ratios, while Austria could continue to strike ducats until the end of 1865.

The Vienna Convention decided not to establish a fixed ratio, but to permit only the coining of gold crowns and half-crowns, the crown being valued at 0.50 to the pound of *silver*. The idea was that the *gold* content could be adjusted in line with market changes. This rather clumsy expedient appears to have been ineffectual.

### Later developments

As explained in the next chapter, Austria had long periods of inconvertible paper money but resumed payments in 1858–9 for six months until war broke out with Italy, while in 1866 Austria went to war with Prussia and withdrew from the *Munzverein*. Meanwhile business interests were dissatisfied with the arrangements: although they wanted a single currency they could not agree on which it should be. The 1867 Paris Conference concentrated their minds on the need for 'universal money' i.e. to join the Latin Monetary Union, and a conference in 1868 passed a resolution favouring the gold standard.

The North German Federation prohibited new issues of paper money in 1870 and when, in 1871 a unified Germany was established following the Franco-Prussian War, a new national currency standard was introduced, the mark. The coinage acts of 1871 and 1873 adopted the gold standard on the British standard. This change was facilitated by the receipt of reparations, and was to precipitate the collapse of bimetallism.

In 1875 the Prussian Bank became the Reichsbank, a central bank which effectively had sole note-issuing powers. The law did not prohibit other banks from issuing notes, but the conditions were such as to make the business unattractive.

## Italy

The various states which make up what is now Italy had used about ninety different currencies, but in 1847 there was a partial move towards economic union. The Kingdom of Sardinia (created at the Congress of Vienna in 1815 from Sardinia, Piedmont and Liguria, which included the trading city of Genoa), Tuscany and the Papal States entered into a tariff union, but Lombardy and Venetia were kept out by the Austrians, and the Kingdom of the Two Sicilies (including Naples) chose to remain outside. Leghorn retained its status as a free city, but in spite of having to deal with a wide variety of currencies, had a discount bank only from 1836, and still had no deposit bank. The province of Tuscany had twenty-four different currencies, towns having their own coins struck to different standards.

Italy was unified politically in 1861, and steps were quickly taken to unify the currency if not (at first) the banking system. During the transitional stage four currencies, the Napoleonic lira of Piedmont, the new lira of Parma, the Austrian florin of Lombardy and the escudo of Rome were accepted. Other currencies were exchanged into one or the other of these.

In August 1862 the Sardinian lira, equal in value to the Napoleonic French franc, became the national currency, and a bimetallic system at the French 15:5 ratio was introduced. This move, following the 1848 example of Switzerland, effectively paved the way for membership of the Latin Monetary Union which was to be formalised in 1865. A new coin, the silver escudo, equal to 5 lire, was minted and replaced the Roman escudo which was equal to 5.32 lire, and the decimal system, already fairly widely adopted, became universal.

There was still no true central bank or monetary authority. Regional banks continued to issue notes and performed some central banking functions. The Sardinian National Bank absorbed some other state banks to form the Banca d'Italia, which became the leading bank without taking the formal role of central bank.

The new Italian government had inherited substantial debts (2.4 billion lire), mainly from Piedmont. There was a financial crisis in France in 1864, followed by the UK Overend Gurney crash of 1866. In 1865 banknotes constituted only a tenth of Italian money supply. In May 1866 the Banca Nazionale del Regno lent 250 million lire to the government, but was relieved of its obligation to convert its notes into specie: *Il Corso Forzono* or forced circulation. (This experience was not confined to Italy: the French had a similar period a few years later, Austria had a long tradition, while Russian currency was almost continuously inconvertible from 1786 to 1897.) Gold soon went to a 20 per cent premium, but this proved to be the highest level reached. The notes of other banks became convertible into BNR notes, which served as reserve assets for other banks.

*Il Corso Forzono* ended in 1881, after which the notes of the six issuing banks exchanged at par. There was no real check on the temptation for each bank to over-issue, and in 1891 the government had to forestall a liquidity crisis by lowering the reserve requirements. There followed an enquiry into the banking system, and in 1893 the Banca d'Italia was formed as a merger of the Banca Nazionale nel Regno with two note-issuing banks in Tuscany. The others, the Banca di Napoli and the Banca di Sicilia, were brought under state supervision, while the Banca Romana went into liquidation.

## Switzerland

Switzerland had fewer problems than Germany or Italy. The Federation of Cantons had been recognised as independent of the Holy Roman Empire in 1648, but were occupied by Napoleon's forces from 1798 to 1803 when a monetary system based on the French franc was imposed. When the occupation ended coinage rights reverted to the individual cantons, which issued a wide variety of coins, leaving the Federation without a unified monetary system. In 1848, coining powers were transferred to the federal government. In the discussions leading up to this measure, the 'French' cantons wanted to adopt the French monetary system, while the 'German' ones wanted to follow Germany. However, Johan Jakob Speiser,[4] representing the German speaking canton of Basel, successfully pointed out that the French had a single system, while the Germans still had three different systems.

The UK Royal Commission on Decimal Coinage report of 1857[5] took evidence on the experience of other countries, including Switzerland. The evidence included a letter from William Brown MP to a banker, Augustus Lemonius,[6] which ends:

> I believe your partner, Mr Zwilchenbart and Mr Speiser, of Basle, were prime movers in conferring the benefit on Switzerland.

The US National Monetary Commission of 1909 includes a paper on the Swiss banking system[7] and discusses inter-cantonal bank clearing:

The first step toward introducing a healthier system into these affairs was taken by the adoption of the concordat, a result of the endeavours of Bank Manager Speiser, of Basle. Under this agreement, made in 1862, the solvent banks pledged themselves to accept one another's notes in payment, and started a kind of clearing and circulating system amongst themselves. In arranging this concordat the primary object was to put an end to a state of things in which the notes of any bank were accepted only at a discount outside its own canton.[8]

This was opposed by 'smaller concerns in the central and eastern parts of Switzerland' who had been excluded. It led to an idea 'of adapting the Scotch system to the needs of Switzerland' (there are in fact closer parallels with New England: see Chown 1994, ch. 20).[9]

Elsewhere the National Monetary Commission report refers to W. Speiser in connection with a dispute with Geering on the factors affecting the Swiss exchange rate. He 'laid chief stress not on the adverse balance ... in mercantile transactions but on ... the international movement of capital' – effectively French direct and portfolio investment into Switzerland (Landmann[10] says both theories are untenable).

There were, it seems, major disputes in 1894 and 1899 on who had the right to issue banknotes. Ten different proposals were submitted to the Bundesrat, including '(2) observations and proposals by Herr W. Speiser'.

# 10 The Austro-Hungarian empire as a monetary union

## History to 1914

## Introduction

The Austro-Hungarian empire was created in 1867, and became a rare (and arguably then unique) example of a monetary union between two otherwise independent countries sharing monetary sovereignty based on fiat money rather than gold while retaining independent and fiscal policies and borrowing rights. It broke up in 1919, an early 'monetary disunion', after which most parts of the former empire suffered hyper-inflation (see Chapters 24–6) and the three stages of this history have many lessons for later times, particularly for the former Soviet Union and its Eastern European neighbours, and indeed for the European Monetary Union.

## Earlier history

Austria, the centre of the Hapsburg empire, had a turbulent eighteenth century, with the War of the Austrian Succession (1740–8) and the Seven Years War (1756–63), and following the Napoleonic Wars the empire gave up certain previous overseas territories, still finishing up with an area substantially larger than present-day Austria. The 'Holy Roman Empire' was no more, and what remained took shape as a centralised hereditary monarchy.

There had been a monetary reform, the so-called 'Convention Currency', following the Convention with Bavaria of 21 September 1753. After a series of monetary adjustments, the basis of the coinage was a silver 20 gulden coin, a gulden being divided into 60 creuzas, and the gold ducat.

Austria first issued paper 'legal tenders' in 1762 to help the financing of the Hapsburgs, and again issued paper money during the Napoleonic Wars. The value of banknotes in circulation increased from 32 million gulden in 1794 to 1,060 million in 1811, when state bankruptcy was declared. The value of copper coins was reduced to a fifth, except for those that were worth more simply as copper. Various regulations governing debts protected creditors and ruined debtors. The old legal tender banknotes were replaced by redemption notes (*Einlösungsscheine*) in the ratio one for five.[1]

The Austrian National Bank was formed in 1816 to facilitate the exchange of these government notes, which had been trading at around 346 paper florins per 100 silver florins, and which were then exchanged into 2.5m per cent government bonds at par, interest (but not, it seems, principal) being paid in silver. Government bonds were exchanged on the basis that holders of 140 nominal received 100 in 1 per cent government bonds and 40 in (apparently) convertible banknotes with an option of taking shares in the bank.[2]

'With the close of 1847 terminated a thirty year period … shareholders and the public might contemplate with a feeling of satisfaction what had been achieved in this stretch of time.' There was 'an unimpeachable circulating medium' and 'the Austrian monetary system since 1820 had been on a stable basis'. The bank had (apparently) been profitable and had paid good dividends, but this, says Zuckerkandl, was based on interest from the Government.[3] Renewed efforts were made to stabilise the currency in the 1850s, but the war in 1859 resulting in the independence of Italy made this impossible.

Under the Vienna Convention of 24 January 1857, the right to the coinage of full legal tender silver, and of gold, coins was conferred on private individuals – gold coins were forbidden to be made legal tender in any of the states. Silver coins, but not gold, were to be legal tender in all the states. Austria could continue to strike ducats until the end of 1865.

Members of the Convention were forbidden to issue legal tender notes unless they were freely convertible into silver. The Convention (between Austria, Liechtenstein and the states of the German Customs Union) was to be valid until the end of 1878 and then to be renewed for five years at a time. The Austrian gulden or florin became the currency unit, divided into one hundred parts eventually referred to as 'new creuzas', although the old creuza was one sixtieth part of the former currency. The conversion was on the basis of 1.05 of Austrian currency to 1 unit of the Conventional currency.

> The paper money and banknotes of each state were permitted to circulate in the other states so long as 'adequate' provision was made for their redemption in full legal tender silver coins.[4]

As noted in Chapter 9 above, the Vienna Convention decided not to establish a fixed ratio, but to permit only the coining of gold crowns and half-crowns, the crown being valued at fifty to the pound of *silver*. The idea was that the *gold* content could be adjusted in line with market changes. This rather clumsy expedient appears to have been ineffectual. Austria (and Liechtenstein) left the union in 1867 at the time of the monetary reform discussed below.

The revolutions of 1848 could have led to the break-up of the Austrian empire, or at least its reorganisation as a loose confederation, but the new emperor brought matters under his control. Austria suspended payments and although it again seemed, in 1866, that specie payments might be resumed the following year, more government paper (declared legal tender) was then issued to finance a war against Prussia and Italy.

## The Austro-Hungarian empire

Defeat by Prussia in 1866 effectively put an end to Austria's pretensions to dominate a Central European empire, and the *Ausgleich* or Compromise of 1867, which created a full monetary and customs union between the Hapsburg empire and the Hungarian monarchy, was not so much a federal union between two previously independent states but an arrangement accepting Hungary's independence and sovereignty while maintaining the political and economic benefits of unity. The two states remained autonomous regions but with a common defence and foreign policy, but the two countries had separate budgets, each contributing to certain common expenditures, including debt service.[5]

In 1867 the Austrian coinage was based on the silver Convention thaler equal to 1.5 Austrian florins[6] while the Hungarian coinage was based on the silver forint with 70 per cent of the silver content.

Marc Flandreau quotes Bela Foldes as arguing that this was not an optimum currency area, as Hungary

> was more rural, Austria more industrial, so the time profile of economic shocks varied from one country to the other: seasonalities were more pronounced in Hungary. In addition, the structure of credit involved a larger share of long term instruments in Hungary while 'capitalist Austria' worked with short term capital: as a result each part's 'monetary transmission mechanism' was very different.[7]

There was a two-tier fiscal system, with a common budget, funded mainly by customs duties, to finance the armed forces and the diplomatic service. There was usually a deficit, funded in principle but usually only after prolonged argument, by the two countries on a 70/30 basis. Some common debt outstanding in 1867 was serviced on the same basis, and intended to be amortised over a period. Austria and Hungary also had national or 'special' budgets, essentially running their own tax and expenditure policies, and deficits could be financed by 'special' debt subject to approval by each country's parliament.[8]

Hungary immediately took advantage of this provision to raise loans, partly to develop a transport infrastructure, but Austria did not issue long-term loans until after 1876. Hungary at first borrowed on the Vienna market, which, perhaps surprisingly, ignored the 'internal' currency risk and demanded only a small premium. It was, it seems, fairly easy to place

Hungarian paper during the earlier period which was one of financial euphoria, *Grunderzeit*, but the collapse of the Vienna stock market in 1873 almost precipitated the bankruptcy of the Hungarian state. The government had guaranteed the bonds of a railway company, but when called upon to meet its guarantee simply did not have the cash. The crisis was contained, and when it was over the government renewed its borrowing strategy. It then had to borrow abroad, and foreign markets required a gold guarantee on Hungarian paper. This gave the Hungarians an incentive to stabilise the currency, and they therefore became, in the period 1892 to 1914, more enthusiastic than the Austrians for the strict gold standard.

Although the Compromise had been silent on the question of banks of issue, Hungary undertook, by a supplementary agreement of 12 September 1867, not to create one and, in effect, to permit the inconvertible notes of the Austrian National Bank to circulate in Hungary (in late twentieth-century terms this was the 'Belgium/Luxembourg' rather than the 'European Central Bank' solution). Given that this issue had been dealt with outside the formal Compromise, the Hungarian parliament would have power to repudiate it, and the Bank needed assurances that this would not happen. The Hungarians were prepared to agree, provided that their government was granted a *pro rata* overdraft facility, and that the Bank opened an autonomous office in Budapest – which it refused to do. The Hungarians became even more insistent after the Vienna Stock Exchange crash of 1873, but the opportunity came when the Bank's charter came up for renewal in 1876, giving the Hungarians a bargaining power which they could use in conjunction with a threat to set up an independent National Bank of Hungary.

On 1 July 1878 the Austrian National Bank became the Austro-Hungarian Bank, with offices in Vienna and Budapest, with a governor appointed on the joint nomination of the Austrian and Hungarian finance ministers, and two vice-governors, one from each country. The shares were owned 70 per cent by Austria and 30 per cent by Hungary.

### The coinage

Initially the basis of the coinage was, in theory, silver standard, but the Bank also issued inconvertible paper money. The financial crisis of 1873 appeared to remove the chance of an early stabilisation programme, but eventually in the same year the collapsing value of silver brought the silver coinage, quite by accident, into line with inconvertible paper money, both having fallen against gold.

Between 1876 and 1879 it was possible to profit by buying silver, having it coined in Vienna and exchanging the coins for banknotes of a higher value. To check such arbitrage opportunities, the right of minting was removed from private citizens in 1879. There was said to be a 'floating exchange rate' but, while silver and paper florins traded at par, the exchange rate with a gold standard country such as the UK or Germany was simply a function of the gold/silver ratio.

The government nevertheless had an incentive to create money up to a point by buying and coining silver, and there appear to have been some interesting arbitrage opportunities for the individual and strategic trade-offs for government. Because the Austria-Hungarian Bank had large stocks of silver, this effectively put a floor under the exchange rate.

There was also a hidden profit on the gold portion of the reserves: 'In the absence of a legally established or prescribed ratio, the bank had been appraising its stock of gold in florins of the Austrian standard of according the gold-silver ratio of 1 to 15½.'[9] In 1892 this was revalued at 18.22, and the gain taken to surplus: a manoeuvre the Bundesbank tried to repeat to meet the 'convergence criteria' of European Monetary Union at the end of the twentieth century.

In 1890, the machinations of the silver lobby in the United States having temporarily achieved a recovery in the price of silver, the florin began to rise. There was another opportunity, this time successful, to stabilise the currency, even though the Argentinian collapse of 1890 alarmed speculators.

## Return to gold

Germany had adopted the gold standard in 1871, helped with reparations from France, but when Austria-Hungary abandoned the silver standard in 1879 it lacked the reserves to adopt a formal gold standard. There was technically a paper standard until 1892, but the relationship between the paper and the gold gulden (German) and the forint (Hungarian) was managed and kept fairly stable, in the range 115–125:100. In 1892 the gold krone or korona (half the value of a gulden) was adopted as the standard: this involved a 16 per cent debasement, and there were early teething troubles. However:

> The German economist, Knapp,[10] regarded the Austrian currency system of from 1878 onward as a model, in that scarcely any metal was in circulation, while the bank of issue through its foreign portfolio and reserve guaranteed the exchange and at the same time husbanded the reserves of the nation.[11]

Attempts were made to stabilise the situation in 1892. The intention was to adopt a formal gold standard on 1 January 1900, and the Austro-Hungarian Bank immediately began building up gold reserves. These rose from 108 million crowns in 1890 to 1920 million in 1900. In the event the gold standard was never formally adopted, but the paper crown was in practice convertible at this gold rate from 1892 until the outbreak of war in 1914.

In 1899 the bank's charter was renewed, but to reflect Hungary's strengthening economy, Austria and Hungary were given equal representation, with each appointing a deputy vice-governor as well as a deputy governor, and Hungary claiming a larger share of the profits. The charter was again renewed in 1911: it was meant to expire in 1919 but other events intervened.[12]

Before a formal gold standard could be introduced, larger gold reserves were needed. How could the purchase be financed given that, given market conditions, it would be impossible to raise an international loan? Government securities had risen in value, thanks to the perceived success of the stabilisation programme, and this gave an opportunity for a profitable conversion of the outstanding paper- or silver denominated debt. These reforms, and the reorganisation of the debt, restricted the ability of the two governments to raise short-term finance, and significantly enhanced the power of the Austro-Hungarian Bank at their expense. There was considerable public discussion about the value of the bank's franchise. It was argued that it suited the bank to be seen to have introduced the gold standard in practice, while the politicians were still debating about theory.[13] This continuing political dispute meant that the issue of formalising the gold standard had not been resolved by 1914, when it became irrelevant.

Flandreau culls some lessons from this history. At the first stage, Hungary was able to raise debt on the Austrian market as the Austrians, unlike the rest of the world, accepted that the two countries' currencies were at par. Once the Austrian market was saturated Hungary had to tap the foreign market, which normally required a gold guarantee. The very fact that an increasing proportion of the Hungarian debt was denominated in gold imposed a discipline: 'increasing the share of foreign currency denominated debt might be seen as a optimal commitment technology as this reduces the country's incentive to inflate its paper debt away'. By 1892 Hungary had become the 'hard money' member of the partnership.

# 11 The Latin Monetary Union

## Introduction

At the end of the Napoleonic Wars, as in 1918 and 1945, the monetary systems of Europe were in need of reform, and generally the postwar chaos encouraged a spirit of cooperation. France, after its disastrous experience with the assignats, had introduced a bimetallic system in 1803 and imposed it on certain occupied territories. In 1814 the Netherlands abandoned this imposed French system, but when the Belgians revolted against the Dutch in 1830, they reverted to the French system. Switzerland (1848) and Italy (1861) also chose to adopt it after their own monetary and political unions. Several countries therefore had, for practical purposes, identical coinages, so that there was already the nucleus of a monetary union. At that stage this raised no problems of principle, as all the currencies were based on a metallic standard. If this standard had been gold *or* silver there would have been no problems, and the countries would have simply enjoyed the practical advantages of having coins of identical weight and a 'foreign exchange rate' of par.

However, because the standard was bimetallic, there was a problem arising from the period of silver shortage discussed above in Chapter 8. International agreement was needed to deal with this, and in the event the problem was turned into an opportunity, the great adventure of Latin Monetary Union, and the series of conferences which might have let to a unified monetary system, at least for the Western world. The Americans would probably have joined, if only the British and the French could have got their act together. Unfortunately, politics rather than economics dominated the proceedings, and they didn't. With the British and the Americans aboard, a Germany united under Bismarck would surely have joined in, and the problems of the 'silver' countries might have been resolved more quickly.

## The problem of small change

As explained in Chapter 8, the gold/silver ratio had fallen to the point at which in bimetallic France (and the United States) full value silver coins were starting to disappear from circulation. The first country to react to this was Switzerland, which by then had based its currency on the French silver franc standard. French gold coins, though not legal tender, circulated freely, putting Switzerland onto a *de facto* bimetallic standard from which silver was being forced out of circulation. In 1860 the Swiss responded by making gold legal tender, and by reducing the silver content from 0.900 to 0.800 fine of its subsidiary silver coins of two francs and less, without changing their weight and appearance.

Meanwhile in France there had been complaints about the shortage of small change and the over-abundance of gold as early as 1850, but a commission came to the conclusion that the changes were temporary. The only practical response was the issue of five franc gold coins in 1854 which, in spite of their inconveniently small size, replaced the disappearing five franc silver coins. Economists debated whether bimetallism should be abandoned, and in 1857 a commission considered both the adoption of the UK 'token silver' solution and a change in the ratio. Their actual recommendation to tax silver exports was rejected by the government.

The Italians, however, did adopt the 'token' approach, and their monetary reform of August 1862 provided that coins of less than five francs should be struck at a fineness of 0.835. These, like the Swiss coins, gained circulation in France. France itself took only limited steps, and only in May 1864, providing that the 50 centime and 20 centime coins should be struck 0.835 fine, the 1, 2 and 5 franc coins continuing in principle to be struck at the 0.900 fineness, but virtually disappearing from circulation. Belgium did not take any steps to produce coins at the reduced fineness, and Belgian silver coins also disappeared from circulation.

The obvious problem was that the Swiss and the Italians were issuing coins with a silver content less than their face value and collecting a useful additional seigniorage profit which could be enhanced if the coins concerned circulated in other countries. International agreement was needed.

## The conference of 1865

In response to this problem France called a conference in Paris in 1865. Eight questions were put to it by way of an agenda by the French delegate. With the assistance of the other delegates a ninth question was added:

> 9. With respect to the five-franc piece would it be advisable to reconsider the bimetallic standard?
>
> (Redish 2000, 192, 206)[1]

There was considerable support for the introduction of the gold standard: this was resisted by France, but the conference soon began discussing issues beyond the immediate problem, and sought to create a uniform and universal coinage, the Latin Monetary Union. The initial members were France, Italy, Switzerland and Belgium, and although it is perhaps the classic example in history of a monetary union, we must remember that it was based on a metallic currency, and that the four participating countries already had substantially the same monetary arrangements.

The treaty on Latin Monetary Union came into effect on 1 August 1866, and was to continue until 1880, and be renewed for further periods of fifteen years (unlike the later European Monetary Union, divorce provisions were built in to the original arrangements). The four original members were soon joined by the States of the Church (also in 1866) and Greece and Bulgaria (1867).

The treaty[2] did have to deal with the 'small change' problem the conference was convened to address, and under its terms the four countries agreed that they would coin only gold pieces of 100, 50, 20, 10 and 5 francs, together with silver coins of 5, 2, and 1 franc, and 50 and 20 centimes. Other coinages were to be withdrawn from circulation by 1 January 1869. The subsidiary silver coins (2 francs and less) would be issued on a 0.835 fineness, each member state would be permitted to mint such coins to the value of 6 francs per head of population, they would be legal tender within the Union only up to 50 francs (Article 6), although 'The state issuing them should receive them from its inhabitants without limit', and free minting of silver was abandoned. French and Italian coins were already on this standard: Swiss coins at 0.800 fine would be retired by the beginning of 1878 (Article 5). This has been described a 'fictitious double standard' but was in fact very close to being the UK model of a gold standard with a subsidiary coinage. Honour was perhaps satisfied by maintaining full value for the 5 franc piece (Article 3): this apparently innocuous gesture to tradition was later to create major problems.

The Latin Monetary Union did far more than solve this original 'small change' problem: it also created a substantial single currency area to the great convenience of travellers and traders.

Significantly, the treaty makes no mention of banknotes. There appear to have been no restrictions on their issue, and it was left to the discretion of the individual banks. In practice, and in sharp contrast with the United Kingdom, paper money was little used in the participating states. Recent experience with the assignats was hardly encouraging, but if the participants at the conference had expected a major expansion of paper money, there would have been a major political issue about who (government or domestic banks) had the right to print how much, who was to enjoy the consequent seigniorage profits, and how these rights and profits would be allocated between participating countries. Paper money would certainly have become a major issue had the UK joined, or seriously considered joining, but the continental European members apparently did not foresee any immediate problems, nor realise that note issues might, not long hence, form a significant part of money supply. The UK had, in the circumstances, nothing to lose from silence.

(When EMU was introduced in 2002, seigniorage was to be allocated on the basis of GDP, rather than on the actual note circulation. This would have given an income advantage to the UK, where credit cards were widespread, and a disadvantage to Switzerland, which made more than average use of paper money, had either been members.)

Henry Russell, the leading American historian of the events, wondered why

> France should worry over the introduction of a few Swiss coins into her territory displacing national coins and then form a treaty making all coins of three states legal throughout the territory.[3]

but agreed that this 'was the first important monetary meeting on international lines, the only one that ever resulted in a treaty' (Russell 1898, 28). It was not, of course, to be the last.

### The conference of 1867 – world money?[4]

Following on the success of the 1865 conference, Louis Napoleon, seeking to extend the French name and influence, called a further conference in 1867 to discuss a far more ambitious project, a uniform world monetary system. As we shall see, politics and personalities would influence events more than rational economic analysis, although then, as now, plenty of the latter was offered. Bismarck for instance 'probably had no disposition at this time to "Frenchify" the coinage of the new empire, even had it been convenient to do so ... he regarded the plan for international coinage as a Napoleonic dream' (Russell 1898, 116–7).

Although there was to be a real political battle, there was also (as with European Monetary Union) a simple technical solution, beneath the dignity of politicians who were (in both cases) more concerned with grand gestures and spin doctoring than with solving practical problems for their citizens.

The gold content of the sovereign was worth 25.2 francs, and unity could have been achieved with two simple steps:

- The UK would devalue the pound (by only 0.83 per cent) to make the sovereign worth exactly 25 francs (this would have involved the cost of reminting the gold, but not the silver, coins).
- The French and their Union partners would replace or augment their basic 20 franc gold 'napoleon' with a 25 franc coin, but make no other change in the substance of their monetary arrangements.

The Americans could, and would, have joined in: the half-eagle of 5 dollars would (had any been minted) be worth 25.85 francs, or £1.025. With an adjustment of around 3 per cent, it could have been brought into line with either the sovereign or a 25 franc coin: both, if only the Europeans would get their act together. The Americans were starting to reintroduce a gold coinage after the 'suspension' (greenback) period during the Civil War: they were keen on monetary union, would have been happy to reduce the value of the dollar by the amount needed, but wanted a quick decision while there was still little gold coinage in circulation and before the cost of re-minting became prohibitive. John E. Kasson, presenting his report to Congress in May 1866, supported a uniform system of coinage:

> The only interest of any nation that could possibly be injuriously affected by the establishment of this uniformity is that of the money changers – an interest which contributed little to the public welfare – while by diversity of coinage under and of values it adds largely to private accumulations.
>
> (Russell 1898, 35)

(He recognised that transaction costs, rather than exchange risks, were the real problem.)

At the conference, the US argued for the 25 franc piece, pointing out that:

> such a coin will circulate side by side everywhere and in perfect equality with the half eagle of the United States and the sovereign of Great Britain. These three gold coins, types of the great commercial nations, fraternally united and differing only in emblems, will go hand in hand around the globe freely circulating through both hemispheres without recoinage, brokerage or other impediment. This opportune concession of France to the spirit of unity will complete the work of civilisation she has had so much at heart and will inaugurate that new monetary era, the lofty object of the international conference, and the noblest aim of the concourse of nations, as yet without parallel in the history of the world.
>
> (Russell 1898, 76)

(There was to be a similar neat relationship, very briefly, in late 1999 when the dollar and the euro were at par with each other and both were equal to 100 Japanese yen. The key difference was that these were highly volatile rates: the euro had fallen by 15 per cent, and was to fall further, while the yen had risen by 13 per cent over the previous year.)

The French did not rise to this. They feared that a 25 franc coin would compete with their standard gold napoleon of 20 francs. They would have to bear the cost of re-minting, and, more seriously to the politicians, might lose out on their objective of being seen to impose a French standard on the world. Napoleon

> was quick to see that if the United States adopted for their half eagle the weight and fineness of the English sovereign, as Secretary Chase was proposing, it would not only be of great advantage to England but would compel France to change her whole coinage system without getting any glory from it.
>
> (Russell 1898, 25)

If the British had given a strong and positive lead, they could, allied with the Americans, surely have forced it through. If the French had indulged in their national sport of intransigence, the British could have upstaged them by acting unilaterally. They could have adjusted the weight of the sovereign so it was worth exactly 25 francs, having previously agreed with the Americans to set the value of the half-eagle at the same level. Even if the French and their LMU partners insisted on retaining the 20 franc coin, some of the advantages would have been achieved, and they would eventually have had to come into line.

It was not to be. The British, then as later, waffled. After lengthy courtesies and expressions of goodwill, the UK delegate, Mr Rivers Wilson, did a superb performance as 'Sir Humphrey':

> So long as public opinion has not decided in favour of a change of the present system, which offers no serious inconveniences, either in wholesale or retail trade, until it shall be incontestably demonstrated that a new system offers advantages sufficiently commanding to justify the abandonment of that which is approved by experience and rooted in the habits of the people, the English government could not believe it to be its duty to take the initiative in assimilating its coinage with those of the countries of the continent.
>
> But the English [*sic*] government will always be ready to aid any attempt to enlighten and guide public opinion in the appreciation of the question and facilitate the discussion of the means by which such an assimilation so advantageous in theory may be effected.
>
> Thus while consenting to be represented at this Conference the English government has found it necessary to place the most careful restrictions upon its delegates; their part is simply to listen to the different arguments, to study the situation as developed in discussion and to report to their government … they cannot vote for any question tending to bind their government or express any opinion to induce the belief that Great Britain would adopt the convention of 1865.
>
> (Russell 1898, 73–4)

The conference ended on 6 July with, in effect, only a resolution to meet again as soon as the different states had reported back.

## The UK Royal Commission

Following the 1867 Conference the UK set up a Royal Commission on International Coinage, which quickly produced a detailed and well researched report, looking at the cost saving to the business community, encouraging small business to export and the advantages of 'promoting commercial and social intercourse, and thus drawing closer the friendly relations between different countries'.

> Smaller manufacturers and traders are deterred from engaging in foreign transactions by the complicated difficulties of foreign coins …

by the difficulty in calculating the exchanges, and of remitting small sums from one country to another. Anything tending to simplify these matters would dispose them to extend the sphere of their operations .... One large dealer ... said very fairly that the adoption of a common currency would facilitate the competition of other importers ... from which ... it is obvious the public would benefit. ... The convenience ... to persons travelling ... too obvious to require remark.

(Report 1868, vii–viii)[5]

However, the Commission agonised over the difficulties of adjusting salaries and rents, and whether the change 'would be tantamount to a legal permission for every creditor to rob his debtor of 2 pence in the pound' (less than 1 per cent – trivial compared with the adjustments of twentieth-century inflation) and in the end caution won the day. (Against this, supporters argued that under existing arrangements, British travellers carrying sovereigns incurred losses because these were often accepted as being equal to 25 francs, when the real value was 25.20!) Again, the loss was less than that imposed on modern travellers using the electronic facilities of credit cards.

## The question of the gold standard

Bimetallism was still an issue, but not, at the time of the conference, a major one. Had it been quietly abandoned, as it nearly was, Latin Monetary Union would have survived and might, eventually, have attracted the wavering potential adherents. It was not to be: politics took over. A majority of countries (Holland dissenting) decided in principle to adopt the gold standard, in the rather simplistic belief that this had contributed substantially to British prosperity, while Laughlin (1892, 153) suggested that, but for the Franco-Prussian war, France would have been on gold by 1870.

The only other true 'gold standard' country represented was Portugal. Their delegate, Count d'Avilla, thought his government would have no objection to making the change, but naturally England would have to set the example. The true gold standard was also supported by Belgium, Switzerland and Italy, but opposed by the Banque de France and the Rothschild interests, both of which were loath to forego lucrative arbitrage opportunities.[6] The French government appears at first only to have supported bimetallism as a negotiating tactic hoping to 'give way' to gold in return for other concessions. Parieu, the vice-president and 'guiding genius', was a convinced gold monometallist, but 'his object was to suggest the easiest means for [coordinating] other systems with the French on any standard so long as France was the centre of the unification' (Russell 1898, 55).

Russell even suggests that the mention of silver was an afterthought, and that a gold standard was taken for granted. Writing in 1898, two years after silver had been a key issue in the US Presidential election, his pro-gold view is clearly and frequently expressed in his writing.

# 12 The collapse of bimetallism

## Introduction

In the event, the silver/gold situation had changed. In the 1860s silver had been the overvalued currency, at risk of being driven out of circulation, but in the early 1870s 'dollar shortage' became a 'dollar surplus', so to speak: the price of silver began to fall. It was no longer true that the LMU countries were on a *de facto* gold standard with a token subsidiary silver coinage: thanks to the status of the 5 franc coins, gold would have been driven out, threatening the existence of the bimetallic system to which France and the United States were, for very different reasons, attached. Although the collapse of the silver price was a key factor in the collapse of the talks on monetary union, there was nothing during the conferences and in the extensive writings of the 1860s to hint at the emotional and political overtones the issue of bimetallism was later to acquire.

The Germans, victors in the Franco-Prussian War, observing that the British were economically successful, and that the British were on a gold standard, drew the probably erroneous conclusion that the second fact caused the first, and decided that they too must introduce a gold standard. This they did, on the British model, partly financed by French reparations. The chief supporter of gold was Ludwig Bamberger, 'virtual founder of the Reichsbank', but he was opposed by Bleichroder, who

> knew how to appeal to Bismarck on this highly technical issue. In 1874 he warned him that the early introduction of an exclusive gold standard would make Germany dependent on the British gold market, which the British defended by raising rates.[1]

Germany adopted the gold standard on 4 December 1871, redefining the mark as 5.532 English grains of fine gold: this did not quite fit in with anyone else's system, as a 20 mark coin was worth about 2 per cent more than the sovereign. Surely if there had been a firm British lead, Germany would have made this small adjustment to help spread the idea of a universal coinage.

Germany immediately set about buying up gold, and inevitably, the silver price collapsed, the ratio falling to 16.6 by 1875. This modest initial fall was enough to damage bimetallism beyond repair, but the debate was to continue for the rest of the century.

The French were furious, and there was a vast political campaign in the United States where the silver mining states succeeded in stirring up 'silver' as a highly emotional issue. It has indeed been argued, persuasively, that *The Wizard of Oz* is really an allegory of money.[2] France was forced to suspend free mintage of silver, and the members of the Latin Union limited the coinage of silver to 6 francs per head of population. As discussed below, there were major repercussions in India and parts of the Far East operating on a silver standard.

Not everyone believed the change was permanent, and even the great Walter Bagehot in December 1876, a few months before his death, considered that

> The rise in price in silver which has just taken place is as local as the fall which preceded it ... Indeed such perturbations as a rise of 20 per cent, and then a fall to the old level in a single year ... would have caused a vast derangement of transactions.[3]

He was wrong about the course of the price – but very right about the consequences.

## The end of bimetallism

In September 1873 the French government decreed that only 250,000 francs of silver coins should be minted every day, and reduced this to 150,000 francs in November. In October the Belgian government suspended the free coinage of silver, and in November 1873 Switzerland asked France to convene a meeting to discuss what measures should be taken.

The conference met in January 1874. The Swiss favoured the adoption of a formal gold standard while the French and Italians thought that limitations on the issue of silver coins would be sufficient. A large number of 5 franc coins had been minted between 1867 and 1873, and with the rise in the ratio redeeming them at face value in gold would have created a loss. The other countries concerned had substantial holdings with the equivalent Italian five lire coins. The conference agreed limits on the coinage of silver 5 franc pieces. The Belgians, Swiss and Italians coined their ration out of silver bullion bought for gold, earning a seigniorage profit in so doing. The French, however, continued to permit the free coinage until June 1875, and the following year imposed a waiting period of about two years between delivering silver to the mint and receiving the coins. France (August 1876) and Belgium (December 1876) suspended coinage of the 5 franc piece.

There was a further conference in 1878. The agreement of 1865 was due to expire in 1880, but meanwhile because of the rise in the price of gold the problem of subsidiary coinage had solved itself. The problem had gone into reverse. France had accumulated large holdings of silver coins struck by the other countries, who would be faced with considerable expense if they were required to redeem them at face value. There was thus a 'limping gold standard' (Redish 2000, 201).[4]

## Conclusion

The Latin Monetary Union broke down, not because it was not a 'political union' and not, directly, because of the collapse of bimetallism. At no stage, not even in 1785, were the French committed intellectually to the principle: what began as an uncontroversial minor technicality, and later a mere bargaining counter, became inadvertently a political and emotional commitment. There was a real problem in that the value of the silver coins had become half their fiat value. There was a seigniorage profit to be gained from putting them into circulation, but an even larger loss to the issuer if they were redeemed or used for the payment of taxes at fiat value. Where coins could be used internationally, competition between different issuing authorities would have created problems, but these could surely have been resolved by commercial agreement. There would have been similar problems but on a larger scale, as and when paper banknotes became as widely used in the LMU countries as they were in the UK. Finally, discussions on 'optimum currency areas' seem irrelevant to 'gold standard' conditions: they are key to relationships with the silver-based East, discussed in a later chapter.

# 13  The United States in the nineteenth century

## Introduction

Although the United States is not an obvious case study of a monetary union, it has some surprising lessons for us: as a new country, with a federal constitution, it began its existence with a single currency which, but for the interlude of the Civil War, has continued until today. The history as outlined in this chapter has (at least) three lessons for our purposes.

### The US as a monetary union

The birth of European Monetary Union prompted Hugh Rockoff to ask:[1] 'How long did it take for the United States to become an optimal currency area?', while Michael Kouparitsas[2] goes further: 'Is the United States an optimum currency area?'

Rockoff says that

> Throughout the first 150 years of the US monetary union, at least, the United States was wracked repeatedly by bitter regional disputes over monetary policies and institutions ... what was good monetary policy from the point of view of one region, was sometimes bad policy from the point of view of another ... In short, an economic historian who is looking for illustrations of the cost of relinquishing monetary autonomy can find them in abundance in the United States.

while Kouparitsas points out that the US has only really had a 'single currency' since the passing of the Federal Reserve Act of 1913. Rockoff argues that this may have been an example of regional pressures within a non-optimal currency area, citing opposing views on this question. Advocates and opponents of European Monetary Union have looked hard at the similarities, and the very significant differences, between US and European circumstances.

### The Civil War as a monetary disunion

The Civil War is an example both of a 'monetary disunion' and one of the earlier experiments with inconvertible paper money, and also contradicts the idea that monetary union makes for a lasting peace.

### Bimetallism

As in France, bimetallism became an emotional political issue, but for rather different reasons. To a modern economist, this is odd. As in the UK, but in contrast to continental Europe, paper money and bank deposits were major components of the money supply, and the main monetary issue was, or should have been, not bimetallism but the role of banks in creating money.

In the United States support for bimetallism came from certain thinly populated silver producing states: Arizona, Colorado, Idaho, Montana, Nevada, New Mexico and Utah. On the US political system such states have the same representation (two) in the Senate as those, such as California and New York, with a much larger population. They allied themselves with the 'soft money' lobby, who had tasted blood with the greenbacks, only to see prices falling sharply in the run-up to the resumption of gold payments in 1879, and continuing through what used to be called the 'Great Depression'. They regarded free coinage of silver as second best (or as the 'sound money' General Walker [1888] commented, 'second worst'). For much of the period when Europe was debating Latin Monetary Union, and indeed when the so-called 'Crime of '73' was perpetrated, the issue was not in fact particularly relevant, as from 1861, when the Civil War began, until 1879, long after it was over, the Americans had an inconvertible paper currency, the 'greenback'.

## The history

This chapter weaves together these three threads, but only gives the relevant parts of the history. There is a more general account in Chown 1994, chs 18–20;[3] reprints of key documents (1838–48) can be found in *Early Origins of American Banking*,[4] and Friedman and Schwartz[5] is the classic study of the later period.

### Early history

The British government in London had taken little interest in the monetary affairs of its colonies. The thirteen continental colonies which were to form the United States had patched together separate currency systems which were at par neither with the British system nor with each other. There was a notorious shortage of sound acceptable coins such as the gold sovereign and the Spanish peso, and these were supplemented with various types of unreliable paper money and such expedients as cowrie shells.

The American Revolution had been financed by printing continental bills of credit, which experience left the Founding Fathers, who were to build a new monetary system from scratch, with a deep distrust of paper money. In 1785 Congress adopted the dollar as currency, and the Constitution of 1787 gave the exclusive power of *coinage* to the Congress. It was silent about *bank money* (notes and deposits), and the federal government and the states were to dispute their roles for much of the next century.

Alexander Hamilton's *Report on the Establishment of the Mint* (1791) recommended the double standard of gold and silver, but seriously underestimated the problem of fixing the ratio. The Mint Act of 1792[6] set the total weight of the silver dollar at 416 grains (371.25 grains fine) and that of the gold eagle ($10) at 270 grains (247.5 grains fine) giving a bimetallic ratio of fifteen. Both had unlimited legal tender, creating the classic 'Gresham' problem which was also to be faced in Europe.

Until 1819, this undervalued gold only slightly, and gold eagles and half-eagles were in fact minted from 1795. When the UK started to build up gold reserves to prepare for the resumption of specie payments in 1819, the relative gold price rose to the 'French' ratio of 15.5, and gold coins disappeared from circulation in the US, being replaced largely by banknotes, many of them issued by dubious banks. Paper money and bank credit was to play a key role in US monetary disputes.

In 1819 Congressman William Lowndes (a namesake of the British Secretary of the Treasury who was involved in Isaac Newton's 1696 currency reform) proposed and chaired a committee to examine the monetary system. This discussed the British system of token silver, and instructed William Crawford, Treasury Secretary, to report on the state of the banking industry. His 1820 report[7] advocated increasing the value of gold coin by 5 per cent (a ratio of 15.75, just above the French specie point) to bring them back into circulation, identified excessive note issues by banks as a major problem, and examined in some depth the possibility of a fiat paper currency which, he said, should meet the following tests:

1　That the power of the Government over the currency be absolutely sovereign.
2　That its stability be above suspicion
3　That its justice, morality, and intelligence be unquestionable
4　That an issue of the currency be made not only to depend upon the demand for it, but that an equivalent be actually received
5　That an equivalent can only be found in the delivery of an equal amount of gold or silver, or of public stock
6　That whenever, from whatever cause, it may become redundant, it may be funded at an interest a fraction below that which was surrendered at its issue.

Difficult tests to meet! He says that 'every attempt which has been made to introduce a paper currency has failed'.

The Treasury produced a detailed report on the relative value of gold and silver dated 4 May 1830,[8] Gallatin recommended a moderate devaluation,[9] and most advisers recommended the then market ratio was 15.625. As so often in these monetary matters, 'political considerations triumphed',[10] and the Act of 1834[11] changed the ratio from 1:15 (too low) to 1:16 (too high), by reducing the gold content of the eagle ($10) from 247.5 grains to 232 grains – a devaluation of 6.26 per cent. 'It was very clearly pointed out in the debates that the ratio of 1:16 would drive out silver' (Laughlin 1892, 64), and readers will not be surprised to learn that, as an inevitable result of this legislation *silver* coins now disappeared from circulation, their place being taken by Spanish and other foreign coins which, not having 'legal tender' status, could pass in trade in accordance with their actual bullion value.

To deal with this, in 1853 a short Act to Devalue the Subsidiary Silver Coinage[12] was passed, reducing the silver content of coins other than the silver dollar. This, says Laughlin (1892, 79), was a practical abandonment of the double standard in the United States: 'There was virtually no opposition, even though its real purpose was openly avowed in the clearest way in the House'. He quotes from Mr Dunham's speech: 'We have had but a single standard for the last three or four years. That has been, and now is, gold. We propose to let it remain so, and to adapt silver to it, to regulate it by it'. Laughlin adds that

> We have heard a great deal in later years about the surreptitious demonetisation of silver in 1873 ... the real demonetisation ... was accomplished in 1853 ... The Act of 1853 tried and condemned the criminal and after waiting twenty years for a reprieve ... the execution only took place in 1873.

This was, in substance, the British 'subsidiary coinage' solution, but it was not popular. The pressure for change was to come in part from silver mining interests. This price of silver, which had been (and was to revert to) $1.29 per ounce on the bimetallic system fell, in terms of gold, to $1.16 by 1876 and to 78 cents by 1893.

## The development of banking

Meanwhile, banking was, or should have been, the main monetary issue. Leaving aside the short-lived Bank of Pennsylvania, the Bank of North America was the first to commence operations in January 1782, joined in 1784 by the Bank of Massachusetts and the Bank of New York, these three being the only banks in the new country when the Federal Constitution came into operation in 1787. All survived into modern times, the first two after mergers, the last (still) remaining as an independent entity.

A new country needs a central bank. Alexander Hamilton, first Secretary to the Treasury, had a duty to 'receive, keep and disburse the money of the United States' but lacked the physical means of doing this except through collecting agents, and the three banks in December 1790 presented to Congress his 'Report on a National Bank', recommending the formation of a bank on the lines of the Bank of England. Congress, he believed, had the right to promote such a bank.

Hamilton belonged to the Federalist party, which believed in a strong central government, and in spite of opposition by Jefferson and Madison on 'states' rights' grounds, the bill incorporating the Bank of the United States passed both the House and the Senate. President Washington, rejecting the advice of the Attorney General and the Secretary of State that the Act was unconstitutional, signed the bill into law on 25 February 1791. It did not define the 'business of banking', but limited 'trading' to bills of exchange, gold or silver bullion, or goods pledged for loans and not redeemed. When the original charter expired in 1811, renewal was disputed, and the bank suspended payments in 1812.

Meanwhile, the number of private banks in the United States increased to ninety in 1811, and to 250 in 1816, the first failure being in 1807. There was virtually no control over small state banks, which were, quite literally, 'a licence to print money' with no effective limit unless and until there were net redemptions of notes, the underlying security proved unrealisable, and the bank failed.

The War of 1812 had to be financed, but European capital markets were closed to Americans, and the federal government still had no direct taxing powers. The war was more popular in the Middle and Southern states, and banks there provided, directly or indirectly, most of the funds. In 1814, Thomas Jefferson predicted a breakdown of the banking system and in August that year, following a British attack, banks in Washington and in Baltimore suspended payments, with Philadelphia and New York following soon after. Specie payment was only renewed in 1816, when Congress resolved that taxes must be paid in specie, or notes of specie-paying banks.

### The Second Bank of the United States

The Second Bank of the United States was chartered for twenty-one years in 1816, but was dissolved after a bitter dispute, the 'Bank Wars', between the bank's head, Nicholas Biddle, and President Andrew Jackson. The dispute was partly, but not wholly, between the West, favouring an expansionist monetary policy, and the 'sound money' men of the Eastern financial establishment.

There were major economic differences between regions, and as with Latin Monetary Union, a uniform currency does not necessarily mean a uniform money: the Founding Fathers had (understandably) failed to provide for the then-unforeseen development of coinage substitutes such as banknotes and deposits. The federal government had the sole right to issue *currency*, but the states claimed the right to regulate the *banks*, a function they often let go by default.

The early United States had a love–hate relationship with banks and banking. Although a necessary convenience providing the financial requirements of a rapidly growing economy, they reflected a bastion of privilege and a source of improper profit for fat cats whose activities were inconsistent with a modern democracy.

### Regional differences in banking practice

The Panic of 1819 placed great strains on the US banking and financial system[13] (Russell 1991, 49) and had led, in the agrarian South and West, to experiments with the issue of inconvertible notes. The banks could only stop runs by suspending payments. Notes continued to circulate, but at varying discounts, leaving the holders with financial losses.

The Western states had large numbers of small banks, most of which were, following the Panic, insolvent. The states reacted by revoking their charters, replacing their role with state-controlled 'relief banks', whose inconvertible notes were given a constitutionally dubious quasi-legal tender status. Their history was 'brief, controversial and generally undistinguished' (Russell 1991, 50).

Southern banks, typically larger and better capitalised with branch networks, also suspended payment but continued to operate, with smaller discounts. Russell (1991) argues that this was a successful experiment, with noteholders carrying part of the portfolio risk. The Second Bank eventually forced resumption: Virginia and South Carolina in 1823, and the others during the following five years.

After the Second Bank closed in 1834, the US had nothing approximating a federal central bank, and bank regulation was left to the states. The mood of the country favoured hard money and treated banks in general, and paper money in particular, with suspicion. Various methods of bank control were adopted at different times and in different places.

From 1829 New York required its banks to subscribe to a 'Safety Fund', an early version of deposit insurance: the rules were modified following the crash of 1837. During 1840–2 there were eleven failures, with debts other than notes of over $1 million, and the law was changed to relieve the Safety Fund of responsibility for deposits or any debts other than notes. Indeed, between 1836 and 1860 the character of banking changed as *deposits* began to substitute for banknotes. Chaddock[14] (1910, 333) comments: 'evidently banks did not realise until the panic of 1857 that deposits now constituted the danger point in banking and must be covered by a reserve as well as notes'.

### Free banking

In New England, banks had on the whole been well managed and continued to grow in number. Some states introduced free banking legislation in 1838 by which anyone could in principle obtain a bank charter, subject to strict reserve requirements. A bank had to hold a 100 per cent reserve against its notes in the form of mortgages or state bonds and an additional 12.5 per cent in specie (the specie requirement was repealed in 1840). A bank could not raise funds for commercial lending by issuing notes, although there was undoubtedly a profit from the operation. The reserve requirement was technically flawed, as the value of the state bonds held as security could fluctuate with interest rates and perceived quality, and at least in New York, there was no reserve requirement for *deposit* liabilities. Of eighteen states which adopted free banking by the 1850s, some took deposits into account, while others permitted part of the reserves to be held as deposits in other banks.[15] One method of generating a multiplier effect was to purchase state bonds at a discount and to deposit them with the state, which insisted that its bonds be valued at par.

## The Civil War

The belief, widely held by EMU supporters, that a single currency ensures a lasting peace is contradicted by the history of the Civil War. This was, in our terms, a 'monetary disunion'. The Confederate states issued their own eventually worthless currency, while in the North gold and silver money was temporarily replaced by inconvertible greenbacks. Californian banks are said to have issued gold-backed notes or 'yellowbacks' (Chown 1994, ch. 27), but if they did no specimens appear to have survived.

Meanwhile the silver issue was overshadowed by the crisis of 1857 and the Civil War: specie payments were suspended, gold went to a substantial premium in terms of greenbacks, and this wartime emergency measure (like so many of its kind) survived the war, actually remaining in force for nearly seventeen years. One side effect was to drive the subsidiary silver coins out of circulation. The value of the silver dollar was 96.9 cents in terms of gold: when the gold value of the greenbacks fell below this figure it was worth melting down the smaller coins.

In 1869, the Civil War having ended, John Jay Knox, Controller of the Currency, was put in charge of a plan to reintroduce metal subsidiary coins, and codify the conflicting laws dealing with the operations of the United States Mint. His recommendations included the effective abolition of the silver dollar, the relevant paragraph being headed in capitals.

## The silver dollar: its discontinuance as a standard

These recommendations were incorporated in the Coinage Act of 12 February 1873, which was to be described in pro-bimetallist literature, and handed down in American folklore, as 'The Crime of '73'. Myers[16] suggests that the legislation *did* receive thorough congressional scrutiny, but was hardly noticed by the press and public. The Treasury was preoccupied with the crisis of that year, while, as resumption was still six years in the future, the question was of little practical importance.

By the end of the war prices had doubled in terms of greenbacks: if resumption was to be at the old parity, they had to halve. Remarkably, they did, and it was. During the war the gold price had risen more or less in line with the GDP deflator. After the war, though, the gold premium fell, distorting purchasing power parity, derived largely by investor expectations of resumption. This was perhaps the last time the 'expectations' trick worked: it certainly did not for Winston Churchill!

After much debate, the Resumption Act was passed on 14 January 1875, providing that from 1 January 1879, greenbacks were to be redeemable in coin. Gold reserves were accumulated, by December 1878 the premium on gold finally disappeared, and 'Resumption Day' was a non-event.

The measures of 1873 were followed by the long recession known (at least to historians writing before 1931) as the 'Great Depression'. The victims were both industrial workers and farmers. As Myers[17] points out,

> To the farmers and the workers whose incomes were falling ... it seemed self-evident that what was needed was more money. It is so clearly a matter of common sense that more money is good for the individual that it seems to follow as a matter of logic that more currency is good for the country.

## Bimetallism again

Although resumption was intended to be on the basis of the *de facto* gold standard which had existed since at least 1853, bimetallism remained a live issue. Laughlin (1892, 93) says that, had silver not been legally demonetised in 1873,

> we [i.e. the US] would have found ourselves in 1876 with a single silver standard, and the resumption of specie payments on 1 January 1879 would have been in silver, not in gold; and 15 per cent of all our contracts would have been repudiated. The Act of 1873 was a piece of good fortune, which saved our financial credit.

Congress debated several measures aimed at increasing the price of silver and the stock of money, two separate but connected aims. A Commission of Enquiry was set up on 15 August 1876 to enquire into various monetary matters. Its majority report came down in favour of bimetallism and the remonetization of silver. The minority referred to this view as 'an illusion and an impossibility'.

### The Bland-Allison Act

The Bland-Allison Act became law on 28 February 1878 (the veto by President Hayes having been over-ruled by two-thirds majorities of both houses) and provided that between $2 and $5 million of silver was to be coined each month at the 'old' ratio of 15.5. The market rate was over 16 and rising sharply. Silver was to be legal tender, silver certificates could be issued and silver could not be used to redeem gold certificates. The House version of the bill would have permitted free coinage of silver: this provision was deleted by the Senate, which added a clause by which the administration was instructed to convene an international monetary conference to determine the ratio (Laughlin 1898, 184–5).[18]

The later Sherman Silver Act of 1890 required the Treasury to buy $4 million of silver each month, but not necessarily to coin it. Grover Cleveland, elected president in 1892, was inaugurated on the day of a Wall Street crash. Brogan says of him: 'There was not much room for ideas in Cleveland's massive head but when one had battered its way in it could never be dislodged'. Cleveland became the leading 'gold bug', but his administration coincided with the worst (and final) phase of 'The Great Depression' and the Free Silver movement became a major political issue.

The 1896 election was fought on this issue between the Republican McKinley and William Jennings Bryan of Nebraska. Bryan won the Democratic nomination with his famous speech to the party convention, presided over by the inappropriately named Governor of Illinois, John Peter Altgeld.

> You came to tell us that the great cities are in favour of the gold standard; we reply that the great cities rest upon our broad and fertile plains. Burn down your cities and leave our farms, and your cities will spring up again as if by magic; but destroy our farms and the grass will grow in every city. ... If they say bimetallism is good but that we cannot have it until other nations help us, we reply, that instead of having a gold standard because England has, we will restore bimetallism, and then let England have bimetallism ... we will answer their demand for a gold standard by saying to them: You shall not press down upon the brow of labour this crown of thorns, you shall not crucify mankind upon a cross of gold.

After a vigorous campaign, Bryan lost, and the Democrats were not to regain power for sixteen years. It also marked the end of the 'Great Depression', and of bimetallism as a serious political issue. The gold standard was now the supreme arbiter of a system of convertible paper currency in the United States and most of the civilised world. The 'golden age of the gold standard' was to last for all of eighteen years.

It has been said that 'there are three roads to madness, love, ambition and the study of bimetallism'; Bryan might well be an example. He appears to have died insane, and certainly shortly before his death in 1925 acted as prosecuting counsel for the State of Tennessee in its notorious case against Mr Scopes. A bemused world watched, as the state sought to invoke a fundamentalist law to prevent this unfortunate schoolmaster from teaching biology as a science.

Between 1896 and 1913, US wholesale prices rose nearly 50 per cent: an average of 2.5 per cent per annum, the then highest ever peacetime rate, and without any debasement or other form of monetary cheating. The world had simply found more gold, in South Africa, Alaska and Colorado, so that the supply of monetary gold almost doubled during the period. On the 'demand' side the absorbtion of monetary gold, as countries had switched from a bimetallic to a gold standard, had been completed.

Any period of rising prices is likely to generate a boom and bust cycle, and this was no exception. The panic of 1907 had several causes: Thibaut de St Phalle (1985, 47)[19] particularly draws attention to 'a lack of a centralised banking institution able to come to the aid of any bank in difficulty'. There were also real factors such as the enormous insurance claims following the San Francisco earthquake in April 1906, and the need to finance an unusually large harvest. At the end of 1906 London banks refused to discount any more American paper, and:

> there were problems caused by the lack of any central organisation: scattered reserves, lack of clearing facilities, absence of any lender of last resort. Excessive individual banking dependence meant that in times of panic each bank acted independently to protect its own liquid position. If a run started in one bank all the others would attempt to collect large amounts of cash simply to protect themselves against a similar run.

The National Bank Act allowed banks to deposit part of their reserve requirements with other banks in major cities, notably in New York, where 'pyramided reserves' were often used profitably to finance stock market loans. Prohibition of inter-state banking (a relic of the Bank Wars) made it difficult to transfer money quickly from one part of the country to another. The crisis came to a head with the failure on 22 October 1907 of the Knickerbocker Trust. Banks, at first in New York and later more generally, refused to repay depositors in gold, which went to a 4 per cent premium over deposits. J. P. Morgan successfully organised a pool of banks to support the market (see Friedman and Schwartz 1963, 156–63; de St Phalle 1985, 46–8). Restrictions on cash payments were removed in January 1908.

A National Monetary Commission, comprising nine members of the Senate and nine of the House, was set up to study the banking system in the United States and various other countries, and to make recommendations about changes to the banking system. They failed to produce a workable plan. This was not for want of research, and I have found their published reports to be an invaluable reference source for the student of money and to include much material which almost certainly would never have been translated into English but for their efforts.

A group of New York bankers, together with Senator Nelson Aldrich and other congressional supporters, met in secret at Jekyll Island and drafted a Banking Bill, 'the Aldrich plan' (Congress was not told that Wall Street bankers had had any part in drafting it). This would have created a National Reserve Association with a single central bank (de St Phalle 1985, 50). There was another delay until the Glass Owen Bill was approved by Congress as the Federal Reserve Act of 1913, a few months after the death of J. P. Morgan, who, it was said, had alone saved the situation in 1907. One of the first governors of the Federal Reserve Bank, an important player behind the scenes, and the first historian of the bank was Paul Warburg.[20]

**Part III**

# The silver countries, Russia and the sterling area pre-1914

# 14 The collapse of bimetallism in the Eastern silver countries

## A 'monetary disunion'?

### General introduction

The collapse of the silver price and the end of bimetallism had dramatic consequences for those countries, in the East and in Latin America, which based their currencies on silver. In, effect there was a major 'monetary disunion' between the 'gold' and 'silver' countries, when the sharp fall in the relative price of the latter suffered a forced devaluation caused by events in Europe and America events totally unrelated to their own economic needs. In modern terms they suffered from a 'disease of the reference currency'.

The gold price of silver fell from $1.33 (a ratio of 15.74, the bimetallic 'specie point') in 1871, to $1.17 (17.88) by 1875, recovering to $1.22 (17.22) in 1876. Not everyone believed these changes were permanent but the really dramatic fall was yet to come. The price was 65.4 cents in 1895 and hit a low of 52.8 cents (a ratio of 39) by 1902. It recovered to 61 cents (34) by 1907, later falling to 50 cents (42). In effect, the silver countries of the East, and Latin America saw the value of their currencies halve.

The silver countries took a long time to react. India took the lead and moved to a gold exchange standard in 1893; the American rulers of the Philippines introduced the gold standard in March 1903; Siam (now Thailand) introduced a gold exchange standard on 25 November 1902 and a full gold standard in 1908. A currency committee in the Straits Settlements had recommended a gold standard in 1893, the project was then shelved because of opposition by the local British community, but a gold exchange standard, modelled on that of British India, was finally introduced in January 1906. There were plenty of anomalies between neighbouring countries. French Indo-China retained monometallic silver while when the Netherlands adopted a gold standard on 6 June 1875, three and a half years after Germany, Java (Dutch East Indies) followed under the Currency Act of 28 March 1877. Glyn Davies makes a perceptive comment:

> Such a fall in the value of the legal and undebased coinage of a large group of countries comprising more than half the world's population

*Table 14.1*   Bimetallic ratios, 1890–1914

| Year | Yearly low | Yearly high | Yearly average |
|---|---|---|---|
| 1890 | 18.1 | 21.5 | 19.6 |
| 1891 | 19.9 | 21.5 | 20.7 |
| 1892 | 21.3 | 24.7 | 23.5 |
| 1893 | 24.1 | 29.7 | 26.3 |
| 1894 | 29.4 | 34.6 | 32.3 |
| 1895 | 29.8 | 34.4 | 31.3 |
| 1896 | 29.6 | 31.4 | 30.3 |
| 1897 | 31.4 | 39.3 | 33.9 |
| 1898 | 33.0 | 37.4 | 34.7 |
| 1899 | 32.3 | 35.1 | 34.1 |
| 1900 | 30.9 | 34.6 | 33.0 |
| 1901 | 31.6 | 37.5 | 34.4 |
| 1902 | 35.8 | 42.9 | 38.8 |
| 1903 | 33.1 | 42.7 | 37.7 |
| 1904 | 32.7 | 36.6 | 35.4 |
| 1905 | 30.8 | 36.8 | 33.6 |
| 1906 | 28.2 | 31.8 | 30.2 |
| 1907 | 28.8 | 38.6 | 30.9 |
| 1908 | 34.6 | 42.5 | 38.3 |
| 1909 | 37.5 | 40.5 | 39.4 |
| 1910 | 35.5 | 40.3 | 38.0 |
| 1911 | 35.8 | 39.4 | 38.0 |
| 1912 | 31.5 | 37.2 | 33.4 |
| 1913 | 31.8 | 35.8 | 33.9 |
| 1914 | 33.6 | 42.3 | 36.9 |

was without precedent a neglected aspect of the costs of the international gold standard and of the supremacy of sterling.[1]

This chapter discusses the contrasting experiences of some of the Eastern countries (leaving Japan and Korea, and the Latin American countries, for later) and outlines some of their earlier history.

### Note on sources

Kann[2], in spite of his title, looks beyond China, while Spalding[3] is a useful source of further information on several countries. Two anonymous sources have details and documents on money in the British colonies, Anon (1848)[4] and Royal Mint (1915).[5] Information on, and illustrations of the actual coins can be found in Stewart Lockhart (1895),[6] who catalogued the Glover Collection of 'Chinese, Annamese, Japanese and Corean coins', while Wicks[7] could be consulted by those interested in the earlier history.

## India

India was the first mover and the best documented example, Indian monetary questions having fascinated British economists from Sir James Steuart, who in 1772 recommended the use of paper credit as a method 'for correcting the DEFECTS of the present CURRENCY', to Maynard Keynes, 'Indian Currency and Finance' (1913).

There had been many local varieties of money circulating in India until, in 1835, the East India Company was given the right to mint its own silver rupees and half rupees which had full legal tender status and were generally accepted. Gold was not legal tender. In 1858 the coinage rights reverted to the British Crown, but with no change in the monetary arrangements or standard[8] (Report of the Indian Currency Committee 1892: 28–9).

The falling value of silver amounted to an unexpected and unwanted depreciation in the currency. The rupee (165 grains of silver) had been worth 22.39 pence, in terms of British gold currency, at the bimetallic ratio of 15.5:1. By 1893, the value had fallen to about half that, and was effectively floating with the price of silver.

Following the Report of the Indian Currency Committee (the 'Herschel Committee'), the Indian mints were closed to silver on private account, leaving the rupee effectively on a gold exchange standard. Rupees, or rupee notes, were supplied, against gold, at 16 pence per rupee and in 1899 the British sovereign was declared legal tender at the same rate, i.e. 15 rupees. Although the formal standard was gold, the silver rupee remained for practical purposes the circulating coinage of India. These coins were legally a subsidiary token coinage, and although sharply devalued, were trading at above the value of their bullion content (at least as long as the ratio remained above 21.7). Indeed they were, both in theory and practice, valued on exactly the same basis as paper rupees, a concept which puzzled contemporaries.

Irving Fisher (1920: 43)[9] quotes Sir David Barbour's story about the British Commissioner who asked an Indian merchant about how serious was the fall in the rupee. The merchant said he had never heard of the fall in the value of the rupee, but his Calcutta agents were very concerned by the rise in the price of gold.

A. J. Balfour (later British Prime Minister) said at the Mansion House, London, 3 April 1895:

> What is the British system of currency? I fix my attention on those parts of our great empire ... under the rule of the British Parliament. ... You go to Hong Kong and the Straits Settlements, and you find obligations are measured – in silver; you go to England, and you find that obligations are measured – in gold; you stop halfway, in India, and you find that obligations are measured ... in something which is neither gold nor silver – the strangest product of monometallist ingenuity which the world has ever seen – a currency which is as arbitrary as any forced

paper currency which the world has ever heard of, and which is as expensive as any metallic currency that the world has ever faced, and which, unhappily, combines in itself all the disadvantages of every currency which human beings have ever tried to form.

(Rothwell 1897, 246–7)[10]

A few years later, Maynard Keynes was to make his first contribution both to public policy and to monetary analysis on the questions of Indian currency. Describing the 1893 system as it was operating twenty years later, he summarised its main features.

(a)    The rupee is unlimited legal tender but [legally] … inconvertible
(b)    The sovereign is unlimited legal tender at £1 to 15 rupees …
(c)    As a matter of administrative practice, the government is … willing to give sovereign for rupees at this rate; but the practice is sometimes suspended …
(d)    the government will sell in Calcutta … bills payable in London in sterling at [not less than] 1s 3 29d/32d per rupee.

The fourth of these provisions is the vital one for supporting the sterling value of the rupee and, although the government has given no binding to maintain it, a failure to do so might fairly be held to involve an utter breakdown of the system.[11]

Keynes gives a list of events, and an analysis of the 'complicated and peculiar' legal position. Kemmerer[12] also discusses the crisis of 1907–8, and the 1913 Royal Commission, while H. Stanley Jevons (son of W. S.) gives a rather later perspective.[13]

## Siam

Siam (now Thailand) had used a cowrie shell currency but King Mongkut ('Anna's King') introduced a silver coinage based on the tical (or 'baht') with a silver content three-fifths of the Mexican dollar. When their purchasing power depreciated with the fall of silver, the effect 'became painfully apparent, not only to the Siamese trading and commercial community but also to the Siamese Government' which 'had seen her revenue expanding, but had been able to perceive few, if any, of the benefits which might naturally have been expected from such a satisfactory financial feature', and had to meet the increased cost of servicing gold-related debt.[14]

The government reaction shows a pattern of trying to fix an exchange rate when the 'reference currency' was effectively floating: a policy doomed to failure. On 27 November 1902 (when silver hit its first low) the mint was closed to the free coinage of silver, and would issue ticals only against the deposit of gold with its London bankers and at a rate of exchange to be ascertained. The rate was initially fixed at 17 to the British pound, compared with a market rate (based on the relative value of gold and silver) of 21.75, so that banks needing to repay depositors could not obtain silver coins. The rate soon had to be changed to 20, but by luck rather than judgment silver then began to appreciate, and between then and August 1903 there were about a dozen small adjustments, mostly upwards, in the value of the tical. There was an increase in imports and a fall in exports. There were two further adjustments before the rate was set at 16 on 16 November 1905, in the hope that this would remain stable. As modern readers would expect, it was not to be, and following a shortage of silver in 1906 the value was raised to 15 (temporarily at par with the Indian rupee) and later to 13.5.

The Gold Standard Law came into force in November 1908, based on an official rate of 13 ticals to the pound sterling. The government had sole power to issue currency, but the mint would sell coin to anyone against the tender of gold bullion. It had been intended to introduce a gold 'dos' or 19 tical gold piece, but this plan was interrupted by the war. Meanwhile the silver tical was made unlimited legal tender with an assumed value of 0.558 grams of pure gold, with a let-out if the market value of the silver exceeded this.

During the First World War certain provisions of the Act were suspended, the silver content of the tical was reduced from 900 to 650 fine, and in 1919 the gold value was adjusted to 0.610 grams to protect the subsidiary silver coinage. Further measures proved necessary, and in 1920 the silver content of the (technically subsidiary) silver coins was further reduced.

## Straits Settlements

During the nineteenth century, a wide variety of coins circulated in the British South-East Asian colonies (Singapore, the Malay States, British North Borneo, Labuan and Sarawak). These were mainly 'dollars' of various types and origin, including the 'pillar dollar' showing the Pillars of Hercules but with the legend *plus ultra* replacing the classic *ne plus ultra*, to reflect that since ancient times lands *had* been discovered further West! Silver rupees, the Dutch rix dollar, the kobang and various other dollars also circulated.[15] The East India Company, which administered the territories until 1867, declared the Indian rupee legal tender and tried, unsuccessfully to force the currency on the inhabitants, but after control was transferred to the Colonial Office the rupee was decreed to be no longer legal tender and was replaced with Hong Kong dollars, silver dollars of Spain, Mexico, Peru and Bolivia, and 'any other silver dollar to be specified from time to time by the Government in Council'.

Subsidiary coins including copper were at first supplied from Hong Kong, but the Mint there was closed in 1868, and from 1871 certain subsidiary coins (less than $1) were specifically struck by the Royal Mint. In 1890 the Mexican dollar became the main coin, later alongside the British 'trade dollars' mainly struck in India. A 'British Dollar (374.4 grains of fine silver, slightly lighter than the Mexican dollar) was introduced in 1897 and a Straits Settlement dollar in 1902. The Hong Kong and Shanghai Bank provided a reliable banknote currency as the main bank of issue from its formation in 1865.

This was essentially a silver standard, and these colonies, like their neighbours, suffered from an effective, but for them irrelevant, devaluation as the gold price of silver fell. In 1893, after the closing of the Indian mints, the Colonial Office instructed the Governor to set up a currency committee. Most witnesses, with the exception of Chinese traders, agreed that 'the fall in exchange has been disadvantageous to the Settlements'.[16] The twelve members divided equally between gold and silver, and nothing was done. In 1897 the Singapore Chamber of Commerce appealed to London for a fixed exchange standard, 'the havoc caused by the continuous depreciation of the gold value of silver induced the Straits Settlements to clamor for a speedy remedy simultaneously with, but independently from, China'.[17]

The sub-committee recommended a currency based on the gold sovereign, with a Straits dollar of 2 shillings as a subsidiary coin struck (like English silver and the Indian Rupee) underweight in silver. The plan was to be kept secret, and adopted simultaneously by the Federated Malay States. It was criticised by the FMS president because of the expense, the danger of counterfeiting, the difficulty of keeping the secret, and the problem of getting the native population to accept seriously underweight smaller coins.

The plan was shelved, and there were no further developments until 1902 (when the silver price hit its temporary bottom). At the request of the Chamber of Commerce the Straits Currency Committee (including the ubiquitous Sir David Barbour) convened. Much of the evidence was heard in London and gave more weight to the views of English merchants than of Chinese traders.

The Settlements did not suffer from India's problem of a large public debt in gold, but the salaries of senior officials were fixed in sterling, and the cost of imports from 'gold' countries had risen sharply. The silver standard was also said to have discouraged the investment of foreign capital.

Following the recommendations of the committee, a gold exchange standard, modelled on that of British India, was introduced in January 1906, and under an Order in Council of 22 October the sovereign was made legal tender at 2s 4d per dollar, the latter remaining the standard coin.

## China

Sources include Wen Pin Wei,[18] Eduard Kann,[19] G. Vissering,[20] and (up to 1895) Frank H. H. King.[21]

The early history of Chinese currency, and indeed of China, is complex, but copper 'cash' (round coins with a square hole, through which the coins could be strung together) were the main circulating medium for two millenia. The earliest paper money dates back to the Song dynasty, and possibly earlier, and became the predominant form of money, at least for business transactions, during the Yuan dynasty (1271–1368). Notes were variously issued by provincial governments and, later, by banks, and there were the usual problems of over-issue.[22]

Silver was used from earliest times, generally passing by weight, often in the form of ingots, 'cakes', or tablets. Tibetan silver coins date from 1632, at about the time that traders started bringing foreign silver dollars into China. Exports of tea and silk greatly exceeded imports, and the balance was settled in silver. The Spanish carolus (1788–1808) was particularly popular. 'Imitations' were officially tolerated for a time but were often struck with debased silver. The habit of 'chopping' or marking a genuine coin dates from this period.

The reform of 1895 began at the end of the war with Japan and was 'rudely interrupted by the *coup d'état* of 1898 and a reaction came with the return of the rule of the Empress Dowager'. There were rather disparagingly, 'many suggestions ... characterised by a lack of knowledge of monetary principles and of the actual conditions and needs of the country'. Hu Chu-fen, mayor of Peking had suggested a uniform coinage in gold, silver and copper and the foundation of a note-issuing government bank but these sensible suggestions were 'doomed to failure right from their inception'.

Sheng Hsuan-huai (a.k.a. Sheng Kung-pao)[23] put forward detailed proposals based on the Chingping tael as the monetary unit, with a central mint at Peking and branch mints elsewhere. He wanted to establish a Chinese-owned national bank and to issue gold coins. Imperial sanction for this was given in February 1897 but the project was never implemented. Yang Yi-chi, a junior official, then advocated the English system of (gold) pounds and shillings, but wanted to prohibit the export of gold through Shanghai. Kann regarded these proposals as naive.

The war indemnity due to Japan was settled by 7 May 1898, computed in English money, paid in gold in London and financed by foreign loans denominated in gold standard currencies. During 1895–1901, China had accumulated gold debt of £120,000,000 and the exchange rate began to decline in late 1901. In 1902 the idea of a gold standard was reconsidered. The Mackay Treaty with the UK provided that 'China agrees to take the necessary steps to provide for a uniform national coinage which shall be legal tender', and there was a similar provision in a US treaty of commerce of the same year.[24]

By 1914, the basic coin of China was the copper cash, a silver coin based on the tael, which Wen Pin Wei tells us 'must not be mistaken for real bimetallism ... [which] requires free coinage of two metals ... both of which are legal tender ... the cash is a standard coin; the tael an uncoined unit of weight.' Regulations issued in 1910 specified the silver dollar as the currency of China, minting rights being vested solely in the central government. In 1914 the yuan became the standard coin.[25] China remained on a silver standard, but on what was by then a relatively stable though 'devalued' ratio. This was to have consequences in the 1930s.

# Hong Kong

Hong Kong, like China, remained on the silver standard well into the early twentieth century. There had been a wide variety of coins circulating in the South-East Asian colonies, but a 'British dollar' was introduced in 1897 and a Straits Settlement dollar in 1902. The Hong Kong and Shanghai Bank provided a reliable banknote currency as the main bank of issue from its formation in 1865.[26] The main silver currency (in 1919) was the British dollar (374.4 grains fine silver, slightly lighter than the Mexican dollar), but banknotes had circulated widely since 1872. Spalding refers to a 'curious' anomaly in 1916, when the export of silver was prohibited,[27] while Muhleman,[28] describing the world's monetary systems in 1908, refers to Hong Kong as 'the exchange point between gold-standard and silver-standard countries'.

In 1842 attempts were made successively to impose various silver dollars, and then the East India Company's gold and silver coins, on Hong Kong, as legal tender. The Chinese traders continued to transact the business in silver by weight.

Following the Australian gold discoveries, Australia joined the United Kingdom gold standard, with silver being legal tender only up to 40 shillings, and a proclamation of 1852 extended this to Hong Kong, intended as a step towards a gold standard throughout the East. Another proclamation, of 1853, held Hong Kong to have a gold currency with subsidiary coins of silver and copper as in the UK. This had no effect, and a legal decision declared that a contract made in dollars could be enforced in that currency. In 1863 Hong Kong was formally recognised as being outside the British currency area, former proclamations were cancelled, and the Mexican and other silver dollars were declared the sole legal tender. The British authorities did not give up the battle completely, and tried to put a 'British dollar' into circulation, to extend the British sphere of influence in the East. These again failed to attract the interest of the Chinese, and the mint set up to strike them had to be dismantled.

Banknotes had been issued by the three major banks operating in the colony since 1872, including small denomination 1 dollar notes which the Chinese accepted as a satisfactory substitute for the silver dollars to which they were accustomed.

Problems arose in 1916, during the First World War. The price of silver rose sharply in London, and both Europe and India were attracting dollars from Shanghai and Hong Kong. The government of Hong Kong had to prohibit the export of silver, 'and the following curious result was witnessed'. The Chinese wanted silver dollars to send to Shanghai and were therefore prepared to take less than, say, $5 for a 5 dollar note, which was equivalent to saying that silver was at a premium or a note was at a discount, which of course was a complete reverse to the usual position.[29]

Hong Kong therefore remained on a silver standard alongside China, but in spite of the efforts of the colonial power never became involved in any fixed gold exchange rate.

# 15 Japan and Korea

## Introduction

Japan had had little commercial contact with the rest of the world during the Togukawa period (*c.*1600 – 1868) and her experience was rather different from that of other Far Eastern countries. The silver question was not a major issue, and the country made a relatively simple transition to a gold standard in 1897. Korea, under Japanese rule for much of the relevant period, makes an interesting contrast.

## Early history

Copper coins circulated from 708 to 958 AD, and the 'twelve antique sen' known to numismatic historians[1] appear to get successively smaller, as one might expect. It appears that each successive issue was 'cried up' to ten times the face value of its predecessor: an intriguing early example of 'inflation tax'. There followed six centuries during which there appears to have been no official Japanese coinage, although Chinese coins were widely used.

Around 1600 effective control of Japan was obtained by the Togukawa family as Shoguns, with the Emperor as a figurehead. The 'revolution' was begun by Nobunaga (1524–82) aided by his allies Hideyoshi, who was Regent from 1584 until his death in 1598, and Ieyasu, who secured the dominace of the Shogunate by 1615 and died in 1616. These three allies founded a dynasty which was to continue until 1868. For much of the Tokugawa period, foreign intercourse was severely restricted, but there was a major reform of the coinage.

## Currency at the time of the Meiji Restoration

The modern history of money and banking in Japan begins with the opening of the country to Westerners following Commander Perry's Edo raid in 1853 and the opening of Yokohama as a treaty port on 1 July 1859.

Tamaki[2] (whose main topic is banking) says that the in the early days of the treaty ports the Mexican silver dollar was the universal trade currency in the East, but that until 1873 taxes in Japan were paid in rice, which was 'the real currency' of the country.

> The standard coin available in Japan was the *ryo*. ... many of the coins were debased and much of the paper devalued. The *han* [regional government] issued paper money, *hansatsu*, which circulated locally. The *bakufu* [national government] issued coins. There was little understanding of the danger of isssuing more paper than was required, and of Gresham's Law.

In 1868, the year of the Meiji Restoration, the goverment realised the urgent need for reform of the monetary system, and in 1869 announced that it would adopt a silver standard with supplementary gold coins. It soon changed its mind and issued new regulations, based on the gold standard, on 10 May 1871. A new yen gold coin weighing 23.15 grams was introduced, and a silver 'yen', on the same weight and fineness as the Mexican dollar, was also issued (as a trade dollar) for the Treaty Ports.

Tamaki begins his study of the Japanese banking system with these words:

> Eleven of the top twenty international banks in the world in 1992 were Japanese and yet on July 1859, when the treaty port of Yokohama was finally opened to importunate westerners, Japan had no companies which could undertake modern banking business.[3]

### 'Arbitraging' the bimetallic ratio

> The most astonishing result was the outflow of gold from Japan. The bakufu did not understand that gold in Japan was, in relation to the world, too cheap. In June 1859 ... the parity of exchange ... was 1:6.44 [cf. 1:15 elsewhere] and between 100,000 and 150,000 of *ryo* of gold was drained out of Japan before Western diplomats persuaded the *bakufu* authorities to change the coinage in 1860.[4]

On the same incident Jevons cites

> the most extreme instance which has ever occurred. At the time of the 1858 treaty, European traders discovered that the ratio in Japan was 4 to 1. Great profits were made – for a short time. ... At the time of the treaty of 1858 between Great Britain, the United States and Japan ... a very curious system of currency existed in Japan. The most valuable Japanese coin was the kobang ... a thin oval disc of gold. ... It was passing currency ... for four silver itzebus, but was worth in English money 18s.5d., whereas the silver itzebu was equal only to about 1s.4d.

Thus the Japanese were estimating their gold money at only about one third of its value as estimated ... in other parts of the world. Not surprisingly, the early traders made hugh profits before 'the natives' withdrew gold from circulation. A complete reform of the Japanese currency is now [i.e. 1875] being carried out, the English mint at Hong Kong having been purchased by the Japanese government.[5]

In such a situation it always pays to look at numismatic sources, which can be relied upon to give accurate information on the actual coins in circulation. Krause and Mischler[6] give details of the actual coin weights (there is more information, and excellent illustrations, in Stewart Lockhart[7] and Munro[8]), and they say that until 1870 the system was 16 shu = 4 bu = 1 ryo, but that during this period there was 'no fixed exchange rate' between gold, silver and copper coins. However 'from time to time the government would declare an official exchange rate, but this was usually ignored'.

### The currency reform of 1871

The Currency Act of 1871 introduced a new currency, the yen, divided into 100 sen. This was originally on a silver standard (the silver coins weighed 25g .800 fine per yen; the gold yen weighed 1.67g .900 fine, an implied ratio of 13.3) although the Act contemplated an eventual change to gold. A new mint was set up at Osaka. In the following year the National Bank Act of 1872 came into force based, for some reason, on American principles. The Dai Ichi ('number one') Bank was set up in 1873, followed by many others.

### The post-restoration inflation 1876–9

From our point of view the main effect was a large number of local banknote issues. There was an expansion both of banknotes and of inconvertible government notes. The *samurai* class were given ¥174 million of bonds in commutation of their stipends. In spite of this increase in money supply the notes kept most of their value until 1875. However, by 1879 national notes caused inflation and a depreciation of 34 per cent against gold and 21 per cent against silver (Tamaki 1996, 37). Tamaki does not explain this discrepancy, but it in fact simply reflects the fall in the price of silver (to a ratio of 17.88 in 1879) following the collapse of bimetallism.

### The specie shortage 1881–5

Partly because of this, Count Matsukata, the minister of finance, visited Europe in 1881 to study central banking techniques, and following this the Bank of Japan was established in 1882, the constitution based on that of the National Bank of Belgium.[9] Tamaki mentions the discussions on the merits of British and American banking techniques, and the role of the Scot, Alexander Allan Shand of the Chartered Mercantile Bank, who was recruited as adviser (on a cabinet minister's salary of ¥500) in August 1872.

Note issues of the Bank of Japan were expanded until in 1899 they became the only notes to constitute legal tender.

## The gold standard

Following victory in the Sino-Japanese War (1894–5) Japan received an indemnity of ¥360 million payable in sterling. Matsukata used the Chinese indemnity to bring Japan onto the gold standard in 1897, and the notes became convertible into gold.[10] The coinage unit was the yen (2 pun) of 0.75 grams of pure gold, and the standard coins were 10, 20 and 50 yen. This was half the old standard: previous gold coins passed at twice face value. Subsidiary silver coins, of old and new issues, continued to circulate, but the silver yen gradually exchanged at par for gold yen. Japan's credit rating rose, the country was able to borrow on favourable terms in the international market and there was a large inflow of foreign capital.

## Korea[11]

The first Korean (iron) coins were issued in 996, and during the next nine centuries there were a series of monetary reforms, none of which appears to have produced a uniform and stable monetary system. Paper money, in imitation of the Chinese yuan, was introduced in 1401 and continued to be used for two centuries.[12]

From 1633 to 1891 the principal Korean money was the copper yopchon, a cast round coin with a square hole issued in thousands of varieties and widely counterfeited. This was supplemented in parts of the country by a nickel coinage, but the (British) head of customs, J. McLeavy Brown, insisted on duties being paid in silver.

The first attempt at reform came in 1891, when Korea was under Japanese domination, and a Japanese adviser introduced a coinage based on the Japanese system. In 1897, Korea having regained independence, a Russian adviser, Alexieff, produced a plan to eliminate Japanese yen, and a coinage law of February 1901 prohibited these, replacing them with a coinage based on the Japanese system but called the whan.

None were struck, and in 1904 during the Russo-Japanese war Japan signed a protection treaty with Korea, and a Japanese adviser, Baron T. Megata, was brought in. The Japanese system was formally introduced. The Seoul office of Dai Ichi Ginko took over the role of central bank and issued banknotes, handing over this role to the Bank of Korea in 1909. In 1910 Korea was annexed and remained under Japanese rule until a US military government took control in 1945, handing over to a Korean government in 1948.

# 16 Latin America in the nineteenth century

## Introduction

The Napoleonic Wars precipitated the perhaps already inevitable collapse of Spanish control of Latin America, but in contrast to the birth of the United States,

> Independence proceeded, *cabildo* by *cabildo*, following the organisation of a system that concentrated everything in towns. There was no united opposition to imperial taxation, no Continental Congress. ... There were no colonial institutions analogous to the assembly of the English colonies that could provide a coherent framework for the ordering of conflict. The independence movement rapidly assumed the character of a civil war.[1]

There are three related monetary themes:

- the break-up of an old (colonial imposed) currency area (a 'monetary disunion') following the collapse of a political union;
- various moves towards monetary unions that mostly didn't happen; and,
- in common with the Far East, there was a forced devaluation or 'monetary disunion' caused by the collapse of bimetallism. This paralleled the similar developments in Asia.

## The road to independence

As with the British colonies that were to become the United States, the colonial powers, Spain and Portugal, did not take the monetary affairs of these far away places very seriously. There was a fairly adequate circulation of Spanish silver, supplemented by a wide variety of foreign coins. As each country became independent, it began issuing its own currency, retaining the silver (or bimetallic) standard inherited from Spain or, in the case of Brazil, from Portugal.

The new countries typically sought to manage their own monetary affairs, and showed little interest in cooperating with their neighbours in monetary unions, in spite of their economic similarities and a shared language and culture. Indeed, their patterns of behaviour soon diverged. Some of the newly independent Latin American states had recourse to inconvertible paper money, acquiring habits which they have found hard to break. Others, which remained on a silver standard, suffered the same problems as the Far East when the price of silver fell in terms of gold: these were postponed, but eventually made worse, because its major neighbour and trading partner, the United States, was effectively on an inconvertible paper standard from 1861 to about 1878, i.e. during and after the Civil War. Mexico is the best documented example of this effect but other countries have similar, but in some ways contrasting, experiences.

## Early experiences with paper money

Argentina, Brazil, and Chile almost immediately, and Colombia, Guatemala and Peru rather later, had recourse to paper money, a habit which continued into the twenty-first century. Although they were technically 'off silver' they did not, during the nineteenth century, indulge in an excessive over-issue of paper, there are no examples of hyper-inflation, and when convertibility was restored the previously inconvertible paper money retained at least some residual value. This pattern was similar to the UK 'suspension' and the winning side in the American Civil War, but contrasted with the experience of revolutionary France, the American Confederate states, and indeed the twentieth-century history of Latin America!

John Parke Young's study of Central America[2], written in 1925, compares the different experiences of five countries: Guatemala, Salvador, Honduras, Nicaragua and Costa Rica. He is best on the period 1914–23, not discussed here, and omits Panama which had, for most of his period, been part of Colombia. His teacher, E. W. Kemmerer (himself a major contributor to monetary history) says in the introduction that

> One of the nearest approaches that can be made ... to the advantages of the laboratory method ... is in the study of currency reforms in small countries whose economic life is simple. ... Herein lies one of the principal services of the present book. Central American countries are all small. ... The ten year period 1914–1923 ... is particularly favourable for the study of fundamental monetary laws under simple conditions.

The country examples described below confirm the diversity of international monetary experience, and a major comparative study (by a reader of Spanish) could well extract some subtle lessons. Deane and Pringle, though, are not encouraging, saying that 'the monetary history of Latin America is very much its own ... it seemed to offer few monetary lessons to those colonies [that cast off independence] only this century'.[3]

The implications of paper money were discussed in a conference paper by Guillermo Subercaseaux (1909),[4] Professor of Political Economy at the University of Chile. He distinguishes between paper money introduced 'as a product of progressive and calm deliberation of monetary institutions', or alternatively as the results of crises, whether 'a shortage of money by the state' or a 'monetary crisis specially affecting banking institutions'. There are also brief accounts in Muhleman 1908, while Deaver (1970) discusses Chile.

## Argentina[5]

Argentina became formally independent in 1816, but the revolutionaries had briefly captured the Potosi mint in 1813 and struck 8 real ('sole') coins there: these were the first non-Spanish coins in the region. Following various provincial coinage issues, there was a national issue of 8 reales (subsequently renamed the peso) from 1826.

The Bank of Buenos Aires was formed in 1822, and its banknotes were at first actually worth a slight premium over gold, but in 1826, when the country was at war with Brazil, its notes were declared inconvertible and the bank was taken over by the government. By 1828 the paper peso was worth only 7 to the gold peso, fell further to 32 by 1840, but stabilised at about 25 by 1856. In 1867 there was a resumption and a reconstruction on this basis of 25 paper pesos for 1 gold peso, a dramatic depreciation, but modest by later standards.

In 1875 Argentina adopted a gold standard by which all comers could bring gold bullion to the mint to be coined into gold pesos which were unlimited legal tender, silver being legal tender only for limited sums. The silver peso was effectively demonetised, following the 1873 example of the US silver dollar. In practice though, Del Mar says 'there was neither mint nor national coinage'.[6] The legislation also accorded full legal tender status to the gold coins of several other countries, including the UK and the US, on the basis of their bullion content. The whole exercise would appear to have been a gesture rather than a real reform, as the circulating medium really consisted of 500–600 million dollars of bank notes.

The experiment did not last, and on 16 May 1876 the 'resumption' was 'suspended' and gold went to a 30 per cent premium: by 1891 paper had so depreciated that 230 paper pesos were worth 100 gold pesos. In 1899, when economic circumstances were favourable, the exchange was fixed at 44 centavos gold for 1 paper peso, and new notes were issued on a gold basis and steps were taken to fix the rate for depreciated paper money at this figure. Subercaseaux (1909, 36) adds that about half the outstanding 518 million pesos of notes remained unguaranteed: he describes the country as 'emerging from the regime of heavily depreciated paper'. A US-style 'national banking system' was inaugurated in 1881: the latter was liquidated in 1891 and replaced by the Banco de la Naçion Argentina.

## Brazil

Portuguese rulers had been minting and issuing coins specifically for Brazil, on a system of 120 reis = 1 real, the standard 960 reis coin being at par with the Spanish 8 real, an arrangement reminiscent of the initial stages of the Latin Monetary Union. When Brazil became an independent empire in 1822, this coin appears to have been debased slightly to 26.89 grams .896 fine or 24.09 grams of fine silver. From 1833 a new unit, the rubreis of 1000 reis, was introduced with a more substantial debasement: the (non-existent) 8 real coin would have weighed 19.73 grams of fine silver. Brazil became a republic in 1889 with no change in the monetary system.

Paper money developed in a pattern similar to Argentina. Notes of the Bank of Brazil date from as early as 1808, when the country was still under Portuguese rule. Apart from the 1813 issue from captured mines, there was virtually no gold or silver coinage, leaving copper coins as the only metal money into which notes could be changed. In 1820 the notes had depreciated, but later the government guaranteed the notes and made them legal tender. In 1846 the gold value of coins was reduced in line with the depreciation of paper. The exchange rate was fairly stable until 1898, when there was a sharp fall followed by a reconstruction in 1906 (Subercaseaux 1909, 36).

## Chile

In Chile, the system was at first bimetallic in principle – but exclusively silver in practice. Commercial banking began in 1860 and developed rapidly. Banknotes became inconvertible during the war with Spain in 1865, and in 1878 specie payments were suspended, with a policy of 'forced circulation'. Inflation was modest at first, and Subercaseaux refers to issues of '*billets fiscaux*' with legal tender status. The paper peso fell on the London market from its 1879 rate of 42 pence to 12 pence by 1894, but the silver peso had itself fallen to 23 pence because of the fall in the price of silver.

In 1895 a gold standard was adopted on the basis of an 18 pence peso, since when 'this enterprising republic has endeavoured ... to recover from the depreciated paper currency regime but has not yet succeeded' (Muhleman 1908). Gold sovereigns remained legal tender at 13.33 pesos: the premium on gold remained in the range 15–70 per cent. There were unsuccessful attempts to restore a metallic standard in 1879 and 1928.[7]

## Colombia

Colombia[8] first issued paper money in 1811 to finance a revolutionary war, but after becoming independent in 1821 confirmed the former Spanish monetary legislation. 'Gran Colombia' was initially a confederation with Ecuador and Venezuela which broke up in 1830. All three countries were in the 'silver' group for most of the rest of the century.

In 1847 a decimal system was introduced on the basis of a silver granadino of 10 reales, exactly equivalent to 5 French and LMU francs, and a gold condor of 10 pesos, on the LMU ratio of 15.5, effectively 'dollarising' the country by adopting the weight standards of the Latin Monetary Union.

Colombia opened its first bank in 1871, and after 1875 banknotes (initially convertible) soon replaced disappearing metal coins. In 1881 the Banco Naçional opened with the exclusive right of note issue, and in 1886 issued 4 million pesos on the orders of the government on its promise to redeem in silver, and these became the only legal money of the country. At first these traded near parity, but following huge issues during the Civil War of 1899–1902 the paper peso fell from $1 to about 1 US cent.

## The 'silver' countries and the bimetallic problem

The countries described above all went through periods of (comparatively mild) inflation based on unconvertible paper money, but eventually attempted, with mixed success, to stabilise on a gold standard. Bimetallism was not an issue for them, as it was for those which remained on a silver standard. Their experiences paralleled those of the Eastern countries, but with the important difference that their main trading partner (the United States) was at the key time on an inconvertible paper standard.

## Mexico[9]

Mexico, as one of the world's largest silver producers, had had an impeccable monetary record. In 1824, on becoming independent, it adopted, as the peso or dollar, the old Spanish 'piece of eight' (reale), also the ancestor of the US dollar. This circulated widely as a trade coin, and was indeed legal tender in the United States until 1857. A decimal system introduced by the law of November 27 1867 confirmed the formal bimetallic system (at a ratio of 16.5 compared with the French 15.5) in force since 1675. Given the ratio, little gold was struck and Mexico (silver mining being its second largest industry) was on a *de facto* silver standard.

All was well until the silver price collapsed, and although the peso had the same silver content as the US dollar, the exchange rate with the gold standard US fell to 48.5 cents by 1900. This unintended devaluation had the usual consequences, as Mexico's external debt (about $240 million) and the peso cost of servicing it doubled, and the peso exchange rate (directly tracking the gold price of silver) became very volatile. Kemmerer (1916, 484ff) says the currency uncertainty was discouraging foreign investors – but surely there would have been buying opportunities? He stresses the uncertainties which an unstable exchange created for the government budget, the inhibitions on imports and the rise in prices of imported goods, the excessive stimulation of the export trade and exploitation of Mexican resources, and the increasing problem of meeting gold obligations.

A series of commissions were set up, liaising with other silver standard countries, notably China. They both submitted notes asking the United States to cooperate, saying that sixteen silver standard countries had imports (1902) of $575 million, mostly from gold standard countries. An American Commission was appointed in 1903 and produced a two-volume report[10] favouring a gold exchange standard for these countries. Against this it was argued that existing arrangements improved competitiveness and stimulated exports, and as in the United States the silver industry pleaded its case.

In November 1904 a currency reform plan provided that the existing silver peso of 24.4391 grams of pure silver would remain legal tender, but valued at 0.75 grams of pure gold, equal to 49.85 US cents. Fractional coins would be struck to a lower standard as token coins.

## Central America

The five territories of Central America (Guatemala, Salvador, Honduras, Nicaragua and Costa Rica) became independent in 1821, initially as a federation, the Central American Republic, but this broke up in 1838 (it seems that the Governor of Guatemala settled for the security of his limited position there rather than fighting it out for the big prize).

At first, the Spanish system more or less continued, based on the silver peso of 25 grams divided into eight reals, and a gold onza equivalent to 16 reals. Various foreign coins circulated.

### Guatemala

Guatemala had issued coins in colonial times, and after the break-up of the Federation used a range of countermarked coins, only introducing its own coins in 1859. Meanwhile, a wide variety of foreign coins circulated, and in 1840 the government refused to accept debased Peruvian and Bolivian coins, extending the ban to certain Spanish coins in 1845. In 1851 US dollars were declared 'legal tender' at par with the peso. The falling ratio forced the US to reduce the silver content of the silver coins in 1853: Guatemala adopted the 'exchange control' route of severely limiting the export of silver coin.

In 1869 Guatemala adopted a decimal system based on a silver real of 25 grams .900 fine divided into 100 centavos instead of eight of the old reales. Gold pesos replaced the onzo at a ratio of 15.51. In 1871 the weight of the silver peso was increased to 25.40 grams, but they were exported and replaced with 25 gram coins, mostly from Peru and Chile. Coinage of the 'pesos fuertes' was discontinued in 1878 and the old standard was restored in 1881.

In 1873, when the bimetallic ratio began to rise, gold coins, as elsewhere, began to disappear from circulation. The Guatemalan peso declined from par with the US dollar to about half by 1895. Barrios, president from 1892 to 1898, issued depreciated coins.

The first step in the restoration of a sound currency was to restore 'choice in currency', permitting contracts specifying any currency to be enforced. Paper money retained its legal tender quality, and the rate was fairly stable at about 100 paper pesos to 1 gold peso. In 1905 a new central bank was formed, but was soon converted into a private concern. New gold pesos, equivalent to the US dollar, were authorised but apparently not struck, and in 1907 the unit was redefined so that a 5 peso coin was identical in weight and fineness to the UK sovereign.

The Banco Naçional de Guatemala was founded in 1874 out of funds received from the confiscation of church property, its notes being legal tender and guaranteed by the government. It suspended specie payment in 1876. Following the theft of silver reserves by a group led by an army officer, the banks were relieved of their obligation to redeem their notes in gold and silver: convertibility was restored in six months.

Barrios, 'who became President in 1892, by the only relatively free election ever held in Guatemala', overspent, and in 1897 borrowed 1.5 million pesos from the (by now six) banks to pay arrears of government salaries. The banks were at the same time relieved of their obligations to convert until the beginning of 1898. Billetes were full legal tender. After the inevitable default Barrios was assassinated.

# 17 Money in Russia before the Revolution

## Introduction

Russia is well worth the attention of the monetary historian, being the first country to 'decimalise' in 1704 and, leaving aside China and John Law's short experiment, the first to make sustained use of inconvertible paper money, from 1768. The earlier history of feudal Russia reveals interesting parallels, and contrasts, with the West's experience of local currencies and 'moneys of account'.

## Early history

During the early feudal period Roman silver coins circulated in the Kiev area and near the Baltic: Roman gold coins, widely used in oriental trade, do not seem to have penetrated north into Russia. These were followed by Cufic, Sassanian and Byzantine coins and later by Western silver deniers, including some Anglo-Saxon coins and their imitations.

In 1237–40 Russia was conquered by the successors of Ghengis Khan, but Alexander Nevsky (1220–63) of Novgorod (an entrepot for silver) paid a voluntary tribute, remained independent and defeated the Swedes in 1240.[1] Imports of silver fell sharply in the twelfth to fourteenth centuries, and there was a 'coinless period' when few silver coins circulated. The larger silver coins introduced in the Western Commercial Revolution did not penetrate into Russia, and the main form of money became large silver ingots, or grivnas, sometimes supplemented with 'leather money'.[2]

The Muscovite dynasty gradually established its control of Russia, notably under two Ivans – the Great (1462–1505) and the Terrible (1533–84). In the fourteenth and fifteenth centuries the basic coin was the denga, with the characteristic oval shape struck from flattened wire. These were issued both by Great Princes and their feudal vassals, until a currency reform in 1534 introduced a unified currency system throughout Russia, based on the kopeck, which was to retain its weight of 0.68 *grains* for about a century.

## The time of troubles

Ivan the Terrible died in 1584 and was succeeded by the simple-minded Theodore I (1584–98) whose brother-in-law Boris Godunov acted as regent and eventually succeeded him. After his death a series of 'false Dmitrys' claimed to be the murdered son of Ivan,[3] and Vasily IV Shuysky (1606–10), presided over a terrible time for Russia. Swedes (invited) and Poles (uninvited) seized Russian territory, and war costs stripped the treasury bare of silver. The silver kopeck was reduced in value to 0.46gr, and for the first time gold coins were introduced in the form of 'dengas' and 'kopecks' of the same oval 'wire money' shape and weight as the silver coins but passing for ten times their value.

Michael Romanov (1613–45) then founded a dynasty destined to hold power until the Revolution of 1917. The concept of 'Russia' needs to be interpreted liberally, sometimes incorporating Ukraine and Belarus, which shared the Orthodox faith and Cyrillic alphabet but whose languages came to diverge from that of what is now Russia proper. From time to time they were conquered by, or allied with, the two neighbouring Catholic powers of Poland and Lithuania.

## The first roubles

By the end of the seventeenth century the silver kopeck, its multiples and its half (pollina) and quarter (denga)[4] were the main currency, but foreign coins also circulated freely. Ducats and thalers from Poland, Saxony and Silesia, called 'yefimoks', were generally current at half a rouble and used by merchants in Ukraine, Belarus and the Baltics rather than in Russia proper. The Russian treasury had the profitable habit of calculating duties in kopecks, but requiring payment in yefimoks (thalers) at an artificial rate of exchange.[5,6]

Mikhail Fedorovich (1613–45) produced kopecks 'of thaler fineness' – i.e. .960 – both saving the cost of refining and increasing seigniorage. His successor introduced the first rouble coins, mostly overstruck ducats, and mainly used to meet local expenses in a war to free Ukraine from the Poles. 'Exchange control' was imposed in 1649 – all thalers had to be surrendered to the treasury. Attempts to strike Russian roubles were frustrated by inadequate machinery.

There was an ill conceived attempt at reform in 1654, based on keeping silver kopecks in circulation alongside devalued roubles, and 'copper yefimki'. Spassky (1967, 126) comments that 'The authors of the reform … with their superficial knowledge of copper circulation in other countries ventured to turn copper into silver based on the naive "theory" of the almighty Tsar.'

## The 1701 reform of Peter the Great

The history of modern Russia really begins with Peter the Great (1689–1725). His currency reform of 1701 was inspired by a visit to London, just after the Great Recoinage of 1696, where he met with Isaac Newton,

Warden (and later Master) of the Mint. He accustomed the public to smaller coppers and fractional silver, devalued the silver rouble to half its value, making it equivalent to the German thaler, and divided into 100 kopecks which were correspondingly reduced in weight to 0.28g.[7] This was the world's first decimal coinage system, and was much admired by foreign merchants, who urged their own governments to copy.[8]

## The debasements of Catherine the Great

Catherine II (the Great, 1762–96) was a German princess who was for seventeen years married (but by no means faithful) to the future Peter III. When he succeeded in 1762 she quickly had him deposed and took his place. She inherited, and implemented in 1763–5, a plan prepared by Count Peter Shuvalov to reduce the fineness of the silver coins. The silver rouble was reduced in value to 24g .750 fine and the gold was debased by 21 per cent, giving a bimetallic ratio of 15. She rejected the other part of his plan, which was to double the face value of the existing copper coinage. The coins which had been prepared under Peter III were simply overstruck with original values.[9]

In 1768 'there was nothing but copper money in circulation',[10] and in 1790 Count Platon Zubov proposed doubling the face value of the copper coins (Shuvalov's scheme of thirty years earlier) and they were 'cried up' in value, the 5 kopeck being overstamped 10 kopeck.[11] The standard of the *silver* coins then remained unchanged for a century and a half until the Revolution, with one small adjustment in 1886.

## Banking and paper money

In 1768 Catherine the Great issued Russia's first paper money. Two 'assignation banks' were authorised to issue notes up to 1 million roubles against a cash cover of copper money. Catherine's promise that these notes would be forever redeemable and would never be appropriated by the government was not kept, and many more were soon printed. In 1786 the issue was increased to 50 million, of which 26 million was lent without interest to the government. The notes were called 'assignats', anticipating the term to be used by the French a couple of decades later. There was a suspension of payments in 1787; this continued, with occasional attempts at reform, for over a century until 1897.[12] According to Seligman (1921, 31) the rot set in with the war with Turkey, and depreciation began in 1790 when 100 million roubles were in issue, and by 1796 there were 150 million roubles in circulation and the paper rouble had lost a third of its value against silver, falling during the Napoleonic wars to one quarter.

Catherine's son, Paul I, succeeded her in 1796, bitterly resenting that his mother had usurped the throne which he should have inherited from his father, who had been deposed and killed when he was eight years old. His attempts to deal with the financial mess, including a (meaningless) ceremonial burning of unissued assignats, appear to have been unsuccessful, but recent research by Valery Shishanov[13] has uncovered new information. Assignats had been extensively forged, and to maintain public confidence forged notes had been redeemed without publicity but at a high cost. There was a plan to replace old assignats with new, to reduce forgery and help the government to discover how many notes actually existed. Those which had been lost could be eliminated from the national debt. The plan was interrupted by the death of Paul, but Alexei Ivanovich Vasiliev, who became Russia's first minister of finance in 1802, continued with the project and a substantial volume of notes was printed and delivered to the bank. The project was aborted, perhaps because the value of the old assignats had risen and it was felt inadvisable to risk public confidence, but mainly because of the need to print and issue further 'old' assignats.

In 1817 the government tried to restore stability, funding the liability by issuing bonds payable in assignats in an attempt to fund the liability, but this had a limited success and the government was forced to issue foreign loans. In 1827 Cancrin, minister of finance, said he would take paper roubles for taxes at 3.6 paper for one silver rouble, an effective partial repudiation of public debt. In 1829 the value of the silver rouble was formally fixed at 3.5 paper roubles, and in 1834 the assignats were replaced by new government notes known as 'roubles credits' based on a silver reserve fund: effectively Russia was back on a silver exchange standard, and convertibility was temporarily restored in 1840. The gold '10 rouble' coin by then passed for 10.30 roubles, in line with the Latin Monetary Union bimetallic ratio of 15.5. This fairly stable period was interrupted by the Crimean War, when gold again went to a premium.

The State Bank of the Russian Empire received its charter on 31 May 1860, and began operations in 1861 backed by a foreign loan, but there was a further suspension of payments in 1863 following the Polish Revolution.

In 1887 plans began to resume specie payments at 1.5 paper for 1 silver rouble, and in December 1895, as a first step to introducing a gold standard, the gold 5 rouble coin was cried up to 7.5 roubles in line with the paper money and paper was accepted at this ratio.

The gold standard, brought in by Count Sergei Witte 'in the face of strong opposition by members of the public' became effective in 1897. The State Bank now had note issuing powers, but had to maintain 50 per cent gold backing up to a limit, and 100 per cent thereafter. The content of the silver rouble did not change, but with the collapse of bimetallism the price of silver had fallen and the bullion value was now only about 0.75 in terms of gold (or paper) roubles. Some silver coins (25 kopecks and less) were struck in .500 silver as deliberate 'token' coins on the UK and European model. In a possible attempt to come into line with the Latin Monetary Union, some coins were struck in 1902 with a stated value of '37.5 roubles, 100 francs'. This gold standard continued until the outbreak of war in 1914.

# 18 The British empire and the sterling area

## An accidental monetary union?

### Introduction

The British empire, a far flung group of very diverse territories, some rich, many poor, is not an obvious optimum currency area, but by the late nineteenth century most of these countries effectively used British 'sterling' currency based on the gold sovereign, and had British-type banking systems (the notable exceptions were Canada, which used the dollar, and India and other Asian territories which were on a silver standard). Was this a monetary union, or simply a group of countries under the hegemony of the United Kingdom? There were elements of both, but significantly, if there was a monetary union, neither its creation nor its dissolution were ever discussed as serious policy issues.

Union or not, it continued for about twenty-five years after 1945, surviving two devaluations of sterling and retaining (more or less) free payments in an exchange control ridden world, even though an increasing number of the members were politically independent and completely free to choose their own currency arrangements. By the end of the twentieth century, though, the countries of the former Commonwealth had dozens of independent currencies, following a long period during which there was a peaceful, undramatic but still highly instructive break-up of what had been a currency area. This is discussed in Chapter 48.

How did it start? The London government took surprisingly little interest in the monetary arrangements of the colonies until a specific problem was discovered in 1825, and in due course the UK Coinage Act of 1870 was formally extended to bring many imperial territories into the UK currency zone. In 1909 Australia opted out of this arrangement, establishing independent monetary sovereignty, while retaining the link with sterling until 1967. Currency boards were set up in various colonies to provide local money with a firm peg to sterling: these too were eventually abandoned when the independent ex-colonies set up their own currency systems. Some chose to retain their links with sterling; others (sooner or later) went their own way; while some Caribbean territories (including those which remained colonies) simply switched their peg from sterling to the US dollar to reflect closer economic ties.

In 1931 Britain left the gold standard, and the dominions (other than Canada) retained, and others developed, a link with sterling, becoming a 'type 2' monetary union based on fiat money – the sterling area. If this was ever a currency area (optimum or not) it came under even more strain following the 1949 sterling devaluation, started to fall apart when many member countries chose not to follow the 1967 devaluation, and effectively came to an end when the UK imposed exchange controls on the outer sterling area in 1971, and floated sterling in 1972. The break up of the monetary union known as the sterling area caused as little fuss as its casual and almost accidental creation.

## Early history

The currency arrangements of the American colonies before the Revolution could charitably be described as 'benign neglect'. There was no attempt to incorporate these colonies into a 'monetary union' of any kind, nor indeed to ensure that they had a proper currency, and although the early United States had many monetary problems at its birth, leaving the British empire was not one of them.

The other colonies, which did not revolt, fared little better, and any monetary problems they had were ignored until 1825 when a Treasury minute of 11 February 1825 expressed concern that the rate used for calculating the value of Spanish dollars used for army pay differed from the value at which they were taken in trade. Officers had 'the option of receiving their pay either from the military chest ... or through their agents in England ... they have the full benefit of the ... exchange when it is more favourable ... and the advantage of the army rate when it is less so'. This was followed on 23 March by an Order in Council stating that in colonies where the Spanish dollar is used, British silver money should be legal tender at 4s 4d per dollar, in the Cape of Good Hope and Ceylon where paper rix dollars were used, silver at 1s 6d should be legal tender for each such dollar.[1]

English silver coins had, since Lord Liverpool's reform, circulated at a fiat value above the silver content, and 'this currency would not be liable to be withdrawn, by private speculation, from the colonies'.[2] They did circulate at the fiat value, and the rates at which they would exchange with foreign coins actually circulating was set in the ratio 103:100, to take account of the estimated cost of returning the silver coins to the UK. Other Orders quoted deal with setting these rates, and the 1848 publication (see note 1) is a useful source on currency practices in the various colonies at the time. The (anonymous) author says (on page 35) that 'the expectations' [of the authors of the 1825 measures] 'were not realised' because the ratios were miscalculated, and in the event foreign coins rather than sterling, gold or silver, continued to be the main circulating medium.

## A New Zealand incident

In 1844 the Governor of New Zealand had insufficient funds, and could not persuade Lord Stanley to speed up transfers, to pay salaries and other expenses. The local bank could not advance more than £2,000 and demanded between 12 per cent and 15 per cent interest, so he solved his problem by issuing bills of £1, £5, £10 and £50 value, redeemable in a year at 5 per cent interest. The correspondence is published as a House of Commons paper,[3] which shows that he was instructed to take no such action. Fortunately, it took weeks to get instructions to the Governor, Admiral Robert Fitzroy, who had been captain of Darwin's *Beagle*, and was later to be the first head of the UK Meteorological Office having a 'sea area' named in his honour. He comes across in the published correspondence as a man of initiative and resource who applied 'the Nelson touch', ignored his instructions (or lack of them) and simply did what was needed. Fortunately the telegraph, the scourge of pro-consular independence, had not been invented. There are some parallels with the much earlier 'playing card' money of Canada, but by this time, of course, any good public servant would be familiar with the concepts of paper money.

A little later, in 1847, the first step was taken to introduce a currency board in New Zealand, this being regarded as 'the perfect Colonial test case' for the concept. The board would hold 100 per cent cover in external assets, gold, silver and British government securities, and was prohibited from holding New Zealand securities. It started operations in June 1850, and the Union Bank of Australia was required to cease its note issues by October 1852. The arrangement was distrusted in New Zealand, which had 'bad memories of an earlier, inflationary issue of government notes' (Schuler: probably a reference to Fitzroy's initiative).

Meanwhile, while the 'test case' was being prepared, the concept was adopted in Mauritius as an emergency measure. The Mauritius Bank failed in 1848 following a UK financial crisis and a fall in the price of sugar. The surviving Mauritius Commercial Bank relinquished its note issuing rights in exchange for cheap funding, and a currency board was formed with the right to issue notes convertible into silver Indian rupees.

## The Coinage Act of 1870

Article 4 of the UK Coinage Act 1870 defined legal tender to include: gold coins for any amount, silver for 40 shillings, and bronze for one shilling (banknotes were covered by different legislation).[4] This Act was extended to various colonies beginning with Fiji (1881)[5] and, notably, to New Zealand and the Australian colonies (1896): coins struck at the Royal Mint in England then became legal tender throughout a large area. (British gold coins, indistinguishable except for a small mint letter, (S, M or P) had been struck at three Australian mints, from Australian gold, since 1871, but silver coins were all imported from the Royal Mint.) There was an extension to a wider range of colonies in 1898,[6] but with a larger legal tender limit for silver coins. In the same year, it was suggested that the British government should share seigniorage with the local governments, and failing agreement on that Sir David Barbour (whose name figures prominently in my earlier book) was asked to report on an independent currency for the Nigerian colonies. His report was rejected.

Following the 1870 legislation, British silver coins began to circulate in the colonies, and from 1909–11 £1,259,450 of UK silver was issued for West Africa, actually more than was within the UK itself.[7] (Gold sovereigns, and indeed the pound note, were too 'heavy' for local needs: as Peter Bauer pointed out much later, the habit of burying money in cocoa tins continued even when paper money supplemented coins: this, and the appetite of termites, did much to reduce effective money supply.) Although silver coin was legal tender in the UK only for sums up to £2, large deposits from the colonies were in practice accepted at par, and the amounts now in circulation led to fears that these would be repatriated during bad crop seasons.

British silver coins had, since 1816, been deliberately struck at a silver content worth slightly less than their face value, but following the collapse of bimetallism the silver value was much less – and, more seriously, falling. The British government had issued silver coins at a useful (potential seigniorage) premium over their cost, but had an obligation to redeem the coins at face value when the price of silver had fallen. The profitable activity of providing a coinage had, unexpectedly, become a highly risky undertaking.

An Order of 1911 relating to South Africa added two provisos to the Coinage Act, one providing that a coin may be proclaimed to be current only in a 'specified part of His Majesty's dominions', and the other extending the definition of legal tender coins to those struck in Pretoria.[8] South African coins are only in fact recorded from 1923.[9]

## Currency boards

The Emmott Committee[10] was set up to advise on the 'surplus silver' problem, and reported in June 1912, recommending the setting up of currency boards. The West Africa Currency Board was set up the same year, and issued both banknotes and coins in West African pounds, one to one, against UK currency, while British coins were gradually withdrawn (base metal pennies, halves and tenths had been issued locally since 1905 to provide small change). Gold coins disappeared from circulation, often to be used as jewellery.

The Board was required (initially) to keep 75 per cent of its reserves in gold, and the rest in 'securities', in practice interpreted as external assets, mainly British government securities. In 1920, when the UK reacted to a rising silver price by halving the silver content of the coins, the WACB issued nickel-brass coins.

The East African Currency Board was set up, along the same lines, for Kenya and Uganda in 1919. They had previously used Indian rupees, and the Kenya government had also issued rupee silver coins against sterling securities. As their bullion value was now less than their fiat value, there was a profit on production and issue, but a corresponding liability to repay at face value in sterling, resulting in a serious loss when the price of silver fell sharply. The Currency Board issued British shillings at two per rupee, and the EACB extended its activities to the former German colony of Tanganyika, which had become a British mandate, and in 1923 offered to issue shillings in exchange for German silver coins. They hit a variant of the 1870 'silver' problem: its price having fallen, the Board lost EA£1.5 million. Zanzibar joined in 1936, and during the 1939–45 war the Board provided currency for previously Italian-occupied territories.

## Australia

Banknotes had been issued in Australia early in the nineteenth century. New South Wales (1893) and Queensland (1866) issued treasury notes. The various colonies came together as the Commonwealth of Australia in 1901, but there is no record of any subsequent private bank issues.

The Australian Coinage Act of 1909 effectively replaced the UK Coinage Act, which was in 1911 proclaimed not to apply in Australia. In 1910 the Commonwealth issued treasury notes, the first being overprinted on un-issued notes of various private banks. From 1911, Australia issued its own coins, but remained on the UK system and at par with sterling. The parity was not affected by the introduction of a decimal coinage in 1960, but the link with sterling was broken in 1967 following the devaluation of that year.

To summarise, by the early twentieth century, Australia (*de facto*) and most other British territories (*de jure*) operated a UK-type currency system, but as this was on the gold standard, there were no real problems of principle, as the currencies were locked into a 'fixed rate' system.

Muhleman[11] gives an account of the world's monetary systems in 1908, and describes Canada as having an ideal money and banking system on the gold standard. Although gold was produced 'in the absence of a mint ... United States coin and British sovereigns were equally legal tender'. In the West Indies, British gold coins were legal tender but US money was also used: banks had limited note-issuing powers. (Muhleman comments that a mint was about to be established: it did in fact open in 1908.) British Honduras, though, had 'a dollar system identical with that of the United States'. The South African colonies, although gold producers, relied on gold coin from the UK and Australia and silver from the UK Cape Colony, and permitted banks to issue legal tender notes secured by government bonds; West Africa used British money.

## The development of the sterling area after 1914

On the outbreak of war in 1914 the gold standard was suspended and wartime exchange controls became an issue. A 'gold exchange standard' was reintroduced in 1925, but abandoned in 1931 during the Depression. The sterling area now took on a specific meaning as a 'type 2' monetary union of countries using fiat currencies without precious metal backing. In addition to the countries of the British empire, Egypt, Estonia, India, Iraq, Latvia and Portugal immediately (September 1931) pegged their currencies to sterling, with Thailand joining in August 1932. Others joined later, and at various discounts (for a list see League of Nations 1944, 51),[12] the two lowest being Iran (March 1936, 68 per cent of old parity) and Japan (January 1933, 57 per cent).

The 'sterling area' then became a 'type 2' monetary union based on fiat currencies rather than gold. A hard core of countries were effectively on a sterling exchange standard, and an outer group chose, because of trading or banking connections, to make common cause with the UK for the defence of their currency, and all became known as the sterling area. Although at this stage there was no formal membership, the Scandinavian and Baltic countries, Egypt, Iraq, Portugal and Siam could be regarded as shadowing sterling quite closely, while Japan, Argentina and Greece simply used sterling as their main intervention currency.

Australia had left gold in 1929, and in January 1931 pegged to sterling at £A130 to £100, but after sterling depreciated, altered the rate to £A125, where it remained until 1967. New Zealand first pegged at £NZ100 but changed to £NZ124 in January 1933.

Peacetime exchange controls were imposed by some members of the area – Denmark, Estonia, Greece and Portugal – in 1931, to check capital outflows, followed by New Zealand in December 1938 (League of Nations 1944, 167).

In 1939, when UK exchange control was reintroduced, formal membership was limited to the Commonwealth, excluding Canada, and in spite of all the currency upheavals and restrictive practices in the world as a whole, transactions within the sterling area could be made freely during the postwar period. At that stage if at no other, it was a genuine monetary union (or an example of dollarisation), accepting the Bank of England as the arbiter of monetary policy. Eventually, though, it fell apart with as little drama or forethought as had accompanied its birth: the story of the 'disunion' is told in Chapter 48.

# Part IV

# The early twentieth century and the collapse of the gold standard

The triumph of fiat currencies

# 19  Introduction to the early twentieth century

Parts IV and V deal mainly with the postwar inflations and currency reconstructions, the attempt to return to the gold standard, and the monetary implications of the 1929 crash and subsequent Depression. The present chapter builds a bridge from the nineteenth century, and shows that the 'golden age of the gold standard' wasn't quite so golden.

Between the two world wars, the most notable event from our point of view was the break-up of the Austro-Hungarian monetary union, probably the nearest precedent in this history for the EMU, and the very different experiences of the successor states. Later chapters cover the Nordic Monetary Union and its wartime and postwar vicissitudes, the Russian Revolution (including two monetary experiments), the short-lived return to gold, and the experiences of Nazi Germany.

## Money before 1914

My earlier *History of Money* mainly covered the period to 1896, a year which marked the end of the Great Depression and the start of a period of stable prosperity which, even though it lasted only eighteen years, is looked back on as a golden age by those who yearn for the (apparent) simplicities of the gold standard.

Was the 'golden age' so stable? During the period wholesale prices rose in the US by nearly 50 per cent, and in the UK by 26 per cent. The world had simply found more gold, in South Africa, Alaska and Colorado, so that the supply of monetary gold almost doubled during the period. On the 'demand' side the absorbtion of monetary gold, as countries had switched from a bimetallic to a gold standard, had been completed.

Whatever would have happened had peace continued, it fell apart in 1914, and was certainly stable at least in comparison with the turmoil which was to follow. The gold standard was eventually to be abandoned and replaced almost universally by inconvertible fiat money.

## The United States after 1896

The year 1896 saw the end of the first American 'Great Depression', the defeat of Bryan and the enthronement of the gold standard as an international monetary system.

A Monetary Commission was set up in January 1897. Its four-hundred page report was largely the work of Professor D Lawrence Laughlin.[1] The Gold Standard Act (Kross 1969–83;[2] and see National Monetary Commission[3] 1909–10 vol. 33: 610) was passed in March 1900, confirming the gold dollar as the standard of value, with silver as a subsidiary coinage. The Treasury was authorised to issue 2 per cent gold bonds which could be used by banks for the issue of their currencies. As a sop to the silver interests, section 14 of the Act provided that 'the provisions of this Act are not intended to preclude the accomplishment of international bimetallism wherever conditions shall make it expedient ... at a rate which shall ensure permanence of relative value between gold and silver'.

The 1907 crisis had affected London: a run on the reserves was reversed by a 7 per cent bank rate, which had squeezed the domestic economy. These eighteen years had otherwise been stable, with little to interest the monetary historian.

> In the days before the War all who studied the English financial system ... contemplated it with admiration, mingled a little with awe. London, they said, was the financial centre of the world, the banker of all nations. ... A mountain of credit of unprecedented size was reared up internally upon the reserve of the Bank of England, and that reserve was amazingly small. ... Even the big bankers were a little awe-struck in contemplating the system for which their institutions were a part. They had read about the great panics of the nineteenth century ... and shuddered to think of what would happen in the event of a great European war. They shook their heads at the smallness of the gold stock ... it is not surprising that when the crisis came, it was they ... and not the public, who lost their nerve. The credit system was even greater than they thought.
>
> (Feavearyear 1931, 299)[4]

# 20 The Great War and its aftermath

## Finance on the outbreak of war

The year 1914 began with the British financial system, based in the City of London, said to be the envy of the world, but its weaknesses were shown up when everything changed during the two weeks beginning with the Austrian ultimatum to Serbia on Sunday 26 July. The stock market collapsed next day with several failures. Bank rate was raised from 3 per cent to 4 per cent (a routine increase), many stockbrokers were hammered and the Stock Exchange was closed on the Friday. In the resulting panic interest rates rose to between 8 per cent and 10 per cent, while banks, other than the Bank of England, refused to pay out gold.

It was time for yet another suspension of the Bank Charter Act, and sure enough on Saturday 1 August, Cunliffe, Governor of the Bank of England, called on the Treasury. He received a 'Treasury Letter', 'an untidy hand-written letter signed by Asquith and Lloyd George'[1] like those of 1847, 1857 and 1866, giving an indemnity against any excess over the legal fiduciary issue but with (as in 1866) the requirement that bank rate be raised to 10 per cent.

Monday was August Bank Holiday and the banks were then closed for a further three days, reopening on Friday 5 August. Prompt action was taken authorising the Bank of England to discount approved bills without recourse, thus restoring the liquidity of the market. On 6 August Parliament passed the Currency and Bank Notes Act, empowering the Treasury to issue currency notes. During the week of the extended 'bank holiday' the printing presses had worked overtime: the £1 note (Waterlow) was issued on 7 August and the 10 shilling note (De la Rue) a week later. The notes were known as 'Bradburys', being signed by John Bradbury, Permanent Secretary to the Treasury. All these events took place in the space of two weeks.

Gold ceased to circulate and was replaced by these treasury notes. Formally, although private bankers pressed for suspension, sterling remained technically convertible. The young Maynard Keynes had said 'The future position of the City of London as a free gold market will be seriously injured if at the first sign of emergency specie payment is suspended', and the Governor, Cunliffe, agreed. In practice it became regarded as unpatriotic to demand gold, and the Bank 'saw to it that every obstacle was put in the way of the man in the street getting gold sovereigns' (Deane and Pringle 1994, 55).[2]

The formal structure of Government/Bank of England relations was maintained, but this still left scope for indefinite credit financing. Prices more than doubled by the end of the war. The South Africans were required to sell newly mined gold at the official price, a 1916 order under the Defence of the Realm Act (DORA) prohibited the melting down of gold coin, and there were a series of measures, at first voluntary, to requisition US and Canadian securities held by British investors.

There were similar phenomena in other countries, nearly all of which went off gold, and the widespread abandonment of the use of gold for monetary purposes actually led to a fall in its real value. But there was little scope for international arbitrage because of wartime restrictions, and surprisingly little evidence of any widespread hoarding of sovereigns. Exceptionally, Sweden's decision to return to gold in 1916 put a serious strain on the Nordic Monetary Union.

After the emergency measures on the outbreak of war, the dollar/sterling exchange rate fluctuated wildly, but in 1916 was stabilised at $4.76, compared with its parity of $4.86, with the help of support funds provided by J.P. Morgan.

## After the war

After World War I ended in November 1918, prices initially fell. In the UK the Cunliffe Committee recommended deflation and the restoration of sound credit position. Their conclusions are criticised in Feavearyear:

> the Committee had no idea of the width of the gap which existed ... between the value of the pound and the value of the sovereign's weight of gold either in England or elsewhere. In parallel circumstances in 1811 the whole political and financial world had had clearly before its eyes the price of gold bullion and had thrashed the matter out ... The history of the period from 1820 to 1830 was written plainly in the pages of Hansard for all to read but nevertheless the Committee recommended deflation.[3]

This, he suggested, was because nine of twelve members were traditional bankers, whose main concern was to get back to doing their old business in their old ways.

In early 1919, the Bank of England stopped supporting the exchange rate, and this was followed by an embargo on gold exports. It was intended to be short-lived, but was to last for six years (Deane and Pringle 1994, 55).

There was a world-wide postwar boom followed by a major collapse in 1920. UK Wholesale prices (1914 = 100) had risen from 240 at the end of the war to 323 by March 1920. Prices had doubled in America; those in France had risen fivefold and its exchange rate had fallen to a third of its prewar value. German experience (so far) was similar.

The postwar stock exchange boom came to an end in March 1920, and prices fell by 25 per cent in the following six months, wholesale prices now fell and unemployment rose. During the early stages of the boom bank rate had not been used as a weapon, would in any case have been ineffective, and was unnecessary to protect gold reserves during the embargo. The rate, long constant but irrelevant at 5 per cent, was raised to 6 per cent in November 1919 and to 7 per cent in April 1920. During the slump of 1919–20 UK prices fell to 197 (there had been similar booms and busts in 1720 and 1825, which may or may not give some comfort to the long wave theorists).

In 1920, UK silver coins began to be struck from silver only 0.500 (instead of 0.925) fine. This was precautionary: they had had a bullion value of less than fiat (face) value for a century, and in spite of rising prices the 0.925 coins were still not quite worth melting down.

## International conferences

The League of Nations set up an International Financial Conference in Brussels in September and October 1920. It was not a success, but did launch Montagu Norman's campaign for every country to have a central bank (Deane and Pringle 1994, 57). Sir Dennis Robertson[4] commented that

> A number of wise and well disposed men met ... to give advice on what should be done. Several ... had been well trained in economic theory, and knew therefore ... that ... a certain state of the country's money glands was an *essential condition* [and that] the bad state of the world's money glands was due to the inordinate demands made by Governments upon their peoples and upon each other. The latter part of this second truth they were not allowed to disclose.

Their advice was 'as much use as recommending a drowning man to keep dry'.

After a period of deflation, the Supreme Council of the Allies set up an International Economic Conference in Genoa in April 1922. Thirty-nine countries came, but not the Americans.

> From today's vantage, it may seem surprising that ... European countries chose to peg their currencies to the pound, rather than to the dollar and gold, waiting until Britain resumed the gold standard. ... But America had just been transformed ... to a creditor nation after exorting $11 billion of capital during the war.[5]

'The Genoa conference voted for the so called gold exchange standard'; 'The Genoa conference also called for international cooperation between central bankers in running the new gold system. Specifics were to be decided at a ... meeting which the Bank of England was invited to convene'.[6] That meeting was aborted by the reparations problem and the sensational collapse of the mark.

# 21   Germany and the great inflation

## Introduction

Germany's wartime inflation followed about the same pattern as that of other belligerents, prices rising fourfold by 1919. Keynes speculated against the mark too early, with near-disastrous consequences. Although prices then fell in the UK, France and elsewhere, others had different experiences. Austria was the first to suffer hyper-inflation (October 1921–August 1922) prices rising seventyfold, and the same problem hit Russia in December 1921, and then, after Germany, Hungary in March 1923.

## The German hyper-inflation

In Germany, prices (1913 = 100) reached 7,030 in June 1922, a doubling over six months, but only actually hitting the '50 per cent per month' definition of hyper-inflation[1] in August 1922. By late September the mark had lost all value and 'became almost eliminated ... as an instrument of domestic and foreign payments'.[2, 3] By November 1923, prices were 1,400 billion times the prewar level.

The French assumed that inflation had been engineered by the Germans as a means of avoiding reparations, and on 11 January 1923, 60,000 French and Belgian soldiers invaded the Ruhr in an attempt to enforce payment. Workers, encouraged by the government into passive resistance, went on strike. The French operated the mines and factories themselves. In spite of the warnings of Max Warburg, the government printed money to pay the striking Ruhr workers, thus ensuring the final end of the reichsmark. The reparations issue was in fact to dominate monetary and political developments in Germany.

The early stages of inflation actually gave the economy a boost, mainly through the influence of 'hugely negative' real rates of interest. Even during the later stages farmers, and industrialists with substantial debt, benefited, and 'the cheaper mark created a bonanza for foreign investors who bought German properties at bargain prices arousing resentment against the banks who executed these deals'.[4]

## Expedients

Meanwhile contracts were based on stable foreign currencies or included a depreciation clause. Borrowers issued 'stable value' loans 'based on rye, coal, potash and the like', while the government issued dollar treasury notes and 'the so called gold loan, payable in dollars'. There had to be arrangements for putting savings and insurance contracts on a gold mark basis, and for inter-bank transfers of dollars.

During the inflation, Max Warburg organised a temporary bank, 'the Hamburg Bank of 1923', which issued gold-backed notes. This was helped by a dollar loan from his brother Paul's International Acceptance Bank in New York.

## Reconstruction

How was the currency to be reconstructed? Bresciani-Turroni[5] discusses (417) a project by the Minister of National Economy for monetary reform as early as July 1922. This was the work of a committee of foreign experts. Havenstein had written in April 1922 that 'the problem of restoring the circulation is not a technical or banking problem; it is ... the problem of the equilibrium between the burden and the capacity of the German economy for supporting this burden'.[6] He took the view that reparations was the key question, and argued that no solution was possible without a moratorium and 'alluded to the failure of the recent intervention of the Reichsbank in the exchange market; 230 millions of foreign exchange had been uselessly sacrificed without ... preventing the continued depreciation of the exchange'.

Bresciani-Turroni refers to, and supports, what he calls the 'English' view that the main cause was the budget deficit. He discusses the collapse of national finances in some detail: some excise taxes were adversely affected by currency movements (436).

Schacht (see note 3) suggests that a return to gold was technically impossible: there were no reserves and, pending a resolution of the reparations problem, no loans were available. In any case (when he wrote in 1924) only the US and Sweden were on gold and, at least until the UK resumed payments action by Germany, 'would lead to the outflow of ... gold and impair the very basis of the new currency'.

'It was only on August 20th 1923 that the system of increasing the railway fares little by little at varying intervals was abandoned. The multiplication system was adopted' (Bresciani-Turroni 1937, 443). But there were still delays in applying the multiplier. 'Only when the disintegration of the monetary system was already complete did the government decide to "valorise" the payment of those taxes which were collected in arrear' (444) based on gold values (11 October 1923).[7]

Various proposals were put forward for monetary reconstruction. One was for a roggenmark, linked to a commodity, in this case rye, but this itself was regarded as too unstable. Another was for a gold note bank authorised to issue notes with a 2:1 reserve ratio. These were rejected in favour of a 'land bank'.[8]

A new government under Gustav Stresemann declared martial law in August 1923, a move directed mainly against communists. Hitler, Goering and Ludendorff made their first attempt to seize power in early November: the Munich Beer Hall Putsch. Hitler was arrested and convicted, but served only nine months in prison.

On 12 November 1923 Dr Hjalmar Schacht was given the task of stabilising the German currency. Max Warburg 'predicted the rentenmark would fail tempting France to introduce the franc in occupied territories. Instead good new money drove bad old money' (Chernow 1993, 233).

The president of the Reichsbank, Rudolf Havenstein, died just a week later on 19 November, and after a battle with Karl Helfferich, Schacht became president on 22 December.

The Rentenbank was formed by decree of 15 October 1923, with a capital of 3.2 billion rentenmarks, each of which was worth 1,000 billion ($10^{12}$) old reichsmarks. Rentenmarks began to circulate on 15 November and the reichsmark was demonetised on 20 November 1923. (This 'dropping of noughts' as such achieves nothing except a saving in printer's ink: there are many Latin American examples.) The new bank was backed by mortgages and debentures secured on German property and business assets and bearing interest at 6 per cent, and issued bonds in multiples of 500 rentenmarks. After reserves of 800 million, the balance was divided between the government and the Reichsbank (part of this operation was effectively a capital levy). The Reichsbank was forbidden to lend to the government, and the Rentenbank could only provide 1.2 billion marks. This forced drastic measures to balance the budget. Inflation was immediately checked, but there was an 'implacable choice between credit crisis and currency ruin'. The rentenmark appears to have declined by 15 per cent (again, Schacht is intriguing rather than fully informative).

Joan Robinson's review of Bresciani-Turroni (see note 5) is an excellent commentary on the main theme: 'causes and consequences'. She is sceptical of the view 'that the stabilisation of the mark in November 1923 indicates that inflation can be stopped at any moment if the quantity of money is strictly controlled', and points out that the mark ceased to function as a 'store of value' in autumn 1921, as a 'unit of account' in that latter part of 1922, but 'never ceased all together to function as a "medium of exchange" but it was to a large extent displaced by foreign currency and the "stable value" instruments of various kinds which were improvised'.

### The Dawes Plan

In 1924 there was a conference in London under the chairmanship of General Charles Dawes of the United States. This resulted in proposals to lower the aggregate burden of reparations and to take a first mortgage on

German government revenues from certain taxes. There was also some control over the Reichsbank and the railways. An Agent General (S. Parker Gilbert, an American) was appointed to gauge Germany's ability to pay. A £30 million 'international loan of unprecedented size' 'was arranged' 'that would ultimately allow Germany to pay reparations with borrowed money thus starting the fatal carousel of global lending that would spin dizzily for a decade then collapse' (Chernow 1993, 273). There was indeed a short-lived boom in 1925. Part of the Dawes plan involved the independence of the Reichsbank and an eventual return to the gold standard. On 1 September 1924 the temporary rentenmark was replaced by the reichsmark, equivalent in value to the prewar gold mark. This was a gold exchange standard with a 40 per cent backing, of which three quarters had to be in gold.[9]

Chernow 1993[10] discusses the relationship between the Warburg family (particularly Max), the Nazis and Dr Schacht. Melchior and Keynes also come into the story: Keynes wrote a memoir on Melchier, and of course had strong views on reparations.[11] Max Warburg, a director of the Reichsbank, the (unofficial) financial adviser to the City of Hamburg, was one of the most influential private bankers in Germany. He was also (he thought) a friend of Dr Schacht, the latter being prized by Hitler 'as a respectable figure who could hoodwink foreign financiers ... the only Aryan who could outswindle the Jews'. Schacht never joined the Nazi party, but professed to believe Hitler's promises and indeed passed these on to his Jewish friends, some of whom may have believed them (Chernow 1993, 376).

# 22 The temporary return to gold and the Great Depression

## The return to gold

UK restrictions on the export of gold and silver were due to expire in 1925, and in 1924, the market assuming that the powers would not be extended, the dollar exchange rate rose quite sharply. In the same year the Treasury had appointed a committee, ostensibly to consider amalgamating the issue of the Treasury and Bank of England issues, but which in fact spent much of its time discussing the restoration of the gold standard. Meanwhile Sweden, 'tired of waiting', had returned to gold in March 1924.

Churchill, the Chancellor, announced in his budget speech on 28 April 1925 that the Bank of England was to have a general license to deliver gold for export against legal tender money. A couple of weeks later the Gold Standard Act of 1925 was passed. This introduced a 'gold exchange standard'. The public would not be entitled to convert bank notes or currency notes into gold coin, and the right to have gold bullion coined at the Royal Mint was reserved exclusively to the Bank of England. The Bank would be required to sell 400 ounce bars of gold (about £1,700) to the public in exchange for notes, a measure sufficient to check the excessive use of the printing press. This was effectively Ricardo's 1816 'Proposals for an Economic and Secure Currency'.[1]

Other countries adopted or re-adopted the gold standard, and by the end of 1928 it was virtually universal.[2]

> In most countries this step followed quickly, though in the case of France it was long delayed owing to the necessity to France (or more strictly to M. Poincaré) that M. Poincaré should first be given another three years' lease of office.[3]

The last paragraph of the first edition of Feavearyear (1931, 333) (written while the UK was still on gold) points out that the history of the pound was continuous from King Offa to 1928 with no real break but with a continuous, if moderate, depreciation. However, the French franc (then 124 to the pound) and the Italian lire (92) were originally at par, while the German mark had totally collapsed. He concludes his book: 'Against these examples, the history of the English standard appears eminently respectable.' It was not to last.

The terms at which the UK had returned to gold are said to have implied a pattern of exchange rates which left British industry at a competitive disadvantage compared with Germany, the United States and other countries. There had also been significant changes in the international distribution of gold. In 1913, Britain had held 9 per cent of the world's monetary gold. By 1925 this had fallen to 7 per cent, while the North American share had risen from 24 per cent to 45 per cent. This also put the UK at a comparative disadvantage, although the Depression of the 1930s was a world-wide phenomenon.

## The Great Depression and the end of the gold standard

The Wall Street Crash of 1929 and the failure of the Hatry empire were early symptoms of a general collapse of the world monetary order. A generally declining confidence in banks and a move to liquidity (i.e. gold) reached panic proportions with the failure of the Creditanstalt on 31 May 1931. There was a run on Germany in particular, and following the collapse of the deutschmark on 13 July speculators, as is their wont, turned their attention to sterling (the MacMillan Committee Report was published that day, which may or may not have been relevant). The Labour Party, then in government, split, one wing going into opposition, leaving Ramsay MacDonald and Philip Snowden to head a National (coalition) Government. They accepted American loans, the terms of which were criticised as a 'bankers' ramp'.

The Bank of England actually ran out of gold, and on 19 September 1931 the gold standard was suspended. The Gold Standard (Amendment) Act 1931 stated that 'until His Majesty by proclamation or otherwise directs sub-section 2 of section 1 of the Gold Standard Act 1925 shall cease to have effect'. Bank rate was raised but sterling depreciated. The Japanese yen was the next target: the gold standard was suspended on 14 December (Kindleberger 1984, ch. 20).

The German left opposed any devaluation, even to follow sterling with the slogan 'no tampering with the currency', an early indication of the fear of inflation which was so valuable to Germany in the post-1945 period.

The United States, Canada and some European countries remained on gold. The European 'gold bloc' countries (France, Belgium, Holland, Italy, Poland and Switzerland) entered into an agreement for mutual cooperation, but the French franc was devalued in 1936. The other Commonwealth countries, together with Portugal and the Scandinavian countries, constituted themselves informally into the sterling area, and immediately after the suspension of the gold standard sterling fell, reaching a low of $3.457 in February 1932.

On 12 May 1933 the Thomas Amendment to the Agricultural Adjustment Act gave the President power to reduce the gold or silver content of the dollar by up to 50 per cent. The Gold Reserve Act of 1934 completed the process, effectively putting the United States on to a gold exchange standard, and devaluing the dollar from 23.22 grains ($20.67 per oz) to 13.714 grains ($35 per oz).[4] The Silver Purchase Act of 1934[5] directed the Treasury to buy silver at $1.29 per ounce, a major subsidy to the silver mining industry, still a powerful lobby. The main monetary effect of this measure was on China[6] but the United States embargo on gold exports certainly raised the price of gold, which eventually stabilised $35 an ounce (where it remained until the days of President Nixon). The pound appreciated to $5 but fell sharply to $4.03 (where it remained until the days of Sir Stafford Cripps). At the outbreak of the Second World War, exchange controls were imposed (where they remained until the days of Margaret Thatcher and Geoffrey Howe).

# Part V

# Monetary chaos in the 1930s

# 23   The Russian Revolution and after

## Introduction

Russia, like its European neighbours, abandoned the gold standard (rouble/gold parity 51.455 US cents) in 1914. There were then five increases in the authorised note issue, and although some gold continued to circulate until 1916, it was increasingly hoarded, while silver also later disappeared from circulation. Wartime inflation was very similar to that of other combatants: prices rose from 100 in 1913 to 315 by March 1917 just before the Revolution. Inflation then accelerated, and by July 1921 the index reached 8 million.[1]

According to Laurila,[2] a mainly numismatic source, at the beginning of 1918 about 27.5 billion roubles of banknotes should have been in circulation, twenty times the prewar circulation. That year new notes were issued, including 5,000 and 10,000 rouble values, and in February cancelled bond certificates were authorised for use as currency by 'impeccable' persons living in Russia. By the end of the year prices had risen, and barter (a persistent feature of Russian economics) was commonplace.

Soviet notes were first issued in 1919, including stamp-like 'notes' of 1, 2 and 3 rouble denominations, and by 1921 100,000 rouble notes were issued. At the end of 1921 there was a dropping of noughts, one new rouble equalling 10,000 old ones, and new notes were issued in 1922. At the beginning of January 1923 two more noughts were dropped, which 'made the situation significantly clearer. Now most foreign bank notes, bonds used as money and temporary mediums of payment could be withdrawn from circulation and the use of them from that point could be prohibited by law.'[3]

The Soviet Union was a command economy, and its monetary history is of little interest to us until its collapse, with the exception of two incidents, one in 'White' Russia and the other in the Soviet Union as part of the New Economic Policy.

## The National Emission Caisse (North Russia) 1919

During the Civil War the British and other allies supported the northern (anti-communist) provisional government which was based in Archangel.

There was a problem as to how the allied forces were to obtain currency to meet local expenditure. The simple solution was to import goods and to sell them for local currency. Hanke and Schuler comment:

> Indeed on occasion the allies were so desperate for notes that they dumped goods on the market for less than they had paid.[4]

This comment begs a lot of questions. At what rate of exchange does one calculate that they had 'lost money'? Thus, if there had been no money at all, the problem would have been solved by barter (paying local workers with imported food, clothes or tobacco) and barter is notoriously inefficient. Even the inadequate mixture of notes, many of which were forged, may have been better.

There was then a fascinating experiment in creating an alternative currency, devised by Dominick Spring-Rice who was attached to the allied forces as a financial adviser, and who liaised closely with Maynard Keynes, then based at the UK Treasury. The provisional government established a new agency, the National Emission Caisse (North Russia), the first president of which was a British banker, Mr Harvey, and which issued notes at a fixed rate of 40 roubles to the pound sterling guaranteed by all the assets of the government. The notes could only be acquired with foreign currency, at the appropriate rate of exchange, and the Caisse was required to keep at least 75 per cent of the issue on deposit with the Bank of England, investing the balance of 25 per cent in the bonds of the provisional government. This presumably was a political compromise; the authors do not say, although they do refer to it as 'one defect' of the currency scheme.

This was effectively a currency board operation, costs being more than covered by the deposit interest, and profits were to be shared with the provisional government. The British government kicked the operation off by buying 100 million roubles in notes for sterling. The notes were printed in a rush, basically using old tzarist note plates, but failing to delete all the insignia, which had to be blotted out by hand. There were about 600 million roubles of old notes in circulation in the area, and the exchange rate was initially fixed at 48 old roubles, or 40 new roubles for £1.

There were said to be 2,000 separate issues of rouble banknotes, 'Czarist, Kerensky, Bolshevik and local White', and it was said that all the issues exchanged at the same rate. By mid-April 1919 the circulation of the old notes had fallen from 600 million to 300 million, and 'good money drove out bad'.

The war with Germany having ended, the allies decided to pull out of the Russian Civil War, and the Caisse was closed on 4 October 1919. Notes held by the army were destroyed (they failed to burn so were dumped at sea) and a book entry credit was made at the Bank of England. The Caisse continued to redeem notes and moved its operations to London.

As the Soviet Union consolidated its position there was (technically) a 'monetary union' as the Russian rouble system was extended (for which read imposed) on three other republics in 1923 and after that to a total of 12 republics and the three Baltic states. This is of no technical interest from our point of view: the break-up is far more fascinating.

## The Chervonetz

Meanwhile, in 1922, the Soviet government introduced a parallel currency, the chervonetz, which was not legal tender but traded at a free price against the rouble. It was informally linked to gold, and from November 1922 the state bank issued chervonetz notes 25 per cent backed by gold and 'stable foreign currency'.[5] These notes were exchangeable for 8.6026g of gold .900 fine (7.74234g of fine gold)[6] and circulated alongside less stable rouble notes as part of the New Economic Policy. On 4 February 1924 smaller denomination gold rouble notes (10 gold roubles = 1 chervonitz) were issued, and from 10 March 1924 old roubles were exchanged on the basis of 5,000 per gold rouble. In 1937 the gold guarantee was dropped, but in any case who would have dared invoke it in such a police state?

During the 1930s the chervonetz remained the main unit, but there was a major currency reform in 1947, when all banknotes were declared invalid and replaced with 'beautiful and well printed' 1, 3, 5, 10, 25, 50 and 100 rouble notes. In 1961 a further nought was dropped, one new rouble equalling ten old ones, and nominally worth about £1.[7] The reform, unlike previous ones, involved the withdrawal and replacement of the (token) coins, and in fact an increase in the production and circulation of such coins.[8] There were no further formal changes until the end of the Soviet Union.

The subject of money in a command economy is outside the scope of this book, but David Woodruff [9] gives an interesting account of the politics of this period, and the origins of the significant and persistent difference between 'cash' and 'cashless' money in the Soviet economy.

# 24 The monetary consequences of the break-up of theAustro-Hungarian empire

## Introduction

The Austro-Hungarian empire was created in 1867, and the resulting 'monetary union' is arguably the first example of two countries formally agreeing to share monetary sovereignty, while otherwise maintaining separate economic policies.

Chapter 10 summarised the monetary history to 1914, and the problems of wartime finance lead into what is surely the classic example of the dissolution of a monetary union followed by the contrasting and instructive histories of how the various successor states suffered (or in one case avoided) and recovered from hyper-inflation. The history as a whole illustrates many themes in this book: the fall of the Credit Anstalt was a consequence of these events.

## Finance during the 1914–18 war

The Austrian crown had, at the beginning of the war, been worth 20.25 US cents on the basis of the gold 10 corona weighing 3.3875g .900 fine, the silver corona weighing 5g .835 fine (a ratio of 13.5) and were by now token coins with a fiat value several times their bullion value.

As elsewhere in Europe, the gold standard was suspended on the outbreak of war, and

> On August 4 [1914] decrees authorised the disregarding of statutes ... forbidding advances to the state ... The provisions for a 40% gold cover ... were suspended ... the bank ... received permission to suspend publishing weekly statements ... The condition of the bank was thus concealed until ... December 31 1917.[1]

When figures were eventually published, it was clear that from end 1913 to end 1919 note circulation increased from some 2.4 billion to 54 billion crowns, or 2,179 per cent, while advances to the state increased from zero to 42 billion crowns. The gold reserves virtually disappeared, mostly to

Germany. Garber and Spencer say that the war effort was financed mainly by sales of war bonds, typically 5.5 per cent at 96. The bank lent up to 75 per cent of face against these bonds at 5 per cent 'and continued to do so even in November 1918 when the bonds sold at only 60'. By the end of the war the value (of the paper crown) was 12 to the dollar or 8 cents, clearly a recipe for a future inflationary disaster.

Czechoslovakia opposed this inflationary policy, and took steps to prevent the bank making loans within its territory. One perverse result of this was that Czech citizens, holding cash rather than bonds, actually suffered more from the general inflation.

## Exchange controls[2]

During the war there was a substantial increase in the banknote circulation, but the exchange rate held comparatively firm. In February 1916 an association of banks in Vienna tried to exercise control over exchange rates. Not all banks were members, and on 19 December 1916 formal exchange controls were introduced, administered by a *Divisenzentrale* under the auspices of the Austro-Hungarian Bank. Controls were strengthened on 18 June 1918: Young suggests they had been successful in maintaining the exchange value of the crown during the war. In April 1919 control of the *Divisenzentrale* was moved from the Bank (which was about to be liquidated) to the Austrian Ministry of Finance, but it was less effective in dealing with the more rapid depreciation, and an illegal market developed. Controls were relaxed in October 1920, reintroduced in December 1921, tightened up in July 1922, and relaxed again after December 1922, by which time Austria was in the grip of hyper-inflation.

Under the terms of the control, Austrian banks maintained separate *Ausland* (external) and inland accounts. At the end of 1921 *Ausland* currency was worth twice the restricted currency, but the rates moved together during the subsequent fall.[3]

## The end of the Austro-Hungarian empire

Before the war the Austro-Hungarian empire had 50 million inhabitants in an area of 676,000km$^2$. After the war, the various ethnic groups within the empire sought independence, with Allied support. Following the Czechoslovak revolution in October 1918, the old monarchy quickly fragmented (with some accretions from neighbouring territories) into Hungary, Poland, Czechoslovakia, the Kingdom of the Serbs, Croats and Slovenes, and Romania; and some territory was ceded to Italy, leaving Austria with just 6.5 million people in 84,000km$^2$.

The Austrian rump proclaimed the German-Austrian Republic, but the empire, like the later Soviet Union, had developed close internal economic links behind a common tariff, and early attempts to maintain the old trade patterns were resisted. The Allies maintained a trade embargo against Austria and Hungary, but not the other states. Czechoslovakia, Hungary, Romania and the Kingdom of the Serbs, Croats and Slovenes raised tariffs. Other problems were caused by distrust of the currency, and much inter-regional trade was conducted in barter.[4]

Austria, again like the later Soviet Union, at first attempted to maintain a monetary union with the successor countries. In January 1919 the Kingdom of the Serbs, Croats and Slovenes called in all Austro-Hungarian notes in the territory and over-stamped them with a national symbol. Czechoslovakia followed, and Austria itself was forced to take its own steps to over-print notes in March 1919.

> However many notes of the bank were withheld from stamping ... to escape fiscal measures, or because it was considered that the notes would be more valuable with the real or forged stamp of another country. A lively trade sprang up in these notes and they commanded a premium.[5]

All the successor states had to take steps to create their own independent monetary systems. Austria had similar reparations problems to the Germans, and had to adjust from being the central power of a large country to becoming a much smaller one with what had become an overblown bureaucracy. This was a major cause of the Credit Anstalt crash.

## The treaties of St Germain and Trianon

The problems were addressed at conferences leading to treaties which approved, and required, the stamping of banknotes in the various territories, but there continued to be movements of notes across national borders, often with easily forged stamps. Obviously, the notes moved to countries where the purchasing power was greatest: most seem to have finished up in Hungary and Romania, one estimate suggesting that half the crown notes exchanged in Romania 'originated outside the new borders of that country and bore forged stamps'.[6]

## The liquidation of the Austro-Hungarian Bank

The various governments were required by the treaties to hand over the crown notes they collected to the liquidators of the Austro-Hungarian Bank. Notes issued before 27 October 1918 were regarded as obligations of the Bank, later issues being a claim against the successor governments. Liquidators, appointed in August 1920 (held up for the ratification of various treaties), did not begin work until April 1921, proposing that each country should take on the assets and liabilities of the bank held within the territory, recognising that a proportion of the loans would prove irrecoverable. Claims representing banknotes were calculated on a statistical basis, giving a lower figure than that of the number of notes claimed to have been stamped.[7]

### The economic consequences

The following passage from Garber and Spencer (1994, 7–8) is relevant to any break-up of a monetary union:

> As successor states in a formally unified currency zone sequentially introduce their own currencies, massive cross-border flows of the old currency typically follow. Arbitrage of two different sorts drive these flows.
>
> First, the real value of the old currency may differ in two successor states. In a currency reform, the old currency is typically exchanged for the new currency at a pre-set conversion rate; goods prices are also converted into the new currency, but not necessarily at the same rate. If price controls for goods or assets differ across countries, or if prices respond more sluggishly in one country than in another to initial differences in conversion prices, currency will move across borders to take advantage of the resulting price differential.

They go on to say that other effects will depend on the causes of the break-up, and what share of the revenue sources is inherited by each successor State. A deprived one may require an inflationary policy inappropriate for its more fortunate neighbour. The break-up of the currency zone is then inevitable, and markets will react in anticipation.

Discussing (1994, 6) the problem of avoiding a 'monetary disunion', Garber and Spencer comment that although the successor states 'shared a common currency, they did not share equally in seigniorage or in the need for inflationary finance'. The Austrians continued an inflationary policy to which the Czechs and the Hungarians objected strongly.

The example shows that currency separation, when it is needed, can happen very quickly. 'The Serb, Croat, and Slovene authorities for example started their initial stamping operation within six weeks of the creation of their state.' There was also an advantage in being a first mover, especially where the immediate solution adopted was to ensure that only banknotes over-stamped with the appropriate national stamp were legal tender within the country. The stock of money

> was determined by the rules governing the stamping operation, and the ease with which the stamps could be forged. The real demand for the new currency dictated where the notes would be smuggled in and fixed with a forged stamp or smuggled out and stamped elsewhere.

Meanwhile, 'states that are late in breaking away from a currency union may have more than their share of the old notes dumped on them'.

Arbitrage opportunities can best be eliminated by simultaneous currency reforms throughout the full monetary union, and Garber and Spencer point out that a note exchange is an opportunity to remove any monetary overhang. This lesson was remembered in the post-1945 Western European reconstructions and (occasionally) in the break-up of the former Soviet Union, but was ignored in the monetary reunification of Germany. They conclude:

> Finally currency reform will succeed in creating a stable medium of exchange only if it is accompanied by sound fiscal and monetary policies. It is not necessary for fiscal restraint to precede currency reform if the new monetary authorities are constrained effectively in their ability to extend credit to the state. In each of the successor states of the Austro-Hungarian empire fiscal equilibrium was contained as a consequence of the currency reform rather than as a pre-condition for it.

# 25 Austria after the break-up of the Austro-Hungarian empire

## Austrian monetary policy

In Austria, notes of various denominations from 1 to 10,000 kronen were over-stamped *Deutsch Österreich* in various colours (not only the red mentioned in the decree) but most also exist further stamped *Note echt, Stempel falsch*.[1] Other notes were issued *Ausgeben nach dem 4 Oktober 1920*.

Joseph Schumpeter,[2] then aged 36, returned from the German Coal Socialisation Commission on 15 February 1919 and was appointed Minister of Finance on 15 March. (One of his first actions was to sign the 'Schumpeter *Verordnung*' on the overprinting of banknotes.) He resigned, a victim of a 'political execution' on 17 October 1919. His own account says little about his role, for which we have to turn to biographies by Stolper,[3] Allen,[4] and März[5]. Stolper says that he was a 'technical minister without a party affiliation and ... without a power base of his own',[6] but Allen uses almost identical words to describe the *general* status of the *Staatsekretär* who did not have a seat in Parliament.[7] The appointment was on the initiative of the socialist group, fellow students of Böhm-Bawerk, and notably Otto Bauer, leader of the Austrian socialists, who appeared to know that Schumpeter was essentially a liberal pro-market economist without being aware of his views on international affairs.

Specifically he was opposed to the official government policy of *Anschluss* (union with Germany), although he had apparently flirted with the idea of monetary union with France. He would have preferred to keep the old empire in a customs and monetary union, perhaps regarding it as an 'optimum currency area'.

A year earlier Schumpeter had written a paper on 'The Crisis of the Tax State',[8] in which he discusses how modern capitalist society had developed from feudalism. Pure economics, he says, ignores government. Capitalist society needs government and government needs taxes. He was one of the first to recognise explicitly that there is a limit beyond which taxes produce diminishing and eventually negative returns.

Schumpeter submitted his first budget on 1 July 1919, before peace conditons were known: Austria was to be left with three quarters of imperial war debt, and there would be a deficit of 60 per cent of expenditures.

On September 27 he submitted a six-point *Finanzplan*[9] to cabinet. It was rejected by the cabinet a few days later, but published by Schumpeter on 16 October. The next day the Allies announced the terms of the peace treaty, and the cabinet formally resigned. Most were reappointed, but not Schumpeter and Bauer. 'The original version is considerably more outspoken than the published version ... a thoroughly pessimistic document.' 'Vintage Schumpeter'. The six points in the plan were:

1   'A massive capital levy' to eliminate the overhang on capital assets. (Bauer wanted to use it to transfer assets to the state as part of his key socialisation ideas: see below.)
2   A plan to stabilise exchange rates, but not (unlike Churchill) at the prewar parity. He wanted 'neither further inflation nor deflation, but rather the maintenance of the status quo'.
3   He 'proposed a new central bank ... completely independent of the government and unrelated to the state's need to borrow'.
4   More and higher indirect taxes.
5   To restore the conditions by which Austrian industry could borrow abroad.
6   Large private capital imports, without which the rest of the package would not work. It would reduce both inflation and the deficit. Increased Austrian exports would follow and could be used to service the deficit.

The main dispute was over socialisation. Otto Bauer wanted to use a capital levy to finance this, and initially accepted that the policy was intended 'to improve the productivity of ... enterprises'. [They would] 'not need resources from the budget, but rather would make a profit'.[10] Schumpeter was concerned to eliminate the monetary overhang: 'the operation ends in the furnace in which all cash and titles which fall into the hands of the state must be burned'. He initially accepted Bauer's other principles but protested vigorously when on 17 June the Socialisation Commission began plans for a financial institution to funds public corporation deficits. There were other arguments about deficit financing while the central bank was honouring bonded debts, most of which were held by Germans.

Allen says he 'tried to explain his position by stating "Krone ist Krone"'. 'He recognised that its value differed, so that those paying 1909 debt with 1919 kronen benefitted greatly. ... the remark seems heartless and unsympathetic to those who had lost and were losing all through inflation.'

Stolper says that 'Krone ist Krone' was actually the heading of the editorial in the *Neue Freie Presse*. The *Verordnung* was challenged and upheld in the Constitutional Court in 1924: the plaintiffs argued that notes were meant to have the same gold value as prewar notes, and/or repayment in worthless paper money was expropriation.

Schumpeter himself[11] gives a somewhat different view of events, explaining that the policy was facilitated, rather than determined, by the League. Its three points were:

- A liberal programme of establishing as much commercial freedom as possible, removing price controls, and limiting direct government activity.
- Stabilising the crown, rather than attempting to restore its value.
- Going for stability first, and hoping to balance the budget out of the readjustment of values. An independent bank of issue was, on this approach, the necessary first step. 'The problem of the bank of issue was attacked months before the League of Nations loan became a certainty.'

His political position was weakened by the so called Kola affair. Schumpeter, as Finance Minister, had used Richard Kola as his agent to procure foreign currency, where necessary on the black market. Kola had also been involved in selling large blocks of shares in the biggest Austrian company, Alpine, to the Italians, which of course also brought in needed foreign currency. Alpine, whose shares appreciated threefold, was high on the list of companies Bauer wanted to socialise. Bauer planned to use this to discredit Schumpeter. 'The facts did not matter; the accusation did.'[12] In the event the Socialisation Commission did not accomplish anything: the affair might even be regarded as a scapegoat for Bauer's own failure.

Allen suggests that if Schumpeter's brief tenure achieved anything it was in delaying socialist policies. Otherwise 'productivity would have fallen, recovery would have been much slower, and much of industry would have moved ... to the public sector'.[13]

His friend Gustav Stolper[14] summed up:

> My personal opinion is that Schumpeter failed because of his boundless ambition, which he wanted to use not in the scientific, but rather in the political field. If he succeeds in concentrating once more on scientific work, he will, with his intellectual capacity, soon overcome this unpleasant intermezzo.

## Austria's hyper-inflation

Although Austria received some international aid, many proposals were, for various reasons aborted[15] and the government, attempting to alleviate poverty caused by unemployment, ran a very large budget deficit, financed by the government selling treasury bills to the Austrian section of the Austro-Hungarian Bank. From July 1920 to June 1921 expenditures of 70.6

bn were financed by 29.5bn of receipts (42 per cent) and 41.1bn of new money (58 per cent). The next year was even worse.[16] The note circulation increased sixfold from March 1919 to January 1921, when serious inflation began. From then until August 1922 the note circulation increased by a factor of 39 (20 per cent per month) while prices rose by a factor of 110. 'The "flight from the crown" occurred as people chose to hold less of their wealth in the form of the rapidly depreciating crown, attempting instead to hold foreign currencies or real assets.'[17] Exchange controls were introduced with the (vain) aim of preventing people 'evading' the inflation tax.

Negotiations for a foreign loan continued through 1921, but the revenue which would have provided the backing was already mortgaged. The situation became more serious in December, and some credits were promised, but most of these fell through. 'It was expected that Austria would accept financial supervision by a commissioner appointed by the League of Nations. However the Vienna government pleaded that the internal political situation made such foreign intrusion impossible at the moment.'[18] By August, though, they would accept anything, but the Allied governments, 'tired of loaning money to Austria', referred the question to the League of Nations.

Negotiations with the League led to the signing of three protocols in October 1922, one reaffirming the sovereignty of Austria, another setting out conditions for an international loan of 650 million gold crowns (585 million net, or about $120 million, was actually raised) and another setting out Austria's plan for economic reconstruction. This included an undertaking to set up an independent central bank (actually formed on 14 November) without power to finance the government, which therefore had to balance its budget.[19] The League would appoint a commissioner resident in Vienna to supervise.

By then confidence had already been restored, apparently occasioned by little more than a League of Nations promise of help, and (a very interesting point) a couple of months before help was actually confirmed. In August 1922 the currency had stabilised at 77,000 per dollar, while prices peaked at 20,090 (January 1921 = 100) in September, actually falling for the next three months. The note circulation, however, continued to increase (about fourfold) for the next couple of years as velocity fell and notes again became credible as a store of value.

### The schilling

Stabilisation 'was not achieved via a currency reform', which took place 'long after the exchange rate had been stabilised and was surely an incidental measure'.[20] In December 1923 Austria introduced a silver schilling coin, with a value of 10,000 of the (now stable) paper crown as a kind of temporary 'dropping of noughts' exercise. The coins, which had unlimited legal tender, came into circulation in June 1924, and were popular. Although the silver content was worth less than the face value (80 per cent according to

Schumpeter), many were hoarded and went out of circulation. The numismatic evidence shows that in 1923 and 1924 some gold 20 and 100 kronen coins were struck to the prewar standard.[21]

Indeed, in a market-driven example of 'choice in currency' the new unit soon took over, *de facto*, from the old, and in December 1924 the schilling was legally adopted as the Austrian currency unit. The gold schilling was established with a content of 0.21172086g of fine gold.

> Thus a new currency has been added ... the gold value of which was determined more or less by accident ... It is regretted ... that ... a unit could not have been selected which was in closer harmony with some of the other leading currency units – such as the dollar, pound, or franc.[22]

Memories of Latin Monetary Union!

# 26 Other former members of the Austro-Hungarian empire

The other countries of the Empire shared a pre-1918 history with Austria: Romania and Bulgaria, also discussed below, had based their currency on the Latin Monetary Union system.

## Hungary[1]

Hungary declared itself a republic on 16 November 1918, but the first Karolyi government was overthrown by Bolsheviks in March 1919. They in turn were overthrown by a Romanian army, and the Horthy government was established in August 1919.

Hungary did not over-stamp its notes until 18–27 March 1920, after the treaty of Trianon. Fifty per cent of the notes were retained as a forced loan at 5 per cent. Crown deposits made before 8 March appear to have been exempt from the levy, but a later decree of 18 December 1920 froze 20 per cent of resident deposits).[2] There were two complications.

First, the Bolshevik regime had had access to the plates for printing 1 and 2 crown Austro-Hungarian banknotes, and used them to print what was known as 'counterfeit money'. (These were eventually honoured by the government at par, while the larger denomination 'white notes', printed on white paper under their own authority by the Bolsheviks, were redeemed at 25 per cent of face value. Dornbusch[3] says they lacked the blue paper used for Austrian notes and used white paper: 'Issue of money in the name of the Soviet government did not succeed, even when the death penalty was threatened'.)

Second, Hungary as the last such state to stamp notes, did not have the advantage of surprise, and had at that time a stronger exchange rate than Austria. (According to Dornbusch, the Hungarian currency was separately quoted in Zurich from January 1920, but notes were only over-stamped in March 1920.) The arbitrage opportunities were inevitably exploited.

'If weak government was the chief reason for failure to stabilise Austria, the same cannot be said for Hungary.' The League of Nations noted that after the right resumed power Hungary had 'A strong, stable and drastic government' (Dornbusch).

There was an attempt at stabilisation in August 1921, when Hegedus, a banker, was appointed Finance Minister with full power. It was stressed 'that a depreciating exchange rate increases budget deficits and thereby feeds money creation'. The stamped notes (and certain other currencies) were replaced by the new State Note Institute set up by the Ministry of Finance to replace the Hungarian section of the Austro-Hungarian Bank. This had limits on its note-issuing rights, but although Hungarian prices had been fairly stable until about August 1921, advances to the government resumed that October.

Like Austria, but a little later, Hungary suffered hyper-inflation. Prices increased from 4,200 in March 1921 to 8,100 in January 1922, reaching 21,400 in August (the peak of the Austrian inflation). From then until March 1924 they increased by a factor of $100^4$ (see Dornbusch for a discussion of the political reasons why Hungary could not follow the clearly successful Czech example).

Again the League of Nations (see Dornbusch who quotes League sources) played a key role in the currency reconstruction.[5] The worst year was 1923, and in April the government requested the Reparation Commission to release the country from its obligations under the Trianon treaty, so that assets would be available to provide security for external loans. This was conditional on an approved loan agreement, which could not then be arranged. The League sent a team to Budapest in November 1923, and in February 1924 the Commission notified the League that it would remove the liens on Hungary's resources, and rescheduled payments, and similar arrangements were made with countries which had subscribed for relief bonds.[6] On 17 April laws adopting the plans for reconstruction were passed. As with Austria, a loan of 250 million gold kronen (twenty years with a 7.5 per cent coupon at 87.5) was arranged in July 1924, actually after prices had stabilised.

A central bank was set up with a constitution similar to that of Austria. The bank was required to maintain a reserve of 20 per cent for the first five years, rising in three stages to 33.3 per cent. Reserves could be maintained in gold, or in currency or bills of exchange 'in countries where the currency is relatively stable'.[7] Whatever that might mean, the krone was in fact stabilised against the pound sterling, which had then not yet returned to gold. The rate was set at 346,000 kronen to the pound, but subsequently improved to 341,000 (71,000 to the dollar) at par with Austria. Later sterling (and the Hungarian currency) improved against the dollar, and (it seems) the Austrian krone. Chart 31 in Young 1925 shows how the value of currency in circulation rose from $20 million to over $60 million by mid-1925. The currency certainly became acceptable again in trade.

> The stabilisation of the krone has been one of the outstanding events in Hungarian reconstruction, and has been of great benefit to the industry and prosperity of the country. When the currency was fluctuating rapidly the economic life was deranged. ... Since the country now has a definite unit ... transactions are carried on with a greater degree of

certainty. The government's revenues ... have increased more than expected. The country has recovered remarkably from the chaotic conditions prevailing at the first of 1924.[8]

The Hungarian pengo was introduced at the beginning of 1928, after White had written.

## Poland

Postwar Poland was created out of territory which had been occupied by Austria-Hungary, Russia and Germany. Its case was more complicated, as money circulating included Austro-Hungarian crowns, Russian roubles, German marks and Polish marks issued by the Polish State Loan Bank which had been established by the Germans in German occupied Poland. The war with Germany having ended, Poland continued to be at war with Soviet Russia until 1920. The Polish mark became legal tender on 15 January 1920, larger denomination crown notes were exchanged in April, and the smaller ones in June.

There was the inevitable deficit, financed by borrowing from the State Loan Bank. From January 1922 to December 1923 the note issue increased by a factor of 523, while a flight from the mark and sharp rise in velocity meant that prices rose by a factor of 2402.[9]

Hyper-inflation came to a sudden end in January 1924. Sargent says 'Unlike the cases of Austria and Hungary, in Poland the initial stabilisation was achieved without foreign loans or intervention': a foreign loan was arranged much later, in 1927. The experience was similar – 'The two inter-related changes were a dramatic move toward a balanced government budget and the establishment of an independent central bank that was prohibited from making additional unsecured loans to the government.'

A new currency unit, the gold zloty, equal to 1.8 million paper marks or 19.29 US cents, was created, and the note circulation increased by a factor of 3.2 during 1924. This is what one would expect; during 1922 and 1923 prices had risen four times as fast as the note issue, and with returning confidence velocity simply returned to normal.

Young[10] goes into rather more detail, but was writing before the Polish reconstruction was really complete. In 1919 the mark was regarded as an emergency currency, eventually to be replaced by the zloty ('zloto meaning gold in Polish'), equal to the gold franc, which would be issued by a state bank to be created after the budget was balanced. Meanwhile it was used as a theoretical unit for certain accounting purposes.

In 1923 the Polish government issued bonds, half in zlotys (initially on the basis of 1,400 marks per zloty) and half in marks, and in June that year began converting statistics into zlotys. Young is intriguing rather than informative, and says that the value of the zloty 'was determined differently at different times, but was based generally on a combination of the price of rye and other commodities, with exchange rates for Swiss francs'.

Bank Polski, successor to the State Loan Bank, began circulating zlotys in early 1924, and in February began exchanging marks for zlotys at the now stable exchange rate. The British adviser E. Hilton Young (later Lord Kennet) had insisted that budgetary reform must precede the establishment of the bank. The bank itself was financed with public subscriptions, and the full 100 million zlotys was raised though with some difficulty. Profits after paying an 8 per cent dividend were to be divided between the government and the bank. The bank was required to hold a 30 per cent minimum reserve against note issues in gold or 'foreign paper currencies which are not subject to great fluctuation', whatever that might mean.

A tax was imposed on the note issue at a rate varying inversely with the gold cover: a 'novel feature'. There was a provision in the statutes (article 47) by which notes would become convertible into gold at a date to be fixed by an order in council.

The currency was thus neither convertible nor pegged in any formal sense. The zloty did in fact depreciate from late 1925, and in autumn 1926 was about 72 per cent of its original parity. Prices rose about 50 per cent: Sargent attributes this to 'the government's premature relaxation of exchange controls and the tendency of the central bank to make private loans at insufficient interest rates'.

## Czechoslovakia[11]

Czechoslovakia became an independent state on 28 October 1918, the first step in the collapse of the old Austro-Hungarian empire. A National Assembly (nominees being appointed by the political parties pro rata to their strength in the 1911 elections) was convened for 14 November and Thomas Masaryk was elected president. The country's status was confirmed in the various postwar treaties, a constitution was adopted on 29 February 1920, and a general election was held on 18 April 1920.

Czechoslovakia had been part of the Austro-Hungarian monetary system, and its main circulating medium was banknotes issued by what had become the Austrian Central Bank. The treaty of St Germain, 10 September 1919, was to require countries which were formerly part of the Austro-Hungarian empire to over-stamp its notes. Jumping ahead of this, and indeed of its political status, the new nation took prompt steps to protect its monetary arrangements. Plans were passed in secret on 25 February 1919, and next day the frontiers were closed (until 9 March)[12] to give an opportunity to over-stamp Austro-Hungarian notes already circulating in its territory. About 8 billion crowns were over-stamped, 2 billion being retained as a forced loan, carrying interest at 1 per cent (receipts for these could be used to meet the capital levy). After 9 March, only stamped notes were legal tender. These were later exchanged for Czechoslovak crowns.

Given the subsequent Austrian inflationary experience, this was just as well. By a law of 10 April 1919, the fiduciary issue was strictly limited.[13] The Ministry of Finance created a banking office which took over the branches of the Austro-Hungarian Bank, and effectively became the bank of issue. Initially, this had no reserves, but these were obtained by loans, transfers from the Austro-Hungarian Bank and a 'patriotic appeal' to turn in gold for notes. The effect was sharply deflationary, and in 1922 the value of the crown rose from 2c to 3.5c. The banking office was due to be replaced by a central bank in 1925 (when Young was writing).[14] He gives details of the proposals.

A capital levy was imposed at rates between 1 per cent and 30 per cent (on property over 10 million crowns). There was also an increment tax on the increase in wealth from the beginning of the war to March 1919, at a maximum rate of 40 per cent (on increments in excess of 10 million crowns).

Dornbusch refers to Czechoslovakia as 'the outstanding example of a country that upon entering statehood and democracy avoided hyperinflation' and 'stopped inflation even before it started'. In his version legal tender status was denied to the (*sic*) '25, 200 and 100,000' crown notes churned out by the Austrian printing presses, and Finance Minister Rasin introduced the measures described above. He also mentions exchange control and the surrender of external assets, with a choice of selling at the current Prague rate or lending to the government at 4 per cent, repayable in the original currency after four years. Rasin 'had planned to go much further. His initial plan was for an 80 per cent withholding of notes and a major appreciation forced with an external loan to back the currency' – effectively a 'big bang' approach, preferable for a new state than a 'steady fever leading to recurrent wage fights'. The new Czech currency opened in Zurich at a premium of 60 per cent over Austrian notes. Rasin's attempt to restore the prewar parity produced the inevitable sharp deflation, and after November 1921 the currency was freed to appreciate. There was a tight money policy and a real appreciation. The deflationary aspects were admitted to have been a mistake, but by 1925 unemployment was moderate while prices and the exchange rate were stable. Rasin did not live to see this: he was assassinated in January 1923.

## The Kingdom of the Serbs, Croats and Slovenes[15]

This kingdom comprised parts of the empire with some occupied territories. Most of the currency was Austro-Hungarian crowns, but with a substantial mix of Serbian dinars, Montenegran perpers and Bulgarian leva. A decree of 12 December 1918 banned the import of Austro-Hungarian notes into Serbia, and this was extended to the rest of the kingdom the following month, when notes already in the country were called in and over-stamped with the national emblem.

The stamp was easily forged, and a year later, November–December 1919, the operation was repeated with an adhesive stamp. As the government could not detect all forgeries it had to accept some falsified notes.

Validation was accompanied by a 20 per cent levy compensated by a ten-year 4 per cent loan and stamped crowns were exchanged for dinars at a rate of 4 to 1 (5 to 1 taking account of the levy).

A National Bank commenced operations on 1 February 1920, taking over the assets of the Serbian National Bank and the local branches of the Austro-Hungarian Bank. As with its neighbours, it was an independent joint stock company with the sole right to issue money, and was prohibited from lending money to the government. Three quarters of the shareholders were Serbian. There was moderate inflation. 'The dinar depreciated by 840 per cent between 1919 and 1923 but appreciated by 37 per cent during the ensuing two years and remained stable at about 56.6 dinars to the dollar after the second half of 1925.'[16]

## Romania[17]

The modern monetary history of Romania begins with Russia's defeat in the Crimean War and the 1859 union of Wallachia and Moldavia as an autonomous nation under the Ottoman Empire. In 1878 the treaty of Berlin recognised full Romanian independence, and brought the province of Dobrudja under Romanian rule. Transylvania, annexed by Hungary in 1848, remained outside, to be reunited only on 1 December 1918.

In 1859 the currency of the newly independent state appears to have consisted mainly of Austrian ducats, and in spite of an early decision (18 November 1859) to adopt the French decimal system there were years of debate[18] before a new national monetary system, based on the leu, was established on 4 May 1867. The leu was defined as 0.3226g of gold .900 fine or 5g of silver .835 fine, and Romania joined the Latin Monetary Union in early 1867.[19] The National Bank of Romania was formed in 1880, and in 1890 the country abandoned bimetallism and adopted a gold standard[20] with Charles Rist as technical adviser.

After the war, postwar Romania was enlarged to include Transylvania and parts of Hungary, Austria and Russia (these were Bessarabia, part of Moldavia until 1812 when it was occupied by Russia; Bucovina, part of Austro-Hungary since 1775; and Banat, increasing the country's area from 120,000 to 295,000m$^2$), thanks to 'the immense success of Ion C. Bratianu at the Paris peace conference in obtaining a recognition of the maximum Romanian national gains'.[21]

Austro-Hungarian crowns and Romanian lei circulated, including some issued during the German occupation. Over-stamping began in June 1919 with a small tax to cover costs, and in August 1920 crowns were exchanged for lei at 2 to 1, and roubles were converted at varying rates. The government ran surpluses and the National Bank of Romania survived the war. Prices rose more than in the SCS or Czechoslovakia, but there was no hyper-inflation. On 19 May 1925 the bank signed a commitment to return to gold with a 33 per cent cover within twenty years.

# 27 Germany and Austria in the 1930s

## Introduction

Germany, having recovered from its hyper-inflation, was hard hit by the depression and problems associated with reparations, and the success of many Nazis and communists in the September 1930 election foreshadowed the political disasters that were to come. Germany still remained on gold but was having serious problems of adjustment.[1] In Austria, which had had similar postwar problems, and the problems of the break-up of the empire, the Credit Anstalt crash precipitated a financial crisis affecting the world, and notably Germany.

## Credit Anstalt

Schubert[2] looks at 'the experience of a country that is right in the eye of the storm', to help us learn from the mistakes of history, using modern economic theory and looking at the links between the bank failure and the currency crisis. It is well worth reading from that point of view. Vienna, once the political and financial capital of 50 million people, saw this shrink to 6 million, and banks, having to choose 'between accepting an economic reorientation based on the new political boundaries or trying to adhere to the economic structure of the pre-War period', opted for 'business as usual' and sought to preserve their influence in the successor states rather than accepting painful downsizing (Schubert 1991, 35). Their judgment was also affected by the trauma of hyper-inflation. The 'universal' nature of the Austrian banks also made them vulnerable: 'British banks were created for people who had money while Austrian banks were created for people who needed money,'

Schubert (1991, 25) suggests that the bank statements may have been manipulated as far as back as 1925: the 'crisis' only hit when the publication of the 1930 balance sheet in May 1931 revealed a huge loss. There was a substantial run on deposits and a reconstruction (33) which was remarkably generous to the shareholders. The National Bank followed the Bagehot Rule, discounting bills on a large scale and threatening the fixed exchange rate system (53–4). The treasury had no funds to contribute to the capital of Credit Anstalt, who had to borrow from other Viennese banks: tax revenues were declining during the recession. The government could not borrow from the central bank, and money borrowed from the BIS which kept them going only for six days to 5 June.

## German exchange controls

German exchange controls were introduced in August 1931, which, it was argued, 'may be judged a success in thwarting an economically purposeless capital flight and in preserving the integrity of the national monetary standard' (Ellis 1941, 282). When the UK went off gold, Germans publicly announced their decision against devaluation (174) and controls were used to support an unrealistic parity. Ellis (182–5) has some intriguing references to the repatriation of German bonds as a method of evasion, obtaining a windfall profit on the export of capital and, in 1932, a deliberate attempt to use this to create an export subsidy.

Hitler came to power on 30 January 1933, and exchange control, 'in creating an authority against the decisions of which the law offered no redress the political predecessors of Hitler, nurtured an institution which paved the way for totalitarianism' (Ellis 1941, 289).

Devaluation in September 1931 would have precipitated a currency flight, but by the summer of 1933 devaluation might have worked. Some German trade enjoyed *de facto* devalued rates under the controls, and

> capital flight was under control, debt service had proceeded satisfactorily and there were clear signs of an economic recovery in Western Europe. ... After 1933 it is difficult to discover justification of exchange control as a monetary and financial measure; its aims became 'ulterior'.
>
> (Ellis 1941, 283)

The Nazis (unlike the Austrians) regarded the economic calculations as irrelevant: 'even if the case were conclusive to these authorities that exchange control entailed net economic losses it would have been retained' (Ellis 1941, 289).

In 1934 Schacht initiated his New Plan and set up a system of controls on imports. Importers could only buy foreign exchange against 'devisen certificates' which were strictly controlled and eventually used as the basis of a series of bilateral payment agreements (Ellis 1941, 211).

In March 1933, Max Warburg was one of the two Jewish members of the eight-member advisory board on which he had served since 1924. They both supported the reappointment of Schacht, but the advisory board was dissolved six months later. Warburg's biographer Chernow discusses the subject from the point of view of this leading Jewish family.[3] In 1931 there was 'imposed' a 25 per cent flight tax on capital shifted abroad. After 1932

German citizens 'could only convert blocked marks into other currencies at a steep discount, but would skim 96 per cent of the amount in question by the end of the decade' (Chernow 1993, 400 – the source does not give details of the regulations). These regulations were of particular concern to Jews who wanted to emigrate. The Nazis were at one stage in favour of encouraging an exodus, 'which they thought might spread anti-semitism abroad, especially if the refugees were poor'. In August 1933 the Haarvara Agreement[4] was negotiated between Palestinian Jews and the Nazis. Under this:

> departing Jews would deposit their marks in blocked accounts in Germany. A year later, they would receive an equivalent amount in Palestine pounds. The hitch was that the Jews had to use those blocked marks to buy German machinery, pipe, fertiliser etc. The Jewish immigrant was repaid with the proceeds when German goods were resold in Palestine. It was a mutually beneficial if bizarre business: goods from Nazi Germany were helping to build Jewish Palestine while Palestinian Jews created German jobs.
>
> (Chernow 1993, 400)

## Nazi plans for a European monetary union

The Nazis planned to impose a 'monetary union' on postwar Europe, in which they, of course, expected to be a 'Greater Germany'. In 1940 Walther Funk, the economics minister, announced that after the war the bilateral arrangements would be phased out in favour of a payments union, with multilateral clearing administered by a clearing office in Berlin. The union would continue to have bilateral arrangements with other countries, notably the United States. Gold would not be used and 'it was Germany's answer to Britain's "fortified" sterling area. It was also the first blueprint for the economic union of Europe.'[5] Gold would be irrelevant and there was no provision for a central bank. Keynes was asked to broadcast, discrediting the idea, but refused, saying there was no point in trying to outflank the Germans 'by offering the blessings of universal free trade and the gold standard'.

## Appendix: Austrian exchange control

Austria had had exchange controls during the First World War, and for a time during the upheavals following the break-up of the Austro-Hungarian empire. The experiences of the 1930s are covered in detail by Howard Ellis[6] in his Austrian chapter. The initial exchange control decrees were very strict and comprehensive, and indeed 'to anyone uninitiated' they 'would appear to ensure an entirely adequate apparatus for the regulation of foreign payments' (Ellis 1941, 37). The defects were 'on the one hand an intolerable severity, and on the other the possibility of legal and illegal evasions'. Below, I discuss the loopholes using modern terminology, and it is particularly interesting to see how Austria escaped from exchange control between 1932 and 1935. In 1938, though, Austria was incorporated into Germany and eventually became part of the German exchange control system. Austria was not, until then, a totalitarian country and its monetary arrangements are, for our purposes, more interesting than those of Germany.

### Loopholes

The law gave the national bank a monopoly of foreign exchange, required that holders of assets had to be offered for sale within eight days, and that exporters had to inform the bank of the payment conditions and could be required to make it a deposit of a guarantee that the proceeds would be surrendered. Substantial fines could be imposed (Ellis 1941, 38). 'It is surprising, however, that illegal evasion should have been resorted to at all, in view of the many possibilities within the law.'[7]

The first loophole is that exports were permitted against foreigners' (frozen) schilling assets. The rights and wrongs of this were fiercely debated, and commercial organisations argued that this procedure enabled export industries to remain competitive and that there was no 'real' loss. The authorities argued that this limited their control of imports, and 'permitted a speculative market on blocked Schillings abroad, a market said to be narrow and subject to disastrous price declines on small decreases in demand'. They also said that many such blocked accounts may belong to Austrians who had transferred their accounts to foreigners in anticipation of exchange control. If these could now be used for exports, such people could be enabled 'to complete the intended capital flight by means of real goods'.

The clinching argument, of course, is the use of blocked balances as an alternative to transactions which brought foreign exchange into Austria. As Ellis points out,

> What the spirited journal discussions apparently missed was that this question involved not simply a particular practice but the whole matter of exchange control. The advantages to exporters cited by proponents of 'exporting in Schillings' were real enough; but after all the 'advantage' of reducing its commercial debt was precisely what exchange control was designed to prevent.
>
> (Ellis 1941, 41)

Another loophole involved the purchase of internationally traded securities. An Austrian could buy goods in Austria, sell them abroad and be paid in blocked schillings. These could be invested in domestic securities or real estate or (as above) applied to exports. At first, the usual vehicles were internationally traded Austrian schilling bonds such as those issued by the League of Nations. In October 1931 the Vienna quotations were at a 20 per cent premium above the foreign quotations. There were arguments in the press about Austria 'following Czechoslovakia, Germany and Hungary in requiring the sale of privately held securities for government'. Austrians, it was said, held a higher proportion of their wealth in foreign securities than the other countries. The proposal was not, as feared, incorporated into the third Divisen Act, and the fourth prohibited foreign securities being accepted in payment of exports. This procedure, effectively a parallel market, continued into the period of more liberal exchange controls. Indeed, in April 1933 the authorities prohibited dealings in Swiss railway bonds, which had become the standard vehicle, but the effect of this measure was predictably to switch attention to other stocks, including British consols. Effectively there was a quasi-legal route for capital flight at a discount.

Alongside these sophisticated parallel markets there were straightforward illegal black markets, both in the border villages and in the cafés of Vienna. In a rare attempt to check this, the national bank withdrew the issue of 1000 schilling notes.

Apart from what we now call 'leads and lags', various types of legal false invoicing were current. Some Austrians went so far as '*even* to found in a foreign city a holding company to originate billings for goods which had never been imported' (my emphasis), which will hardly surprise a postwar reader! Some foreign firms were induced to send Austrians blank printed invoices.

For all this avoidance and evasion, it was hardly surprising that exchange control failed in its objectives: it is perhaps more surprising, given the known predeliction of bureaucrats, that it was essentially relaxed. Before looking at how it was unscrambled, we need to consider the role of bilateral trading agreements which became widespread in prewar- and an important part of immediate postwar monetary arrangements.

By 5 February 1932, when Dr Kienbock took over as president of the National Bank, trade via exchange controls had virtually ground to a halt. The first step was to permit Austrian exporters of wood products (whose markets had suffered from the sterling devaluation) to sell the foreign exchange proceeds to importers of mineral oils, who could pass on the extra cost as there was no competing domestic production. This 'private clearing' arrangement was extended to other affairs of industry. Transactions were subject to specific consent, and a 'raw material quota' had the effect of requiring a proportion of foreign exchange to be surrendered to the National Bank. There was also a fiction that only 'additional' exports were eligible for this treatment (this 'additional' concept was also used by Germany – needless to say all exports were additional) and transactions had to include high commissions and a risk premium against the possibility of not securing permission. This arrangement 'resulted at first in a welter of quotations for one and the same foreign money' (Ellis 1941, 48). Naturally there were opportunities to arbitrage, legally or illegally, between these rates and new opportunities for evasion were created.

On 17 July 1932 the Vienna Bankers' Organisation was appointed the official agency for private clearing, and this paved the way for a move towards an 'official' free market at which the schilling traded at a discount to its gold value. As clearing agreements were wound down the raw material quota was reduced and eliminated, frozen accounts were liquidated and rations of 'official' exchange were reduced and the 'quota' rate effectively became the real exchange rate at which Austria's business was carried on. Effectively this was a devaluation: the whole course of events was very much trial and error; the events can be regarded as a subtle and perhaps politically acceptable alternative to a straight devaluation.

> The eventual official recognition of Schilling depreciation, which had always been contemplated as a calamity, scarcely aroused a word of comment even in financial circles and the general public remained happily ignorant of the fact.
>
> (Ellis 1941, 47)

On 21 November 1932, allocation of 'official' reserves for travel outside Austria was suspended: travellers, like by then everyone else, had to obtain foreign exchange through the private clearing market. On 6 December the quota was finally abolished. Importers, though, still had to pay a premium to liquidate adverse balances with France, Italy, Romania and Switzerland. Authors, annuitants and dependents still received remittances from abroad at the low official rate of exchange. These anomalies were removed by the decree of 6 April 1933. There were still blocked balances, but by June 1934 the market discount on these was negligible. For most practical purposes exchange control had been abolished, while the schilling had been devalued and floated.

# 28 Scandinavia and the Baltic states
## The Nordic Monetary Union

## Introduction

The central theme of this chapter is the Nordic Monetary Union which, unlike the Latin Monetary Union, was founded on a gold standard and did not face the problems of bimetallism. Following the outbreak of war in 1914, though, it became a 'type 2' union with each member in principle having the power to print inconvertible paper money. As such, it came under strain first when Sweden, as a neutral, accumulated gold and resumed minting in 1916, and again with the general if temporary return to gold in the 1920s.

The chapter begins with some earlier history which includes periods of inconvertible currency and a remarkable example of a 'monetary disunion', when Russian-controlled Finland managed to establish a currency system independent of a Russia then in the throes of a banknote inflation. It ends with a short account of the Baltic states, during their brief period of independence from both Germany and Russia, by way of a prelude to their experiences in the Soviet 'disunion'.

## Some earlier history

### Sweden

The basic Swedish coin was the silver riksdaler divided into 48 skilling. Sweden was an early country to issue banknotes, and to suffer suspensions of payments at various times. The 'Swedish Bullionist Controversy' of the mid-eighteenth century is interesting if perhaps irrelevant,[1] and there was a forced circulation of debt certificates in 1792, after which silver convertibility was restored at a depreciated rate. Another followed the 1802 war with Russia, and the monetary system was reformed in 1830 on the basis of 4 riksdaler risgalds (paper) = 1 riksdaler species (silver), but with 32 skilling to the riksdaler risgalds. The currency was decimalised in 1855, and a stable silver standard continued on this 4:1 basis until the gold standard was introduced in 1873.

## *Finland*

Finland had been conquered by Sweden in the twelfth century, and became a Grand Duchy under the Russian empire as part of an 1809 peace settlement after Sweden's defeat by Russia. Swedish money was, after some discussion of alternatives, supplanted by the rouble in December 1809.[2] There were some locally issued banknotes, and Swedish money continued to circulate. Postwar inflation continued in Sweden until 1834, but the value of Swedish paper money fell less in Finland, giving arbitrage opportunies which the authorities tried to prevent by prohibiting the use of Swedish money.

Russian paper money was inconvertible until 1840, when 3.5 paper roubles became equivalent to 1 silver rouble and Finland took the opportunity for its own monetary reform. Inflation was curbed, the silver rouble became the *de facto* as well as the legal currency of Finland, and Finland issued its own banknotes on a substantial scale. A Finnish proposal to issue silver coins of 3, 6, and 9 copecks 'to correspond to the most common small Swedish notes' was rejected by Russia.[3]

### *Finland's own money: an unusual 'disunion'*

In 1854, during the Crimean War (when Russia was flooding the market with paper money, which had legal tender status in Finland), the Bank of Finland also had to suspend the conversion of banknotes into silver, and sought a 'monetary disunion' from Russia. In 1859 Fabian Langenskiold, Minister of Finance, petitioned the Russian government that Russian paper money should be accepted in Finland not at face value, but at a market value published by the Bank of Finland and based on bourse quotations. This was rejected, but the incidental suggestion that Finland should have a smaller monetary unit than the rouble was (surprisingly) accepted: Talvio comments that

> the granting of a monetary unit for Finland was unique in Russian history. ... By giving Finland a currency of its own, the rulers of the Empire furthered its development into a state which later was also able to assert its own political independence.[4]

After some discussion it was decided to call the new unit the silver *markka*, weighing 5.1828g and valued at a quarter of a rouble, divided into 100 *penni*. Banknotes were issued, and appear to have been convertible.

Following the collapse in the value of silver and the crisis of bimetallism, Sweden and Denmark (1873) and Norway (1875) adopted the gold standard, and Finland followed in 1878, introducing a gold standard based on the gold markka. Thereafter Russian and Finnish silver coins circulated only as small change, being legal tender only up to 10 markka.

## Nordic Monetary Union

Sweden and Denmark (which then incorporated Greenland and Iceland) adopted the gold standard in 1871, and took the opportunity to bring their coinages into line by a treaty of 18 December 1872. The following year they were joined by Norway, creating the Nordic Monetary Union, based on the gold krona of 0.44803 grams of .900 fine. Gold coins were legal tender in all three countries: silver was, on the UK pattern, a subsidiary coinage with limited legal tender. Banknotes were strictly only legal tender in the country of issue, but were generally accepted in the others.[5] Although coins were struck to the same standards, numismatic sources show little similarity between the design of the coins or notes: notes of Denmark and Norway are rare, suggesting that only Sweden had any extensive issue.

### The First World War and the end of NMU[6]

All three members suspended the gold standard in August 1914, and the NMU became a more interesting 'type 2' monetary union based on inconvertible currencies. In Norway and Denmark prices rose to about 300 per cent of prewar, more or less in line with the UK, and all shared in the 1920–1 recession. There were only fairly minor deviations in exchange rates.

### The Swedish gold-exclusion policy

Sweden was an exceptional case, being able, as a neutral, to accumulate gold. Early in the war prices rose in Sweden like everywhere else, but towards the end of 1915 the exchange rate hardened and gold began to come in. Its currency was, during the war, at a premium (ranging from 10 per cent to a peak of 34 per cent in November 1916) over other currencies, including the US dollar, and, a rare monetary event, its gold coins passed at this premium over their bullion value. The country had no need for exchange controls, and resumed specie payment in January 1916. This created an arbitrage opportunity for foreign governments, which could, on 'gold standard' rules, require the Riksbank to buy their gold for Swedish currency at the official conversion rate, and to pocket the premium. Apart from the loss to the government (Swedish exports were effectively being sold at a discount where this route could be used) the effect was to inflate the money supply. The classic gold standard adjustment could not work symmetrically as other European countries were 'off gold'.

Sweden then began its 'gold-exclusion policy'.[7] In February 1916 a new law released the Riksbank from its obligations to buy gold, and from April the mint no longer had to coin gold. (Notes remained convertible, and could still legally be redeemed in gold, although this was of course unattractive in practice.) Lester points out that 'The Riksbank still had the right to buy as much or as little gold as it wished and at whatever price it cared to offer. The Bank was not bound by any rules.'[8] He adds that the Riksbank did not seem to understand that its policies could affect inflation, and that its gold transactions were motivated solely by profit to the Bank without regard to the broader interests of the country. Certainly, in spite of the policy, money supply rose by 62 per cent, and prices by 65 per cent, between early 1916 and late 1917.[9]

This unprecedented and possibly unique policy put an interesting strain on the Nordic Monetary Union. 'The exclusion policy could not be applied immediately to Scandinavian gold coin on account of the Scandinavian monetary convention.'[10] Sweden was still bound by its terms to accept gold coin from Denmark and Norway. These countries had also abolished free minting, but their governments could buy gold in the open market, coin it and send it to Sweden. So long as the exchange rates remained around par there was no incentive for the central banks to do this, but in August (Denmark) and September (Norway) the differential widened sufficiently to make the exercise worth while.[11] Deaver says that there were protests by the Riksbank, and a formal agreement to stop the practice in July 1916. Young only mentions a conference in April 1917, and implies that the problem continued until autumn. Kindleberger says that Germany shipped gold to Denmark or Norway, where it was minted and re-exported to Stockholm, until 1917 when the traffic was stopped.[12] Whatever the details, it was inevitable that, even in wartime, someone would find a way to arbitrage differentials.

The Riksbank in fact continued to buy substantial quantities of gold in the open market (at least ensuring that it rather than its neighbours enjoyed the profit), and money supply continued to expand. At the end of the war prices reached 370, broadly in line with the rest of Europe, in spite of Sweden's apparent advantages as a neutral. Again, as elsewhere, prices then fell sharply until late 1919 when they started to rise again.

## Postwar experience

### Sweden

During the next period the countries had contrasting experiences. In neutral Sweden prices[13] had been fairly stable in the range 150–165, and the exchange rate had been close to the prewar parity of 26.8 US cents, for two years, and the country led the return to gold at the prewar parity without (immediate) problems. Norway and Denmark returned to gold at an inappropriate parity, with consequences described in Lester.[14] He argues a monetary case linking recession with an over-valued exchange rate. Finland (not a member of the monetary union), whose currency had depreciated the most, accepted this and returned to gold at current rates.

Sweden's central bank, the Riksbank (the world's oldest) was owned by the state but was politically in 'a peculiar position'.[15] The government had no control over its management, except to appoint the chairman. The other six directors were appointed by the Riksdag (parliament) on the basis that all political parties were represented. The Riksdag authorised the Riksbank to suspend payments in August 1914, 'but only for a ... brief period of time', usually for a parliamentary session but sometimes less. It was the Riksdag which pressed for an early return to gold (at the prewar parity) and 'deliberately pursued a course of deflation'. The powerful Swedish trade unions, represented by the Social Democrats, the largest party, supported the return to gold, but wanted nominal wages to be held – i.e. for real wages to rise. Export industries pressed for the krona to be linked to sterling rather than to gold, but the Social Democrat 'members were quick to grasp' that the proposals would reduce real wages. The Labour movement would consider any deviation of more than (say) 10 per cent as *force majeure*.[16] Rydbeck, writing immediately after the event, and before UK resumption, says that it was the Social Democrats who forced the resumption of gold payments on 1 April 1924, and recognised that meanwhile the move tied Sweden to American financial policy. There is interesting material here for supporters (or opponents) of independent central banks. In February 1924, Sweden declared that Danish and Norwegian money was no longer valid in Sweden. The Nordic Monetary Union was over.

### Denmark

Denmark enjoyed an inflationary boom in 1922–4, but the cheap krone was sucking in imports. In late 1923 an exchange equalisation fund was established with the help of a foreign loan, 'but it was not clear exactly what function this fund was to perform since ... [policy on the krone] was undetermined at that time'. In January 1924 bank rate was raised to 7 per cent and credit was generally tightened.[17] Cassel said it was too little too late. There was the usual dispute about the appropriate parity: being 63 per cent, one school suggested 75 per cent, and at one stage parity with the English shilling (90 per cent) was suggested. The hard money men wanted parity with high interest rates to keep prices down. The law of December 1924 in fact provided for a rise in parity from 65 per cent to 70 per cent over two years and gave speculators the usual one-way option. Cassel had predicted that the gradual-appreciation policy would fail. On 15 December 1925 the currency act was changed to require support at 23.8 US cents (just under 90 per cent of parity) and on 1 January 1927 Denmark returned to gold at the pre-war parity. Lester implies that the policy was speculator driven, but surely the government missed the chance for a profitable bull squeeze? (Lester 1939, 200). Denmark suffered a recession between, and additional to, the two suffered by the rest of the West.

### Iceland

Iceland, under Denmark, had its own currency from 1778 to 1820:[18] it became part of the Scandinavian Monetary Union with Denmark. When

Iceland achieved home rule in 1904 and sovereignty in 1918, the Danish Coinage Act continued to form the basis of the currency until 1925: the National Bank of Iceland became the sole note issuer in 1927.

## Norway

In November 1923 Gustav Cassel had recommended that Norway stabilise at 60 per cent of parity, and 'spoke disparagingly' of monetary policy 'in a way that aroused resentment and hurt national pride'. The Bank Governor (Rygg) responded by saying that Norwegians had brought their currency back to par a hundred years before, and was 'legally and morally bound' to do the same again.[19] From November 1923 parity became an over-riding aim of policy, and to many complaints bank rate was raised to 7 per cent.

A foreign exchange committee was split, but reached a compromise at 24 to the UK pound, reporting unanimously in January 1926 that a long-term solution was impracticable and recommending provisional stabilisation at the then current level. The central bank did not comment for three months and meanwhile the krone appreciated by 10 per cent. Again there was a speculative attack, forcing the krone up, even though the currency had been over-valued.[20] In February 1926 parliament passed a bill for the prewar parity. The inevitable recession was followed by the election of a socialist government in January 1928, followed immediately by a flight of capital and the fall of the government. The gold standard was formally introduced from 1 May 1928.

## Finland

Finland had not been a member of the NMU, and had won independence from Russia after the Revolution. By 1923 the markka was only one eighth of its prewar value. There was a temporary return to the gold standard, and public pressure for this to be at the old parity. In August 1923 Eli Heckscher[21] sent his report to the Bank of Finland, recommending a return to gold at its then current exchange rate. Gustav Cassel concurred, and a committee set up by the Bank of Finland so advised in April 1925. A law of 10 December 1925 effective 1 January 1926 formally devalued the markka to 39.7 to the US dollar, or 13 per cent of its prewar parity. The Bank had managed the rate at about this level for the previous two years, a period during which prices were stable, and the return to gold had no adverse effects on business. Finland enjoyed a period of prosperity based[22] on the domestic market. Talvio,[23] though, points out that the period of prosperity lasted only until 1928, and Finland went off gold in October 1931. This was a 'temporary' measure regularly renewed by Parliament until 1963, when a new currency act was introduced.

### The Baltic states[24]

The three Baltic states, Estonia, Latvia and Lithuania, have fiercely held on to their respective identities in spite of long periods of foreign, mainly Russian, occupation. All three, Russian territory since the eighteenth century, were occupied by Germany in 1915, but became independent after the end of the war.

Before 1915, the currency had been the Russian rouble, which the occupying Germans sought to replace with reichsmarks, valued at 2.16 per gold rouble or 1.66 per paper rouble. Roubles were hoarded, and when a double pricing system was unsuccessful in luring roubles from the populace, the Germans restricted supplies of sugar and salt, selling them only for gold.

The Germans then took to printing money in the form of 'ost roubles'. 'The similarity to the Russian currency was ... intended to deceive the people' who treated it, correctly, as fiat money. It fell to a modest discount. Russian money was prohibited by law.

In April 1918 the ost rouble was replaced by the ost mark, nominally worth half an ost rouble. No new coins were issued, iron kopeks and pfennigs serving as small change. 'During and as a result of the occupation the standard of living ... dropped to abysmal depths.'[25]

Towards the end of the war, the three countries declared their independence, but had to suffer parts of their territory being occupied at various times by the new Red Army or the Germans. During, and indeed after this transitional period, many different currencies circulated, but the larger value imperial Russian notes seem to have been regarded, irrationally, as a good store of value.

### Lithuania

After Lithuania finally became independent the German mark and pfennig were renamed auksinas and skatikas without any change in monetary arrangements in the period 1918–1922.[26] The value of the auskinas fell to 8,775 to the dollar by 28 November 1922, but the German mark was by then worthless.[27] Several other currencies continued to circulate: Karys says that 'the currency of revolutionary Russia ... presented the greatest single hindrance to Lithuania's economic recovery', and on 1 October 1922 Lithuania established a new currency, the litas, containing 0.150462g of pure gold and hence worth 10 US cents (changed to 13.4 cents in 1934). Various types of auksinas, marks and roubles were exchanged at market rates. All debts and taxes due in these currencies were cancelled and revalued. Notes were backed by gold: the highest per capita circulation was 69 litas at a time when the US figure was $190. Notes were convertible into gold in minimum amounts of 20,000 litas. There was no mint until 1936, and no gold coins appear to have been struck. Silver and copper-aluminium coins were issued in 1925.

## Latvia

Latvia set up a provisional government, which had to move to Liepaya when the Soviets occupied Riga. This government, which issued a currency based on the rublis of 100 kapeikas, at par with the Soviet rouble, returned to Riga in May 1919. In March 1920 the Latvian rublis became the sole legal tender, but depreciated in value and was in July 1921 supplemented for trade purposes by the gold frank as a unit of account (not a coin). Stability was restored in August 1922 when this, renamed the lat (plural latu) became the official currency, creating a gold exchange standard.

## Estonia[28]

Estonia declared independence in 1918, but part of the country was for a time occupied by the Red Army. 'The same banknotes were in circulation in both parts of Estonia, but within the framework of two completely different financial systems.'[29] The provisional Estonian government resolved to establish its own currency in November 1918, and on 14 December the Finnish markka (then equal in value to the German mark, which had not then begun its slide) was declared to be legal tender. Rates were fixed for the Russian currencies: the east rouble was valued at 2 marks, a czar rouble at 1.50, a duma rouble at 1.25 and a kerensky rouble at 1.00.[30] Given the delays (described in Leimus) in getting Estonian banknotes printed, the government issued redeemable 'fidelity notes' carrying interest at 5 per cent. These, together with Tallinn clearing house receipts, also became legal tender. On 2 May 1919 the Estonian mark was declared to be the sole legal tender. It was stable for a time at 375 to the US dollar, but later declined.

Estonia only followed the 1922 financial reforms of its neighbours when Strandman became Minister of Finance in 1924. In June 1924 the gold standard was introduced on the basis of the gold kroon containing 0.403226g of pure gold. This was never issued as a coin but was used as a unit of account. 'As the English recommended ... the United Nations Organisation' (*sic*) was asked for help. Loans of $3,848,000 and £676,000 were obtained. The reform legislation was enacted on 3 May 1927, effective 1 January 1928, the loans effectively underwriting the gold standard. The Bank of Estonia became independent, with the sole right to issue banknotes, which were legal tender and backed by loan assets. Treasury notes were meant to be phased out, but in practice continued to be issued.

Although the gold exchange standard appears to have continued in all three countries until the war, it may have had little practical significance. The Baltic states were 'allotted' to the Soviets by the Molotov–Ribbentrop Pact, and invaded by them in 1940. The Germans occupied them from 1941–4, after which the three countries remained reluctant members of the Soviet Union until its collapse in 1991.

# Part VI

# Bretton Woods and its collapse

The postwar monetary order

# 29 Money after the Second World War

## General introduction

The early postwar period of European economic history includes many interesting events which set the scene for later developments. At the end of the war the monetary systems of continental Europe were in chaos, the countries concerned were desperately short of internationally acceptable means of payment, and felt themselves forced to impose rigid exchange controls which themselves seriously inhibited trade.

The war had ended in 1945 with the United States, undoubtedly the world's strongest economy, still on the gold exchange standard, and with sterling still at its prewar parity with the dollar. Neither country had suffered serious inflation or currency problems, but during the war there had been, for practical purposes, no private trade: all foreign transactions were closely controlled by governments, and this emphasis on control continued into the postwar period. The United States held two thirds of the world's monetary gold, partly acquired during the 1930s but augmented by wartime payments for supplies to the Allies.

There was, inevitably, a major attempt to create a stable and rational postwar monetary order, and to avoid a repeat of the interwar inflations and (particularly) depressions. There were three patterns during this period. Those countries which had been occupied by the Germans, and the Germans themselves, having seen their currencies destroyed by inflation or otherwise, had recourse to currency reconstructions. Switzerland exceptionally had, like the United States, retained a sound and strong currency. The United Kingdom (and the Republic of Ireland, which had not taken part in the war but which had retained a currency union with the UK) had experienced only mild inflation, but suffered the same shortage of international reserves as its continental neighbours, and had to face the special problem of the sterling area.

### Bretton Woods

The Atlantic Charter (1941) and the Mutual Aid Agreement (February 1942) had set the scene, including economic undertakings agreed essentially between the British and the Americans, and a group of international financial experts meeting at Bretton Woods in July 1944 proposed two new organisations for the postwar world: the International Monetary Fund (IMF) and the International Bank for Reconstruction and Development (IBRD or World Bank). The 'Bretton Woods system' of fixed, but adjustable, exchange rates was to dominate monetary events until it collapsed in 1971, and influence thinking for many years after. Although not strictly a monetary union, it might be regarded, at least in its time, as the most successful of the 'half-baked' solutions. Chapter 30 gives a general account of the creation of the Bretton Woods system, followed by more detailed discussion of events in Western Europe and the UK.

## Monetary reform in Europe

Germany and the occupied countries had, typically, suffered a collapse of their monetary arrangements. There was too much money in circulation, too few goods to spend it on, and most of what was available was price-controlled. To avoid runaway inflation while restoring market incentives and mechanisms, action was needed to remove surplus purchasing power and to start phasing out rationing and price controls. The first country to act was Belgium in 1944, followed by Denmark, the Netherlands, Norway, Czechoslovakia, Finland and Austria. Germany had a more comprehensive, and highly successful, reform in 1948. After the reconstructions, described in Chapter 31, most established relatively stable currencies, although with tough exchange controls and, at first, rigid bilateral trade arrangements. Indeed, and perhaps because they had to rebuild from scratch, many of them recovered from the war more quickly than the victorious and never-occupied UK. The chapter also discusses Hungary and Greece, which were less lucky, actually suffering hyper-inflation after the war. Their contrasting experiences have some lessons, although they were typical neither of postwar events nor of hyper-inflation.

The United Kingdom had a different pattern, and because of its relation-ship with the United States, and the problems arising from the sterling area, played a key role, in the early years, in the move towards multilateral payment arrangements. Chapter 32 deals with the period to 1951, including some disastrous premature initiatives and the sterling devaluation of 1949. Chapter 34 takes the UK story up to the abolition of exchange control in 1979.

Meanwhile Chapter 33 describes how the rest of Europe was struggling to revive trade in the face of what was perceived of as a 'dollar shortage'. During the first four years to about 1949 (the 'bilateral phase') pairs of countries entered into a complex network of bilateral payment agreements in an attempt to make at least some trade possible, and this was followed by the 'multilateral phase'; a series of attempts, eventually successful, to create a multilateral payments system within Europe. This phase was virtually complete by 1954, and by 1958 Western European countries essentially had more or less sound monetary systems, based on convertible currencies and designed to facilitate international trade. Exchange controls were to persist for many years, but mainly served to regulate capital movements and restrict personal travel. At the end of this period many of the ideas that were to lead to the concept of monetary union had been developed, and the long and continued debate between the virtues of 'fixed' and 'floating' exchange rates was given a good airing.

Chapter 35 describes how the Bretton Woods system (arguably an essay in 'monetary union') collapsed. This stimulated interest in some form of monetary union in Europe, specifically within the Common Market, which had been born in 1957. This leads us into Part VII, where Chapter 36 gives an account of the long and painful path towards monetary union and of two periods, the 'Snake in the Tunnel' and the European Monetary System, when a substantial degree of fixed exchange rates was achieved, at least for a time. It can be argued (Chapter 37) that the EMS collapsed because of a botched monetary union between West and East Germany, but by then the first steps had been taken towards an ultimately successful European Monetary Union, described in Chapters 38–41, which are perhaps the core of this book.

# 30 Bretton Woods and the IMF

## Introduction

The Bretton Woods conference effectively agreed on a financial system for the postwar world, and this led to the creation of the IMF and the World Bank. The 'Bretton Woods system' of fixed but occasionally adjustable rates, although falling far short of even attempting to be a world-wide monetary union, worked well enough for a couple of decades, effectively collapsing in 1971. Its end, discussed in Chapter 36, gave a new focus to moves towards European Monetary Union.

## The Bretton Woods conference[1]

This historic conference was dominated by two rival 'plans'[2] which had been published in 1943, by teams from the British and US treasuries, led by John Maynard Keynes and Harry Dexter White respectively (although Keynes had had an office in the Treasury since 1940, his position was not that of a civil servant and he drew no salary).

Those interested in the complex diplomacy of the period, and the strains which beset the Anglo-American 'special relationship' will find an excellent account in volume III of Skidelsky's biography of Keynes.[3] There were several overlapping issues. The Americans wanted to, and did, help with Lend-Lease and later the American Loan, but (thought the British) wanted to make the British first draw down their already depleted international reserves. They distrusted the sterling area, fearing it might be adverse to America's trade interests, and indeed it seems that Roosevelt did have a plot to devalue the dollar by letting sterling rise from $4.03 to $5.00. Skidelsky discusses the disputes within the UK about postwar monetary arrangements, Keynes distrusting floating and favouring multilateral payments and the Schactian system of bilateral agreements (2000, 228–230).

### The Keynes Plan

The basis of the Keynes Plan[4] was a proposal for an International Clearing Union with funds of some $26 billion which would make overdraft facilities to members, using *bancor* as a unit of account. The value of bancor was to be fixed in gold (which had once been described by Keynes as a 'barbarous relic'),[5] while the par value of national currencies would be set in bancor. The fund would in effect have the right to create bancor, which would not be automatically redeemable in gold. Each country would be assigned a quota of loans which it could receive from the fund, but debtors would face increasing penalties as they drew on their quotas.

The burden of the 'adjustment process' (a key issue in discussions then and since) would fall on creditors who could in effect have indefinite bancor liquidity forced on them, and be required to take measures to expand credit, revalue their currencies upwards, cut tariffs and extend international loans. Bordo and Eichengreen (1993, 33) comment that 'this reflected Keynes' preference for rules over discretion', a comment which could also apply to the proposals requiring countries to maintain permanent capital controls to prevent speculation. There was a clear and deliberate expansionary bias, reflecting the Keynes of the *General Theory* (which was, in spite of its title, a then much-needed tract on the *special* problem of recession) rather than the more symmetrical balance of his earlier works. Richard Gardner, writing in 1956, commented that

> there was little recognition ... that other causes besides the failure to maintain full employment could produce balance of payments disequilibria. ... This bias in an inflationary direction might well provide a difficulty when the Keynes plan was presented to the United States.[6]

### The White Plan

In contrast, the American White Plan[7] gave more emphasis to stable exchange rates than to expansion. It envisaged the creation of a United Nations Stabilisation Fund to which each country would contribute a quota of gold and its own currency, to a total amount of only $5 billion. Support would be given to a deficit country by permitting it to sell its currency to the fund in exchange for that of another member so that, unlike the Keynes 'overdraft' concept, there would be no net expansion in world liquidity. He proposed the *unitas*, equal to ten United States gold dollars, as the international unit of account in which countries would be required to declare their par value, and that this par value could only be changed if there was a 'fundamental disequilibrium' (a term which was to become important in later developments) of the balance of payments. A change of less than 10 per cent could be made after consultation with the Fund while a larger change would require the approval of three quarters of the membership. Debtor countries which exceeded their quotas could, as with the Keynes Plan, be put under pressure to mend their ways, but there was to be less call for creditors to contribute to the adjustment. However, a proposed 'scarce currency clause' would in effect permit the

Fund to ration the use of the currency of the surplus country by means of exchange controls.

### The birth of the IMF

Even at the height of the war, time was still found for intense negotiations between the British and the Americans leading to a compromise 'Joint Statement by Experts on the Establishment of an International Monetary Fund' published in 1944. This served as a draft for the Bretton Woods conference, which in turn produced the 'Articles of Agreement of the International Monetary Fund'. The British had to give up the concepts of overdraft facilities, the International Clearing Union, and 'bancor', and had to accept an initial fund of $8.8 billion compared with $26 billion proposed by Keynes and $5 billion by White. For their part, the Americans accepted that countries should have greater flexibility to set their own exchange rates, and to impose controls on capital movements. The Fund would *not* have discretion to interfere with domestic economic policy or to make explicit conditions on credit drawings, and the 'scarce currency clause' was included. The British request for postwar financial assistance was left for later negotiations.

The International Monetary Fund was duly formed, and began its operations on 1 March 1947. Members were required to declare a par value and maintain it within a 1 per cent band, but could change it by declaring a 'fundamental disequilibrium', with the consent of the Fund. They were permitted under the articles to continue to use exchange controls for a period of three years, which in practice turned out to be much longer.

Most countries, pressured by the IMF for a quick decision, and apparently in the misguided belief that any imbalances were structural, rather than the result of differential wartime inflation, adopted their prewar parities.

Thirty-two countries declared official par values in December 1946 and others joined later. Apart from the United States as the key currency country, most of the major countries involved were in Europe, the exceptions being Canada and Japan. The original parities held until September 1949, when the UK devaluation was followed by several other countries. Canada initially devalued from parity to C$1.10 = US$1.00, but later floated. Italy and Japan set their initial parities for the first time in that year.

There was then a long period of stable exchange rates at least in the major countries: apart from the floating of the Canadian dollar, the only adjustments to parities in the major countries between 1949 and 1967 were devaluations in France (1957 and 1958) and minor revaluations by Germany and the Netherlands. There were more adjustments in other, mainly smaller countries. Edwards and Santiella[8] analyse forty-eight selected cases, mainly in Latin America, Africa and Asia.

The IMF aimed at stability, and less successfully, to permit free currency movements and to outlaw exchange controls. Article VIII sections 2, 3 and 4 required currencies to be convertible for current account transactions, but

Article XIV section 2 permitted derogations for the first three years of the system, while Article VI.3 permitted capital controls.

Although the founders of the IMF had envisaged a speedy move towards (relatively) free trade and payments, exchange controls were to persist for some time, most countries entered into bilateral agreements with their trading partners, and it was not until 1958 that even limited convertibility was restored. Because of this, it could be argued that until then the full Bretton Woods system was not in operation: it was to meet its test during the following decade. The founders had envisaged a system of equal currencies: what actually happened was a dollar version of the gold exchange standard. The United States was the only country operating at capacity, and the 'dollar shortage' was assumed (wrongly) to be a permanent feature of the world.

The Bretton Woods system at this stage was effectively a dollar exchange standard which, as the US dollar was linked to gold at a fixed price of $35 per ounce, amounted to a *gold* exchange standard. The United States had maintained a stable economy with only moderate inflation, and (as with the Germans some years later) was 'exporting' this stability to the rest of the industrialised world. However, the gold exchange standard was on a precarious basis, as the other countries had effectively given up their rights to convert their dollar reserves into gold, leaving the United States as the only country which could effectively create a 'banking multiplier' of acceptable paper reserves. The postwar recovery of world industrial activity had expanded, and what was then thought of as a 'dollar shortage' really had at its basis an artificially low price for gold.

# 31 Postwar monetary reconstructions

## Introduction

Some countries, including the United States, the United Kingdom and Switzerland, finished the war with their domestic monetary systems substantially intact. Most continental European countries were less lucky: there was too much money in circulation, too few goods to spend it on, and most of what was available was price controlled. To avoid runaway inflation and to restore market incentives and mechanisms, action was needed to remove surplus purchasing power and to start phasing out rationing and price controls.

The first country to act was Belgium in 1944, followed by Denmark, the Netherlands, Norway, Czechoslovakia, Finland, Austria, and finally Germany in 1948. Hungary and Greece suffered hyper-inflation after the war. The hyper-inflations as such are described fully in the source cited:[1] this chapter deals mainly with the reconstructions.

## Belgium

The liberated countries reconstructed their currencies more or less immediately. When the Belgian government was restored to Brussels in September 1944, the circulation of notes had risen to 164 billion francs, there were few goods in the shops and these were price-controlled. It was essential to remove the surplus purchasing power, and this was done by blocking part of the excess and then allowing a controlled release of some of these balances. The problem was analysed, and plans were made, between May and September. Belgian prices were compared with those in the UK and Switzerland, so that a realistic rate of exchange could be calculated. It was decided to let wages rise 30–40 per cent, and that a note circulation of 80–85 billion francs would be needed. A new currency was printed in England, and an exchange rate of 176.6 to the pound agreed. The stock exchange was closed and holders of bank deposits were permitted to withdraw only 2,000 francs per week.

After business hours on Friday 6 October 1944, it was announced that all notes over 100 francs were to be demonetised, and had to be handed in during the following week (coupon 11 in the ration book was used as control). Small notes and coins were not affected. Heads of households were permitted to exchange 2,000 francs per person into new money immediately against coupon 12.

Of the surplus, 60 per cent was converted into 'temporarily blocked' accounts, which were gradually released, and 40 per cent into 'permanently blocked' accounts later converted into a 3.5 per cent compulsory loan. Blocked balances could be used to pay special war taxes, apparently intended to mop up 'undesirable' balances, and eventually to retire the compulsory loan.

Kindleberger says that of 300 billion francs in outstanding notes, 10–13 billion were never turned in. Circulation after reform was 57.4bn in October, rising to 75bn by year end. Meltzer, writing very soon after the events, says that currency and deposits increased from 45bn in 1939 to 155bn by liberation.

The size of the allowance in Belgium encouraged the better off to do deals with those who did not have 2,000 francs. The exemption of small notes, which continued to circulate at face, created a secondary market. There was a similar problem in Austria. In some countries (not specified), frozen balances were transferable, but could not be withdrawn in cash. This also led to a two-price system.

Other countries followed suit, using broadly similar techniques. Metzler[2] gives more information, and the key figures for money supply as shown in Table 31.1 below.

## The German currency reform of 1948

The later German reform was more comprehensive and interesting. The key information is to be found in the Colm-Dodge-Goldsmith report,[3] submitted by its authors to General Clay on 20 May 1946 and which was the basis of the reform. It was actually published much later, in 1955. Appendix O, by Lloyd A. Metzler, which set out events in other countries, was only published in 1979.[4]

*Table 31.1*  Key figures for money supply

|  | *Austria* | *Czechoslovakia* | *Belgium* | *Netherlands* | *Denmark* |
|---|---|---|---|---|---|
| Prewar level | 1.0 | 0.10 | 0.30 | 1.3 | 0.50 |
| Before conversion | 9.0 | 120 | 100 | 5.5 | 1.25 |
| After conversion | 2.5 | 0.20 | 0.42 | 1.0 | 0.87 |
| June 1946 | 4.2 | 0.40 | 0.70 | 2.0 | 1.50 |
| Personal allowance (US$, approx.) | $15 | $45.60 | $10 | $20.80 | $3.75 |

*Source:*  After Metzler 1979

Metzler says that 'the desire to eliminate German holdings of a country's currency and to reduce the holdings of war profiteers and collaboration was occasionally a more important motive … than internal reform'. This meant prompt, rather than considered, action.

Lutz[5] comments that postwar Germany, before reform, was a barter economy: workers worked three days and spent the rest of the week foraging (he gives figures), and to deal with this situation the 1948 reform was more comprehensive than those in other countries. There were two parts to the reform package, originally meant to be simultaneous: 'monetary reform' and 'equalisation of burdens'.

## Monetary reform

A new currency, the deutschmark (DM), was created, into which money and monetary assets, including *all* debts were converted at the rate of 10 old RM = 1 new DM. Every individual was permitted to convert a 'Kopfgeld' of RM60 into DM60 at 1 for 1. Wages, other contracts and prices were carried over into the new system at par but money supply fell to a tenth. This ratio was critical: too little money would have produced a massive recession, while too much would have renewed inflation, stimulated a flight away from the new money, and destroyed credibility, making it difficult to repeat the operation. It was a once-for-all opportunity which had to be, and was, seized successfully.

In the event, there *was* renewed inflation (Schmiedling says that velocity was under-estimated), but stability was restored after a rise in prices of about 30 per cent. This suggests that the essential tight control over retained money supply after reform was effective. The authorities may also have had plans to counter a recession by an easier policy; a difficult task, given the then institutional structure.

The Colm-Dodge-Goldsmith report (221) discusses the advantages of writing down over blocking. 'Blocking only postpones the final solution, leaves uncertainty and invites constant political pressure for de-blocking'. Against this, blocking 'permits adjustment to changing economic conditions'. The report goes on (222) to analyse the level of write-down required, and explains how 'a substantial error in the initial figure can be corrected'.

There was an obvious potential injustice between private debtors and creditors, particularly where the debtors owned 'real' assets. Kindleberger says that the Germans on the team wanted to exclude private debt, but 'the point was of minimal practical importance since … private debtors had, for the most part, paid off their creditors' (by implication very cheaply with debased money). This injustice was addressed in the second part of the package, 'equalisation of burdens'.

It is not clear what happened to banks, insurance companies and other financial institutions, given that Germany had a sophisticated privately owned financial system. Monetary assets and liabilities both shrank to a tenth. Real assets were adjusted under the equalisation of burdens measures.

The report (232–3) discusses 'complementary measures' for adjusting organisations, commenting that: 'the present German banking and financial system ... is too dense and complex for the smaller amount of business that will be available after the war'. Later events proved this wrong.

### Equalisation of burdens

The *Lastenausgleich*, or capital levy, was intended to equalise the burden of the reform as between owners of real and monetary assets. This was imposed at a rate of 50 per cent, compared with an effective 90 per cent confiscation of monetary assets. It took the form of an interest-bearing mortgage, and the proceeds were paid into a fund to assist those who had lost out, one way or another, in the war and its aftermath, a fund which seems to have been managed on a discretionary basis.

The Colm-Dodge-Goldsmith report explains (226–7) why the 50 per cent figure was chosen, and says

> the mortgage should be measured in such a way that it will reduce equities by 50 per cent of the values which they had before the scaling down of money claims. In other words, the mortgage will (a) replace the written-down part of private mortgages, and (b) reduce the owner's equity by a further 50 per cent.

Unless this procedure was followed, owners whose property was heavily mortgaged prior to the operation would receive windfall gains.

According to Kindleberger,[6] 'At the last minute, the American authorities insisted on separating monetary reform and *Lastenausgleich*, leaving the latter to be enacted by the German authorities by 31 December 1948.' It did in fact come into effect on 2 September 1948.

## Hungary

Hungary and Greece were less lucky. The second Hungarian hyper-inflation (so far) holds the world record: prices rose by a factor of $3 \times 10^{25}$. By the peak, 15 July 1946, the number of ordinary pengo notes in circulation reached $76 \times 10^{24}$. 'At the official rate of exchange, the total note issue could have been purchased for \$23,245 (or approximately \$2,300 on the black market).'[7]

Hungary was in transition towards becoming a communist state, although at this time the Smallholders were the dominant party in parliament. The country was under the supervision of the Allied Control Commission (which in this part of Europe was dominated by the Soviets), and the circumstances 'led some to conclude that the hyper-inflation was designed to achieve a political objective – the destruction of the middle class'.

One complication, which Bomberger and Makinen say led earlier scholars such as Cagan astray, was the concept of the 'tax pengo'. This had its origin with the indexed deposits which the government required Hungarian banks to make available, and meant that some holders of money were (in the event only partially) protected against inflation, and that the government had to accelerate money growth even faster than would normally have been the case. Because of this factor, tax pengos became very popular, and between January and April 1946 there was a very sharp rise in the deposit to note ratio. On 21 May 1946 the minister of finance was authorised to issue tax pengo banknotes which at first could only be used for the payment of taxes. Each note had a term of two months and would lose its value on the expiry date if it had not already been used for tax payments. On 13 June the tax pengo notes were made available to cover payment for public utility bills, rail fares and other state services, and the government began to use the notes to pay farmers for produce suppliers. From 23 June the government made all its payments in tax pengo notes.

Faced with a major hyper-inflation, which had already self-destructed, the Hungarian government launched a stabilisation programme, prepared in large part by the Communist Party. The government undertook the programme on its own initiative, and not at the instigation of the United Nations or the Allied Control, and without the benefit of large foreign loans. However the United States had returned to Hungary $32 million of the Central Bank gold reserve expropriated by the Nazis, which arrived, with much publicity, on Adolf Hitler's old personal train on 6 August, and this, supplemented by $12 million of gold from domestic sources, gave 517 million forints, or more than 100 per cent, backing for the initial note issues.

A new currency unit, the forint, was introduced to replace the pengo. The normal pengo was exchanged in a ratio of 400 octillion ($4 \times 10^{23}$) pengos to one forint, and the (allegedly indexed) tax pengo at 200 million to one. The forint had a theoretical gold content, and was required to be covered by gold to the extent of 25 per cent of its face value, but was not actually convertible into gold or foreign currency.

The Central Bank was also prohibited from lending, directly or indirectly, to the government, and an initial hundred per cent of reserve requirements was imposed on commercial banks. Prior to 31 July 1947, not more than one billion forints in notes could be issued by the Central Bank. This limit was in fact exceeded by December, and on 1 January 1947 the formal ceiling was removed.

Although this brought hyper-inflation to an abrupt end, and from 1 August to 31 December prices rose only 6 per cent, the money supply again increased. At the end of August 1946, 356 million forints were in issue, but this increased to 1,992 million by the end of 1947.

### Greece 1944–6[8]

Greece suffered a hyper-inflation from 1943 to 1946, which was cured, after two failures, at the third attempt.

### The first attempt

The first attempt to cure the hyper-inflation took place on 11 November 1944, and comprised a monetary reconstruction, coupled with a limit on the government's borrowing. Old drachma were converted into new in the ratio of a 50 billion to one, the new drachma being theoretically convertible into British Military Authority pounds but only in amounts larger than 12,000 drachma or £BMA200. The latter were also legal tender, an interesting if inconclusive example of two currencies having legal tender status in one country.

The second part of the package limited the government's overdraft at the Bank of Greece to 2 million drachma, a figure exceeded within two months and subsequently ignored. No measures were taken to reform taxes or to cut government expenditure, and although the rate of inflation fell sharply, the official price index rose by 140 per cent in the seven months to May 1945, while the price of the gold sovereign rose by 800 per cent. Taxes yielded less than one sixth of total revenue.

### The second try

The first half-baked package had little effect, and on 3 June 1945 Kyriakos Varvaressos, 'a prominent economist, was named as a sort of economic czar'. He interpreted the failure as 'a lack of effective state control over the economy and inadequate assistance from abroad'. Such a diagnosis is hardly likely to lead to a successful prescription! On 4 June, the day after his appointment, he took steps to devalue the drachma, accelerate foreign aid, raise wages, impose wage and price controls, and reduced all prices by one half. To meet the budgetary cost of these measures he imposed a substantial tax on rented accommodation, which had in any case been the subject of price control. Prices actually fell sharply in June, rose slightly in July and substantially in August, after which the monetary and fiscal situation deteriorated even further. Mr Varvaressos resigned in September.

### Success at last

The third, and successful, attempt to solve the problem was taken under British initiative, and the Anglo-Hellenic Convention was agreed on 24 January 1946. British experts were called in to prepare a realistic budget, to improve the tax assessment and collection arrangements, and to increase to realistic market levels the price at which foreign aid goods were sold while certain taxes were adjusted for past inflation. A five-member currency committee, including British and American representatives, was appointed, and their unanimous consent was required before the Bank of Greece could issue any notes. This proved effective, and the Bank of Greece managed to maintain a fixed exchange rate with both the dollar and the pound sterling, and to restore gold convertibility: Makinen comments in a footnote that

'Greece was then one of the only countries in the world with an internal gold standard. In no other stabilisation programme was gold convertibility restored.'

To finance this package, the British government cancelled the loan of £46.5 million made at the beginning of the war, releasing a charge over half the reserves of the Bank of Greece. There was an additional loan of £10 million as cover for the note issue, and the United States provided $80 million.

This package was immediately effective. The Bank of Greece stabilised the currency with open market sales of gold sovereigns, prices actually fell slightly, and the budget moved towards balance. However, civil war broke out in September.

# 32  The UK 1945–51

## The United Kingdom in the postwar world

Although the United Kingdom had ended the war with its currency intact, and had no need of the reconstructions described in the last chapter, it had serious problems (partly because of the sterling area arrangements), and played a key role in the European monetary history of the early postwar period. Initially, under pressure from the Americans, the UK sought to lead the way towards convertible currencies, but the moves were, in the circumstances of the time, premature.

The newly elected Labour government under Clement Attlee began with Hugh Dalton as Chancellor, and Maynard Keynes as effectively chief negotiator and adviser. There were financial problems – and expensive aspirations to create a Welfare State. Keynes hoped to persuade the Americans to put up $6 billion as a free gift, and in the event secured $3.75 billion as a loan. Although under Article 14 of the Bretton Woods Agreement, the UK was permitted to postpone making sterling convertible for five years, the Americans insisted that 'the UK must, as a condition … rejoin the international community without discrimination against the USA'.[1] The US loan agreement, which Congress ratified by a slim margin on 15 July 1946, gave the pound a year to become convertible, and required the sterling balances problem be addressed.[2]

The dangers of premature convertibility were well aired: Cameron Cobbold (a director, later Governor, of the Bank of England) warned that 'the proposed … convertibility would resemble a return to the rigidities of the Gold Standard', but Dalton argued that Bretton Woods offered a combination of 'stability and flexibility … with the ultimate right to resign from the IMF … and with the concept of "fundamental equilibrium" '.[3] Dell says that Keynes sympathised with an autarkic view, quoting him as saying that 'free trade' combined with international mobility of capital, was more likely to provoke war than keep peace, and 'let goods be homespun whenever it is reasonably and conveniently possible, and, above all, let finance be national' – but Keynes had actually written these words in 1932.[4]

### The sterling balances

The sterling area continued in being, and transactions in sterling within this area were unregulated. Apart from this, exchange control then applied both to resident and non-resident holders of sterling, and there was perceived to be a danger that dollars would leak from the area if the UK became too involved with more flexible arrangements in Europe. To deal with this some sterling accounts were designated 'transferable accounts' which could be transferred between countries only with specific Bank of England consent.

There was a serious problem with the sterling balances. During the war certain countries – India, Egypt, the Sudan, Iraq, Portugal and Argentina – had sizeable sterling claims on the United Kingdom, which was reluctant, and indeed unable without precipitating a financial disaster, to release these in a form in which they could be converted into dollars. Claims by the old Dominions were re-negotiated and partly written off. Another problem discussed at the time was 'unrequited exports' (compare the 1930s Austrian parallel), by which British industry was producing goods not in return for convertible dollars nor for imports from other countries, but simply as a reduction in outstanding debt.

The traditional prewar trade pattern had been triangular: the UK ran a deficit with the US, financed by surpluses with India, Australia and West Africa which in turn were net exporters of primary products to the United States.[5] After the war the UK deficit became chronic and general, with deficits for the two immediate postwar years of ($US, billions):

|              | 1946 | 1947 |
|--------------|------|------|
| World total  | 5.8  | 7.5  |
| Of which US  | 4.2  | 5.4  |

The United States, fearing that a collapse of the European economy would be exploited by the Soviet Union, launched the Marshall Plan on 5 June 1947. Robert Triffin, then director of the IMF Exchange Control Division, looked forward to an integrated Western Europe dedicated to eventual multilateral payments. Ernest Bevin, the British Foreign Secretary, found this approach too 'continental', in that it ignored the UK's central position as the economic bridge between the Western and Eastern hemispheres.

The sterling balances grew during 1946 and 1947, as British food and raw material imports were partly supplied without immediate cash payments. There was a commitment under Clause 10 to 'adjust' these balances: Keynes suggested the UK block old balances, but this was resisted by the Bank of England. The (temporary) return to convertibility on 15 July 1947 removed Britain's 'most important bargaining counter'.[6] India held about one third of the balances and was negotiating independence.

The government discussed whether it would be possible to float sterling, although this would have been inconsistent with the Bretton Woods agreement. Dalton, the Chancellor (finance minister) and a former academic economist, favoured stable rates, aided where necessary by government intervention, arguing that the problems of the interwar period had been caused by competitive devaluations which damaged British industry and British exports. Dell says that this fear arose from a misinterpretation which was 'far too influential on policy then and subsequently ... the government might have asked itself how long it could hope to sustain exactly the same value of sterling against the dollar, $4.03, as had obtained pre-war'[7] (Dell 1996, 41).

### *The premature dash for convertibility*

Sterling became (briefly) convertible on 16 July 1947, honouring the undertaking given in connection with the American loan. The experiment, coinciding with the introduction of the Marshall Plan in June 1947, lasted only seven weeks: it was a disaster.

Gold and dollar reserves (including the undrawn part of the US and Canadian credits) had already fallen in the year to 30 June 1947 from $7bn to $4.7bn, partly accounted for by drawings from the sterling area and, after February, by the operations of the transferable account area. After sterling became convertible, the monthly drain rose to $498m: at this rate, had the pound remained convertible, reserves would have been exhausted by mid-September.[8]

Sterling convertibility was abandoned on 20 August 1947: 'the system of transferable accounts will be modified ... so as to make it possible effectively to control dollar outpayments'.[9] Exchange controls, on non-residents as well as residents, therefore continued.

## The sterling devaluation of 1949

Meanwhile on 12 November 1947 the British Chancellor, Hugh Dalton, introduced a budget increasing consumer taxes and intended to defend the country against inflation. He refused to take the advice of the Treasury that he should cut food subsidies, thinking it was politically impossible. Unfortunately, he had inadvertently leaked a fairly trivial point to a journalist, had admitted this and resigned the same day. Ben Pimlott[10] tells the story, and quotes an American commentator as having said that if similar standards of ethics were applied in Washington there would not be enough members of Congress left to make a quorum, and dismisses the suggestion that Dalton had engineered an excuse to leave his demanding post. Dalton was replaced by Sir Stafford Cripps, who, whether or not he was really an 'iron chancellor', certainly gave the impression of austerity and regarded his main task as being to restore the balance of payments. Cripps was to introduce another austerity budget the next April.

Dell quotes Cripps as saying 'I am beginning to wonder if we are not paying too high a price for the luxury of the sterling area: we are certainly paying too high a price for the luxury of not blocking the sterling balances.'[11] Meanwhile the current account moved back into surplus, although Germany was recovering more rapidly. By the end of 1948, though, the United States began to suffer a recession, and the situation deteriorated. The possibility of floating sterling was discussed during 1948. Alec Cairncross is quoted, again by Dell, as having said 'If you have hard currencies and soft currencies the natural thing to ask yourself is whether you should try and make the hard currency softer and the soft currencies harder by changing their relative price', and indeed Cairncross appears to have been the first of the government's economic advisers who advocated devaluation – before the end of 1948: by March 1949 Robert Hall and Edwin Plowden had decided that devaluation was inevitable.

Cripps was opposed to devaluation, and the Bank of England took the view that there was a serious risk that the politicians would not follow a devaluation with the necessary deflationary 'consequential measures' (a term much used at the time in any discussion of devaluation). Cripps in particular made every effort to prevent the devaluation of sterling being discussed in any international forum: the US executive director of the IMF responded to one such effort by saying that if devaluation could not be discussed by the IMF, what was the IMF for?

Certainly, by April 1949 informed economic opinion both inside and outside the government thought that devaluation or floating was inevitable.[12] In July Cripps was taken ill and had to go to Switzerland for treatment. Prime Minister Attlee took personal charge of the Treasury with the help of Harold Wilson, Hugh Gaitskell and Douglas Jay, three young economists who had been brought into government at the suggestion of Hugh Dalton, still influential behind the scenes. They, and indeed Dalton himself, had come round to the idea of devaluation, but the decision was not taken in Cabinet until 29 August and the pound was not actually devalued (from \$4.03 to \$2.80) until 18 September when Cripps was back. Some 'consequential' deflationary measures were taken, and although the cabinet lacked the stomach to do all that should have been done, the rate of inflation did actually fall. Reserves had fallen to £330 million but increased by 70 per cent in the following nine months, the UK's competitive position had improved and the external position became much clearer after the end of the Korean war. The IMF and other European countries had been given little notice of the devaluation, but many countries followed shortly afterwards.

# 33 Europe 1945–58

## Bilateral to multilateral payments

### Introduction

After the war there was a chronic shortage of internationally acceptable reserves, and the rigid exchange controls then felt necessary to protect them hindered the recovery of international trade. During the first four years of 'the bilateral phase',[1] pairs of countries entered into a complex network of bilateral agreements in an attempt to make some trade possible. Tew points out that the term needs substantial qualification, and explains the typical pattern of agreements by which pairs of central banks exchanged currency at a fixed rate, up to a defined limit, known as the 'swing'. Once this was reached, settlement had to be in gold or dollars.

Although each country tried to export enough to pay for its necessary imports, Europe's trade recovery was slow. Once countries reached the limit of their 'swing', trade between the countries concerned could grind to a halt for months. It had become urgent for European countries to develop more flexible means of payment,[2] and to create more generalised purchasing power while accepting the perceived need for each country to protect its reserves by strict exchange controls.

### European compensation arrangements

The First Agreement on Multilateral Monetary Compensation was signed on the initiative of the Committee for European Economic Cooperation (an early forerunner of OECD) on 18 November 1947 by France, Italy and the Benelux countries with eight 'occasional members'. Each member reported its credit positions with the other participants to the Central Office (managed by the Bank for International Settlements) which worked out the best multilateral compensation available without prejudicing the net position of any country. Such 'first category compensations' were settled automatically while 'second category compensations', which would increase a national balance, required mutual agreement. This was ineffective: at the clearing in December 1947, only $1.7 million of aggregate debts totalling $762 million were cleared.

In October 1948, after the Marshall Plan had been introduced, the first two intra-European payments agreements were reached along similar lines but extended to all members of what by then had become the OEEC. There was American aid to be distributed, and the Americans hoped that some of this money would help stimulate intra-European trade and replace dollar imports. This 'indirect aid' would, it was hoped, make some of their dollars at least work twice as hard and help to target the 'scarce' dollars into the hands of those countries most in need of them.

The IEPA had similar first- and second-category compensation arrangements but few payments were in fact made. The second IEPA began operations in July 1949 with some increase in drawing rights, and there was a new provision that about a quarter of them were multilateral. The multilateral drawing rights were used only after first category compensations had been matched. Belgium was a special case, and as it had a surplus with the rest of Europe more than sufficient to finance its deficit with the US, it became the first Western European country to balance its books. About half its credits were matched.

## Continental Europe after the British devaluation

The French had devalued in January 1948 and were censured by the IMF for introducing a multiple currency system.[3] The British government had had extensive discussions on devaluation with the Americans, but the IMF was given less than twenty-four hours notice, and most foreign governments even less. Within the next six months, many other countries – with the notable exceptions of Switzerland and Japan – devalued. The fall against the US dollar was:

| | |
|---|---|
| Greece | 33 per cent |
| UK, Denmark, Finland, Netherlands, Norway, Sweden, Denmark, Egypt | 30 per cent |
| France | 22 per cent |
| Germany | 20 per cent |
| Belgium, Portugal | 13 per cent |
| Canada | 9 per cent |
| Italy | 8 per cent |

For a time it seemed that these changes had brought exchange rates to a sustainable level and, that, helped by heavy American spending on arms during the Korean War, the 'dollar shortage' might disappear. There were even suggestions that some of the devaluations might be partially reversed: Canada did in fact float its currency in October 1950, after which it rose in value. By 1951, though, American consumption (and the price of raw materials) fell, the 'problem' seemed to be reemerging, and European policy returned to a restrictionist bias.

## The move to convertibility 1950–8

It still took over a decade to move from a strict bilateral to an effective multilateral basis for settlements. Each country had its own 'currency area', the sterling area being the largest and most successful example, and each appears to have been afraid of 'loopholes' by which they could lose gold or dollars to multilateral partners without obtaining any corresponding benefit.

The key problem was that exchange rates were again out of line, and given the disparity between the United States and immediate postwar Europe, it was (at that time) argued that the world was not ready for free markets and that any attempt to devalue to an equilibrium point would have risked hyper-inflation. This still leaves the key question of why one 'exchange control' country suffering from a 'dollar shortage' should not be trading with one similarly placed. (Compare the discussion in Chapter 24 of Austria and Hungary in the 1930s, their inconvertible currencies being at a similar discount on gold.)

Kindleberger[4] quotes Harrod as saying that the 'dollar shortage' was 'one of the most absurd phrases ever coined ... and one of the most brazen pieces of collective effrontery that has ever been uttered'.

## The European Payments Union

This arguably was the first serious attempt at multilateral clearing, and came into operation in July 1950 at the end of the second IEPA. At the end of each month each participating country surrendered all its bilateral surpluses and deficits to the union administered by the Bank for International Settlements. The BIS could then calculate the net position of each country, which would be added to or subtracted from the unsettled position at the end of the previous month to give an accumulative net position within the Union. Although most of the net amounts were settled in gold or US dollars, some settlement was in the form of 'credits'. The proportion that could be settled in this way was, until July 1954, calculated with reference to the relationship between the cumulative deficit or surplus and the country's quota. In July 1954, the rules were simplified and 50 per cent of all balances could be settled in credits.

## United Kingdom initiatives

Further progress towards multinational payments was made in the mid-1950s as the result of two initiatives by the United Kingdom: the re-opening of the London foreign exchange market and the relaxation of exchange controls. Until May 1953, dealers in the London foreign exchange market were only permitted to deal with a foreign counterparty in the currency of the country concerned, with the one exception that arbitrage was permitted between US and Canadian dollars. The restrictions were gradually relaxed so that by the end of the year dealings, including spot arbitrage, were permitted in a defined range of currencies. A little later the list of countries was extended, and forward transactions could be carried out for up to three months. The Bank of England could now stand back from the operations of the market, intervening only to preserve the spot value of the currency (Tew 1977, 42).

Exchange controls, although strictly enforced against UK residents, were similarly relaxed. Sterling held by certain countries with which there had previously been a bilateral arrangement was simply treated as transferable sterling, which meant that it could be freely sold to other countries outside the dollar block. The whole nonsense of '57 varieties' of sterling began to unwind, and transferable sterling itself did actually trade at a small discount in Zurich. The discount widened in 1954, but virtually disappeared when the UK Chancellor authorised the Bank of England to intervene in the market to preserve its value.

Tew refers to this period as the 'binary phase'. Much of the world was covered by two currency areas within which multilateral settlements were possible, although the two were kept apart by exchange controls. One, of course, was the dollar area, and the other (sometimes referred to as the 'soft' currency area), represented a greatly expanded European Payments Union, which effectively included the whole of the sterling area as well as the colonial empires of the Belgians, Dutch, French and Portuguese. This effectively included most of the non-dollar, non-communist world, with the partial exception of Japan where some discrimination continued. Bilateral agreements still continued between some pairs of countries, but these were of little practical importance and the negative impact on foreign trade was fairly small.

In December 1958 the United Kingdom and Germany removed all discriminations against foreign holders of their currencies, retaining exchange controls only on transactions between residents and the rest of the world. Restrictions retained by other European countries were becoming less important, being superseded by these multilateral arrangements of the type envisaged by the founding fathers of the IMF. It had taken all of thirteen years to remove this really serious impediment to international trade, and a further couple of decades before exchange controls (another deterrent) finally disappeared. The aims of the IMF had unfortunately been defeated by an excessive preoccupation with an attempt to maintain fixed exchange rates. The restrictions were far more damaging than the relatively minor uncertainties, occasioned by the period of floating rates, which was to follow, but attention then turned to removing these obstacles under the development of a single currency for Europe. It would be an over-simplification – but possibly a useful one – to quote this as an example of a period of fixed rates creating a yearning for the flexibility of floating, and vice-versa.

**Early moves towards closer European union**

While all this had been going on there were early moves towards closer links between European countries. The Council of Europe was set up in 1949, followed by the Schumann Plan and the foundation of the European Coal and Steel Community in 1951. Other early initiatives mainly concerned defence, the end of the formal occupation of Germany by the allied powers (with the notable exception of the Russian zone) and the creation of the Federal Republic. In 1953, J. W. Behan, the Dutch foreign minister, proposed a customs community between the six ECSC countries and Belgium, the Netherlands and Luxembourg as 'Benelux' began coordinating their own economic policies. In 1955 a treaty established the Western European Union, and the Messina Conference set in motion the launch of the Common Market.[5]

# 34 The UK 1951–79

## Introduction

Europe was now starting to move towards multilateral payment arrangements. The UK continued to have an important, though diminishing, role in monetary developments in Europe, and this chapter covers the period from when the new Conservative government of 1951 began to think about convertibily, to the eventual abolition of exchange control in 1979. By then, continental Europeans were taking the dominant role, and the first steps towards monetary union.

## The 1951 UK Conservative government: Butler and 'ROBOT'

The postwar Labour government was defeated in 1951, and Winston Churchill, the new Prime Minister, appointed R. A. Butler as Chancellor, with the support of a strong economic team: Sir Arthur Salter as Minister of State for Economic Affairs, Lord Cherwell as Paymaster General[1] and Donald MacDougall (later Sir Donald) as adviser. Butler, soon discovering that he had inherited a crisis, revived the long-neglected interest rate weapon, raised bank rate from 2 per cent (but only to 2.5 per cent), cut imports and rescheduled the armaments programme.

There was still an obligation to restore the convertibility of sterling, and a second, very interesting, attempt was made to achieve this. An escape plan, ROBOT,[2] was presented to Butler on 14 February 1952 as he prepared for his first budget. Sterling would become convertible for non-residents (although exchange control would remain for residents) but would be allowed to float, ignoring the Bretton Woods band.

> Convertibility at a floating rate was a simple principle. It was also a revolutionary principle. Fixed rates enforced discipline on governments and were the cornerstone of the new world economic order ... [they] were] designed to prevent the competitive devaluations which, some believed, had been an important cause of the 1930s depression.[3]

The project raised several questions. The economists on the team managed to explain to the politicians that only a float from strength would work, and that this meant domestic deflation. Was this politically acceptable?

What was meant by 'floating'? Should it be really free with no support from the reserves, or should it be supported within a (published or unpublished) band – what was later to be called a 'dirty float'? Should the existing parity ($2.80) be maintained or should there be 15 per cent bands, implying a possible fall to $2.38? Bolton had written to Salter,[4] 'one price ... must not be brought under the general principle of free market movements: that is the sterling-dollar rate'. He suspected that without support it would fall below $2.40. The Treasury's wish for a free float was eventually watered down, under Bank of England influence, to a plan for a 10 per cent margin each way – $2.52–3.08.

It was proposed that, to deal with the sterling balances, 80 per cent of sterling area, and 90 per cent of other, balances would be blocked and eventually turned into (low) interest bearing bonds. There would be 'special arrangements' (a public relations fudge?) for India, Pakistan and Ceylon, while Australia and New Zealand were told that if they did not accept, they would be excluded from the sterling area and its more favourable regime for UK source investment. The concept of 'overseas sterling', which alone was freely convertible, would be extended to include the unblocked part of the balances, i.e. sterling held by dollar area residents, earned in current transactions by other foreigners, or held by sterling area central banks (Dell 1996, 168).

There were arguments between supporters and opponents within the Treasury and the Bank of England, but Butler was told 'there was no alternative'. The reserves were draining fast, and given that it would be impossible to support a fixed rate for long, it was better to act in good time while he was still in control of events.

According to Samuel Brittan, ROBOT was vetoed by Churchill 'against his original inclinations' on the advice of Cherwell,[5] and writing in 1964, he goes on to make an interesting comment, highly relevant to later discussions on EMU, on

> the enormous power of fashion in economic policy. In the early 1950s the idea ... of leaving sterling to its own devices was advocated by [those on] the Right wing ... every Conservative Chancellor before Mr Selwyn Lloyd seriously considered letting the pound float. ... If no one took the plunge it was through lack of nerve rather than doctrinal inhibitions. [These views were opposed by the left] as a false solution that did not get to the root of our difficulties.
>
> Today [i.e. 1964] ... any thought of touching sterling is denounced ... as irresponsibly extreme [even for official Labour] and economists who

believe in floating rates (mostly moderate Lib-Labs in their politics) are
treated almost as bomb-carrying Bolsheviks.

(In *Steering the Economy*, 1969, an enlarged second edition, on page 119
the end of this passage was changed to 'were treated as eccentrics, remote
academics, or far-out radicals (or worst of all "Powellites")'. There is also, it
seems, a 'power of fashion' in invective!)

## The switch to multilateral payments, 1954–5

On 22 March 1954 the UK abolished bilateral arrangements and extended
transferable account status to virtually all countries outside the sterling and
dollar areas.[6] From the point of view of foreigners there were then just two
types of sterling, convertible 'American account' sterling and transferable
account sterling which was *de facto* freely exchangeable at a discount which
soon became fairly modest. Exchange control continued for UK and other
sterling area residents, who had to make capital investments via a separate
'investment currency' market, which traded at a premium.

On 24 February 1955 Chancellor Butler announced that he had authorised the Bank of England to use wider discretion in carrying out exchange
policy and managing reserves. In practice the Bank intervened to buy sterling for dollars, supporting the currency and preserving the discount at less
than 1 per cent. Such a move had to be coordinated with European
Payments Union partners, but they were not ready. Butler's decision on
convertibility was supported by the Bank of England, which still opposed
floating. The Treasury still favoured convertibility at a floating rate, particularly given that 'non-residents could convert sterling so easily'.[7] There were
sterling crises in 1955, 1956 and 1957, all caused by the shortage of
reserves, the level of which was typically in the ranges $2–3 billion, about
three months imports and less than the $4 billion liability of the sterling
balances.

## The move to convertibility, 1958

Following the Suez crisis, Prime Minister Anthony Eden resigned on 9
January 1957 and was succeeded by Harold Macmillan. His first Chancellor,
Peter Thorneycroft, tried to control public expenditure but was, with Enoch
Powell and Nigel Birch, to resign spectacularly over this issue at the begin-
ning of January 1958. By now the main currency problem was that
Germany's DM was undervalued. Robert Hall favoured floating coupled
with deflation, but Robbins was against floating from what he regarded as a
position of weakness. Dell comments:

> If British Governments were to wait until the economy was strong
> before floating they would ... find that they had waited until ... there

was no alternative. ... From a purely economic point of view, it was an ideal time to combine the rise in the Bank Rate and the assault on public expenditure with the floating of the pound. There were ... the usual political objections.[8]

While Brittan[9] suggested that

the real tragedy of 1957 is the missed opportunity on the sterling side. In the later sterling crises, Central Bankers used the state of the dollar as an argument against allowing the pound to float. ... If the pound 'went' it was claimed, there would then be a run on the dollar [and a] general flight ... into gold with untold consequences ... 1957 was the last sterling crisis when Britain could have abandoned the sterling rate ... without any risk of rocking the international boat; and the opportunity was thrown away.

On 21 March 1958 Macmillan asked Heathcoat-Amory, who had succeeded Thorneycroft as Chancellor, to prepare a paper on the implications of a floating rate which was opposed by the Bank of England. Robert Hall, Leslie Rowan and Overseas Finance were also against, feeling that

to allow a Macmillan government the soft option of freedom from the discipline of a fixed exchange rate would be a recipe for exchange rate depreciation, inflation and economic irresponsibility of every kind. Once more the opportunity was missed.[10]

In the event non-resident sterling became convertible on 29 December 1958, but without floating and at the old fixed rate of $2.80. UK exchange control continued to be enforced against sterling area residents, and thereafter took the general form in which it was to continue until its abolition in 1979. Dell suggests that the Bank of England had changed its views of floating and now favoured a fixed rate without even the wider 6 per cent spread which would have been allowed under the rules of the European Payments Union, then being wound up.

## Selwyn Lloyd and the 1961 crisis

The general election of 8 October 1959 gave the Conservatives a larger majority. The German currency was still strong, the DM was revalued by 5 per cent on 5 March 1961, was expected to rise further, and the market now realised that the Bretton Woods rates were no longer immutable. Sterling was regarded as a devaluation candidate, and came under speculative pressure in July. Selwyn Lloyd met this crisis by a sharp deflationary package and fiscal measures which do not concern us here.[11] The idea of floating was again canvassed, but Dell says that Macmillan, in his diary for 23 July 1961, questioned whether devaluation mattered. The exchange rate held – for the time being.

## Callaghan and the devaluation of 1967

After Reginald Maudling's doomed 'dash for growth', Harold Wilson won the 1964 general election, and found that he had inherited a crisis. The Labour Party had used the risk of a run on the reserves as a scare tactic during the election campaign, but had no contingency plan for dealing with it. Donald MacDougall recommended devaluation, but the government feared that the Conservatives would accuse them of rushing to Labour's usual 'soft option'. Dell comments (correctly) that devaluation was not in fact a soft option, as it had to be accompanied by deflation – the danger was that the 'government was only too likely to treat it as such'[12] and that it was typical of Wilson to be 'deterred by debating points'. Wilson also feared that a devaluation would encourage speculation every time the government ran into problems. The exchange rate was held, with a struggle, during 1965. On 24 November Wilson suggested floating, but Cromer, Governor of the Bank of England, 'warned that [it] would cause a world financial crisis'.[13]

The subject was aired again at a cabinet meeting on 19 July 1966, at which there was some support for floating the pound, but only when the crisis was over. There was at this stage little support for devaluation to a new fixed rate, the government opting for a standard Treasury deflation.[14]

In 1967, following the Six Day War and the closure of the Suez Canal, devaluation was again discussed: Wilson announced that he was taking personal charge of economic policy, and twice raised bank rate without convincing the markets. The European Commission, reporting on Britain's application for membership, implied that devaluation would be needed, and on 2 November Cairncross (then head of the economic service) told Callaghan that devaluation was inescapable. Callaghan agreed and Wilson accepted his advice, but apparently favoured floating.[15] There was resistance to the idea from France (which feared, wrongly in the event, that the franc would follow) and the United States (afraid that the dollar would be more exposed). The IMF gave standby help but was criticised by its developing country 'clients' for not imposing tough enough conditions.[16] Cabinet approved devaluation to $2.40 on 16 November: a two-day delay in announcing it cost the country $1.5 billion. Wilson made his notorious 'pound in your pocket' speech justifying the change, and the cabinet resisted the full consequential deflationary package. Again the opportunity to float was missed, although the idea had increasing support and Jenkins later thought that it might have been a better solution.[17]

Callaghan resigned as a matter of honour and exchanged jobs with Roy Jenkins. The was to be yet another loss from a mishandled devaluation. Because of the terms of the Basle Agreement of July 1968, holders of the sterling balances were guaranteed the dollar rate, but also enjoyed the higher interest rates paid on sterling as a weak currency.[18]

In his April 1970 budget, Jenkins could tell a story of achievement, but Dell comments that 'the implication must be that if only earlier Chancellors, under less compulsion, had done as much the damage would have been even less and the effect on the British economy wholly salutary, especially if their action had been accompanied by the floating of sterling'.[19]

## The UK: floating at last

The Conservatives were returned in the June 1970 election, but Iain Macleod died within weeks, to be succeeded as Chancellor by Anthony Barber. It was an eventful period, marked from our point of view by the publication of *Competition and Credit Control* and the collapse of the Bretton Woods system. The DM had already floated upwards in September 1969, and on 15 August 1971 Nixon imposed a 10 per cent surcharge of imports into the US and announced that the dollar would no longer be convertible into gold. In a vain attempt to restore fixed rates, new parities were agreed at the Smithsonian Conference in December 1971.

Anthony Barber, in his budget speech of 21 March 1972, made what Dell (1996) called 'the most important statement about exchange rate policy uttered by any Conservative Chancellor since the War',[20] saying that it was no longer sensible to maintain unrealistic fixed rates at the expense of the domestic economy, but added 'there can be no soft option if we fail to get a grip on ever-rising costs'. This, says Dell, 'brought to the government and the House of Commons a sense of combined relief and exaltation', but he comments that 'after a brief and humiliating episode' (the experiment with the Snake) Barber *did* use his freedom as a soft option.

## Geoffrey Howe and the end of exchange control

The Conservatives under Margaret Thatcher resumed power after the 1979 election. Geoffrey Howe, the Chancellor, took an early opportunity to cut top tax rates, and continued a monetarist policy initiated (with IMF encouragement) by Denis Healey. He also took advantage of what Dell calls the 'temporary strength' of sterling to abolish exchange control on 23 October 1979. Dell adds that 'among the costs was that it was at odds with Howe's attempt to control the domestic money supply', which is technically questionable. Harold Lever (and Dell himself) had supported abolition from within the Labour Party 'to provide some offset to the upward pressure on the exchange rate that the oil might otherwise cause'.[21]

Nigel Lawson[22] refers to an article he wrote in *Financial Weekly*, 20 April 1979, arguing the case for exchange control abolition, and claims to have been the one to have persuaded Geoffrey Howe and Margaret Thatcher. He refers to an 'important relaxation' in the 1979 budget – automatic clearance of direct foreign investment up to £5 million, higher travel allowance and the use of sterling finance for third country trade. He claims to have minuted Geoffrey Howe on 4 October, and says that 'Ministers were taken completely by surprise'.[23] He quotes Harold Lever (House of Lords, 17 November) as welcoming 'the end of exchange control which has served no useful purpose, and ... was not even a useful machinery for protection against a run on sterling'. The legislation remained on the statute book: there was an EC Directive of 21 March 1972 requiring members to retain reserve powers. Legislation was finally repealed in 1987.

Howe himself gives credit to 'a splendid IEA pamphlet from John Wood and Robert Miller ... in February 1979 [which] helped to break the intellectual ice-pack'.[24] A review article based on this pamphlet in the *Banker*[25] was submitted before but published just after, the election and in consequence was 'promoted' to being the lead article in the magazine. Based on an earlier Policy Group paper, it agreed wholeheartedly with the conclusion, but discussed the practical problems, ignored by Miller and Wood, of engineering a soft landing. It stressed the need to make a clean break, pointing out that there was far more likely to be a capital flight if investors feared that there was still the mechanism to close the door again at short notice: this could have become a self-fulfilling prophecy. In the event companies which had been holding as much foreign currency abroad as they could persuade the Bank of England to allow, took the opportunity to repatriate and centralise treasury management.

Howe says he had authorised Lawson to 'reassert the arguments during the election campaign' in September. Lawson and 'Treasury officials responsible for international finance' were pressing for abolition. Fred Atkinson, chief economic adviser, 'warned of the risks of this "fairly momentous decision" as he quaintly described it. John Biffen and the Governor too had some cautionary words to offer.' The cabinet was given a few hours notice: 'Michael Heseltine alone objected both on the merits and because the Cabinet had not been consulted'.

Later developments, including the short lived-experiment with the Exchange Rate Mechanism, are discussed in Chapter 36 in the broader context of Europe.

# 35　The collapse of Bretton Woods

## Introduction

The Bretton Woods system was not a monetary union but was, in its day, the nearest approach we had. It carried the seeds of its own destruction and inevitably came to an end. Indeed, to quote Peter Garber:[1] 'The collapse of the Bretton Woods system ... was one of the most accurately and generally predicted of major economic events ... the general outlines at least of the key events from 1967–71 were foreseen, starting from the work of Triffin (1960).'

Ralph Hawtrey[2] can surely make an even earlier claim than Triffin. Writing in 1946, he asked how it is that 'a country incurs not merely a casual and momentary indebtedness but a progressively growing indebtedness?'. His answer, obvious to us now, was very perceptive at the time: 'That may in general be interpreted as a sign that the country's money is *overvalued*' (1946, 7, his emphasis).

Later (33–4) he commented that

> Lord Keynes was not oblivious of the need for international coopera-
> tion to guard against undue monetary expansion. But he hardly
> accorded the need to prominence it merits ... [but when the White plan
> was] put forward, there was no vestige in them of this vital provision.
> Nor does the Bretton Woods plan ... contain any.

In his view (40) 'A country's right to alter the par value of its own currency should never be parted with', and he saw the Bretton Woods limitation as a serious danger, commenting, with prescience, that 'it is as important to avoid being entangled in an inflationary movement ... as that it should resist the contagion of a deflation'.

Another collection of papers, as early as 1961, *The Dollar in Crisis*, edited by Seymour Harris, included contributions from the leading economists of the day.[3] It includes the text of the White House Message on the Balance of Payments and Gold, 6 February 1961.

## The gold price

The first sign of trouble came in October 1960, when a speculative attack forced the free market price of gold up from the official $35 to around $40, causing fears in the United States that such a rise might force foreign central banks to convert their reserves into gold. A 'gold pool' was therefore set up, and until around 1967 succeeded in holding the gold price, but at a cost of some leakage of the United States reserves.

Bordo (1993, 50–2) lists three problems discussed at the Bellagio conference in 1964. First, the adjustment process was neither that of the gold standard nor of exchange rate changes. 'Under Bretton Woods, concern over the unemployment consequences of wage *rigidity* delayed the deflationary adjustments required by a deficit country and together with the use of short-term capital controls considerably muted the automatic mechanism.'

Second, there was a shortage of *liquidity*, which could in the long run have allowed time for adjustment. 'The world's monetary gold stock was insufficient ... unconditional drawing rights were meagre and the supply of US dollars depended on the US balance of payments which in turn was related to the vagaries of government policy and the confidence problems.'

Third, the *confidence* problem 'involved a portfolio shift between dollars and gold ... the probability of all dollar holders being able to convert their dollars into gold at a fixed price declined'. He goes on to discuss in detail two contrasting examples of the adjustment process – the United Kingdom and Germany during the period 1959–67.

### Special drawing rights

These criticisms led to a discussion of the possibility of creating new reserve assets, and in 1968 under the first amendment to the Articles of the IMF, the concept of the Special Drawing Right (SDR) was introduced, although it was held up until 1970 by the French, who insisted that it could only be activated when the US balance of payments deficit was eliminated (Bordo 1993, 67). The SDR, arguably a re-invention of Keynes' 'bancor', was defined as a basket of dollars, yen, DM, sterling and French francs, and was to be used as an 'intervention currency' by certain countries.

### Currency events

The economic situation in the United States began to deteriorate in 1965 when, partly as a result of the Vietnam war, US inflation began to rise and the current account surplus became a deficit. Following the 1967 devaluation of sterling there was further pressure on the gold market, and the gold pool ceased to operate in March 1968: the members of the central banks agreed not to buy or sell gold in the market, but only to trade between themselves at the $35 rate. Other transactions were free. There was much talk about how world liquidity could be restored, and the whole issue of international monetary policy was back into the centre of the public arena.

The Bretton Woods parities had held good, at least in the industrialised world, since 1959, but the sterling devaluation of 1967 affected other countries, and was followed by the devaluation of the French franc by 12.5 per cent on 9 August 1969. The United States dollar was overvalued, and the country was losing gold, and it became clear that the whole structure of rates was under strain. After a political row the deutschmark was revalued by 9.29 per cent on 24 October, but this was too little, too late, and the dollar outflow continued. On 10 May 1971 and in breach of Bretton Woods rules, the Germans and Dutch allowed their currencies to float, and France withdrew from meetings of the Committee of Central Bank Governors in protest. On 15 August 1971 President Nixon suspended the dollar's link with gold, and on 18 December 1971, the Smithsonian Agreement provided for a series of currency adjustments, including an increase in the gold price to $38, a devaluation of the dollar by 7.89 per cent and the widening of the IMF adjustment bands from 1 per cent to 2.25 per cent. On 12 February 1973, the dollar was devalued by a further 10 per cent, and on 19 February the deutschmark was revalued by 3 per cent and the Snake countries effectively floated against the dollar: the end of Bretton Woods and, incidentally, of the Tunnel. The dollar again fell sharply in May 1973, but recovered from August to January 1974, partly because of the Middle East War and the first oil shock.

Even after the 1973 collapse, developing countries 'continued to rely heavily on fixed exchange rates, mainly pegging to specific countries within the spirit of an optimum currency area', only moving to floating rates in the 1980s and 1990s. Figures in *International Financial Statistics* show that in December 1979, 85 per cent of such countries had a fixed regime, but by December 1990 the figure had falled to 67 per cent.[4]

## A retrospective view

Cottarelli and Giannini[5] (1997) give some useful information on different country patterns. They also say

> After the switch from the gold standard to the fiat standard ... matters related to the monetary standard practically disappeared from both theory and policy discussions. In spite of Irving Fisher's famous warning against the perils of fiat money, inflation remained for more than two decades at about 2 per cent in industrial countries ... the world economy developed at an unprecedented pace.

The credit must go not only to Bretton Woods: there was 'widespread scepticism about the effectiveness of monetary policy', and the authorities tried to stabilise interest rates, and did not 'avail themselves fully of the flexibility the fiat standard allowed', a point which had concerned Fisher.

Problems began when in the mid-1960s, growth slowed, and fixed rates were felt to be a constraint on economic policy. This was followed by 'an attempt to fix what by then had become a faltering monetary framework' which was incompatible with the demand for active policies. Conflicts between politicians and central bank governors, many of the latter being dismissed or 'duly subdued'. Inflation inevitably followed, but it was not until 'inflation began to be associated with rapidly mounting unemployment' ('stagflation') that support for activist policies began to falter.[6] There is a similar approach by Giovannini,[7] who asks 'are there predictable cycles in exchange-rate regimes? Can these cycles be predicted in terms of the rules-versus-discretion theory?'

# Part VII

# The road to European Monetary Union

# 36 Early moves towards European Monetary Union

## Introduction

When the Marshall Plan was introduced, in 1948, the Americans took the opportunity to encourage the nations of Europe to unite, at least economically. A decade later, in 1957, the Treaty of Rome launched the European Economic Community between Germany, France, Italy, Belgium, the Netherlands and Luxembourg. The UK at first rejected an invitation to join, and a later application for membership in 1963 was vetoed by General de Gaulle.

During the early years, various proposals were put forward for monetary union, notably by Walter Hallstein in October 1962, but at that time there was little interest: the Bretton Woods system was believed, at least by politicians, to 'ensure' a world of fixed rates, so why did Europe need any special arrangements? The mood changed in 1969, when the Bretton Woods system was visibly about to collapse, and European leaders decided that Europe needed its own system of stable rates as a step towards a new international monetary order.

The first of three major initiatives towards monetary union in the EEC, the Werner Report of October 1970, aimed to achieve monetary union by 1980 and involved the concept of the 'Snake in the Tunnel'. This formally continued until 1978 (when only three members remained) but effectively came to an end a couple of years earlier; most of the currencies floated following the collapse of Bretton Woods.

The European Monetary System, introduced at the beginning of 1979, had its problems, but even though it lacked the disciplines of a genuine monetary union it was, for a time, a success. Exchange rates were relatively stable from 1987 to September 1992, when EMS was derailed following the politically botched currency union between West and East Germany, discussed in Chapter 37.

The EMS had been regarded as a precursor of full monetary union, and the third (and successful) initiative began with the Delors Report of April 1989. This was formalised by the Maastricht treaty of 1991, and European Monetary Union (based on the euro) was completed in January 2002.

Throughout each of these phases the economic and political motives were often in conflict. Exchange controls persisted well into the ERM phase, and inevitably influenced events.

## The Werner Report and the Snake

### The Werner Report

Karl Schiller of Germany had tried unsuccessfully to persuade France and other members to participate in a joint float against the dollar in May 1969. He favoured monetary union as a prelude to political union: H. J. Witteveen, the Dutch finance minister, put it the other way round, saying that political union was a precondition for monetary union.[1] A summit meeting was held in the Hague on 1–2 December 1969, to discuss both the widening the EEC to include other members including European Free Trade Association members, and deepening it in the direction both of political unity and monetary union. Pierre Werner, Prime Minister of Luxembourg, was appointed to chair a commission aiming at achieving European Monetary Union by 1980, based on the harmonisation of monetary policy.

The Werner Report[2] was published in October 1970. During stage 1 exchange rate movements would be restricted, and monetary and fiscal policies would be coordinated. This would be taken further during stage 2, while stage 3 would constitute full union with irrevocable fixed exchange rates, a Community-wide system of central banks and a 'centre for economic policy decision making'. Exchange controls would be abolished, and there would have to be a substantial increase in the European Community budget. This last was to remain controversial even after 2002, and there was the alternative: 'The centre must be able to exert influence over national budgets, particularly on whether they should be in surplus or deficit and by how much, and on how surpluses are spent or deficits funded.'[3] The whole process was to be completed by 1980.

The report was followed by slightly different proposals submitted by the commission, which would itself put forward proposals for what was to be done after the completion of stage one.[4] Political motives were, as ever, an issue. Germany was on record as saying that European Monetary Union would have no chance of success without political union, France then disagreeing. A Council Resolution on 22 March 1971 set out the main principles: the 'total and irrevocable' convertibility of currencies, fixed exchange rates, a system of central banks, a European Monetary Cooperation Fund, and a significant transfer of economic decisions to Community institutions.[5] This was more or less where we were to be thirty years later, but with, at that stage, hardly any serious discussion of the practical difficulties of getting there. The Resolution proposed that stage 1 should run to the end of December 1973, but did not specify a date for the ultimate achievement of EMU.

## The Snake in the Tunnel

On 24 April 1972 the 'Snake in the Tunnel' was set up by the six original EEC members, Germany, France, Italy, the Netherlands and Belgium/Luxembourg. This provided that the maximum margin between any two currencies could not exceed 2.25 per cent, holding them within a 'Snake', leaving the group of currencies effectively centred on the deutschmark, free to float freely against the dollar within a wider 'Tunnel'. (The concept of the Tunnel still assumed some attempt to keep within Bretton Woods parities, but this was about to become irrelevant.) The Snake (whose supporters were dubbed *ophiopholists* by a classically inclined Treasury official) was to have a turbulent history.

In March 1972 Anthony Barber, the UK Chancellor (finance minister) had introduced a more flexible approach to exchange rates, and in May the United Kingdom (with Ireland and Denmark) joined the Snake, but was effectively driven out by market forces six weeks later, on 23 June. Ireland and Denmark also left, Ireland retaining the fixed parity with sterling. Denmark returning to the Snake on 10 October 1972 after a referendum approved EC accession.

Thereafter sterling floated until accession to the ERM. The speculators had tasted blood and hot money, and set out in pursuit of the next profitable defection. In January 1973 the lira came under pressure and the Swiss franc floated on 23 January. Money moved into Germany and Japan, and away from the dollar, which was effectively devalued on 12 February 1973, and Italy left the Snake the same day. On 19 March the deutschmark central rate was revalued by 3 per cent (and by another 5.5 per cent on 29 June) while Norway and Sweden joined the Snake. France left on 21 January 1974 'for six months', actually rejoining over a year later (10 July 1975) but at its old parity. There were abortive discussions in mid-1975 about Switzerland joining the Snake. In March 1976 France again left, and the Benelux 'Worm within the Snake' ceased to operate.

This all meant that at the end of 1973 the second stage of monetary union, scheduled to be effective from the beginning of 1974, was postponed indefinitely. The Snake was scotched, but the concept persisted until 1978.[6]

## Exchange control

Exchange controls, even between member states, had persisted well into the period during which monetary union was being actively discussed. Such controls are quite incompatible with the idea of a single market. Although most of the economic loss from such restrictions is borne by the countries imposing them, their neighbours also suffer some collateral damage from the mis-allocation of resources. The UK scrapped exchange controls in 1979, but some other EC members did not follow for over ten years. Other restrictions on capital movements, such as those imposed, allegedly for 'prudential' reasons, on cross-border institutional investment, continued rather longer.

It may be asked why exchange controls persisted so long. The answer is to be found in public choice theory, which analyses the conflict of interest between governments and citizens. Exchange controls increase the time lag between bad economic decisions and their visible consequences: this is both their attraction to a certain type of politician, and the most serious and subtle way in which they damage the economy.

## The European Monetary System and the Exchange Rate Mechanism

In spite of these setbacks, a meeting in Rome on 12 September 1973 resolved to set up a European Monetary Fund before the end of stage 1, and on 19 October a Paris meeting decided to establish a European Monetary Cooperation Fund before 1 April 1975. This was a much more serious initiative, and a commission set up in 1975 under Robert Marjolin commented

> Europe is no nearer to EMU than in 1969. In fact, if there has been any movement, it has been backward: national economic and monetary policies have never in 25 years been more discordant, more divergent, than they are today.[7]

The Tindemanns Report was described as 'vague' and the general mood in the 1970s was one of pessimism about both monetary and political union. It suggested approaching monetary union on the basis of the Snake and existing treaties. In early 1978 Roy Jenkins, then a European Commissioner, said that he looked for a more important role for EMU, and the creation of more stable relationships within the international monetary system. At a Bremen summit in June 1978:

> Germany, supported by the Netherlands, had always regarded monetary union as the crown on economic convergence, by contrast with France which – together with the United Kingdom and the European Commission – mainly considered monetary unification as the driving force of economic convergence.[8]

On 1 November 1975 the *Economist* published the All Saints Day Manifesto, advocating the introduction of a parallel currency, discussed, with other similar proposals, in Chapter 40.

The Bremen meeting put forward a proposal which would lead to a 'zone of monetary stability', and following this initiative it was decided to introduce the European Monetary System on 1 January 1979 (it was in fact delayed until 13 March because of French problems with the Common Agricultural Policy). The transitional stage was intended to end after two years, but there was no indication of any long-term goal of full monetary union.

The European Monetary System had three aspects:

1  an arrangement for pegging the exchange rates of member countries
2  a system of credit facilities to help defend the rates and
3  a 'European Monetary Fund'.

### The European Currency Unit

The Ecu (European Currency Unit) was introduced on 13 March 1979 as a successor to the European Unit of Account, but had a much more central role, notably in the arrangements for the EMS. The Ecu (like the EUA and indeed like the SDR) was defined as a weighted average of member states' currencies. It was not, at this stage, envisaged that the Ecu would take the place of national currencies. When introduced, the deutschmark constituted about 33 per cent, and sterling about 13 per cent, of the Ecu basket. The composition was amended from time to time, the final changes being in September 1989. As from November 1993 it was 'frozen'; there were to be no more changes, which, incidentally, meant that the currencies of Austria, Finland and Sweden were not included. (When most of the component currencies adopted the euro, the Ecu continued to exist as a basket of the euro, plus the pound sterling and the Danish krone.)

The European Unit of Account had been defined in terms of gold parities, but by 1979 these had become irrelevant. The Ecu was simply defined in terms of a basket of floating currencies, without specific reference to gold or to any currency, such as the dollar, outside the basket.

### The Exchange Rate Mechanism

Steps taken to initiate a 'zone of monetary stability' included the 'Exchange Rate Mechanism' (ERM), in some respects similar to the Bretton Woods system but with more symmetry: strong- as well as weak-currency countries were required to take action to keep their currencies in the basket. The bands (plus or minus 2.25 per cent) were also wider than the 1 per cent of the Bretton Woods system, and there were formal arrangements for realignments within the ERM. Italy joined but with a wider (6 per cent) band.

The EMS had two intervention mechanisms, a 'parity grid' and a 'divergence indicator'. The central parity of each participating currency was defined in terms of the Ecu. Cross rates could then be calculated consistently for the purpose of the parity grid: to use the Bank of England example, if, at central rates, 1 Ecu = DM2.5 and BF40, then the corresponding German Belgian cross rate would be DM1 = BF16. The Banque Nationale de Belgique would be required to buy (*and* the Bundesbank to sell) deutschmarks against Belgian francs at 15.6440, and to sell (buy) at

16.3640. During defined hours on a working day, each central bank would simply hold itself available to deal at these rates: 'The central bank has *only* to respond to requests initiated by the commercial banks: it need take no initiative itself.'[9] ('Only' was later to prove very expensive indeed.) In practice, of course, central banks could and did intervene well before the official limit was reached.

A generally strong or weak currency might be near its intervention margins with several of the others, and in those circumstances the second mechanism, the 'divergence indicator,' would become important. This threshold came into play when the divergence of the currency from the Ecu basket was three quarters of the theoretical maximum divergence which would result from its being 2.25 per cent (or 6 per cent for Italy) from all other currencies (the arithmetic was a little complicated because the currency itself was part of the basket). When the divergence indicator is triggered, the central bank concerned is expected to intervene to correct the divergence. (The Bank of England commented, in 1979, that it was not possible to publish intervention rates directly against the Ecu as 'commercial banks are unable to deal in them', but it did not take long for the banks to find ways of creating efficient Ecu markets in spite of exchange control obstacles.)

Parities could be, and indeed were, changed but there was an important difference from the Snake regime, when parities were declared in terms of the European Unit of Account (EUA), which was itself defined in terms of gold. Currencies would then effectively have been devalued or revalued against gold, or in practice against the US dollar, but under the new regime a change in European parities did not have to relate explicitly to the dollar or any other outside currency.

Commenting on the divergence indicator, the Bank of England suggested that

> Intervention arrangements on the lines of ... the parity grid proved themselves to be technically robust in ... the 'snake' [but] the authorities of several member countries [considered that the system] would be likely to prove more durable and effective if an additional mechanism for identifying the need for intervention were used.[10]

Credit facilities to defend parities were divided into three maturity categories: short term (forty-five days), medium term (nine months) and long term (five years). Different amounts, measured in Ecu, were available within each maturity.

### The European Monetary Fund

Finally, a European Monetary Fund (EMF) was to be established. This Fund would receive a portion of the gold and foreign exchange reserves of member countries, and would issue in exchange deposits denominated in Ecus.

Countries becoming members still had exchange and capital controls, but these were finally relaxed between 1985 and 1 July 1990[11] when a Directive came into force. Greece, Ireland, Portugal and Spain had derogations giving them until 1992 to comply.

A UK cabinet committee, Denis Healey being Chancellor, considered but rejected the idea of joining.[12] Dell discusses the political arguments, and quotes Healey as saying 'I was fairly agnostic until I realised, from long discussions with Lahnstein and others how [the EMS] was likely to work in practice; then I turned against it'.

After Margaret Thatcher was elected Prime Minister, the UK abolished exchange control in 1979, and discussion turned towards exchange rate policy. Should the pound continue to find its own level in markets (a 'clean float'), should it shadow another currency such as the deutschmark, or should the UK formally join the Exchange Rate Mechanism, and actively support and move towards full monetary union? This (amateur) historian has been too heavily involved, professionally and personally, in these issues to be able to offer a suitable perspective,[13] but it does seem worth reminding readers of the 'pendulum' referred to before: there is nothing like a period of floating rates to remind people of the benefits of stability, and vice-versa.

Nigel Lawson as Chancellor chose to subordinate monetary targeting to an exchange rate policy, shadowing the deutschmark as an alternative to joining the ERM (which Margaret Thatcher would not countenance). In October 1990, after much vacillation and resistance from Thatcher, her Chancellor John Major took the UK into the ERM with 6 per cent bands. She 'stipulated the 6 per cent bands and a 1 per cent cut in interest rates as her price for accepting defeat'.[14] This was *after* the decision on the terms of German reunification which was to cause the collapse of the ERM, with expensive consequences for the UK. In September 1992, John Major having become Prime Minister, Norman Lamont, his successor as Chancellor, was forced into an expensive withdrawal.

# 37 The reunification of Germany and the collapse of the EMS

This is an interesting case from our point of view, as a badly conceived monetary union (between East and West Germany) put an intolerable and destructive strain on a larger emerging monetary union to which West Germany belonged.

## German reunification

In 1989 the Hungarian border was opened to East German refugees, and in November that year the German borders were themselves opened, the Berlin Wall was destroyed by a jubilant population, and serious discussions towards reunification began. West Germans had been offering 'welcome money' of DM100 to East German visitors to the West, but Western visitors to the East had had to change a minimum amount of money at official rates in effect as an entry fee. This penalty was abolished at the beginning of 1990, and West Germany set up and subsidised a foreign travel currency fund permitting East German citizens to acquire DM100 for ostmarks at par, and a further DM100 at a rate of 1 per 5, each year, a measure expected to cost DM2.9 billion. East Germans (and ethnic Germans from elsewhere in Eastern Europe) coming West were to receive integration payments.

These were only transitional measures: now that the Eastern Länder of Germany were free to rejoin the West, German politicians in particular were enthusiastically speeding up full and formal reunification. A Treaty of Unification was ratified in May 1990, and the deutschmark was to become the common currency from 1 July – also, as it happened, the starting date for stage 1 of European Monetary Union.

### Economic issues

There were economic questions to be answered, but the politicians took little interest in them. How could East and West Germany acquire a common currency in such a way as to remove the monetary overhang in the East, treating the East Germans equitably but without creating recession in the

East, inflation in the West or both? How could skilled labour be encouraged to stay in, and capital to move to, the East?

An obvious approach would have been a reconstruction of the ostmark by a full-blown currency reform such as that undertaken in West Germany in 1948, finding a suitable exchange rate for the ostmark, using the black market rate of 7:1 as a basis. There would have to be a suitable *Kopfgeld*, a modest ration of currency which each citizen could change at a favourable rate (not necessarily par) to give some protection to East German pensioners and savers.

The East German money supply (in ostmark) was estimated at around 15 per cent of West Germany's (in DM) and an exchange at a rate of 1:5 would have added around 3 per cent to the total money stock, which would still be administered from Frankfurt. Deutsche Bank figures put the value of East German financial assets (cash plus savings accounts) at OM180bn. Based on *their* assumed exchange rate of 3:1 this would represent a 15 per cent increase in German M1, or an 8.6 per cent climb in M2 (a concept closer to the East German 'financial assets'). This inflationary impact would of course be offset by the addition of 16 million 'new Germans' who would need to hold money. We tried to analyse the figures at the time but the long-run impact on prices proved very difficult to estimate. The net effect of a currency reform could be either inflationary or deflationary, and some subsequent fine tuning would be needed.

In the shorter run there would almost certainly be a jump in the price level, as a practically unchanged stock of consumer goods was chased by West Germans with their existing money supply *and* East Germans with a newly created supply of hard deutschmarks. A short-term price jump seemed to us to be inevitable at any likely exchange rate. Fine tuning would have been easier if part of the ostmark balances had been converted into deutschmarks denominated medium-term bonds which could have been redeemed at discretion, and this seemed to us at the time to be a more politically attractive alternative to the economically equivalent blocking of bank accounts.

Another possibility would have been simply to have let the ostmark wither away, encouraging the use of the deutschmark as the *de facto* currency of the East, leaving existing ostmark balances to find a free-market level. Parties to a contract (including a wages contract) would have been free to *specify* deutschmarks, and this could be encouraged, and the ostmark could have ceased to be legal tender for contracts after a specified date.

A Brookings Institution study, 'Christmas in July?', updated from a workshop held in September 1991, gives a good outsider's view of what were then recent events. It concentrates on the 'real' economy, and although it has relatively little to say about the monetary aspects, it gives some interesting figures, including table 4 (page 24) on net fiscal transfer payments for the five years 1990–4. These rose from DM27 billion in 1990 to DM59 billion in 1991 and DM92 billion in 1994. There are figures on investment, and comparisons with Marshall Plan payments on page 25. For comparison, German GNP in 1990 was DM2.4 trillion, as shown in their table 1.

> Making East Germany competitive is a huge task for employers, administrators and management and for the capital stock and infrastructure. The FRG's Germany's traditional mode of economic assistance has been oriented towards capital ... (but) assistance should start with improving the capabilities of the workforce ... (but) because East Germany is being integrated into West Germany's highly developed social security system, East Germans' wages would not be low. With East German wages in 1991 only 20 per cent lower than Japan's ... it will not become a low-wage region competing with any of the South East Asian countries. In 1992 average wage unit costs rose to more than 200 per cent of the West German level by no means low itself.
>
> (Brookings Institution study, 31)

Also obviously, 'skilled workers who are mobile will be attracted to West Germany anyway' (32).

## The events

On 20 March 1990 the West German government agreed to establish a monetary, economic and social union beginning on 1 July, and a few days later voted a supplementary budget including emergency aid to East Germany of DM5.8 billion. The whole supplementary amounts and aids were granted.

The terms of the monetary union were announced on 21 June. The black market rate had been 11. As from 1 July the deutschmark would be the only legal tender in East Germany. Credits and debts in ostmarks were converted to deutschmarks at 2:1, as each individual would be allowed to exchange OM2,000, 4,000 or 6,000 (according to age) at par. Certain claims by non-residents would be exchanged at 3:1.

More seriously, wages, salaries, scholarships, pensions, rents, leases and other regular payments would be valued into 1:1. East Germany established an equalisation fund allocating interest-bearing claims to banks. This was all going to be inflationary, and a horrified Bundesbank (exonerated from blame for this 'political decision') had to take corrective action. Yields on German bonds rose sharply in 1990, and

> the Bundesbank felt compelled to demonstrate its determination to achieve stability. It set monetary targets that gave no room to inflationary expectations. It curbed the unexpectedly high monetary growth, it raised interest rates several times. ... Although the Bundesbank was accused of choking West German expansion and is delaying the turn round of the rest of Europe the capital markets seem to respect its firm

stand. … Nevertheless the government sector's large capital needs put a great deal of stress on the capital markets.

(Brookings, 27–8)

## The effect on the European Monetary System

The Maastricht treaty was signed on 7 February 1992, and some countries needed to ratify it. Problems hit almost immediately. Denmark's voters in a referendum rejected the treaty on 2 June 1992, although this decision was reversed after some amendments, including an opt-out from the single currency, on 18 May 1993. A French referendum on 20 September 1992 endorsed the treaty by the thinnest of margins: the 'petit oui'. There was growing criticism of the treaty in the United Kingdom (which had a derogation) and the poll evidence strongly suggested that, if a referendum had been required in Germany, it would have been defeated. More seriously, the botched German reunification had caused a widespread deterioration in the Maastricht ratios. This was precisely the type of 'asymmetric shock' which can put a stress on a monetary union, and the European Monetary System began to fall apart in July 1992.

Meanwhile there were doubts on how the French referendum on EMU would go and speculators, smelling blood, were out in force. The first to go was Finland, which broke the link with the Ecu on 8 September 1992. Five days later, on the 13th, Italy devalued by 3.5 per cent, and on the 16th, 'Black (or White) Wednesday' (your choice) sterling left the ERM, and Swedish overnight interest rates rose to 500 per cent (annualised). A day later, the Italian devaluation having proved inadequate, the lira was forced out of the ERM, while Spain devalued 5 per cent. Sweden floated on 19 November, followed by Norway on 10 December. On 22 November the central rates of the escudo and peseta were reduced by 6 per cent: there were further falls of 6.5 per cent and 8 per cent on 14 May 1993. The French franc came under considerable pressure but kept its parity.

Only a few months earlier markets had been behaving as though the EMS rates were more or less fixed in the run-up to monetary union, but these factors put enormous pressures on currencies, not helped by the Bank for International Settlements' conviction that exchange rates might be brought into line by changes to domestic costs and prices rather than by a change in exchange rates as such.

Geoffrey Howe, towards the end of his autobiography,[1] comments on the 'tragedy' of the closing phase of Margaret Thatcher's premiership, and her 'ideological hostility' to exchange rate policy and any strengthening of the role of the European Community. He says that 'this double wall of unreason' caused policy clashes, and irrational judgments on ERM policy 'ruptured so irretrievably the solid troika' between Howe, Lawson and Thatcher. The UK actually entered the system under Thatcher's premiership on 5 October 1990 at the wrong time, at the wrong rate, and in the wrong way ... for five years ... almost every key Minister had been consistently agreed on the case for early entry into the ERM. Properly managed it would have been the right move as Margaret Thatcher belatedly conceded to buttress our counter inflation policy. The Prime Minister, almost alone, had resisted that case.

If other counsels had prevailed, he says, we would have been much better equipped to deal with the crisis of September 1992.

Robert Pringle (reviewing Philip Stephens)[2] suggests that Norman Lamont did not realise, until after the event, that he was playing with real money when he threw away some £3 billion of the nation's assets in a poker game with George Soros.

## Another view

Larry Siedentop,[3] in an excellent study of the political problems of the European Union, puts a different and interesting slant on the effects of German monetary union (138). He says that 'the sudden unexpected re-unification of Germany ... created a great fear (*grand peur*) among the French political class', who feared a more powerful Germany and concluded that 'France if it were to be safe must have a hand in the government of Germany', and that the best way of achieving this was to press for a single currency and the European Central Bank. They also had in mind that the European Bank should be politically accountable rather than genuinely independent, and sought the use of the Stability Pact as a means of increasing the power and influence of the Mediterranean bloc. The French, unlike the Germans, wanted to make sure that Italy, Spain and Portugal were included.

Siedentop admits that his story is not the conventional one, and may have something of the conspiracy theory about it. But it does offer a plausible explanation of why and when the economic project looking towards a single currency was blown off course by accumulating what was (from an economic point of view) irrelevant political baggage.

# 38 European Monetary Union
## 1988–99

## Introduction

The last few chapters set out the monetary history of postwar Europe, including some earlier initiatives which might have led towards the European Monetary Union, ending by explaining how the Exchange Rate Mechanism effectively collapsed with a series of economic crises in 1992 and 1993.

By then the Maastricht treaty, the key step on the road to monetary union in 1999, had been signed, and indeed the roots of this initiative go back even further, to 1985, when the Single European Act envisaged the completion of the single market by the end of 1992. The newly appointed President of the Commission, Jacques Delors, wanted to incorporate the concept of monetary union, arguing that France and other countries recognised that inflation could only be dealt with using German-type policies. The deutschmark and the Bundesbank were then the obvious economic anchors of monetary order, but given that a simple surrender to German policies was politically unacceptable, the French were keen to transfer the control of currencies to a supra-national organisation in which all member states would have a say.

## The Delors Report

In June 1988 the European Council set up a Commission of Experts (mainly central bank governors 'acting in a personal capacity') chaired by Jacques Delors, which was to put forward proposals for the Madrid meeting of the European Council in 1989.

The Delors Report,[1] presented in April 1989, was based on the idea of rigidly fixed exchange rates and a single monetary policy conducted by a European system of central banks. It represented a compromise between the pragmatists (at that time Germany, the UK and Luxembourg) who wanted to move forward gradually on the basis of the 'existing achievements' (as it then seemed) of the EMS, and the enthusiasts (France, Italy and Spain) who were in more of a hurry and feared that without institutional changes some countries might lack the political will to bring their inflation rates and general economic performance into line with countries such as Germany.[2] The UK was opposed: 'The British Government did not want to hear of an amendment to the Treaty of Rome', and Margaret Thatcher actually believed that 'neither a European central bank nor a European currency were required for the realisation of EMU'![3]

The Delors Report stressed the need for economic integration and for steps to deal with regional and sectoral differences: 'in particular unco-ordinated and divergent national budgetary policies would undermine monetary stability and generate imbalances in the real and financial sectors of the community'.[4] It proposed three stages of monetary union, a timetable which was more or less followed.

The British House of Lords[5] said that policies would be 'geared to price stability, balanced growth, converging standards of living, high employment and external equilibrium' (para. 16). The British resisted the idea of a supranational monetary institution, regarding it as a step towards eventual full political union. Odd as it now seems, although it was (rightly) said that capital movements must be fully liberalised, 'a common currency was not seen as an essential feature of monetary union, although it might be a natural development' (para. 9).

### The Madrid summit, June 1989

The Spanish prime minister had said that he would seek a full political debate on the Delors Report at the June 1989 summit in Madrid but in the event, although the proposals were agreed (including a decision to start stage 1 on 1 July 1990), this mainly served to sharpen the divide between the United Kingdom government and those of its neighbours. It also split the UK Cabinet; Geoffrey Howe (Foreign Secretary) and Nigel Lawson (Chancellor), supported by the Foreign Office, favouring early accession, with Margaret Thatcher and her advisers bitterly opposed. Another key development was that the French managed to secure the support of the previously cautious Helmut Kohl for a 'fast track' approach. Although Mitterand would go down as the father of the proposal, it was Kohl who, without much support from either the Bundesbank or the German electorate, was to put the most energy into seeing the project through.[6] In September 1989 the Commission made some formal proposals and set up a Committee of Central Banks.

### EMU stage 1

Stage 1 of the Delors concept of EMU started on 1 July 1990, six months later than originally planned. Various alternative proposals had been put forward, the Bundesbank stating that EMU must be based on economic and financial harmonisation between all member states. There was a Spanish proposal to start stage 2 in January 1994 and 'harden' the existing Ecu, as an alternative to introducing a thirteenth currency, such as the UK concept of the 'hard Ecu' discussed in Chapter 40. Spain regarded the European Monetary Institute, which was to be established as stage 2, as the forerunner of the European System of Central Banks.

On 19 March 1991, Governor Pöhl of the Bundesbank advised the European Parliament against premature monetary union, pointing out that the introduction of the deutschmark into East Germany in mid-1990 had been effected 'without any preparations or the possibility of adjustment and thus at the wrong exchange rate'. He added that the result was 'a disaster as the new currency had fully destroyed the competitive position of the area'.[7] As we have seen, one consequence of the disaster, the partial collapse of the Exchange Rate Mechanism, was yet to come.

## The Maastricht treaty

In December 1991 the European Council met at Maastricht and agreed the terms of what became the Maastricht treaty, signed on 7 February 1992, which set out, amongst other things, the framework for full monetary union. It provided that the second stage of EMU should begin on 1 January 1994, by when member states were required to have met certain conditions and to have adopted 'programmes intended to ensure the lasting convergence necessary for the achievement of economic and monetary union in particular with regard to price stability and sound public finances'. It also provided for a European Monetary Institute (EMI), the council of which should be the governors of the national central banks of the participating member states, and that this should ultimately become the European Central Bank.

The treaty laid down four 'convergence criteria' which had to be met by these states if they were to participate in stage 3: it was envisaged that all states, other than those which had a derogation (the United Kingdom and Denmark), which met the criteria would be *required* to join. The procedure in Article 109J provided for taking earlier decisions subject to an absolute deadline:

> if by the end of 1997 the date for the beginning of the third stage had not been set, the third stage shall start on 1 January 1999. Before 1 July 1998 the Council ... shall acting via a qualified majority ... confirm which member states fulfil the necessary conditions for the adoption of a single currency.

At the start of stage 3, the exchange rate would be irrevocably fixed and the EMI would be reconstituted as the European Central Bank with broad powers to determine monetary policy for all the participants.

There was a lot of political juggling, including an opt-out for the United Kingdom and Denmark. David Buchan comments on one potential problem. The United Kingdom, in spite of its opt-out, would be entitled to vote on the position scheduled for 1996 as to whether the project was to go ahead. This would involve seven out of the then twelve members of the Community. 'What happens', he asks,

> if Britain is one of only seven countries deemed economically fit to pass to Emu but London opts out? If only six were both ready and willing to go to Emu the answer seems to be that Emu would remain stalled. A possible solution, but not a watertight one to this potential problem appeared to be found in a protocol to the Maastricht Treaty, which states that no member should act so as to prevent a single currency coming into being.[8]

## The convergence criteria

The 'convergence' criteria (Article 109J and Protocol) were:

*Price stability*    The state must have a sustainable price performance and an average rate of inflation that does not exceed by more than 1.5 percentage points of the three best performing member states.

*Government finances*    The budget deficit must not be 'excessive', defined, possibly naively, to mean that it 'is not the subject of a council decision under Article 104C(6) of this Treaty that an excessive deficit exists'.

*Good standing in the ERM*    The state must have respected the normal fluctuation margins within the ERM 'without severe tensions' for at least the last two years before the examination and shall not have devalued its currency's bilateral central rate against any other member currency on its own initiative for the same period.

*Interest rates*    The state must have had over a period of one year an average nominal long-term interest rate that does not exceed by more than two percentage points that of the three best performing member states in terms of price stability.

There were several intriguing features about the package. Throughout the period leading to stage 3 there was much public discussion on 'convergence', and when the treaty was signed it was assumed that there would be a smooth and gradual transition towards achieving these. The third one, keeping within the EMF bands was, it seems, not expected to give any trouble, and the founding fathers certainly assumed that the convergence requirements, once met, would thereafter be maintained without difficulty. This was not to be, and future 'stability' was to become a major issue.

Even odder was the assumption that for two years after the exchange rates were 'irrevocably fixed' the general public would still be denied the practical benefits of using a single currency. Charles Goodhart has suggested that this was a deliberate political manoeuvre: the Commission postponed what it thought might be the unpopular part of the measure until it would be too late to do anything about it. I took the opposite view, having suggested that the introduction of notes and coins, originally as a 'secondary currency', would achieve most of the benefits for normal (non-politician) citizens without the controversial political baggage, and pave the way for public acceptance.

### The Madrid summit, December 1995

The next major event was another Madrid summit in December 1995, which both agreed the timing of the launch (1 January 1999) and the name 'euro' for the new currency. The names of 'florin' and 'Ecu' were also canvassed, while Chirac, defeated on his first choice, suggested a poll to choose a name.[9] Helmut Kohl commented that 80 million Germans would simply vote for the deutschmark, perhaps not realising the implications of his remark. Showing great enthusiasm but very poor foresight, Kohl also called on the pessimists such as John Major 'to draw inspiration from the leaders of Serbia, Croatia, and Bosnia-Herzogovina, who just the day before in Paris had buried their doubts and reached agreement in the broader interests of peace'. As later events were to prove, they hadn't!

### The Dublin summit, December 1996

At the Dublin summit in December 1996 the design of the new banknotes was unveiled, although it was to be all of another six years before they would go into circulation. Why did it take so long? During the Wars of the Roses it was politically necessary to make quick changes in the names and portraits of the alternating rulers on the coins, and how long did it take to design and print the first billion mark note during the German inflation?

## The Stability and Growth Pact

The Dublin summit in December 1996 was concerned to make sure that these convergence criteria were maintained, and this resulted in the so-called Stability and Growth Pact. The Germans wanted a strict discipline imposed through a European Central Bank, while the French thought that subsequent budgets were a matter of national sovereignty. The Irish compromise involved a two-tier approach. Any member state which experienced a fall in GDP of 2 per cent or more would qualify automatically for 'exceptional' status, while one suffering a fall of 0.75 per cent could argue its case. The 'stability pact' was renamed the 'stability and growth pact'. (This is reminiscent of the fancy and misleading titles made up for tax-raising American tax bills. Any seasoned professional, seeing a bill 'for stability, fairness and growth' knows he is about to read of a systematic assault on the taxpayer.)

Member states will be required to keep budgets 'close to balance or in surplus' over the medium term, and publicly to announce the medium-term budget objectives. If there is a deficit and this is held by the Commission to be an excessive deficit, then a qualified majority will be able to recommend to the state concerned that remedial action should be taken within four months with the intention of correcting the excessive deficit within a year. The excessive deficit will be acceptable if:

- there has been an economic downturn of more than 2 per cent of GDP;
- where the fall in GDP has been more than 0.75 per cent and it can be shown to be exceptional;
- where there has been a major external event which has affected the budgetary position.

If the member state concerned continues to have 'excessive' deficits, the Council of Ministers can require another country to make interest-bearing deposits equal to 0.2 per cent of GDP plus one tenth of the amount by which the deficit exceeds their 3 per cent reference value. It appears to be intended that if the deficit continues these deposits will effectively be confiscated and treated as fines.

The pact provides for fines on a sliding scale, which seem in practice likely to add to the problems they are intended to solve.

The effect of all this is that if a country suffers an asymmetric shock (or pursues unsound economic policies) it will not be able to devalue or increase interest rates following monetary union. In a free and competitive market there will be limited scope for raising additional tax revenue, as tax rates significantly above EU averages will drive business away and reduce the tax base. Deficit financing is ruled out by the stability pact, leaving cuts in public expenditure as the only remaining weapon.

### Fudging the convergence criteria

The Maastricht treaty set out a series of 'convergence criteria' which countries would have to meet if they were to be admitted to the first round of monetary union. The criteria, drawn up in 1991–2, had assumed a rather different Europe from the one actually facing the applicant members in 1997, when they had to be met. The first change was the increase in German interest rates caused by the reunification of Germany, which led (apart from the partial collapse of the Exchange Rate Mechanism) to higher costs of service of government debt and a sharp reduction in the rate of growth in all the applicant countries.

The other (political) factor is that, following the collapse of communism, some (but not all) Eastern European countries had emerged to become serious candidates for membership of an enlarged European Union. Germany (in this context a front-line state) felt that this made political union more urgent, and abandoned its traditional argument that economic convergence should precede monetary union. The German government (but not most German voters) came to regard a broad-based monetary union as the most effective road towards a political federation.

In the event, though, the criteria were held to have been met by all the countries interested in joining with the exception of Greece. In most cases this was achieved by creative accountancy of one form or another, an aspect which caused concern to enthusiasts as well as sceptics. The French figures included a payment of E5.7 billion made by France Telecom to the government, an internal piece of creative accounting, which left a broad deficit of 3.02 per cent, rounded down to the required 3 per cent. Italy levied a special tax for Europe equal to 10 per cent of personal income in December 1997, which counted towards reducing the deficit even though the government promised that it would be refunded at a later date. Even the German government sought to revalue its gold reserves in line with current market prices and bring the extraordinary one-off profit into its budgetary account as 'income'! The Bundesbank rightly and successfully blocked this, but the Germans still included a reclassification of hospital debt. Although only Luxembourg actually met the strict criteria, it could be, and was, argued that this multiple failure could in principle have been compatible with them all 'converging', but at a different level from that assumed. Unfortunately this didn't meet the facts.

It was in the event easy enough to fudge convergence, thanks to the imperfections of government accounting and the preoccupation with gross liabilities (rather than net worth) and gross deficits (rather than savings). The national figures for 1997 had to be submitted to the Commission of the European Union and the European Monetary Institute by the end of February 1998, and on 25 March the Commission published a long-winded, and the European Monetary Institute a rather crisper, report. On 2 May all members except Greece were held to qualify: the United Kingdom, Denmark and Sweden had an opt-out, but the other eleven countries became the initial members of what became known as Euroland. Greece was admitted to the club in June 2000.

### *The presidency of the ECB*

There was a major row over the presidency of the European Central Bank in April 1998. This, too was fudged, with the appointment of Wim Duisenberg for the first half of the eight-year term subject to an agreement that he would 'voluntarily' step down in favour of Jean-Claude Trichet, Governor of the Bank of France.

## Fixing the rate

The Maastricht treaty (Article 1091(4)) provided that the conversion rates of the currency should be 'irrevocably fixed' and that the euro would have the same value as the Ecu at 1 January 1999. This seemed a good idea at the time, as it was assumed that the rates would only be set at the end of 1998. In the event, it was decided to fix the rates between the eleven participating currencies in May 1998, months earlier than the formal introduction of the euro. This created a problem, as the Ecu was still defined as a basket of twelve currencies, three of which, the United Kingdom, Denmark and (it was then assumed) Greece, would not be joining EMU. Currencies in the euro zone constitute only 83.5 per cent of the Ecu basket, and until the end of 1998 the euro was literally indefinable (although its value could be estimated accurately enough from forward rates), and for the rest of the year foreign exchange transactions had to be one of the eleven legacy currencies. But for the wholly artificial attempt to create this one-to-one link, the euro could have been given an immediate valuation in May.

Subject to this transitional problem, there was an effective monetary union with fixed rates between the participating countries, but it was to be another three and a half years before travellers would have the benefit of a common currency, and during this period little progress was made with reducing bank charges for cross-border payments. At the beginning of 2002, euro notes and coins (which few people had actually seen in advance) were brought into circulation to a general (but not universal) welcome. A complex administrative task (for which, after all, there had been plenty of time to prepare) appears to have gone well with few problems, apart from some banking strikes. From an economist's point of view, though, the interesting stage of the experiment was just beginning.

# 39 European Monetary Union

## Policy issues

### Introduction

Much has been written for and against monetary union, and whether or not a particular country should join. The literature is of varying quality, and this is not the place to add to, or even survey it, particularly as the main issues have been discussed in a historical context. This chapter simply gives a highly selective account of what seem to the author to be particularly significant, and perhaps less obvious, contributions.

### *The 1995 Green Paper*

Some of us had been taking an active role in discussions, in my own case as an active member of the Association for Monetary Union in Europe, generally favouring the initiative, but conscious, as monetary economists, of the difficult technical economic issues it raised. We hoped these could be solved, and indeed we regarded a highly critical, but very positive approach as the best way we could contribute. Specifically, we had been waiting for the European Commission's Green Paper,[1] which was eventually published in May 1995, but which turned out to be a serious disappointment. It gave an excellent explanation of the mechanics and timetable, but stated explicitly that (in the opinion of its authors) it was not a matter of 'who' and 'when' but 'how' EMU would happen ('encouragement, not prescription, is what is needed')[2] and it turned out to be more of a propaganda document concerned only with 'possible approaches for encouraging public acceptance of the changeover to the single currency' than an analysis of the serious economic issues. It devoted itself 'entirely to the communication campaign which is needed to bring home to European citizens the advantages of the single currency' (para. 18). Using a term later to become fashionable in describing the antics of politicians, it was all 'spin' and no substance.

The Commission's campaign appeared to be directed against what it regarded as its only opposition: uninformed populist euro-sceptics, untutored on the economic issues. It failed to recognise that there were many technically competent well-wishers who broadly favoured the idea of monetary union but knew it raised problems which, they hoped, would find solutions: the Green Paper ignored their constructive questions.

Economists discussing the 'fixed versus floating' issue ask whether the ability to devalue a currency (or allow it to depreciate in a free float) does or does not give a country a valuable policy tool in today's world of highly mobile capital. Does devaluation 'work' or are its effects quickly neutralised by differential inflation? The only passage the Green Paper allowed itself on economic issues addressed this point – and was wrong. The authors asked:

> But how much autonomy do monetary policies really have today in Europe? ... an autonomous monetary policy is no longer a credible policy option. Member states will only lose a prerogative which in practice they cannot use.
>
> (para. 7)

and

> Some people fear that when their country is experiencing particular difficulties, the exchange rate instrument cannot be used to deal with them. However this instrument provides – mostly temporary – relief only in special circumstances.
>
> (para. 8)

This statement reflects a view which was widely held, even by some economists, in the late 1980s (and often quoted even into the 1990s, by when there was plenty of evidence to the contrary) when it seemed that devaluation would be quickly absorbed in changes in relative prices, giving no long-term structural benefits. By 1995, the shift to greater market competition, the weakened bargaining power of organised labour, the decline in inflation expectations and more effective techniques of domestic monetary control, meant that devaluation no longer led to inflation, but actually achieved a substantial and sustained fall in the real exchange rate and a corresponding competitive advantage. This had been well illustrated by the collapse of the ERM, and was certainly not a matter to be lightly dismissed. (Later events reinforced this conclusion: the sharp fall in the euro against the dollar and sterling was not compensated by a higher inflation, and materially affected the competitive position of the economies.)

### A two-stage EMU?

The various crises discussed in previous chapters stimulated talk about a two-stage EMU. Rather than risk the whole system collapsing, why should not France and Germany, the two key countries, simply fix their exchange rate with no nonsense as to 'bands', whether wide or narrow, and then agree to pursue a single monetary policy? Belgium, the Netherlands and

Luxembourg, which had already been shadowing the deutschmark very closely, would surely have joined in, while Austria had linked its currency to the deutschmark years before EMU accession. The idea was popular in France, but there has been little discussion about the three key questions, such as whether the central banks would them create a mini ECB to cover monetary policy, how the exchange rate would be defended in the foreign exchange markets, and what tests would apply to future applicant members.

## Is the EU an optimum currency area?

Is the European Union an 'optimum currency area'? (The same question could have been asked about the sterling area which functioned perfectly well for many years.)[3] This issue was widely discussed. Daniel Gros,[4] for instance, took a sanguine view: elsewhere in the same issue of the *NIER*, John Arrowsmith and Christopher Taylor are more guarded.[5]

Jacquet,[6] arguing that EMU is 'a worthwhile gamble', comes down narrowly in favour. He rejects 'the current system of stable but adjustable exchange rates' and effectively sides with those economists who believe that the only credible policies are a convincing peg (such as true single currency or a currency board) or a clean float. He also comments that continental Europe has fared less well than the US because monetary policy was too tight, a 'damaging policy-mix error' resulting, of course, from German reunification. 'The focus should now be on making the gamble a success.'

Wyplosz[7] discussed why EMU was likely to happen politically even if the economic arguments are unconvincing. Nations 'like France, Italy and Spain, gradually realised that they had lost control of their domestic monetary policy'. They needed a new institution in which they would have a voice.

Martin Feldstein[8] also discusses the contrast between political will and economic reality: a 'strange mixture of pro-European internationalism and the pursuit of narrowly defined national self-interest', mutually contradictory aims which together 'may propel Europe into a monetary union'. France and others see EMU as an opportunity to escape from German domination. Germany's motives are 'harder to understand': they either see it as a means to reduce the risk of conflict (but, as he points out, monetary union did not prevent the American Civil War) or as an opportunity to reinforce their role as natural leaders of the EU, aided by new allies from its Eastward expansion.

A more recent book by Larry Siedentop[9] looks at the political structure of the European Union from a much broader perspective, and his fascinating account does much to explain what went wrong at the political level. It is an excellent study, although his occasional blame of 'economists' for certain problems suggests he has been talking to the wrong ones! One of his many points is the competition between different, and possibly incompatible, models of the state. The French model is essentially bureaucratic, with centralised power, a large arbitrary element in decision making, and scope for influence by well placed interest groups. The German constitution, in contrast,

> takes enormous trouble to create different spheres of authority – true Federalism which is not, *pace* some Eurosceptics, a surrender of power to some unaccountable super-government but a constitutional arrangement, on the American model, carefully balancing the rights and powers of different levels of government and setting up checks and balances to ensure that no individual or group can exercise undue power. The British model is different again, informal and consensual, relying on precedent and custom and putting a premium on mutual agreement.

One could add that the UK, with a common law system, has a tradition of Parliament and its committees taking apart the small print of new legislation and treaties before approving them, but the French regard this as tedious Anglo-Saxon nitpicking. Why not, they say, just agree broad principles and leave the civil servants to sort out the details? The British, for their part, are horrified by the casual approach taken by others to essential details, and even accuse continentals of ignoring the detailed rules because they intend to ignore them when it suits them: bureaucratic arrogance, rife in certain countries, is tempered by the healthy anarchy of their citizens.

Unfortunately, says Siedentop, the British form of state 'cannot be exported. It is too embedded in a particular social context.' In contrast, the French model, 'with its in-built predilection for power rather than authority', can only too easily be spread across the EU. He has a lot to say on the problem facing those of us wanting to preserve or create a genuine democracy, an open political class, and a state which exists to serve the citizen rather than the other way round. This is not an economic issue as such, but it is important in understanding how easily an economic project can be hijacked by those with a separate political agenda.

# 40 Parallel currency proposals

## Introduction

European Monetary Union was, in the event, achieved by first requiring certain tests of economic convergence to be met, second by irrevocably fixing the exchange rates between the participating currencies, and creating economic rigidities, but only, third, replacing national currencies with actual coins and banknotes in euro after a further delay of three years. The practical benefits, for most people, came only in 2002, ten years from the signing of the Maastricht treaty, and thirteen years after the Delors Report.

Could we have achieved the practical benefits for citizens, travellers and businessmen, more quickly? We could, at least ten years earlier, have begun by introducing an alternative parallel currency which would initially circulate alongside national currencies. This would have secured a large part of the practical advantages to travellers and traders much more quickly – would have enabled the public to become accustomed to the new currency, and might have avoided or postponed some of the irrelevant political problems.

### A summary of the proposals

One group of proposals, notably the All Saints Day Manifesto of 1975 and the 'hard Ecu' of 1990, offered a further advantage, suggesting that a new currency might be so organised as to constitute a sounder store of value than any of the then existing national currencies, thereby speeding up the transition to a stable, inflation-free European economy. Another school, including the *Economist*'s editorial comment on the All Saints Day Manifesto and the Chown/Wood proposals of 1989, preferred to use a basket of existing currencies, on the grounds that this could be achieved quickly and without the need for 'too much panoply and treaty signing'. No new institution would be required, unless and until it was decided to go ahead to the second and final stage of full monetary union with a single issuing authority.

The most commonly made criticism of both versions of the idea suggested that it was illogical that the first move towards a single currency should actually be to add a new one. Fair enough, but the most efficient way of getting from A to B is not always by the obvious straight line route and, as we tried to show, although the proposals add a 'vehicle currency', they substantially reduce the number of cross rates needed for day-to-day transactions.

It is also worth commenting that monetary union, as actually achieved, involved increasing the number of central banks – by two. The European Central Bank obviously adds one to the 'one per country' quota, and the second is accounted for by Luxembourg, which, shadowing the Belgian franc, did not need a central bank until it had to form one to secure a seat on the board of the ECB.

The practical problems (addressed by the supporters rather than the critics) would have been more serious, notably the difficulty of estimating how many notes and coins needed to be produced before we knew how quickly, if at all, the idea would reach critical mass and take off. At what stage would one have had to consider changing vending machines and other similar arrangements, and could we have been sure that the temporary 'vehicle currency' would be the one ultimately chosen for an eventual fully fledged monetary union?

Conspiracy theorists (who credit politicians with a higher degree of intelligence and foresight than those of the rival persuasion) might suggest that there was another factor at work. Some architects of the proposal, mainly committed federalists, may have seen monetary union, not as an economic end in itself and a measure to simplify life for those carrying on business across frontiers, but as a backdoor means of achieving a political objective of creating a centralised government for Europe. They might not have been keen on testing the waters, in case the idea proved unpopular, and they might not share the enthusiasm of the ordinary citizen for a solution which could develop naturally without the need for increased central political control.

## Two earlier 'secondary' proposals

During the 1892 Monetary Conference there was an attempt, though unsuccessful, to broaden the concept of Latin Monetary Union, and an intriguing comment by Russell[1] says that Bengesco, the Romanian delegate to the conference, suggested compromising on a secondary currency, saying that 'while an international agreement [on the US bimetallic proposals] appeared to be impossible, one might easily be arranged on the optional coinage and obligatory circulation in each country of gold pieces equivalent to 25 francs'. Russell comments that this idea fell flat.[2]

A little earlier Alfred Marshall, in his 1887 evidence to the Royal Commission on the Values of Gold and Silver, tentatively suggested that, as gold could no longer be regarded as a stable measure of value, certainly at the national level, there was a case for examining 'the suggestion made earlier in the century' (he does not say by whom) by which the government would publish a 'tabular standard of value' (i.e. a price index) which could be used, optionally, as a unit of account. He assumes that this would be used for long-term agreements, such as mortgages, and does not suggest it as an alternative money. He briefly discusses the advantages, and his conclusion could apply to all secondary currency proposals:

> There are great difficulties to be overcome. ... But failure would do little harm, because it would disturb nothing. Success would diminish much the anxieties of business and the irregularity of employment. And I think the attempt ought to be made.[3]

Marshall includes a brief comment in his *Money, Credit and Commerce* (1923, 30) as an aside in a discussion of index numbers. (Andrew Coleman, in a paper on Australia–New Zealand monetary union,[4] revives the idea as a solution to his question 'Can New Zealand have its cake and eat it?', saying it could by adopting the Australian dollar and introducing a new indexed unit of account.)

## The All Saints' Day Manifesto

On 1 November 1975 the *Economist* published an article by nine economists[5] suggesting the introduction of the 'Europa' as a secondary, and alternative, currency which could in due course become the currency of Europe. The Europa, a predecessor of the 'hard Ecu' would be inflation-proofed. Its value would be a weighted average of the participating currencies but would differ from the European Unit of Account (and its successor, the basket Ecu), in that the value would be adjusted by movements in the consumer price indices of the countries concerned. Indeed, as the *Economist* commented, the Europa would effectively be 'indexed linked securities (called money) not under the control of national governments'. The authors agonise over technical details which a later reader would take in their stride (swamped by the problems of a real monetary union!) but the economic arguments are still interesting. They wanted monetary union to 'evolve in the market place' without 'official edicts and legalistic structures', and their scheme does not 'emphasise labour and capital mobility'.

They point out that a major weakness of the then current Snake in the Tunnel arrangement was 'its non automatic nature and its reliance on political discretion. Monetary union, if it is to succeed at all, must be brought about by a gradual process ... so that nationalist feelings are not provoked by sudden losses of ... national powers'. The authors preferred 'the free play of market forces'.

### *The* Economist's *comments*

The *Economist*, in its editorial comment, welcomed the proposals, but took a rather different line, showing more foresight in regarding an early monetary union as unattainable unless there were to be unimaginably fast convergence of inflation rates and trade union structures, plus social and regional funds set up on an unimaginably vast (and unworkable) scale to balance the currency union ... we have long argued that an optional parallel currency ... introduced by stealth would be a far better method.

The editorial goes on to make some sensible criticisms of the proposals as 'not being by stealth ... too much panoply and treaty-signing, not enough quiet use of the existing EEC unit of account and issuing Europa denominated bonds which would quickly become market favourites'.[6]

Kindleberger[7] says that the Manifesto was based on work by Giovanni Magnifico and John Williamson,[8] who had attacked the Werner Plan in 1971, and proposed a European Bank issuing the Europa as a parallel currency. He also refers to a Study Group on Optimum Currency Areas (the 'Optica' group), and radical critiques by Hayek, Vaubel and Salin.

Others have made similar suggestions from time to time. Lionel Robbins, in his 1979 Mais Lecture, alluded briefly to Irving Fisher's 'compensated gold backing', and suggested that the European Commission 'might embark on the issue for a new money, parallel with existing currencies but guaranteed to be so managed as to maintain a constant value in terms of ... commodities'.

Ten years later James Meade (1990)[9] recommended that a European Central Bank be set up, financed through deposits from the member central banks. The ECB would issue a currency (also called by Meade the 'Europa') in exchange for deposits in national currencies, gold and foreign exchange. Member central banks would peg their exchange rate against the Europa.

The Banca d'Italia also envisaged an 'average Ecu' being issued by the ECB against national currencies. National central banks would agree monetary targets, and any money growth would entail the growth of Ecu reserves. It was not clear how this proposal would work if money demand or supply relationships were to change.

Herbert Giersch (1998)[10] refers to earlier writings proposing a European parallel currency (asset backed, in his version) and discusses the case for it, also suggesting that the dollar might have found such a role. He says that such a currency, to be successful, would have to be regarded as sound, correctly explaining Gresham's Law. He proposed that the euro would need some asset backing, if it were to be as strong as the deutschmark. The EU could then earn seigniorage from its use in other countries, notably the former Soviet Union and other Eastern European neighbours. Within the EU budget deficits would be financed only by index linked bonds: the European Central Bank should issue currency only against such indexed bonds (para. 3 of the German Currency Protection Law of 20 June 1948, which bans index linking, would have to be repealed).

## The Chown/Wood proposals

In 1989 Professor Geoffrey Wood and I proposed[11] that we should immediately encourage the use of the then 'basket Ecu' as a secondary currency. As and when this became established, travellers abroad would only have to carry one 'foreign' currency with them while shopkeepers, hotels and other suppliers of services would not have to cope with a wide range of currencies, but would simply double-price in local currency and Ecu. This would substantially reduce transaction costs, which in turn would encourage more travellers and businesses to use the new system. It would also make it easier to compare prices across frontiers as these became expressed in Ecu, bringing forward another advantage of monetary union as transparent pricing enhanced competition to the benefit of consumers. Our starting point was, of course, that any change should be designed to benefit the citizen, as traveller, trader and investor, rather than to be part of a power play designed to make life easier and tidier for governments.

If this had been adopted (and had been coupled with the type of assault, seriously lacking in the following years, by the European Commission on uncompetitive banking practices), over half of the 'transaction cost' (but of course none of the 'exchange risk') savings could have been achieved within five years – which then would have meant by 1994 – and might actually have brought forward, and would certainly not have delayed, full monetary union. This 'half baked' approach would have more than paid off the transitional costs of monetary union before it even began!

The most often cited benefit of EMU was that foreign exchange losses and costs would be reduced or eliminated. We analysed this, and showed that what business records as 'foreign exchange losses' mainly arise, not from currency fluctuations (which may tend to average out over time) but from bank charges and commissions. These charges were, at the end of the twentieth century and in spite of the development of electronic techniques, significantly higher than they had been a century and a half earlier when Latin Monetary Union was being proposed, partly to eliminate them. The Commission could have reduced these by a positive use of competition policy: in practice, for whatever reason, they always backed off from any serious initiative. Indeed the Commission, although certainly not informed consumers of financial services, appears to have been surprised that in 2000 when euro rates were fixed, banks still charged commissions for converting (e.g.) deutschmarks into euros, while on the introduction of actual euro notes they were still typically charging 2 per cent for exchanging 'fixed rate' currencies. Bank charges on money transfers within the eurozone were still not down to 'domestic' levels, although there is a requirement (which may, knowing the banks, still be honoured in the breach) that charges on various types of transaction (but only up to 12,500 euro) should be brought into line at various dates between July 2002 and January 2006. Big businesses can look after themselves, but this leaves a lot of smaller ones still without the promised transaction costs advantages, and calls into question whether the cost aspect (the real alleged benefit for business and travellers) had really been addressed by the political enthusiasts for monetary union, or whether they had a quite different agenda.

Christopher Johnson,[12] a prominent campaigner for monetary union, came to a similar conclusion to us on costs, suggesting a figure of £2.5 billion or 0.33 per cent of GDP, for the UK, and $25 billion for the EU as a whole.

> About half the total saving will come from the elimination of bid-ask spreads and commissions in foreign exchange dealings ... another 14 per cent will come from the ending of similar charges on banknotes, travellers' cheques and banknotes. Just over a quarter will be due to the reduction of companies' in-house costs, managing foreign exchange risk, and the remaining 10 per cent to a reduction in the cost of cross-border payments.

His later and more sophisticated analysis came to much the same conclusion as ours: about three quarters of costs to business arise from transaction costs and only a quarter from exchange rate fluctuations.

This diagnosis led us to propose encouraging the use of the 'basket Ecu'[13] (predecessor of the euro) as every European's second currency, and the first choice of every foreign visitor to more than one European country. Businesses and regular travellers would keep a second bank account in Ecu, would write cheques in Ecu or carry Ecu travellers' cheques. Any difference between the amount sent and that received (both being in Ecu) across borders would then be clearly and correctly identified as a transaction cost (bank charges), rather than as an 'exchange rate loss'.

These costs, and the time delays (very profitable for banks as they earn interest on the 'float' – money in transit) would then be as transparent as in domestic banking transactions – which may not be saying much. The businessperson or traveller would only need to think in terms of two currencies – their own and Ecu – while a German hotelier or shopkeeper would double-price in DM and Ecu. There would have been fourteen relevant exchange rates instead of the ninety-one that EMU then required, which should have encouraged lower and more competitive transaction costs.

This could soon have achieved many of the benefits of full monetary union quickly, without 'panoply or treaty signing', or having to wait for the very serious economic and political problems to be solved. We could have made a start on the practical problems, and familiarised the public with a new currency. It would have become much easier (although not as easy as with a full monetary union) to compare prices across frontiers, giving some of the benefits of transparency. If the new currency proved popular, people might begin to use it domestically, national currencies might wither away and monetary union would emerge driven, as any good economic initiative should be, by the preferences of the market rather than the machinations of politicians.

## The hard Ecu

Our own proposals paralleled, and were sometimes confused with, proposals by Christopher Taylor and others in the Bank of England, for a 'hard Ecu'. (We preferred the 'basket Ecu' because it could be introduced without any new institutional arrangements: a similar argument to that put forward by the *Economist* editorial in 1975.) On 19 June 1990, John Major, then UK Chancellor, announced his support for the 'hard Ecu' proposal immediately, inspired by a paper 'The Next Stage in an Evolutionary Approach to Monetary Union', by Sir Michael Butler and Paul Richards and published by British Invisibles.[14]

This 'hard Ecu' would have come into play in stage 2 of the Delors Report timetable – that is to say, after all EEC countries had joined the ERM (stage 1), but before Europe had a single currency (stage 3). In stage 2 as modified by these proposals, a European Monetary Fund would have been established which would issue a new common currency, the hard Ecu, which would, unlike the then existing average Ecu, comprise, not a basket of existing currencies, but a new currency – the thirteenth in the ERM – whose value in relation to these existing currencies would be guaranteed by the national central bank owners of the EMF: it would be 'as strong as the strongest currency in the Community'.[15]

One benefit claimed was that the proposal allows an evolution to a single currency – 'stage 2'. Second, it ensures that in stage 2 European monetary policies converge to each other *and* to low inflation, while the EMF would manage hard Ecu interest rates 'just like any central bank – by creating a liquidity shortage which it would relieve at an interest rate of its own choosing'.[16] National banks would in turn have to tighten up policy. The benefits were summarised very clearly by the Governor as follows.

1    first and foremost, it would add an extra counter-inflationary discipline to monetary policy decisions in individual member states;
2    building on the hoped for achievements of stage 1, it would significantly strengthen the forces leading to the convergence of economic conditions in the Community;
3    it would pave a way for a move away from the current position where the ERM anchor is a single country's currency and would bring an element of collective decision making to the ERM;
4    it would provide a common currency that would be used throughout the community, enabling consumers and producers to get used to using a real, new currency.[17]

John Major, who by then had become Prime Minister, pointed out that unlike the basket Ecu it would ensure convergence on the lowest inflation rate, rather than on the average, and would also give time for an EEC central bank to establish credibility.

One objection was that it would, like the basket Ecu, have been an additional currency. There were also minor technical problems. So long as ERM currencies fluctuate within bands, rather than being fixed rigidly, the 'hard Ecu' was unlikely to be the strongest currency *all* the time, and as the method of calcuating its value would have been complicated and its behaviour would have been affected by relative exchange rate variability, it would not necessarily have been stable.

> The new Ecu currency would indeed be superior to any EC national currency, *provided* member central banks agreed to subsidise exchange rate losses in one way or another. But what incentive would national central banks have to subsidise a competitive currency? What would prevent a national central bank from withdrawing its national currency entirely in favour of Ecus to ensure a smooth rather than a panic process of currency substitution?[18]

Vanthoor gives a valuable summary of the history, but his historical objections to a parallel currency are based on his misunderstanding of Gresham's Law:

> Experiences from the nineteenth century indicate that Gresham's Law would be applicable here too, for so long as the Ecu would not be as 'hard' as the Deutschmark as the anchor currency – between 1979 and 1995, its Ecu central rate decreased from 2.51 to 1.91 – the common currency would soon be qualified as 'bad money'.[19]

and again:

> Under those circumstances, the introduction of a parallel currency, proposed by some Member States as an instrument to promote integration was rightly rejected by European policy-makers. As long as this currency is not as 'hard' as that of the economically most prosperous Member State, it would rapidly be qualified as 'bad money' which would be driven out by 'good money'.[20]

There is a double error here. First of all he has reversed the popular summary of Gresham's Law – that 'bad money drives out good', and second, has, like many others, forgotten that the 'Law' is only applicable where both types of money have *effective* fiat value, meaning that the law (which is generally obeyed and enforced) requires them to be accepted on equal terms in trade or for the settlement of debts. If not, 'good money' can and does drive out discredited 'bad money'. There are many examples, from early history to today, where merchants and citizens, distrusting their local currency, choose to use a sound (often foreign) money, in spite of the best efforts of governments to prevent them.

# 41 Exchange control

## Introduction

Exchange controls played an important role in the history of postwar Europe, hindering the development of international markets, but also making it easier for foreign exchanges to persist at inappropriate fixed rates. This chapter, by way of an appendix, goes into a little more technical detail on issues which have already been discussed. One aim of the IMF was to free up capital movement as quickly as practicable, but exchange controls were to remain a serious problem for many years.

Although the UK retained exchange controls until 1979, the Bank of England proved itself very adept at ensuring that they did not hinder the City of London's role as an international financial centre, and for this reason the UK rules are here analysed in detail. Indeed, Mann,[1] explaining that his own detailed analysis is confined to the UK, says that

> A comparative treatment of these matters is neither necessary nor possible. In their kernel the exchange control regulations of the world are identical, though they may differ in detail; moreover to a large extent they are liable to undergo rapid changes. ... A comparative treatment [would have changed this book into] a monograph on exchange control.

## IMF provisions on exchange control

One aim of the IMF was to permit free currency movements and to outlaw exchange controls. Two Articles, Article VIII sections 2, 3 and 4 and Article XIV section 2, dealt with exchange control and both permitted derogations. The text is given below.

### Article VIII (2)

*Avoidance of restrictions on current payments*

(a) Subject to the provisions of Article VII, section 3(b) and Article XIV, section 2, no member shall without the approval of the Fund, impose restrictions on the making of payments and transfers for current inter-national transactions.

(b) Exchange contracts which involve the currency of any member and which are contrary to the exchange controls of that member maintained or imposed consistently with this Agreement shall be unenforceable in the territories of any member. In addition members may, by mutual accord, cooperate in measures for the purpose of making the exchange control restrictions of either member more effective, provided that such measures and regulations are consistent with this agreement.[2]

## Article XIV (2)

### Exchange restrictions

A member that has notified the Fund that it intends to avail itself of transi-tional arrangements under this provision may, notwithstanding the provisions of any other articles of this Agreement, maintain and adapt to changing circumstances the restrictions on payments and transfers for current international transactions that were in effect on the date on which it became a member. Members shall, however, have continuous regard in their foreign exchange policies to the purposes of the Fund, and, as soon as conditions permit, they shall take all possible measures to develop such commercial and financial arrangements with other members as will facilitate international payments and the promotion of stable exchange rates. In particular, members shall withdraw restrictions maintained under this section as soon as they are satisfied that they will be able, in the absence of such restrictions, to settle their balance of payments in a manner which will not unduly encumber their access to the general resources of the Fund.[3]

## Exchange control in the UK

The history of postwar United Kingdom exchange controls can be divided into four broad periods:

1    World War II, until 1947 when the Exchange Control Act was intro-duced;
2    from 1947 until 1958, the period of bilateral payments;
3    from 29 December 1958, when non-resident sterling became convertible, until June 1972 when the sterling area was effectively dismantled;
4    from 1972 until 23 October 1979, when UK exchange control was abol-ished.

During the wartime period virtually all international transactions were under strict government control. The necessary powers were given by the Emergency Powers (Defence) Act 1939 and supplemented by the Defence

(Finance) Regulations of 25 August 1939 and the Amendment Order of 23 November 1939. These were superseded by the Exchange Control Act 1947. Even then, there were formal distinctions between different types of foreign-held sterling accounts: Evitt[4] lists eight types of restricted sterling accounts at the end of 1940.

## Exchange control under a bilateral system

Between 1947 and 1954 tough exchange controls were imposed in the UK, although transactions within the sterling area were (perhaps surprisingly) free, and controls did apply both to resident and non-resident holders of sterling. External transactions were via bilateral agreements made by the United Kingdom with other countries, including those in continental Europe, which also retained strict exchange controls and settlements were made bilaterally.

Some bilateral agreements provided for 'soft' settlement in sterling. There were, apart from the sterling area, 'American account' and 'transferable account' countries, supplemented by a number of 'bilateral' arrangements and a number of 'unclassified' countries. 'Convertible currencies' meant in practice the US dollar, which was fixed to gold and free of exchange control restrictions. However some Swiss agreements, constituting a 'super hard settlement area', required settlements in gold. Apart from Switzerland, the 'dollar area' effectively comprised the United States, Canada and a few Latin American countries.

## The end of the bilateral phase

On 22 March 1954 the UK abolished bilateral arrangements. Exchange control continued for UK and other sterling area residents, but the separate 'investment currency' market, which traded at a premium, the 'dollar premium', was introduced to facilitate outward investment. 'Transferable account' status was extended to foreign holders of sterling in countries outside the dollar area,[5] so that from their point of view there were then two types of sterling, convertible 'American account' sterling and transferable account sterling which was *de facto* freely exchangeable at a discount which soon became fairly modest. These were variously known as 'blocked', 'switch' or 'security' sterling, and were frequently confused, even by bankers and traders, with 'investment currency' used for outward investment. This also gave rise to some interesting arbitrage opportunities such as the 'Kuwait gap'.

On 24 February 1955, Chancellor Butler announced that he had authorised the Bank of England to use wider discretion in carrying out exchange policy and managing reserves. On 29 December 1958 non-resident sterling became fully convertible: thereafter exchange controls applied only to residents.

## UK exchange controls in a multilateral world

Exchange control then took the general form it was to retain until 1979, with very flexible administration designed to 'protect the reserves', while interfering as little as possible with business. Specifically, the Bank of England did all it could to help the City of London to remain an efficient international financial centre. Although the Exchange Control Act 1947 was very widely drawn, and effectively prohibited payments of any kind by UK residents to non-residents without Bank of England consent, general consents, and known practices, permitted a wide range of transactions. Normal commercial transactions, imports and exports, were effectively free, but foreign currency for travellers was severely rationed. The most interesting aspects concerned foreign investment.

### *Outward portfolio investment: the 'dollar premium'*

During this period United Kingdom residents could buy and sell foreign currency securities quoted on a stock exchange without specific exchange control consent via the investment currency market. This derived in theory from a pool of securities held before the war by resident holders of non-sterling securities. Residents wishing to buy foreign securities bought currency from this market at a premium which varied with supply and demand. This 'dollar premium' was expressed as a percentage over the rate of exchange in the official market, and applied equally to securities denominated in marks, pesetas, or any other non-sterling currency. (Australian and other currencies called 'dollars' were *sterling area* currencies to which the premium did not, prior to June 1972, apply.)

### *Direct investment*

The investment currency market initially applied only to portfolio investment. UK companies wishing to invest abroad had to persuade the Bank of England of the long-term benefit to the economy but, having obtained specific consent could then buy foreign exchange at the official rate.

### *Inward investment*

For practical purposes there were no restrictions on investment by non-residents of the United Kingdom. Provided that the original investment had been made in a non-sterling currency, dividends and capital proceeds (including gains) could be freely remitted. UK companies controlled by non-residents did need specific permission (on criteria which changed several times) to borrow sterling, on the principle that if foreigners want to invest in the United Kingdom, they should bring their own money rather than draw on local sources of finance.

### Changes in the operation of the investment currency market

Originally, the seller of foreign currency securities obtained the full amount of the premium on the proceeds. From 7 April 1965 the seller could only obtain the premium on 75 per cent of the sales proceeds: the rest had to be sold for official exchange. This '25 per cent surrender' requirement resulted in a bleeding off from the investment currency pool for the benefit of the official reserves. It was also, in economic terms, a 'tax' (disguised as an exchange control) on switching securities, and as such can be compared with the US 'interest equalisation tax' (which did so much to drive the international bond market to London), which was 'an exchange control disguised as a tax'.[6]

In May 1966 the rules were tightened, and for a time even direct investment transactions had to be financed through the investment currency market. This, coupled with the quarter surrender requirement, pushed the market cost for the premium to over 50 per cent. The Bank of England then used considerable ingenuity to devise procedures to protect the reserves while leaving business with the maximum flexibility to carry out its overseas operations.

Specifically, companies were encouraged to borrow foreign currency to finance their investments. The investing company could pay interest, but profits had to be remitted at the official (non-premium) exchange rate. The loan had to be for a minimum period of five years, and early repayment had to be financed through the investment currency market. At the end of five years the borrowing could be repaid at the official rate, provided that the total repatriated foreign earning returns of capital and extra export receipts equalled or exceeded the repayment plus interest.

## The 1972 break-up of the sterling area

Until 1972, transactions within the sterling area were exempt from exchange control restrictions, although the *legal* position was that the Exchange Control Act 1947 applied only to the United Kingdom. Other sterling area countries had comparable legislation designed, not always successfully, to ensure that the funds of residents of one sterling area country could not bypass their own exchange control regulations by using a back door through another.

When the pound was floated in June 1972, restrictions were imposed on transfers with the rest of the sterling area. There was power to do this under the Exchange Control Acts, with the important exception that the Channel Islands and the Isle of Man were defined to constitute *part of the United Kingdom* for exchange control purposes (although not for tax and many other purposes). Agreement was reached on an exchange control union with the Republic of Ireland, and in January 1973 Gibraltar was readmitted to the 'inner sterling area'.

When exchange control restrictions were imposed on transactions with the outer sterling area there was in effect a windfall gain to holders of Australian, South African and other securities. It was also provided that the 25 per cent surrender rule would *not* apply to transactions in portfolio shares of those countries. Direct investment in the former sterling area territories required Bank of England consent, but where consent was given the investment could be financed at the 'official' rather than the 'investment currency' rate of exchange.

## United States restrictions on capital movements

The United States had no exchange controls as such, but for a time restricted outward capital movements by two separate measures, the 'interest equalisation tax' which applied to portfolio investments, and the 'guidelines program' on direct investments by US corporations. The combined efforts of these two measures produced a result broadly similar to that of the UK exchange control legislation, but were less flexible and contributed substantially to the development of the Eurodollar and the Eurobond markets in London.

### Interest equalisation tax

The interest equalisation tax was introduced on 19 July 1963, not so much to stem an outflow of capital but to isolate the structure of American interest rates from those ruling in the rest of the world. It was cheaper for an international company or government to borrow in the United States than in Europe, potentially imposing a credit squeeze on US industry. The tax was technically an 'excise duty', and was originally introduced at a rate of 15 per cent for bonds having a life exceeding 28½ years and for stocks and shares (the rate on shorter bonds was calculated effectively to produce a 1 per cent differential in interest rates). The rate peaked at 22.5 per cent in 1967.

Interest equalisation tax was indeed an effective and precise measure as applied to bonds, keeping non-US borrowers out of the US bond market – but it led to the development of the parallel Eurobond market. It was much less flexible in the case of shares. The US investor wishing to purchase non-US shares had to contemplate writing off the tax as an irrecoverable cost of purchase: unlike the British dollar premium, there was no effective machinery for recovering the tax on sale or of switching without a penalty. Although the tax was not payable when a foreign security was bought from another US investor, very few securities had a premium market for shares with prior US ownership. The tax was not only clumsy but ineffective. For the first four years of its operation, the 'exemption for prior US ownership' was applied without any attempt to ensure that either the securities that had been held prior to 1963 or that tax had been paid, on the original purchase by the vendors! Dishonest operators bought blocks of British and European stocks, forged certificates of American ownership, and unloaded the stock through the market at a premium. Frauds of this nature were perpetrated on a huge scale until checked on 31 July 1967.

### Restraint on direct investment

The interest equalisation tax was mainly designed to prevent non-American companies tapping the US capital market. The 'voluntary guidelines program' was introduced on 10 February 1965 to limit capital investment by US corporations, and was made compulsory in 1968.

In contrast to the IET, the programme was sophisticated and flexible right from the start, reflecting the exceptional importance of direct investment outflows from the United States. The 1965 programme was the first to set down specific guidelines. Cooperating companies were asked to ensure that net direct investment overseas should be limited during the two-year period 1965–6 to 90 per cent of the allowed actually invested during the three-year period 1962–4. This approach contrasts with the case-by-case application procedure then used by the Bank of England. An American company was simply limited as to the amount it could invest abroad.

# Part VIII

# Money and the collapse of communism

Some monetary disunions

# 42 The collapse of the Soviet Union

## General introduction

The Soviet Union was dissolved at New Year 1992 and the fifteen component republics, the largest being Russia, became independent states. Under the leadership of Boris Yeltsin, democratically elected President of Russia, twelve of them (excluding the Baltic states), formed themselves into the Commonwealth of Independent States (CIS). At first, they all continued to use the Russian rouble as their currency, constituting what was, at the time, the largest monetary union between a group of states otherwise pursuing independent economic policies. Within two years the 'monetary union' collapsed, under what Marx might well have called its own internal contradictions. This introductory chapter describes the political drama from 1985, and although some of the relevant reforms date back to 1987, Russia and the other successor states came into being as essentially command economies with a monolithic banking system, price controls, a substantial element of barter and virtually no proper role for money.

Russia itself began an ambitious programme of reform, but the problems proved too great for a quick fix. Furthermore, for the first two years twelve diverse and newly independent economies were attempting to use a single currency – with twelve central banks having (some) power to create money. Chapter 43 discusses the end of this doomed monetary union, followed by the very diverse subsequent monetary histories of Russia and the CIS states (Chapter 44) and the very different experience of the three Baltic States, which opted out of the CIS, quickly stabilised their currencies, and joined the fast track for EU membership (Chapter 45).

## The Soviet Union from 1985 to 1991[1]

Mikhail Gorbachev became General Secretary of the Communist Party and leader of the Soviet Union on the death of Chernenko in March 1985, and introduced the policies of *glasnost* (political reform) and *perestroika* (economic reform). The former ensured the perhaps already inevitable collapse of communism: the latter was (arguably) a failure. The concepts of monetary reform had by then already been discussed in reformist circles.[2]

1989 was the year of the Velvet Revolution, when communism collapsed in Central Europe. The Polish communist government, forced to concede elections in June, was soundly defeated by Solidarity. Hungary, Bulgaria and Czechoslovakia soon followed, the Berlin Wall came down in November, and December saw the dramatic overthrow of Ceaucescu, the Romanian dictator. Gorbachev notably did not attempt to intervene in any of these countries, but remained determined to reform, rather than destroy, the Communist Party and, significantly, to preserve the Soviet Union as an entity. On 27 February 1990 Gorbachev persuaded the Supreme Soviet of the USSR to approve a system of multi-party politics, and this was ratified by the Congress of People's Deputies on 14 April.

Boris Yeltsin, a reformer, was elected Chairman of the Russian Supreme Soviet in March 1990, and found that he had a better chance of building a power base in Russia than in the Soviet Union as a whole. His opponents reacted by forming a specifically Russian (rather than Soviet) Communist party, and the resulting disputes at first strengthened the hand of Gorbachev. Meanwhile, though, support for the Soviet Union was declining in other republics, and in June 1990 Uzbekistan declared itself an independent sovereign state. Boris Yeltsin took the opportunity to take a similar initiative on behalf of Russia: 'By September when even obedient Turkmenistan declared its sovereignty, this had become the general trend. Everywhere the republican leaderships were calling for democracy and national self-determination.'[3] In most cases, though, there was not so much democracy as an attempt by Communist Party elites to retain power.

In the summer of 1990 a group headed by Shatalin and Yavlinsky produced the '500 Days' report, which 'would possibly have led Russia, or even the Soviet Union, into a proper economic reform'[4] and created the basis for a possible alliance between Gorbachev and Yeltsin. Gorbachev originally supported it but gave way to pressure to adopt a compromise. 'This was like mating a rabbit with a donkey ... a predictably unworkable mixture of radical language and conservative ideas.'[5]

In January 1991 Valentin Pavlov, the last prime minister of the Soviet Union, had confiscated all 50 and 100 rouble notes, which actually did little to reduce total money supply (although it may have achieved other ends), and in April demanded a state of emergency, giving him a chance to increase controlled prices by 65 per cent. This damaged any remaining confidence in the Soviet currency.

Gorbachev, sticking to his 'Soviet' strategy, fought shy of the necessary economic reforms, but in April said that he would work with Yeltsin and began talks with Republican leaders aimed at establishing a Union treaty governing their relations with the Soviet Union. Gorbachev seemed to have the upper hand, until on 12 June 1991 Boris Yeltsin was elected President of Russia with a substantial majority. One of his first acts was to ban Communist Party organisations from roles in administrative and economic organisations in Russia. This did not please Gorbachev, who had been blamed for the economic collapse, and for Pavlov's action in raising the prices of food products in the shops. Although he remained popular abroad, his standing at home was declining and many of his colleagues thought that the problem was too much, rather than too little, reform.

The anti-reformers gathered together in a State Committee for the Emergency Situation but Gorbachev, leaving Yeltsin effectively in charge, went off with his family to his dacha, where he was visited by members of the State Committee, seeking to involve him in their plans. Having failed in this they effectively imprisoned him in his dacha while they planned television broadcasts denouncing the proposed Union treaty. Although the State Committee had access to the main Soviet levers of power, the *coup d'état* failed, partly or perhaps mainly because of Yeltsin's bravery and initiative in famously standing on a tank and announcing his defiance.

The next day, 22 August, Gorbachev returned to Moscow to find that the whole balance of power had changed. Outside Russia, several other republics had refused to be drawn into the activities of the State Committee, while Estonia, Latvia and Lithuania took the opportunity successfully to appeal to the Western world to recognise them as independent states. Gaidar (1999, 64) asked whether 'the swift and total collapse of the Communist Party' (and other agents of government) might not 'simply clear the road for chaos, anarchy, terrible economic ruin and a new dictatorship?'.

Yeltsin was now plainly in charge in Russia, while Gorbachev's Soviet Union had little influence either on Russia or on the other republics. Trying to save the situation, Gorbachev proposed a 'Union of Sovereign States', but others refused to cooperate, and on 1 December Ukraine voted for independence. In October Yeltsin announced an economic programme based on free markets, and in early November banned the Soviet Communist party from Russia, stipulated that Russian ministers had precedence over Soviet ministers, and said he would veto any Soviet appointments he disliked. He also announced a cabinet of reformers, including Yegor Gaidar as finance minister and a deputy prime minister.

The Commonwealth of Independent States (CIS) was formed at a meeting between Belarus, Russia and Ukraine on 8 December 1991. On 21 December it was extended to include all the other republics, excluding the Baltics (Latvia, Lithuania and Estonia) and Georgia, although the latter acceded in 1993.

This was virtually the end for Gorbachev, who had lost his struggle to maintain the Soviet Union intact. On 25 December he appeared on television to announce his retirement and to say that the Union of Soviet Socialist Republics would be abolished at midnight on New Year's Eve! So easily did a formerly much-feared communist super-power meet its end.

On 31 March 1992 all republics within Russia, except Chechnya and Tatarstan, signed a treaty of Federation, and on 1 April a Western aid package of $24 billion, including a $6 billion stabilisation, fund was announced. Yegor Gaidar was appointed acting Prime Minister on 15 June 1992.

# 43 The end of the rouble zone

## Introduction

Although the Soviet Union ceased to exist at New Year 1992, all the republics forming the Commonwealth of Independent States continued to use the Russian rouble. Indeed, in early 1992, 'the ruble was atop the currency hit parade; no other currency served as sole legal tender across so many national borders'.[1] The collapse of a political union had inadvertently created a large and complex monetary union, but for many reasons, including the inherited monobank system and the distinction between cash currency and inter-enterprise credits, this could not last and by 1994 Tajikistan was alone in continuing to use the Russian rouble. Meanwhile Russia 'effectively had no central bank' and indeed 'nothing at all, except the name', while barter had largely replaced money.[2] (Barter is a key factor in Russian economic events: although outside the scope of this book there is an extensive literature, including Shleifer and Treisman,[3] who give a comprehensive overview within a broader economic context.)

## Policy issues

An effectively unified and centrally governed nation state had split up into twelve independent sovereign states (losing three others on the way) eager to pursue their own economic policies, with the largest of them, Russia, dedicated to dismantling central planning, making a complete break with the Soviet system and instituting free market reforms. The institutional framework for a currency union simply did not exist, although during the next two years some players persisted in a doomed attempt to preserve one. A monetary union can have only one single authority with the right to create money: independent states would have to agree to sacrifice a significant part of their newly won sovereignty.

While politicians worried about this, economists had to ask two more fundamental questions: 'is the CIS an optimum currency area?', and if so, 'what institutions would be needed to make it work?'. It is rare and difficult for a true monetary union to exist successfully without a political union, but in this case the break-up of the latter had left the former isolated. Should (and could) the mechanisms for a formal rouble zone be created, or should the various republics pursue independent monetary policies?

The US and the IMF originally supported a rouble zone, although the new European Bank for Reconstruction and Development opposed. Initially each republic took over responsibility for its own financial system, and set up a central bank, based on the local office of what had been Gosbank, but the Central Bank of Russia remained the monetary authority for the whole area, the sole source of banknotes and the clearing house for the area. The other central banks could (and did) create non-cash credit, an important component of the money supply under the Soviet monobank system, which distinguished between cash money used by consumers and credit used to settle accounts between enterprises. When Russia began to create a market economy there was a strong incentive to delay payments and speed up receipts, and other republics would in any case have created extra credit of this type just to keep trade going. There was a 'free rider' problem: the growing level of credit created in other republics and used to buy Russian goods benefited the republic creating the credit, but the resulting inflation was 'exported' to its neighbours. Russia was trying to impose a tight money policy, but no longer had control of its own broad money supply, while the other republics found that cash roubles were being sucked away from them.

Gaidar and his friends had, even in the Soviet days, been looking ahead to see how a market economy could be created, and in his book he explains how the new government was faced with two 'fundamental and quite unpleasant' monetary problems. There was a budget deficit of about 30 per cent of GNP financed by printing money, but with strictly controlled prices concealing inflation and creating a 'monetary over-hang' of the type suffered in postwar Western Europe. The Gaidar group had tried to estimate its size: if liberalisation had been implemented in 1990, prices would have had to rise by about 60 per cent, but after Pavlov's botched 'reform' of January 1991 confidence fell, and between 200 per cent and 250 per cent would have been needed. The main problem, said Gaidar, was finding a politician 'who can get up the political courage to tell the truth, that the state had squandered the people's savings', and had balanced its books by 'seigniorage', 'the simplest and most effective of all existing taxes', although it often leads to the catastrophe of hyper-inflation.[4] Unfortunately, Russia could not simply declare 'unilateral independence' for its money without destroying the complex network of economic relationships between the republics, and during the next two years attempts continued to preserve a single currency.

## The Soviet payments system

The Soviet financial system and payments mechanism were quite unlike anything known in the West, and Russia's attempts to liberalise prices affected all the republics, which had typically specialised in producing goods or even components ('back axles for tractors') for the whole Soviet Union, and for outside demand. Any adjustment to this pattern would have caused economic chaos.

> Under socialism, money was passive. A payment was essentially a recording indicating the fulfilment of a plan target. If payments were not made, the state paid up one way or the other. A socialist enterprise did not bother to confirm whether it had been paid, and the mechanisms for checking payments were in any case inadequate.[5]

Under the Soviet regime Gosbank had fulfilled almost all banking functions, such as they were, but in 1987 further specialised (but still state-owned) banks were set up, and in 1988 cooperative banks were permitted. By 1991 there were about 400 of these, and in December that year Gosbank was wound up, and its central banking functions transferred to the Central Bank of Russia[6] which, at first, had limited functions. Generally, banking remained very primitive.

## Price liberalisation in Russia

After the break-up of the Soviet Union, Russia immediately attempted a dash for economic freedom, but the problems were too great for this to work. Prices were freed on 2 January 1992 and immediately rose by over 200 per cent; wages, though, rose by only 50 per cent. Foreign exchange markets were freed for the purchase of imports but not for capital transactions. In April 1992 interest rates were increased, and there was another once-and-for-all increase of 350 per cent in consumer prices, but after this the inflation rate fell from 40 per cent per month in February to 9 per cent (per *month*). After the sharp January rise inflation for the other eleven months was said to have fallen to 'only' 18 per cent, but this was enough for prices to rise sixfold during the period. In August the exchange rate actually strengthened, and there was talk of pegging the exchange rate at 80 to the dollar. These gains proved unsustainable: 'Gaidar ... had no control over direct off-budget CBR credits ... or CBR loans to so-called commercial banks. In the end, he failed to control the budget deficit as well.'[7]

Gaidar has said that he would have preferred to follow the Polish timetable, with six months of price liberalisation preceding the stabilisation measures, which in the Russian context would have meant unfreezing prices at the beginning of January 1992 followed by changes in the tax system to balance the budget, and then waiting until June to introduce a specific Russian currency; but instead they had to fall back on 'the most risky and controversial' method of launching reform, converting repressed inflation to open inflation liberalising prices, reducing subsidies and introducing a 28 per cent value added tax in place of 'the random and disorganised sales tax'.[8]

Gaidar resigned in December 1992 (he was reappointed deputy Prime Minister on 18 September 1993 but resigned again on 16 January 1994) and the new government of Victor Chernomyrdin, the former chief of Gazprom, 'in its first ten days issued an enormous amount of cheap credits and drastically increased the budget deficit'.[9] Boris Federov was appointed deputy Prime Minister and Finance Minister: he proposed price controls, and had to be dissuaded by Sergei Vasiliev and Andrei Illarionov.

Granville (2001, 98ff) gives a good account of the relationship between monetary and fiscal policy during this period, and points out that there were substantial increases in credits to the other republics. In each of these the local branch of Gosbank had become the national central bank, but without the power to print cash roubles. However they could, on the unusual Soviet type system, create non-cash money, while as a practical matter the Central Bank of Russia continued to provide both cash and non-cash liquidity to Russia's 'near abroad' neighbours.

## Events in other republics

What of the other republics? Table 43.1 shows the general pattern of consumer price inflation (and Table 43.2 restates these as price indices), and although the figures need treating with some caution, they show a significant pattern. In 1990 the reported rate in all republics (still within the highly controlled Soviet system) ranged from 3 per cent to 10 per cent, with 5 per cent for Russia. In 1991, as the economy began to free up, the rate rose sharply to 92.6 per cent in Russia, while the rate as reported in the other republics ranged between 82 per cent in Uzbekistan to 103 per cent in Tajikistan. (Armenia was outside this range at 175 per cent, having taken early steps to liberalise prices in 1991.) Such differences were to be expected in the context of an inflexible economy which is starting to loosen up. Under the Soviet system, relative prices, and inter-regional purchasing power, were way out of line with market realities, and differential inflation was actually to be expected. Substantial adjustments in real earnings would have been needed, and in the absence of floating exchange rates, high inflation made it easier to achieve this (this point is discussed in Chapter 46 in the rather different context of Estonia).

So far so good, but in 1992, the first year of independence (and Gaidar's liberalisation initiatives), there was quite a different picture. Inflation rates ranged from 528 per cent to 1,500 per cent in that year, and from 837 per cent to over 10,000 per cent in 1993. Clearly, 'fixed exchange rates' were unsustainable, but what policy should be pursued? Even if the various republics could agree, what exchange rate policy should the CIS follow? Should there be the multiple arbitrary rates as used under the communist system, or some form of unified floating rate?

Yegor Gaidar and his allies were concerned to 'nationalise' the Russian rouble, but feared that practical preparation for monetary reform would take at least nine months, and it became clear that the Russian rouble would have to follow a different course from the currencies of other CIS states. These could have retained the rouble if they wished, and could have negotiated their share of seigniorage, provided they submitted to a single Russian monetary authority.

*Table 43.1*    Inflation rates during the early stage of transition (%)

|  | 1990 | 1991 | 1992 | 1993 | 1994 | 1995 |
|---|---|---|---|---|---|---|
| Russia | 5.0 | 92.6 | 1354.0 | 840.0 | 204.4 | 128.6 |
| Armenia | 10.3 | 175.0 | 729.0 | 10896.0 | 1884.5 | 31.9 |
| Azerbaijan | 7.8 | 87.3 | 1350.0 | 1294.0 | 1788.0 | 85.0 |
| Belarus | 4.5 | 83.5 | 969.0 | 1996.0 | 1959.9 | 244.0 |
| Georgia | 4.8 | 81.1 | 1500.0 | 7487.9 | 6473.9 | 57.4 |
| Kazakhstan | 4.2 | 90.9 | 1513.0 | 2169.0 | 1158.3 | 60.4 |
| Kyrgyzstan | 3.0 | 85.0 | 855.0 | 1363.0 | 95.7 | 32.3 |
| Moldova | 4.0 | 98.0 | 1276.0 | 837.0 | 116.1 | 23.8 |
| Tajikistan | 4.0 | 103.0 | 1156.0 | 7343.7 | 1.1 | 2133.3 |
| Turkmenistan | 4.6 | 102.0 | 4.9 | 9750.0 | 1327.9 | 1261.6 |
| Ukraine | 4.2 | 91.2 | 1310.0 | 10155.0 | 401.0 | 181.7 |
| Uzbekistan | 3.1 | 82.0 | 528.0 | 885.0 | 1281.4 | 116.9 |
| Unweighted average | 5.0 | 98.1 | 1017.4 | 4925.1 | 1498.9 | 384.4 |

*Table 43.2*    Price indices (calculated from Table 43.1): 1989= 1

|  | 1990 | 1991 | 1992 | 1993 | 1994 | 1995 |
|---|---|---|---|---|---|---|
| Russia | 1.05 | 2.02 | 29 | 276 | 841 | 1,923 |
| Armenia | 1.10 | 3.03 | 25 | 2,765 | 54,872 | 72,376 |
| Azerbaijan | 1.08 | 2.02 | 29 | 408 | 7,705 | 14,255 |
| Belarus | 1.05 | 1.92 | 20 | 430 | 8,850 | 30,446 |
| Georgia | 1.05 | 1.90 | 30 | 2,304 | 151,476 | 238,424 |
| Kazakhstan | 1.04 | 1.99 | 32 | 728 | 9,161 | 14,694 |
| Kyrgyzstan | 1.03 | 1.91 | 18 | 266 | 521 | 689 |
| Moldova | 1.04 | 2.06 | 28 | 266 | 574 | 710 |
| Tajikistan | 1.04 | 2.11 | 27 | 1,974 | 1,996 | 44,566 |
| Turkmenistan | 1.05 | 2.11 | 2 | 218 | 3,118 | 42,458 |
| Ukraine | 1.04 | 1.99 | 28 | 2,881 | 14,433 | 40,657 |
| Uzbekistan | 1.03 | 1.88 | 12 | 116 | 1,603 | 3,478 |
| Unweighted average | 1.05 | 2.08 | 23 | 1,167 | 18,665 | 90,412 |

## The reform of inter-republic payments

From January 1992 the Central Bank of Russia provided cash roubles to the central banks of other republics only through bilateral 'correspondent accounts', but there was no mechanism for dealing with overdrawn accounts. In any case payments were subject to long and variable delays, and there were inevitable free rider problems, and in July 1992 the payments system was reformed by introducing the concept of 'correspondent accounts' in an attempt to produce more effective controls and increase monetary discipline. This was effectively a bilateral system somewhat on the lines of immediate postwar Europe, and once a republic's credit line was reached no further transfers would be made. 'The individual countries were restricted in their ability to export inflation, gain access to additional cash, and collect seigniorage within the ruble zone.' In August, though, this system was relaxed, but the restrictions on trade payments were tightened up, the CBR generally requiring advance payment.[10]

Another key step was taken in July 1992, when the first 'Russian' banknotes were issued, but only in Russia itself. The old Soviet ones, with a portrait of Lenin, continued to be issued to the other republics. This was to pave the way for a monetary reform of a year later designed to ensure the end of the rouble zone.

Meanwhile the central bank presidents, meeting in Bishkek in May 1992, set up an Interbank Coordinating Council and discussed an interstate bank for clearing payments. On 9 October six republics signed the Bishkek Agreement, recognising the rouble as legal tender and delegating the right to print money to the CBR. This was approved in January 1993, but before it could be ratified the rouble zone collapsed. A further meeting in October 1992 discussed trade and payment arrangements, but these were opposed by the CBR as they would have eliminated its control over the destination of cash.[11]

The proposed new arrangements would have permitted every central bank to issue roubles without any control. Aslund is not polite to the IMF, nor to Michael Emerson, then European Union Ambassador to Moscow, whom he accuses, unfairly, of drawing the wrong parallels with European Monetary Union. He suggests that some Western specialists had supported the idea of independent national currencies, perhaps with a multinational clearing along the lines of the European Payments Union of 1950–8. This was not favoured in the CIS, partly because of their experience with the Council for Mutual Economic Assistance.

> The few local supporters of a payments union appear to have acted for tactical reasons. They were interested above all in maintaining the ruble zone, and talks about a payments union fudged the monetary issue and delayed the separation of currencies.[12]

Interestingly, a 2001 article in *Russian Economic Trends*[13] proposed just such a multilateral payments union, on the model of the EPU and with the euro as the accounting currency.

## Early action by other republics

Some of the other republics began to break away from the rouble zone without waiting for Russia to act. Leaving aside the Baltic states, Georgia was the first to declare independence in April 1991, but continued to use the rouble until April 1993, when supplies of cash from the CBR became erratic and the Georgian National Bank introduced a coupon, the menati, at par with the rouble. Azerbaijan had been the first of the republics actually to introduce a supplementary currency in August 1992, and the manat became the main currency in September 1993. Moldova introduced a national coupon in July 1992 (replaced by the leu in November 1993), in March 1993 Kyrgyzstan was reported to be planning its own currency pending the collapse of the rouble zone and actually introduced the som in May 1993 before the Russian action. The same month Kurdistan introduced a new currency helped by an IMF stabilisation package of $62 million, without warning the other republics. Once the banknotes had been printed a political decison to have a national currency could be implemented within a week. This compares with the more than three years that EU citizens had to wait for the practical advantages of monetary union.

## The monetary reform of July 1993[14]

The final collapse of the rouble zone followed the action of the Central Bank of Russia, which, on 24 July 1993, without warning the other members of the currency area, withdrew from circulation all banknotes issued between 1961 and 1992, permitting only a limited exchange into the new notes which had been issued (but only in Russia) the previous year. This forced the hand of the other republics,[15] and was surely a deliberate move to break up the rouble zone.

Belarus, Kazakhstan and Uzbekistan said they would remain in the rouble zone, but would not phase out the notes quite as quickly. Armenia complained that six months notice should have been given: Azerbaijan, Georgia and Moldova brought forward their own reforms.

> When rumours spread that the Russian central bank's employees had been asked to work on Saturday July 17th even individuals in Moscow knew enough to trade old roubles for hard currency.[16]

In September 1993 six of the states signed a treaty on economic union based on monetary union, but it soon broke down over details.[17]

The remaining republics now had to react, Armenia introducing the dram in November 22 1993, the currency only becoming the sole legal tender four months later. The governments of Kazakhstan, Turkmenistan and Uzbekistan were offered the choice of submitting to more stringent control by the Central Bank of Russia or of introducing their own currency. Kazakhstan at first wished to arrange to continue with the Russian rouble, but terms were unacceptable, and the tenge was introduced on 12 November 1993. Uzbekistan adopted a temporary coupon currency, the 'sum', in November 1993 and Turkmenistan introduced the manat on 1 November 1993, with an initial rate of TMM2 = $1.

# 44 The twelve CIS countries following monetary disunion

## General introduction

By the end of 1993 the disunion was effectively complete: each of the CIS countries had its own currency. Table 44.1 gives the exchange rate history as an index number, and the very wide discrepancies are brought home in Table 44.2, which gives the rates against the rouble. These official figures from the IMF are, in the early years at least, distorted by exchange controls (and the black markets these create), but the general pattern is clear and broadly consistent with other sources. Table 44.3, giving price indices, needs to be treated with rather more caution, covering a period of transition from administered to market prices. There were at first substantial one-off adjustments to relative as well as absolute prices: the currencies of a couple of republics held their value better than the Russian rouble, while others fell more dramatically.

## Russia

Once Russia was free of the problems caused by sharing a currency with the 'near abroad', the rouble enjoyed a brief period of stability, but on 'Black Tuesday', 11 October 1994, it crashed by 30 per cent, recovering much of the loss the next day. Yeltsin sacked Gerashchenko as Governor of the Central Bank (he was to bounce back later, keeping the post until early 2002) together with the two key economic ministers, Shokhin and Dubinin. Anatoly Chubais became economic deputy Prime Minister, and Tatyana Paramonova was appointed acting Governor of the Central Bank. There was a real problem of flight of capital.

Russia was not without advice on what to do. The IMF was proposing a 'stabilisation fund' for the rouble, but many of us felt that this would be throwing good money after bad (and this was before the disastrous attempts to defend the EMS against speculative attacks). Geoffrey Wood and I published an article in *Central Banking*[1] suggesting the use of US dollar bills as the *de facto* currency of Russia, and showing how this could be combined with a very cost-effective form of aid. Hanke *et al.*[2] persuasively advocated a

*Table 44.1*  Exchange rates index against US dollar (year end)

|  | 1993 | 1994 | 1995 | 1996 | 1997 | 1998 | 1999 | 2000 | 2001 |
|---|---|---|---|---|---|---|---|---|---|
| Russia | 100.00 | 33.33 | 26.09 | 21.43 | 20.00 | 5.80 | 4.48 | 4.26 | 4.01 |
| Armenia | 100.00 | 18.50 | 18.66 | 17.24 | 15.15 | 14.37 | 14.32 | 13.58 | 13.29 |
| Azerbaijan | 100.00 | 5.91 | 5.77 | 6.25 | 6.58 | 6.58 | 5.85 | 5.61 | 5.39 |
| Belarus | 100.00 | 6.58 | 6.07 | 4.50 | 2.27 | 0.65 | 0.22 | 0.06 | 0.05 |
| Georgia | 100.00 | 7.69 | 8.33 | 7.69 | 7.69 | 5.88 | 5.26 | – | 4.78 |
| Kazakhstan | 100.00 | 11.60 | 9.84 | 8.54 | 8.30 | 7.50 | 4.56 | 4.33 | 4.24 |
| Kyrgyzstan | 100.00 | 74.77 | 71.43 | 47.90 | 45.98 | 27.21 | 17.58 | 16.53 | 16.71 |
| Moldova | 100.00 | 83.72 | 80.00 | 76.60 | 76.60 | 43.37 | 31.03 | 29.03 | 27.93 |
| Tajikistan | 100.00 | 35.21 | 4.25 | 3.81 | 1.67 | 1.28 | 0.87 | 0.57 | – |
| Turkmenistan | 100.00 | 40.00 | 1.23 | 0.59 | 0.57 | 0.37 | 0.37 | 0.36 | – |
| Ukraine | 100.00 | 24.04 | 13.97 | 13.23 | 13.16 | 7.29 | 4.79 | 4.60 | 4.74 |
| Uzbekistan | 100.00 | 4.64 | 3.31 | 1.98 | 1.20 | 0.73 | 0.37 | 0.21 | 0.19 |

*Table 44.2*  Exchange rates index against Russian rouble (year end)

|  | 1993 | 1994 | 1995 | 1996 | 1997 | 1998 | 1999 | 2000 | 2001 |
|---|---|---|---|---|---|---|---|---|---|
| Armenia | 100.00 | 55.49 | 71.52 | 80.44 | 75.76 | 247.84 | 319.78 | 319.18 | 331.65 |
| Azerbaijan | 100.00 | 17.74 | 22.10 | 29.15 | 32.92 | 113.52 | 130.59 | 131.79 | 134.60 |
| Belarus | 100.00 | 19.75 | 23.27 | 21.02 | 11.37 | 11.25 | 4.87 | 1.39 | 1.13 |
| Georgia | 100.00 | 23.08 | 31.94 | 35.90 | 38.46 | 101.47 | 117.54 | – | 119.40 |
| Kazakhstan | 100.00 | 34.81 | 37.73 | 39.84 | 41.50 | 129.38 | 101.74 | 101.82 | 105.76 |
| Kyrgyzstan | 100.00 | 224.30 | 273.81 | 223.55 | 229.89 | 469.39 | 392.67 | 388.43 | 416.90 |
| Moldova | 100.00 | 251.16 | 306.67 | 357.45 | 382.98 | 748.19 | 693.10 | 682.26 | 696.93 |
| Tajikistan | 100.00 | 105.63 | 16.30 | 17.78 | 8.36 | 22.07 | 19.44 | 13.35 | – |
| Turkmenistan | 100.00 | 120.00 | 4.71 | 2.73 | 2.87 | 6.35 | 8.17 | 8.54 | – |
| Ukraine | 100.00 | 72.12 | 53.54 | 61.73 | 65.79 | 125.73 | 106.96 | 108.00 | 118.38 |
| Uzbekistan | 100.00 | 13.93 | 12.68 | 9.23 | 5.99 | 12.55 | 8.33 | 4.84 | 4.76 |

*Table 44.3* Price indices, CIS countries

| | 1993 | 1994 | 1995 | 1996 | 1997 | 1998 | 1999 | 2000 | 2001 |
|---|---|---|---|---|---|---|---|---|---|
| | | | | | | Year end | | | |
| Russia | 100 | 304 | 696 | 848 | 940 | 1,734 | 2,372 | 2,849 | 3,348 |
| Armenia | 100 | 1,985 | 2,618 | 2,759 | 3,373 | 3,329 | 3,399 | 3,413 | 3,501 |
| Azerbaijan | 100 | 1,888 | 3,493 | 3,720 | 3,735 | 3,451 | 3,434 | 3,509 | 3,586 |
| Belarus | 100 | 2,060 | 7,086 | 9,871 | 16,129 | 45,435 | 159,615 | 331,200 | 464,674 |
| Georgia | 100 | 6,574 | 10,347 | 11,765 | 12,624 | 13,533 | 15,008 | 16,058 | 16,941 |
| Kazakhstan | 100 | 1,258 | 2,018 | 2,596 | 2,886 | 2,941 | 3,465 | 3,797 | 4,063 |
| Kyrgyzstan | 100 | 196 | 259 | 349 | 401 | 474 | 664 | 727 | 769 |
| Moldova | 100 | 216 | 268 | 308 | 342 | 404 | 581 | 689 | 751 |
| Tajikistan | 100 | 101 | 2,258 | 3,172 | 8,362 | 8,588 | 11,173 | 17,966 | 20,661 |
| Turkmenistan | 100 | 1,428 | 19,442 | 106,114 | 128,929 | 154,457 | 187,202 | 201,055 | 221,361 |
| Ukraine | 100 | 501 | 1,411 | 1,972 | 2,171 | 2,605 | 3,105 | 3,906 | 4,258 |
| Uzbekistan | 100 | 1,381 | 2,996 | 4,923 | 6,282 | 7,921 | 9,917 | 12,694 | 15,614 |

currency board for Russia, based on a very similar underlying analysis. Auerbach *et al.*[3] use a different analytical approach, while Samantha Carrington[4] envisaged the creation of 'new rubles' which the United States guarantees 'to convert the fixed number of new rubles that are going to be created into US dollars on a one-to-one basis in perpetuity'.[5]

Generally, between 1992 and 1995 there was a sharp fall in the dollar value of the rouble, but a much more substantial rise in domestic prices: the real exchange rate of the rouble actually rose, but this was, arguably, a move towards, rather than away from purchasing power parity.[6]

### *1995–8: deceptive stability*

This period of relative stability began when steps were taken in 1995 to give the CBR more independence and the government began using the issue of GKOs (treasury bills) as the main source of financing its deficit. At first this was successful, and in April 1995 the rouble began to appreciate in nominal as well as real terms, and to deal with this 'competitiveness' problem, the exchange rate policy was changed in July. A preannounced exchange rate band, about 12 per cent wide, was set, initially for three months, and adjusted from time to time to keep the rate constant in real terms.

### *1998: a defining year*

The policy was successful, and at the beginning of January 1998, the rouble 'dropped three noughts', one new rouble being worth 1,000 old roubles, usually a signal that inflation is regarded, by the government, as being under control. The target exchange rate was now set for a three-year forward period, but with a much wider band (15 per cent either side of 6.2 roubles to the US dollar, or a range of 5.25–7.15). Granville says that the attempt by the Central Bank to target both monetary base and the exchange rate, created conflicts.[7]

At first, all continued to go well. The Russian currency held firm within its bands, year on year inflation to July 1998 was 5.6 per cent, there was no major balance of payments problem, and purchasing power parity was not significantly out of line. *Russian Economic Trends* commented, just before the crisis, 'Control of inflation has been one of the few bright spots in Russia's economic and financial performance ... [however] a forced devaluation of the rouble would trigger an immediate renewal of inflation.'[8]

The August 1998 crisis took many people, who were watching the wrong indicators, by surprise. On Monday 17 August Russia, unable to pay its debts, announced a widening of the fluctuation band for the rouble to 6–9.5 new roubles per dollar, a moratorium on foreign currency commercial debt servicing, and a restructuring of domestic debt. Credit rating agencies downgraded all Russian issuers but the markets reacted fairly calmly until the Western press began referring to an 'effective devaluation' of 50 per cent.

This figure was wrong and based on a common arithmetic error: even if there had been an immediate fall to the lower support point (and there was not) it would only have been a devaluation of 33 per cent – the dollar appreciated by 50 per cent against the rouble, but that is not what the press was saying. The real collapse of confidence only came the following week, when there was a technical default on a repayment to HERMES.

How did an apparently stable currency in a country with inflation under control and no obvious balance of payments problem, collapse so quickly? There were serious political problems and chronic difficulties in collecting taxes, while the collapse of the oil price reduced the current account surplus and created a small, but not of itself worrying, deficit in the first half of 1998. The collapse of the Asian Tigers had shaken confidence in emerging markets but although this made the markets more nervous, 'contagion', as such, does not explain the crisis.

The key factor was the extraordinarily high real cost of servicing government debt. By mid-1997 inflation (measured by past rises in price) was down to 17 per cent and the yield on GKOs (treasury bills) had followed the rate down to about 20 per cent (a measure of *future* nominal interest), a real return of about 3 per cent and, so long as the currency was believed to be stable, much higher, even after hedging, in US dollars. Foreign as well as domestic investors were tempted into the market. Perhaps paradoxically, Russian legislation actually inhibited foreign access to the market.[9] From 1996 foreigners were allowed to access the market through 'S' accounts in Russian banks, but our figures showed the procedure gave investors a much lower net (prospective) return than was available to domestic investors. (The latter were mainly banks, who found the operation far more interesting than boring old commercial lending. We suspected at the time that government policy was designed to keep the dodgy banks solvent.) The rules were successively relaxed, as returns rose, and the money flooded in: a study of the returns showed that they were unsustainable and there were all the signs, to those of us who study financial history, of a bubble about to burst.

In mid-1997 the issue price of GKOs (mostly issued for three or six months) gave a *prospective* nominal return of about 20 per cent, a normal enough margin over *historical* inflation rates of 17 per cent, but before this group of issues matured, inflation fell sharply to about 6 per cent, leaving investors with a much more substantial real (corrected for inflation) return – and a corresponding higher cost to government. Treated as a one-off windfall this would not have been too serious, and the anomaly would normally have corrected itself, with interest rates falling in line with inflation rates. In the event, though, nominal interest rates actually *rose* to about 30 per cent (20 per cent real!) by the end of the year. This was followed by an even sharper rise, to over 40 per cent, a sure sign of an imminent default, and on 27 May 1998 a rouble crisis was only averted by raising rates to 150 per cent. So long as the currency remained within its bands (and there was no default), banks and other investors were earning massive dollar returns, and were happily counting present and expected future gains. They would have done better to make the calculation of how many months the Russian government could meet these costs without becoming insolvent. Many, indeed most, market participants failed to recognise a Ponzi trap: the Russian government was in this case victim rather than perpetrator.

The exchange rate fell outside the bands, but any consequent inflation was contained, resulting in an effective devaluation, which, coupled with a helpful rise in the price of oil, led Russia forward into a recovery, only marred by continuing weaknesses in the system of corporate governance.

## Ukraine

Ukraine became independent in August 1991. In September the Gosbank decided to ship no more banknotes to Ukraine, and after Russia liberalised prices in early 1992, the new Ukrainian National Bank (the old Gosbank branch) issued a new currency, the karbovanets (a local word for rouble but sometimes referred to, at this stage, as a 'coupon'). This was nominally at par with the rouble and legal tender only in state stores. It could also be purchased at ten to the US dollar.

Initially 25 per cent of wages and salaries were paid in karbovanets, with the balance in roubles, but food had to be purchased in karbovanets, causing them to be traded initially at a premium value of about 4 roubles. Russia was pursuing a tight money policy and, as more of the new currency was issued, it went to a discount by the end of the first quarter of 1992. Non-cash credits, though, continued to be exchanged at par.

There was the inevitable arbitrage: karbovanets notes were bought for roubles at a discount, deposited in a bank account and used to purchase Russian goods, causing an adverse balance of payments. In May 1992 the CBR introduced its payment clearing mechanism and in September rouble credits to Ukraine were suspended. The karbovanets depreciated, and on 15 November 1992 was declared the sole legal tender of Ukraine. As the table shows, the inflation rate continued to be higher even than that of Russia. In April 1993 restrictions were imposed on the use of cash, and after the Russian currency reform of July 1993 there were wide discrepancies between NBU and free market rates.

The inflation rate fell to 60 per cent in 1995, and to 28 per cent in 1996, and in September 1996 there was a 'nought dropping' operation and the karbovanets was replaced by the hyrvnya on the basis of 100,000 for 1.

Following the Russian crisis of August 1998, there was an effective devaluation: and the intervention bands were widened and changed from 1.8–2.25 hyrvnya to the dollar to 2.5–3.5. Although the currency held its value better than the Russian rouble, bands were changed to 3.4–4.6 in February 1999, and the currency was floated a year later at an initial rate of 5.57.

## Belarus

Belarus, also faced with a shortage of cash, introduced the zaichik ('rabbit', the picture on the 1 rouble note) as a coupon in 1991 for the convenience of consumers. On 25 May 1992 it was reintroduced as a supplementary currency, valued at 10 roubles, in response to budget deficits and a cash shortage, and by the end of the year this represented 80 per cent of currency in circulation. Further cash shortages in May and June 1993 (just before the Russian currency reform) resulted in a discrepancy between credits and cash. There was a speculative activity known as 'the mill', with a profit of over 50 per cent every cycle, and conversion had to be rationed.

In January 1993, in the first of several attempts to re-establish monetary union with Russia, the two countries had signed an agreement that Belarus would rejoin the rouble zone. 'It was estimated that it would cost Russia about 1.5 trillion rubles to get Belarus to join. It would also increase domestic Russian inflation by an unwelcome additional 10 percent.'[10] Belarus notes were intended to be exchanged at one-to-one, although the black market rate was four to one.

In the event it never happened, and following the July 1993 reform, non-Russians had only one day to convert their old roubles to zaichik, and could convert only 15,000 per head (cf. 100,000 in Russia). The zaichik fell against the US dollar while the rouble appreciated. On 18 November the Belarus parliament ratified the CIS economic union and a monetary union with Russia. In August 1994 Belarus dropped three noughts from its currency, and in October plans for monetary union were dropped. Since then Belarus has had the highest rate of inflation and currency depreciation in the CIS. Talk, without action, has continued about a possible economic or even political union with Russia.

## The South-Western republics

### *Azerbaijan*

Azerbaijan was the first of these republics to introduce a supplementary currency in August 1992, and the manat became the main currency in September 1993. There were parallel official and commercial rates until March 1995, when the rates were unified. By the end of 1995 the inflation rate was one of the lowest in the CIS, and since then the currency has been reasonably stable, continuing to depreciate against the dollar but more than holding its own against the euro.

### *Armenia*

Armenia, which had made a premature attempt to liberalise prices in 1991, introduced the dram on 22 November 1993, but the currency only became the sole legal tender four months later. It was initially pegged to the US dollar, but later floated. Armenia had liberalised prices in 1991 (before the collapse of the Soviet Union), but this policy was suspended following a blockade by Azerbaijan. Armenia's economy, based on processing and agriculture, was then adversely affected by political discrimination by its neighbours, but again the currency has remained stable.

## *Georgia*

In Georgia[11] hyperinflation was followed by a successful reconstruction. Having declared independence on 9 April 1991, the country continued to use the rouble until in April 1993 (before the Russian July reform) supplies of cash from the CBR became erratic and the Georgian National Bank introduced a coupon, the menati, at par with the rouble. The rate held for a couple of weeks, after which prices rose sharply and the country quickly collapsed into hyper-inflation: by September 1994 the currency was 5 million to the dollar, and the rouble (which had ceased to be legal tender after the Russian currency reform of July 1993) again became the preferred currency.

Nell gives three reasons for the inflation: the government had monetised a huge deficit of 25 per cent of GDP; Georgian enterprises found it difficult to adjust when Russia decontrolled prices; and Georgia had a corrupt central bank chief who later committed suicide. Shevardnadze admitted that circulating the menati in parallel had been 'a costly error', saying it would take several months to consider rejoining the rouble zone.

In October 1993 Nodar Javakishvili was appointed Governor, and a modern central bank law was passed on 23 June 1995, giving the governor rather than parliament the right to nominate members of the board and the bank the right to introduce its draft monetary policy should parliament fail to discuss it within a three-month period. There was a two-stage stabilisation programme, backed by the IMF. First, in late 1994, the exchange rate was stabilised at 1.3 million coupons per dollar, and at the end of September 1995, when this rate had been maintained for a year, a new currency, the lari (divided into 100 tetras) was introduced at a value of 1 million coupons. By mid-October, 17 trillion coupons, 68 billion Russian roubles and 23 million US dollars had been exchanged for lari, and this became the *de facto* currency, while the dollar continued to be used for some transactions and roubles circulated in border areas. The fiscal deficit remained, although in principle the government could not borrow more than 5 per cent of the average of the previous three years' revenue, and as elsewhere in the former socialist bloc there were problems with the banking system – 'the bad loans come out of the closet when inflation falls'. As the tables and charts show, the currency then remained fairly stable, losing some value against the dollar in 1998 while appreciating sharply against the rouble. In practice, though, the country became substantially dollarised: at the beginning of 2000 foreign currency deposits were 3.8 times higher than domestic deposits.[12]

## Moldova

In July 1992 Moldova introduced a national coupon, replaced by the leu in November 1993. The economy was strongly affected by the civil war, but the currency remained fairly stable until the 1998 Russian crisis, and even then held its value better than the rouble.

## The Central Asian republics

These republics were slow to respond to the problems created by events in Russia, and Michael Kaser[13] discussed the advantages for the Central Asian governments of continuing to use the Soviet rouble. One problem was that rates of inflation, although uniform until 1992, diverged considerably in later years.

### Kyrgystan

Kyrgystan was the first republic to give notice that it would introduce its own currency, the som, which was in fact in operation by 21 May 1993, before the Russian reform. Generally, 200 Soviet roubles were exchanged for 1 som, but deposits in Sperbank were exchanged at 150 as the balances had already been reduced by inflation. With the support of an IMF standby arrangement of $38 million, all controls on current and capital movements were lifted and the currency was allowed to float. The currency was, on the whole, held within a narrow band.

In 1993 the governments of Kazakhstan, Turkmenistan and Uzbekistan were offered the choice of submitting to more stringent control by the Central Bank of Russia or of introducing their own currency.

### Kazakhstan

Kazakhstan, which has a long border with Russia, close economic ties and a substantial Russian population, at first wished to continue with the Russian rouble. There were negotiations, but the conditions that Khazakhstan should a surrender its gold and currency reserves totalling some $700 million and pay interest on rouble credits, were unacceptable.

A new currency, the tenge, was introduced on 12 November 1993 and associated with an IMF standby arrangement for $173 million. Initially sums of up to 100,000 roubles were converted at the basis of 500 roubles to 1 tenge. Bank deposits which had been held on 1 October were also converted, but later deposits and larger cash sums were blocked until their source could be identified (this was a classic feature of 'currency reconstructions'). Businesses were allowed to convert 'normal' balances with, again, the surplus being blocked. The tenge effectively became the sole legal tender, although the dollar was also widely used.

## Uzbekistan

Uzbekistan, faced with the same choice as Kazakhstan, chose in mid-November of 1993 to adopt a temporary coupon currency known as the 'sum'. Initially this was a parallel currency used alongside the rouble, but in early 1994 it became the sole legal tender, although pegged to the rouble one-for-one. In mid-April of 1994 the policy was changed to a managed float. Although Uzbekistan is a substantial producer of gold, its currency has been the weakest in the region. In 1997 a formal system of multiple exchange rates was first introduced and later abandoned.

## Turkmenistan

Turkmenistan introduced the manat on 1 November 1993, with an initial rate of TMM2 = $1. The rate of inflation was 1,750 per cent during the following year, in line with other CIS states. During the next two years inflation continued at around 1,000 per cent, while the CIS average in 1995 was 290 per cent, and in 1996 all but Tajikistan were below 100 per cent. Exchange controls and other restrictions meant that the 'official' exchange rate was largely meaningless. There were separate exchange rates for official government, and for commercial, transactions, and on 19 November 1995 the manat was devalued from 75 to 200 (official) and from 195 to 500 (commercial), but the black market rate fell to 850. The rates were unified in April 1998, but the parallel market premium widened later in the year. Turkmenistan is the only former communist country not to have a stabilisation agreement with the IMF.

## Tajikistan

Tajikistan initially accepted the new Russian rouble. Because of civil war and problems in neighbouring Afghanistan, economic links with Russia and Uzbekistan remained close. There was in effect a dual currency system, based both on cash roubles supplied by the CBR and non-cash bank money created by the National Bank of of Tajikistan. Export earnings were sequestrated and held in a State Foreign Exchange Fund, which was outside the budget and published no accounts. There was a change of government and policy in December 1994, including a tight monetary policy and repressed inflation. In May 1995 a new Tajikistan rouble was introduced. Cash money was converted on the basis of 100 Russian roubles for 1 Tajikistan rouble, but non-cash money only at 1,000 or 1,200. Currency performance remained poor, and a new currency, the somoni, was introduced in October 2000.

# 45  The Baltic states from 1991
## Successful monetary reforms

## Introduction

The Baltic states, Estonia, Latvia and Lithuania, had regarded themselves as occupied countries rather than as part of the Soviet Union, and soon reasserted their independence, introducing their own currencies without waiting for the rouble zone to break up. All three quickly and successfully adopted a 'strong' form of fixed exchange rate, using different pegs and structures, have shown no interest in any form of 'monetary union' between themselves, and are all serious candidates for admission to the European Union. In spite of having stable currencies, prices continued to rise for some years, and the 'Estonian paradox' has important lessons for any country contemplating fixing its exchange rate in similar circumstances.

## A brief earlier history

Estonia regained its independence in 1918, and Eesti Pank, the central bank, was founded in 1919, with the sole right to issue banknotes. The marka, initially set at par with the German mark, was proclaimed the sole currency on 2 May, with an exchange of German, Finnish and Russian currencies. Following the collapse of the German currency (and a milder inflation in Estonia) the currency was reformed in 1928 with the help of foreign loans, and the (gold based) kroon became the currency. Ivar Leimus[1] describes this period, and the physical problems of printing banknotes, but the English summary has little to say on the economics.

Estonia was occupied by the Soviet Union in June 1940, then by Germany in 1941, by the Soviets again in 1944, becoming independent once more in 1991. Latvia and Lithuania also became independent in 1918, were occupied by the Soviet Union in 1940 with a short period of Nazi occupation, regaining their independence in 1991.

## Estonia after the collapse of communism

By the time the Soviet Union was dissolved, Estonia had already declared independence, and was making plans for a new currency, but as Richard

Giedroyc[2] explains, the roots of monetary independence go back even further, to a Soviet currency reform of 1988: Gosbank then hived off its non-central bank functions into five banks with networks of branches, but when these failed to become proper commercial banks as had been expected, Gosbank had to allow independent banks to be formed. Estonia (then still a Soviet Socialist republic) seized the opportunity to form the Tartu Commercial Bank, in 1989 resuscitated Eesti Pank, and introduced separate banking laws. Gosbank retained the sole right to issue banknotes until November 1990 when Estonia managed to transfer the issue of Soviet roubles to Eesti Pank, which soon after also took over the Talinn branch of Vneshekonombank. On 27 March 1991 Estonia set up a Monetary Reform Committee to begin planning for an independent currency, and the country declared its independence on 21 August 1991.

In June 1992 Estonia abandoned the rouble to restore its own currency, pegging the exchange rate at 8 kroon to 1 deutschmark. The reform was greatly facilitated by the return of gold which had been deposited abroad before the war by Eesti Pank (Giedroyc says, intriguingly, that the Supreme Council transferred some standing timber to the bank by way of additional security). When EMU was introduced in January 1999, the rate was adjusted to 15.6466 kroon to 1 euro, but there seems little interest in actually adopting the euro, and in spite of the well established 'fix' it has been suggested that a referendum on EMU entry would actually be lost!

Eesti Pank holds reserves in gold and foreign convertible currency to match notes and coins, deposits of commercial banks, 'foreign loans' and other liabilities. It acts as a currency board, being required to hold 100 per cent of the monetary base in foreign assets (mostly but not all, in interest-bearing deutschmark assets, seigniorage accruing to the banking department. The bank is said[3] to have the right to revalue the kroon (upwards), but devaluation requires an act of parliament. It is also the bank regulator. One issue in setting up a currency board is what parts of the total money supply it effectively guarantees: typically only banknotes are formally backed, creating problems discussed in the chapter on Hong Kong. Estonia decided to back bank reserve deposits, 'partly because there was no effective system of interbank clearing outside the central bank'.[4] Bennett also says that Estonia considered adopting the ECU but it 'would not have been as transparent as a link with a single well-known currency'. (At about this time there was a serious and well worked out proposal to link the currency to that of Sweden,[5] but unfortunately the latter suffered a sharp fall soon after-wards – an averted example of a country catching a 'disease of the reference currency'!)

After the deutschmark peg was introduced, inflation fell from 117 per cent in the first year, to under 30 per cent in the twelve months to June 1995, still high considering the peg to a stable currency. There was a sharp rise (46 per cent) in prices during the two months after the change: this is easily explained as a one-off adjustment, but, surprisingly, prices then more than doubled over the next two years. During discussions in October 1994 some central bank officials suggested to me that inflation would continue at around 50 per cent and thought nothing odd about it!

As the exchange rate itself is fixed, the rise in domestic prices relative to prices in the country to which the exchange rate is pegged implies a substantial rise in the real exchange rate against that currency. Relative prices are likely, in a previously rigid command economy, to be seriously out of line, and a period of adjustment (typically achieved by differential inflation rates, rather than by a combination of price rises and falls around a stable general price level) will be necessary. This is not 'inflation' in the technical sense of a persistent *tendency* for money supply to increase and for prices to rise. One would have expected this process to be completed in a rather shorter period, and a three-year adjustment seems unusual and possibly unprecedented: the 'Estonia Paradox', discussed below. There was another paradox: interest rates remained high, in line with the inflation rate, which seemed to create an arbitrage opportunity for investors. The scope for this was limited by a distrust of the banks in which kroon deposits could be made.

## Latvia

After asserting independence in 1991, Latvia initially suffered a rapid contraction of the economy coupled with inflation and associated with the collapse of the Comecon. On 19 May 1992 Latvia joined the IMF, and in May 1992 the Bank of Latvia, independent of the government, was established, Latvia joined the IMF, and a temporary currency, the Latvian rouble (LVR) was put into circulation. 'At the time various Soviet financial experts foresaw a disastrous end to that experiment – after all, Repse was a physicist and not a "finansist" [*sic*] '.[6] The currency, they said, lacked cover, and the measure amounted to 'economic suicide'. They were wrong, it did work, and in March 1993 a new currency, the lats, was introduced on the basis of LVR200 to one new lats, which held its rate and became one of the world's strongest currencies.

Latvia, having the closest links with Russia of the three Baltic countries, was the most affected by the August 1998 collapse of the rouble, which produced some speculative pressures but no 'real' direct damage. Exports to Russia had of course fallen, weakening some customers, but there had been no serious exposure to the rouble. They had succeeded in holding the currency, but it had been important not to support the failing banks, of which there were several. Monetary targeting would not have been credible, and exchange rate targeting would result in continuing inflation. The adjustment period of some five years was reasonably short.[7]

Inflation having fallen, another problem was created because Latvia was shadowing the 'wrong' exchange rate. The currency held its value and its purchasing power equivalence against the dollar, but appreciated substantially, in real and nominal terms, against the euro, losing competitiveness against the country's main (Western) trading partners. Sooner or later there will have to be a switch to a euro link, but they must get the timing right to avoid being locked into a monetary union at the wrong rate.

There is an interesting, if possibly irrelevant, difference between the coin and note systems in the two countries. In Estonia, the smallest banknote is 5 kroon, about 20 pence or 30 cents, while the largest coin is only worth 4 pence or 6 cents. In Latvia there are coins up to about £2 ($3) with the smallest note, 5 lats, being equal to £5, a pattern very similar to that of the UK.

## Lithuania

Lithuania began its independence with an interim (coupon) arrangement, but in April 1994 linked its currency to the US dollar on the basis of 4 lit to the dollar. The Bank of Lithuania is required to keep 100 per cent reserves in foreign assets and gold against currency and 'liquid liabilities' (presumably including commercial bank reserves deposited with it).

Since June 1994 the exchange rate can be changed but 'only under extraordinary circumstances'.[8] The Bank retains seigniorage, and is the bank regulator. On 2 February 2002, faced with a similar problem to Latvia, the peg was switched from the US dollar to the euro on the basis of LTL3.45 per euro. This appears to have gone smoothly, but Lithuania had already lost competitiveness as the dollar appreciated against the euro, and there was a danger of a further loss if the switch turned out to have been made just before the trend reversed.

## The exchange rate paradox

The 'Estonia currency paradox' seemed, at first, just that. If a country creates a really credible currency board, fixing its exchange rate to a stable currency, one might expect initial sharp adjustments in prices, but how can such high inflation rates persist for so long? There was also the problem of interest rates, which remained high in Estonia to take account of inflation: why did not foreign investors rush in to take advantage of high rates in a deutschmark-linked currency? If they had, domestic rates would have been forced down so that they were substantially negative, in real terms, to investors and borrowers. During a first visit to Estonia it seemed that there was a danger of a policy-induced recession if there was an attempt to counter this, but it turned out that a distrust of banks was sufficient, for a time, to keep the two markets separate at that time. Eesti Pank deposits and securities alone did pay 'DM' rates.

There are two partial explanations. First, a closer examination of the figures reveals wide discrepancies between price rises in traded and non-traded goods, and second, much of the trade was with other former communist countries. Figures now available[9] show that Eastern European currencies in the early 1990s were at a fraction of their purchasing power parity: a huge correction was needed, and this (arguably) would have been needed whatever exchange rate had been chosen. After what had gone before, credibility as such would cause a sharp rise in the real exchange rate. There was a similar underlying pattern in the other former communist countries, but it was not so strikingly obvious.

Eesti Pank quoted figures for February 1999 showing the composition of the Estonian real exchange rate (June 1992 = 1). The disparities are enormous (examples only):

| | |
|---|---|
| USA | 4.914 |
| Sweden | 7.303 |
| Latvia | 0.836 |
| Russia | 1.659 |
| Trade weighted | 3.576 |

Conversations with Eesti Pank at that time suggested that they thought that competitiveness had remained constant, and that the figures had simply adjusted to this target (the Bank of Latvia independently expressed a similar view). They successfully implemented a programme of structural reforms, undertaking the currency reform very early, and commented that Bulgaria was even earlier in the cycle and that perhaps an early move to a currency board makes it easier to force through other economic reforms.

# 46  The break-up of Yugoslavia

## Introduction

Yugoslavia in its old form only really held together under the leadership of Tito. Milosevic, campaigning as a Serbian nationalist, won the leadership in 1987 to the dismay of the other and smaller ethnic groups. Croatia and Slovenia declared their independence in June 1991, and Bosnia and Macedonia followed in 1992. There were wars in Bosnia and Croatia which were settled, at least for the time being, by the Dayton agreement of November 1995.

As with the break-up of the Austro-Hungarian empire, and indeed of the Soviet Union, the successor countries went their own way with different degrees of success. Typically they started their independent careers with, effectively, no monetary organisation and indeed no money, but some of them have emerged with amongst the stablest currencies in South-East Europe, confirming that it is often easier to build from scratch following the complete collapse of a discredited currency than to check and reverse a mere decline. Three of the republics, Bosnia, Croatia and Macedonia, succeeded, with various degrees of formality, in linking their currencies to the deutschmark/euro. In contrast, Slovenia, although the front runner of this group for EU membership, decided against a rigid link in favour of a 'crawling peg', while 'old Yugoslavia' suffered hyper-inflation, followed by a short-lived peg. Montenegro, the junior partner, unilaterally adopted the deutschmark and then the euro.

## Old Yugoslavia

Inflation was a major problem in old Yugoslavia, including periods of hyper-inflation in late 1989, and the break-up of the Federation may have been partly due to Milosevic's initiative in forcing the National Bank of Yugoslavia to make substantial and generally uncollectible loans to Serbian enterprises in 1991. Beginning in 1991–2, Yugoslavia again experienced hyper-inflation, which hit 313 million per cent per month in January 1994, exceeding the previous 1947 record held by Hungary. By then the other republics had broken away: later developments in the Federal Republic of Yugoslavia (Serbia and Montenegro) are discussed below.

## Croatia

Croatia was the first to declare independence, on 25 June 1991, and on the same day the Zagreb branch of the National Bank of Yugoslavia was converted into the National Bank of Croatia. Initially it had no reserves, issued no currency (other than the stock of Yugoslav dinars in its vaults) and had no charter giving it any status or legitimacy. The Croatian dinar was introduced in December 1991, but the country suffered high inflation (about 25 per cent per month) until in October 1993 a spectacularly successful stabilisation programme was introduced. In May 1994, a new currency, the kuma, was introduced. This was not officially pegged, but was unofficially linked to the deutschmark, and fluctuated only between 3.5 to 3.95 per deutschmark. Currency substitution ceased, the demand for the currency was strong, and the National Bank could effectively print money to finance the state without prejudicing stability, using the 'scigniorage' route. In the earlier period the bank was able to build up reserves, which it did with the help of a balance of payments surplus. Jacob Nell[1] says that the NBC used the dinar as a 'sacrifice currency'; the bank said that inflation had to be incurred to build up the reserves necessary to stop inflation. Marko Skreb, interviewed by *Central Banking*[2] said he regarded a stable exchange rate as essential for a highly 'dollarised' economy.

## Slovenia

Slovenia was next, beginning its independent monetary policy in October 1991 with a new central bank, the Bank of Slovenia, and a new currency, the Slovene tolar (SIT). Although there was a strong export-oriented economy, the new bank had no foreign exchange reserves and lacked the ability to defend a fixed rate.

For this and other reasons it opted for a 'managed float'. The decision is discussed in an article by A. Cosar in *Central Banking*, summer 1997. He says that 80 per cent of household savings were denominated in foreign currency, and discusses the difficulties of setting an equilibrium exchange rate. 'A fixed exchange rate would have required an initially very weak tolar to cope with high inflation', but this 'would itself have stimulated imported inflation'. In any case it was expected, correctly, that the reduction of 'exports' to what had previously been a domestic market, would change the equilibrium real exchange rate. There was no financial support from outside, and they were reluctant to relinquish control over interest rates.

These are all arguments against a rigid fix, or currency board type of approach, and as the Estonia example in Chapter 45 shows, particularly important in Eastern Europe. Cosar says that estimates were made of the parameters of the demand for real money balances, and that these 'were far more stable than the supply and demand on the foreign exchange market'. This was perhaps a surprising conclusion in the context of an emerging economy with neither internal reserves nor external help, but it was interpreted to mean that, in spite of the flight of capital, a 'managed float' would be credible. Legally the central bank has independence even to the extent of setting its own goals, and it chose to target the demand for money while taking account of exchange rates and interest rates.

The initial exchange rate was set at 32 SIT per deutschmark, a rate designed to maintain a surplus on current account. Cosar says that 'the main problem was the appreciation of the tolar', but judging by the tables in the bank's monthly bulletin, this seems incorrect. The rate slipped to about 61 by the end of 1992 and 81 by the end of 1994, since when it has been depreciating at a fairly steady 4 per cent per annum. Inflation, though, was rather higher. The bank intervened to keep the real exchange rate under control. Slovenia will probably be in the first wave of former communist countries to accede to the European Union, and the only representative of former Yugoslavia.

## Former Yugoslav republic of Macedonia

Macedonia voted for independence in September 1991, at an early stage of the second Yugoslav hyper-inflation, and the new country faced formidable economic and other problems. Dr Trpeski, Governor of the National Bank, described how these were tackled in a tenth anniversary speech.[3] After months of secret preparation, including printing, a bill to introduce the Macedonian denar was presented and passed on 26 April 1992. The Prime Minister produced the first notes from his pocket, but with the name of the currency omitted. This could not be included before parliament had passed the bill! Initially the denar was equal to the Yugoslav dinar, but an anti-inflationary package produced shortly afterwards fixed it at 360 to the deutschmark – then the official (rather than the black) rate for the dinar, then in free fall. This proved unsustainable, and a currency reform (this time prepared without the need for secrecy) was introduced in 1993. Two noughts were dropped. The National Bank of the Republic of Macedonia was also formed in 1993. The currency tracked the deutschmark at a rate of around 26.5 until July 1997, when it was devalued to 31 denar per deutschmark, a rate which has been maintained. In April 2001 the country was the first in the region to enter into a Stabilisation and Association Agreement with the EU.

## Bosnia and Herzegovina[4]

Bosnia declared independence in 1992, but Bosnia and Herzegovina was only recognised as a successor state following the 1995 Dayton peace agreement. During the war the Bosnian Federation had issued the Bosnian dinar, backed by deutschmark reserves. This circulated in the north, while the Croatian kuna was widely used, with the deutschmark, in the south.

As the constitution required, a new Central Bank of Bosnia and Herzegovina commenced operations on 11 August 1997, with the interesting requirement that the governor is appointed, after consultation with the government, by the IMF and must not be a citizen of Bosnia and Herzegovina or a neighbouring state. The first governor was a Frenchman and he was succeeded by Peter Nicholl, a former deputy governor of the Reserve Bank of New Zealand. The governor also chairs the governing board, which has three other members, one from each of the main ethnic groups.

The CBBH effectively acts as a currency board, issuing convertible marka (KM), at par with deutschmark, against a 100 per cent minimum backing in deutschmark assets (it can now diversify into euro instruments) and the currency is at par with the deutschmark. In 1999, when the euro rates were fixed, the definition was changed so that 1 euro = KM1.95583. As with other deutschmark-linked currencies, such as Estonia, it appears to have been 'persuaded' not to switch to a euro link. Part of the aim is to have the national currency become a symbol of national unity: the policy has been described as 'de-dollarisation'. There were difficulties in agreeing a design for the banknotes, but these were eventually issued in June 1998. Coins followed in December. By the beginning of 2001, the CBBH had repatriated DM2 billion of currency notes back to Germany as they were replaced by the KM. Between July 2001 and February 2002 (when deutschmark banknotes became obsolete following the introduction of the euro) a further DM4 billion was sent back, about one third each being converted into KM, euros and other foreign currencies. The euro is not legal tender in the country, but is freely used.[5]

## The Federal Republic of Yugoslavia (Serbia and Montenegro)

At the time that the other republics were breaking away, Yugoslavia was in the grip of hyper-inflation. To deal with this, in 1994 Dragoslav Avramovic was brought back out of retirement and appointed Governor of the National Bank of Yugoslavia. A new dinar (13 million old dinars) was introduced at par with the deutschmark, and hyper-inflation was eliminated by April 1994 when prices stabilised. Money supply expanded to 1.2 billion new dinars, backed by gold and currency reserves, by the end of July, but then exploded, again because of excessive deficit financing. Inflation rose to 7 per cent per month by November 1994, and the dinar was formally devalued in November 1995, after the Dayton agreement.

After a sharp initial rise in prices the *monthly* inflation rate fell, initially to around 5 per cent, almost disappearing in the middle of 1997 but then rising again. The exchange rate weakened even further: the real exchange rate halved by the time of the reform.

Following the deposition of Milosevic and the lifting of sanctions, a new government initiated a currency reform, tightened fiscal policy and liberalised prices and financial markets. The exchange rate then stabilised, but inflation continued and the real exchange rate approached its former level. Inflation is forecast to fall to 10 per cent per annum by 2003.

Meanwhile, in November 2000 Montenegro unilaterally abandoned the dinar, and the deutschmark (by then a sub-unit of the euro) became the sole legal tender. It had been used extensively alongside the dinar for about a year. A substantial minority in Montenegro favours total independence, and there have been years of constitutional discussions both within and between the two parts of the country, now renamed simply 'Serbia and Montenegro'.

# 47 Transitional and other EU applicant countries

## Introduction

The past few chapters have discussed the break-up of the rouble zone and of Yugoslavia, and the very different experience of the Baltic states. Following the collapse of communism, most of the other Central and Eastern European states are, together with Cyprus, Malta and Turkey, aspiring to join the European Union, and hence the EMU. Meanwhile they have had a wide range of currency policies, and the main theme of this chapter is how each of these will face up to the problems of joining the EMU – and by implication the effect of 'enlargement' on the future of EMU itself. The examples include a fairly undramatic 'disunion' (Czechoslovakia), a currency board (Bulgaria), and an example of a 'wrong reference currency' problem (Turkey).

## The transition from communism

The former communist countries all began their independence with a more or less sharp bout of inflation as price controls were removed, but nearly all succeeded fairly quickly but not painlessly in setting up a credible currency system (the economic effects of the early period are discussed in IMF Occasional Paper 179). Most then linked their currencies with a basket which typically involved a significant mixture of US dollars and deutschmarks, but also in some cases the pound and Swiss franc.

Before accession, inflation rates will need to come down and currencies converge on the euro: some are already there. So far monetary policies have been targeting some variant of exchange rate, inflation rate or money supply, but aspirants will seriously have to take steps to ensure that their real exchange rate is in line: once they have gone in at the wrong rate, it will only be possible to adjust by a possibly painful inflation or deflation, and domestic policies may be further constrained by such EU regulations as the Stability Pact.

It might be thought that it would make sense for some applicant countries unilaterally to adopt the euro, at least as an actively encouraged secondary currency. Some already have *de facto* currency boards linking their currencies either to the euro or to a basket with a substantial euro component. Bosnia and Montenegro, which have currencies at par with the deutschmark (now 0.51129 euro), Bulgaria (was 1000:1) and Estonia (kroon originally 8 per deutschmark, now 4.09034 per euro) would make life simpler for business and travellers if they now simply adjusted their currencies to parity with the euro. Those which are still having to adjust might find their paths easier if they 'euroised' via a currency board on the principles discussed in Chapter 4.

Extraordinarily, though, a report of the ECOFIN Council, meeting in November 2000, specifically stated that

> it should be made clear that any unilateral adoption of the single currency by means of 'euroisation' would run counter to the underlying economic reasoning [*sic*] of EMU in the Treaty, which foresees the adoption of the euro as the endpoint of a structured convergence process within a multilateral framework.

It is hard to imagine any sound 'economic reasoning' that would justify this objection to self-help: ECOFIN's attitude can, alas, be explained in terms of public choice theory, which explains how public policy decisions can be shaped by the private agendas of politicians and bureaucrats – a less benevolent version of Adam Smith's 'invisible hand'.

## Poland

Poland initiated a currency peg based on the US dollar in January 1990, but then suffered an exceptionally high peak inflation at an annual rate of over 1,000 per cent in February. In May 1991 this was replaced by a crawling peg arrangement with a five-currency basket, 45 per cent US dollars, 35 per cent deutschmarks, 10 per cent sterling and 5 per cent each French and Swiss francs. The adjustment, initially 1.8 per cent per month, was gradually reduced to 1 per cent per month and was switched again to a broad band crawling peg in May 1995.

In May 1997 the emphasis changed to broad money targeting, although the target was initially mixed and this in turn was replaced by interest rates targeting in 1998. The country accepted capital account convertibility in 1999, when there was direct inflation targeting based on a two-currency 55 per cent euro and 45 per cent US dollar basket with a rate of crawl of 0.3 per cent a month.

## The Czech and Slovak republics: a monetary disunion

Czechoslovakia began with a five-currency basket but when the Czech and Slovak republics decided to go their separate ways, it was originally intended, at least at first, to maintain a monetary union. Events were against this: those seeking Slovak independence envisaged the creation of separate currencies and many Slovaks, believing that this would happen, and that it would lead to a depreciation of the Slovak currency, transferred deposits to Czech banks or acquired other assets within the Czech Republic.

In an attempt to check a capital flight, the authorities of the two republics announced in October 1992 that they would enter into a currency union for at least the first six months of 1993. This failed, and in February 1993 there was a currency reconstruction. Czechoslovak notes were called in, and stamped appropriately, between 4 and 10 February. Those over 15 could convert 4,000 koruna in cash, but any balance was held in a deposit. It was forbidden to transfer banknotes and koruna deposited securities across borders, and certain withdrawals and payments were restricted during the conversion period.

After the break-up, the Czech Republic adopted a peg with a narrow band against a basket of 65 per cent deutschmarks and 35 per cent US dollars. This continued until February 1996, during which period there was considerable real appreciation of the value of the currency. There were also large short-term capital inflows towards the end of the period after the introduction of capital account convertibility. In February 1996, there was a switch to a broad band peg using M2 growth and interest rates as targets. The exchange rate has floated since July 1997, with monetary policy being based on core inflation targeting.

The Slovak koruna started its independent life at a discount of about 10 per cent to the Czech, and for four years fluctuated around this figure. The currency tracked a slightly different basket: 60 per cent deutschmarks and 40 per cent dollars, switching to a broader band in 1996, and floating in October 1998. At first, the discount narrowed after the Czech koruna floated, almost disappearing at the end of 1997, but widened again, eventually to about 20 per cent, after its own float.

## Hungary

Hungary introduced current account convertibility in the 1980s, and appears to have suffered only relatively modest inflation in the initial period. The initial policy was a narrow float, and there were several devaluations and changes in the composition of the currency basket. In May 1995 a crawling peg with a plus or minus 2.5 per cent band was initiated based on a basket adjusted, after EMU, to 70 per cent euro and 30 per cent US dollars. The crawling rate of devaluation has been reduced to 0.5 per cent.

## Romania

Romania has had fairly continuous inflation, falling from over 100 per cent per annum in 1997 to under 40 per cent in 2001. The currency has tracked inflation, and purchasing power relationships have followed a similar path to more stable neighbours.

## Bulgaria

Bulgaria's central bank began operating as a currency board in July 1997, with a fixed rate of BGL1,000 per DM. Its constitution (Articles 20, 29–30) requires it to maintain 100 per cent backing for the currency including commercial bank deposits with the central bank (essentially M0) and to buy or sell deutschmarks on demand at a rate of plus or minus 0.5 per cent of the official rate. It does, however, retain a supervisory power and powers to act as a lender of last resort (Article 20(2)), although these powers are severely limited by Art 33(2). The fixed rate has now been formally changed to the euro but, again, the actual adoption of the euro has been delayed.

## Turkey

Turkey, with its population of 67 million, is the largest of the applicant countries. On its past record, it would also seem to have the hardest task in getting its monetary arrangements into line, although there have been more positive developments. Inflation had been fairly consistently above 50 per cent per annum, sometimes rising to 100 per cent or more, but well short of hyper-inflation. The Turkish lira depreciated in line, no noughts have been dropped and the rate fell past 1,000,000 lira to the US dollar.

In November 1999 the IMF introduced a stabilisation package, at first successful in stimulating the Turkish economy and bringing inflation down to 30 per cent. The package required Turkey to introduce a 'credible' exchange rate policy, which took the form of a crawling peg tracking the inflation rate. This was achieved, and the currency tracked purchasing power very accurately until October 2000 – but, unfortunately, against the US dollar, presumably thought by the Washington-based IMF to be the 'obvious' target. This coincided with a sharp fall in the euro zone currencies, and Turkey's competitiveness against its major trading partners deteriorated by over 30 per cent – a classic case of the danger of shadowing the wrong currency.

This contributed to, but was not the main cause of, the crises. A liquidity squeeze on November 2000 put some pressure on the banks, but the real crisis of February 2001 was said to have been precipitated by a conflict between the president and the prime minister. There was a speculative attack on the currency and the central bank fell into another classic trap and spent some $10 billion on support operations before the currency was floated on 21 February. Initially the exchange rate fell by 45 per cent but then recovered.

This time the country benefited from another classic lesson: things sometimes have to get worse before they get better. A new government began pursuing a tight fiscal policy, getting expenditure under control and generally liberalising the economy, and all may, at the end of the day, work well.

## Cyprus

The Cyprus pound had been pegged to the 'basket Ecu' for many years, meaning incidentally that it has stood at a premium to the pound sterling, with which it was at par when the peg was introduced after Cyprus became independent, making it one of the highest value units in the world. The peg was switched to the euro in 1999, and Cyprus will face no more (or less) problems than did France or Germany in making the transition.

Cyprus was remarkably slow to abolish exchange controls and interest rate ceilings in 1999, although these had ceased to be practical impediments. We, as advocates of the early adoption of the Ecu as a secondary currency, had suggested to the central bank that there was an opportunity actually to issue Ecu-denominated notes with a credible 'currency board' backing. This would have required a very modest small devaluation to produce a round figure (e.g. C£3=5 Ecu) and if they were in fact used elsewhere as a secondary vehicle currency Cyprus would have earned useful seigniorage. These would have become even more attractive once the euro rates were fixed in 1999. We learnt afterwards that the European Commission had indicated that any such action by an individual applicant country would be regarded as an unfriendly act. It would have been an interesting experiment!

## Malta

Malta broke its link with the pound sterling in 1972, and established the Maltese lira, successfully linked to a basket of currencies. The Central Bank of Malta is required to hold external assets to cover a percentage of its liabilities, including note and coin issues. This minimum percentage can be changed by the minister of finance: it has been 60 per cent for some time, but in practice the bank has normally held around 100 per cent.

In 1999, when the euro exchange rates were fixed, the basket, which had included the Ecu, was adjusted to 56.8 per cent euro and 21.6 per cent each US dollars and UK pounds. Since then, therefore, the Maltese lira has appreciated significantly against the euro, and Malta may have to consider whether present arrangements will produce the right exchange rate on accession.

# Part IX

# The break-up of the sterling area

The contrasting experience
of the French territories and
some recent proposed unions

# 48 The end of the sterling area

## Introduction

Chapter 18 discussed the monetary history of the British Empire, and described the sterling area as an 'accidental monetary union'. Wartime exchange controls in 1914, and the aftermath of the short-lived return to the gold standard in the 1920s, gave it a more formal role, and this continued after 1945 when, even in a world of exchange controls and bilateral payment arrangements, transactions between the UK and the sterling area remained virtually unrestricted. Its end was, as this chapter shows, equally unplanned, unpremeditated and undramatic. Ireland, which switched from a dependent sterling to a euro link with several intermediate changes, is treated in more detail in Chapter 49, and this is followed by Chapter 50 which discusses the contrasting experience of the French colonies. Significantly, silver had by now virtually lost its monetary role, and the 'silver' countries of the East, which had had such problems at the end of the last century, were simply, where relevant, part of the sterling area.

## The early postwar period

Bell[1] gives a comprehensive account of the sterling area during the early postwar period, and describes the degree to which countries were, in 1952, linked into the area. 'Rigidly dependent currencies' were fixed to sterling by currency boards (Central Africa, West Africa, the West Indies and Malaya/Singapore) and most other colonies and protectorates had currency commissioners or a local currency representative operating less formally in a similar manner. In contrast, Australia, New Zealand, India, South Africa and Iceland had considerable independence, while Ceylon, Burma and Pakistan were in a transitional stage. Some West-Pacific islands, although on a 'colonial' type regime, were linked more closely to Australia and New Zealand.

The theory of 'optimum currency areas' requires us to address the problem of how countries with fixed exchange rates adjust to 'asymmetric shocks', and although neither term was in use when he was writing, Bell, in his chapter VI, discusses in some detail how the economies of Ireland, Ceylon, Southern Rhodesia and British West Africa adjusted to shocks such as fluctuations in the price of key exports, and compares them with independent countries, notably Australia, South Africa and New Zealand (ch. VII) which did not maintain 100 per cent reserves and could use monetary policy, albeit with a fixed exchange rate. The Mundell–Fleming 'impossible trilogy' principle tells us that any two, but not all three, of the following are mutually compatible: full capital mobility; an independent monetary policy; and fixed exchange rates. In this case the last two could remain compatible only because capital mobility was still inhibited by exchange controls and the then relatively unsophisticated international capital markets.

The sterling area was at this stage by no means an optimum currency area. The UK, the anchor country (and main arbiter of currency policy) had a serious deficit, and the area also included primary producers dependent on the vagaries of crop yields and the prices of major export commodities, together with surplus countries such as the prosperous Old Dominions, and a range of other countries which a modern economist, advising on whether to introduce a currency board or other 'hard peg', would warn of the dangers of catching a disease of the reference currency, in this case UK sterling.

## The 1949 devaluation

The devaluation of sterling in 1949 was followed by much of the rest of the sterling area, with a few interesting exceptions. Pakistan did not devalue, relying on price inelasticities in the demand for imports and the supply of exports but, as Bell points out, because banking in undivided India had been dominated by Hindus, Pakistani central bankers were inexperienced: although exchange and trade controls 'enabled Pakistan to keep its drawings on sterling balances within desired bounds', they were less successful in dealing with domestic inflation.

Iceland followed the sterling devaluation of 1949 but then devalued by a further 40 per cent in March 1950: Bell, commenting generally on the right of the IMF to intervene (there were no objections in this case) says there would have been a good case for 'fundamental disequilibrium'. He concludes that alterations of parity, together with flexible import and exchange controls, are 'important ingredients in the armoury of managed adjustment weapons'. There were only the three cases in his period, but there would be many more in later years. British Honduras tried to maintain the US dollar parity when sterling devalued in September 1949, but had to follow the devaluation in December 1949 after a flight of capital.

In the 1930s, Australia and New Zealand had devalued their pounds so that £1 sterling equalled A£ (or NZ£) 1.25 ('25 shillings'). In August 1948 New Zealand had revalued back to parity with sterling, but did then follow the 1949 sterling devaluation. During the period there were frequent rumours that Australia would also restore parity with the UK.

## The 1967 devaluation

In 1967 the devaluation of the pound to meet a UK, rather than a general sterling, problem was not followed by those sterling countries whose internal economies were not under the same political management, and this put considerably more strain on the sterling area concept than had its 1949 predecessor. Only the substantial advantage of being on the inside of the exchange control net, with preferential access to the London capital market, helped to hold it together.

Although Bermuda and the Bahamas retained the link with the US dollar, the currency of their main trading partner, the East Caribbean Currency Agreement members followed the devaluation. Barbados proposed an amendment to allow the ECCA to change the parity following any further devaluation of sterling. This was never implemented, and when the pound floated in 1972 Barbados left the ECCA and formed its own central bank. In 1976 the ECCA did switch the peg from sterling to the US dollar.

Many UK residents made currency profits on (exchange control free) investments in Australia, Bermuda and elsewhere, while others were losers on commercial transactions with other sterling countries, notably Nigeria. Nigeria, for instance, was by then a republic and the Nigerian pound could and in the event did divert from its parity with sterling, but (because it was treated as being part of the 'monetary union') there was no forward or futures market on which traders could hedge their position. (Those with Nigerian commitments had sought Bank of England consent to hedge in the US dollar as a proxy, but this permission was refused.)

In practice, the logic of the sterling area system had been falling apart for some years. Although the UK allowed unrestricted payments to sterling area countries, members as diverse as Australia, South Africa and India imposed exchange control regulations even on transactions with other sterling area countries. Others, such as the Bahamas and Bermuda, were essentially 'US dollar' economies (indeed, their own respective 'dollars' were at par with the US) and maintained only such controls as were needed to prevent leakages from the UK and the rest of the sterling area (they also wanted to continue the benefits of free entry of British capital – and visitors!).

## Extension of UK exchange control to the outer sterling area

Exchange controls were fast disappearing in the industrial world, and in those which no longer really needed them were administered without enthusiasm. The transition of the UK to EEC membership would (it was then presumed) have required the country to abolish controls with fellow members, and generally the concept of the sterling area as an exchange control area was hard to sustain.

In 1971, UK exchange control restrictions were imposed on transactions within the rest of the sterling area, although with some concessionary treatment for direct investment. The Exchange Control Acts gave power to do this, with the important exception that the Channel Islands and the Isle of Man were defined to constitute *part of the United Kingdom* for exchange control (although not for tax) purposes, and on 11 January 1973 Gibraltar was readmitted to the 'inner sterling area'. There was a special agreement amounting to an exchange control union with the Republic of Ireland, which continued until 1978 when Ireland imposed exchange controls even on transactions with the UK.

When exchange control restrictions were imposed on transactions with the outer sterling area there was in effect a windfall gain to holders of Australian, South African and other securities. They had been bought, and up till then would have been sold, without the dollar premium, but overnight they became eligible for it. It was also provided that the '25 per cent surrender' rule would *not* apply to transactions in shares of those countries (these technicalities were explained in Chapter 41).

There was little remaining logic in the sterling area, and with sterling floating the larger territories simply went their own way. In any case, the smaller territories, typically colonies with currency board or similar links to sterling, were becoming politically independent. At first, some retained the sterling link but most, sooner or later, established their own independent currencies. Some have become, or have considered becoming, parts of local monetary unions: see Chapter 51, which follows a discussion of the contrasting experience of the former French colonies.

## Money in former British territories

The smaller British territories, having become independent, chose, some sooner and some later, to cut their links with sterling, while the events discussed above removed any logic in having a currency union with a distant country.

## Nigeria[2]

In 1952, following a motion in the Nigerian parliament, J. L. Fisher of the Bank of England was asked to report on whether it was desirable and practical to establish a central bank. He thought the project premature, preferring to 'build from the base upwards'. A World Bank report of 1954 (according to Davies, Eyo says 1953) was more positive and suggested a rejected compromise, first forming a State Bank of Nigeria. In 1957 J. B. de Loynes, also of the Bank of England, produced a 'Report on the Establishment of a Nigerian Central Bank and the Introduction of a

Nigerian Currency', and the bank was opened on 1 July 1959. Nigeria became independent in 1960, and a republic in 1963. During the Nigerian Civil War there were problems, discussed by Eyo (104): there were currency reconstructions, and in 1973 the naira of ten shillings, divided into 100 kobo, replaced the pound.

## Ghana

When Ghana set up its own currency in 1955, the West African Currency Board paid off its own notes as they were withdrawn, winding up its Accra office in 1960. It had followed a similar procedure in 1959 for Nigeria, and ceased operations when Gambia and Sierra Leone became independent.[3] The exit from the currency board created no real problems.

Ghana split off the Bank of Ghana as a bank of issue and ultimately central bank on becoming independent in 1957; Eyo (102) says that 'in contrast' Sir Cecil Trevor had recommended that Ghana set up a central bank immediately.

The other two West African colonies created new currencies in 1970: the Gambian dalasi and the Sierra Leone leone. All four had political and economic problems, including inflation, inconvertible currencies and currency depreciation, but made attempts to pursue stabilisation policies in the 1990s.

## East Africa

The East African Currency Board was originally set up for Kenya and Uganda, but Zanzibar joined in 1936. During the Second World War the Board took over responsibility for Italian Somaliland, Eritrea and Ethiopia when the Italians retreated, and its notes and coins also began to circulate, alongside rupees, in British Somaliland and Aden. At the end of the war Ethiopia established its own central bank. Somalia reverted to Italian administration in 1950, with its own currency board, but established a central bank on becoming independent in 1960; British Somaliland then joined the Currency Board.

# 49 The Irish pound

## Introduction

Although Ireland has been mentioned in several previous chapters, its unusual and interesting history, which includes both monetary unions and disunions, is worth a special mention. When Ireland became an independent state it at first continued its monetary arrangements as if it were still part of the United Kingdom, with its banks retaining (like the Scottish banks) certain limited rights of note issue. Although it then took steps to acquire its own monetary sovereignty, for practical purposes it was in full monetary union with the United Kingdom, operating rather like a currency board.

In 1978 exchange controls were imposed with the United Kingdom, and these continued even after the UK abolished exchange control a year later: there was a complete break in 1986 when the Irish pound was devalued against sterling. In 1987 Ireland joined the Exchange Rate Mechanism, pegging the currency to the deutschmark, and remained within the ERM for some time after the UK pound left it. It had thus moved from one monetary union to another, less rigid, one. From 1993 the Irish pound again floated, until it formally joined European Monetary Union in 1999 and, with the others, adopted the euro as its currency in 2002.

During all this period the closest trade and financial links continued to be with the United Kingdom: Irish experience has, and will continue to have, much to teach us about the nature, significance and relevance of monetary unions, more specifically about the strains whcih result when the main trading partner is not a member of the union.

## Earlier history

The monetary system of Ireland had, like those of the American and other colonies, long suffered neglect or worse from London. Ireland under English rule had its own and generally inferior coinage, and suffered both the first and the worst of Henry VIII's experiments in debasement. James II issued 'crowns' and 'half crowns' made out of gunmetal or pewter with which to pay his Irish troops in his war against William of Orange. When William won and became king, these were called down to a tiny fraction of their original face value. Thirty years later the issue of copper tokens known as 'Woods Halfpence' caused a public outcry, including the full force of the invective of none other than Jonathan Swift, cleric and satirist, who wrote the anonymous 'Drapiers Letters'.

In 1701 the English silver shilling had been proclaimed to be worth 13 pence Irish, and taking account of a later proclamation valuing the gold guinea at 22 shillings and 9 pence Irish, £100 English was nominally equivalent to £108 6s. 8d. (£108.33) Irish. For practical purposes Ireland was on a 'sterling exchange' standard.

The Bank of Ireland, incorporated in 1783, shared note issuing rights with private Dublin and country banks. There was no foreign exchange market except with London and (occasionally) Lisbon.

At the start of the Napoleonic Wars, the UK government 'suspended payments' and banknotes were no longer convertible into gold. The Irish parliament had approved a separate Irish Bank Restriction on 20 April 1797 and the two restrictions were assimilated by a provision in the Act of Union on 1 January 1801. There was no immediate over-issue of banknotes and no significant discount on Bank of England notes, until 1809, but the Bank of Ireland was a little less circumspect: by 1802 the circulation of Irish banknotes had increased fourfold, leading to a sharp depreciation in the Irish pound in 1803, and critics of restriction such as Boyd, Thornton and King succeeded in securing the appointment of a committee to investigate the condition of the Irish currency. Its report, published in 1804, rehearsed many of the arguments that were subsequently to be discussed by the Bullion Committee of 1810.

The Bank of Ireland suggested that monetary policy has no influence on exchange rates, arguing from the 'real bills' doctrine (which holds that credit creation, provided it is against genuine 'trade' assets, does not affect money supply), a fallacy which continued to be current amongst practical bankers well into the nineteenth century, long after it had been discredited by economists.

Henry Thornton successfully argued the 'bullionist' view that the over-issue of money in Ireland had been the prime cause of the depreciation in the exchange, and that the balance of payments deficit was *caused* by monetary policy.

The report received relatively little attention, mainly because the Dublin/London exchange rate did return to par, and exchange rate policy affected only absentee landlords and merchants, rather than the general population of Ireland. The issue was only taken seriously after 1810, when it affected the United Kingdom as a whole.

## The Irish Free State

Banks in Ireland (then part of the UK) had, like Scottish banks, retained note issuing powers following the Bank Charter Act of 1848, with the same proviso that 100 per cent backing was needed for increases over the issue at that time. When the Irish Free State became independent in April 1922, although the main circulating currency was Irish banknotes, Ireland had no more monetary independence than Scotland. This caused no pressing economic problem, but was incompatible with the pride of the new nation. The Irish pound was created as an independent currency in 1925 but was explicitly linked to sterling, and was backed 100 per cent by gold or sterling assets, UK sterling notes remaining legal tender.

In 1926 the government introduced Irish coins – technically tokens – and set up a commission chaired by Professor Henry Parker-Willis of Columbia University, a former Director of Research at the Federal Reserve Board. This recommended establishing a new currency at par with sterling, administered by a Currency Commission (effectively a currency board) and the consolidation of private banknote issues into a national issue. Arrangements were made for Irish pounds to be exchanged for English at the Bank of England without commission. This was 'a British solution to the question of parity and currency and an American solution to the constitution of the governing Commission'.[1]

The existing banknotes were replaced by a consolidated series of notes guaranteed by the banks as well as by the Currency Commission, but these were not legal tender. An annual fee of 3 per cent (more or less capturing the seigniorage) was payable by the banks. These issues, not being very profitable, were phased out after 1943, when the Central Bank of Ireland began operating.

Following another commission of enquiry, the Currency Commission was replaced by a central bank in 1943. Initially, this lent neither to government nor to banks, but continued effectively to act as a currency board. 'Its main policy intervention was as an outspoken critic' of government spending in its 1950–1 annual report, 'which was followed by the early retirement of the Bank's Governor'.[2] Honohan goes on to compare the bank's activities with the criteria for a currency board, and concludes that in spite of successive relaxations it essentially remained one until the 1970s, and retained some characteristics until the end of the sterling link in 1979.

An IMF study,[3] discussing exits from currency board arrangements, says

> the backing rules were relaxed by expanding the set of foreign assets eligible for backing and by lowering, in 1961, the backing coverage to around 75 per cent. In 1965 central bank lending to banks and the government began on a modest scale. After 1971, exchange rate adjustments no longer required legislative change, but could be effected by the Minister of Finance in consultation with the central bank.

## The break with sterling

Another IMF Occasional Paper[4] uses Ireland as an illustration of the effect of introducing capital controls between previously integrated financial markets. In December 1978 effective exchange controls were introduced on transactions with the United Kingdom, and according to an empirical study by Browne and McNelis (1990),[5] based on the hypothesis that 'if economic agents learn how to evade capital controls over time, then the influence of external financial market conditions on domestic interest rates should grow relative to that of domestic money market conditions'. In the event 'there was a permanent wedge in the interest rate parity relationship only in the markets for small deposits and clearing banks, and share accounts in the building societies', and a temporary one in the mortgage market.

## The EMS phase

Ireland had a successful surprise devaluation against sterling in August 1986, but pegged the currency to the deutschmark in January 1987. The collapse of the pound, and its exit from the ERM, meant a loss of competitiveness for Ireland, but the devaluation arguably necessary to cure it risked causing a loss of confidence and would 're-kindle longer-term fears about the stability of the Irish pound and ... drive up interest rates to compensate ... for the greater risk.'[6] Honohan gives a tentative estimate of the cost at £350 million or 1.5 per cent of GNP, and discusses the difference between the central bank figure of £25–35 million and the Comptroller and Auditor General's figure of £915 million.

The Irish pound was finally devalued by 10 per cent on 1 February 1993. The Irish, unlike the British, had retained residual exchange control powers, and these were used to prevent foreigners (notably the British) borrowing Irish pounds and limiting their access to derivative transactions. This did not, of course, prevent them selling Irish pound assets (mostly government securities) and protecting trade positions by leading and lagging, but there was limited scope for pure speculation. Interest rate were kept high, imposing an economic cost. Honohan says that some £14 billion net of foreign exchange was sold for Irish pounds, resulting in a capital loss of £300 million, from which must be subtracted interest receipts of £20–25 million. There were other direct exchequer costs.

The Bank brought into account a £1.58 billion book gain on foreign currency securities (calculated in Irish punt), while the government took a negative of £755 million on the stock of foreign debt (a better measure of the real loss of international economic resources). These figures resulted from the devaluation as such, while Honohan's paper is more concerned with the cost of the delay in devaluing.

## Joining the EMU

Ireland was one of the first round of members of EMU, in spite of close trading links with the UK, which did not join. The fall in the value of the euro strengthened its competitive position against the UK, but it soon became clear that expanding Ireland should on general grounds have adopted a tight money stance, impossible when the approach was incompatible with the policies in continental Europe. If there is to be a later edition of this book, it may well have much to say about Irish experience with EMU.

# 50 The former French colonies

## The CFA franc zone

### Introduction

The French colonies, in striking contrast with the British African colonies, retained their link with the French franc zone, adopting a structure which is neither quite a currency board nor a monetary union, based on the 'CFA franc'. This apparently unique arrangement makes an interesting case study.

The French Caribbean territories of Martinique and Guadaloupe are neither colonies nor independent, but are simply governed as *départements* of metropolitan France, and send representatives to the French parliament. Their currency has been the *metropolitan* French franc, and is now the euro.

The CFA franc was introduced into fourteen French African colonies in the 1940s, initially issued under French authority. In 1955 France devolved local currency issuing rights to the colonies, and in September 1958 most of them accepted the new French constitution, remaining autonomous members of the French community until in 1960 they became formally independent, continuing as members of the CFA franc zone.

All but one of these former colonies divided into two unions, for West Africa and Central Africa respectively, each with its own central bank. Although the two currencies are at par with each other, each is legal tender only within the specific union. The exception is the Cormorian franc, a similar currency with a slightly different history.

After independence, the currency of the Communauté Financière Africaine (CFA) continued to be guaranteed by the French government at a rate of CFAF50 = 1 French franc. In 1994 the rate was devalued to CFAF100, and is now linked to the euro: this makes little practical difference, as the obligation to support the currency remains with France rather than the European Central Bank or the European Union.

### The nature of the CFA franc

Although the arrangement may look like a currency board, there are significant differences. A currency board holds securities denominated in the anchor currency, and can operate without the (formal) consent of the country issuing that currency and without imposing any credit risk on it. In this case, the government (of France) actually issues the anchor currency which guarantees the exchange rate, taking what could in principle be a substantial risk.

Each of the central banks is the issuing authority for a group of otherwise independent countries, creating all the problems of a monetary union, including specifically how member countries can be prevented from 'free riding' by running budget deficits which will ultimately be financed by the French guarantee.

The arrangements technically fall short of guaranteeing a 'hard' fixed rate. There has at times been a black 'parallel' market with the CFA franc trading at a discount. This has usually been small, but it did reach 20 per cent in 1988, and the CFA franc was actually devalued in 1994.

David Fielding[1] has published a detailed analysis of the economics. He concludes that the package of arrangements has been reasonably successful in keeping prices stable, and in removing deterrents to inward investment, but has done less well in coping with short-term adjustments and integrating the economies of the member countries. He concludes:

> The historical accident that is the CFA has served many of its members well: but if the institution is to perform efficiently in the future, its institutions must be based not on its colonial inheritance but on the economic characteristics of its member states.[2]

## Administrative arrangements

Under their (similar but not identical) constitutions, the central banks have the sole power to issue CFA currency, implement monetary and financial policy and regulate banking, and certain government, activities. 'Overall control of monetary creation is sought through the close monitoring and regulation of *the different components* of money stock' (emphasis added). The constitutional powers of the bank are 'very clear; what is not so clear is how effective the central banks actually are in controlling the financial system'.[3]

The French government guarantees unlimited convertibility into French francs, and undertakes to provide the central banks with French francs for CFA francs on demand, but France requires the central banks to hold 65 per cent of their foreign assets in 'operations accounts' with the French treasury, and these accounts are imputed, on a formula, to each member country.

There is no specific requirement, as there would be with a currency board, to hold French franc assets against note issues, but there is a serious attempt to control the overall money supply, as well as just the note issue.

The most important tool of the central banks is their rediscount facilities offered to institutions in member states. These can be restricted and generally used to control credit, but short-term agricultural credit is excluded from the restrictions. *Ratissage* ('raking in') is a reserve power that can require the compulsory deposit of foreign currency assets held in the various states: it is seldom used but removes the temptation to 'round trip' with members building up foreign assets outside the 65 per cent central bank rule and effectively financing them with soft loans from Paris. The central banks must also limit credit to governments to 20 per cent of their previous year's tax receipts.

Fielding refers briefly to a tax on the export of assets, including 0.25 per cent on short-term loan capital, increased by surcharges of up to 0.75 per cent (Congo). There is even a 0.1 per cent tax on assets (a 'Tobin' tax) moving from one member to another, and this can result in multiple taxation of complex financial transactions. There are various exchange restrictions, and member governments 'encourage' banks to invest in the local market rather than in CFA neighbours. 'These regulations are designed to prevent Latin American style capital flight, but they also restrict the movement of capital within the CFA and between the CFA and France.'[4] The arrangements thus fall far short of a single market, especially for financial services.

## The devaluation of 1994

The CFA franc had for many years been freely convertible into French francs at a fixed rate. At first the real exchange rate remained fairly stable, and growth was higher, and the rate of inflation significantly lower, than neighbouring states with different monetary regimes. In 1985, though, the zone then caught 'a disease of the anchor currency' and became less competitive, partly because of falling prices for its agricultural exports but also because the French franc, to which the CFAF was linked, strengthened substantially (and for them irrelevantly) against the zone's trading partners. Growth became flat, real per capita income fell, while current account deficits and external debt rose. Economic performance now became significantly worse than the zone's neighbours.[5]

On 11 January 1994

> the 14 African member countries of the franc zone decided collectively to broaden their adjustment strategy through a large change in the parity of their currencies ... buttressed by a coherent set of macroeconomic and structural policies tailored to the circumstances of each country.[6]

and formed the *Union Economique et Monetaire Ouest Africaine* (UEMOA).[7]

The CFA franc was devalued from CFAF50 to the French Franc to CFAF100, but the Comorian franc (CF) was devalued only to CF75, losing its parity with the other CFAF countries. There is little[8] detail of what should have been a traumatic event: Fielding only mentions the devaluation in the context of its effect on his figures.

## Appendix: territories covered

The CFA franc countries divide into three groups:

### West Africa (Afrique Occidentale Française)

The Central Bank of West African States (BCEAO) covered Benin (formerly Dahomey), Burkina Faso (formerly Upper Volta), Ivory Coast, Guinea-Bissau, Guinea-Conraky (now Guinea), Mali, Mauritania, Niger, Senegal and Togo. All except Guinea, which became a republic, but rejoined the currency union in 1985, became overseas territories of France in September 1957 and formally independent in 1960. Togo originally opted out of the monetary arrangements, but rejoined in 1963. Mali also issued its own currency from 1962–84.

In 1958 the Banque de la République de Guineé (Banque Centrale from 1960) began independence by issuing franc notes, but introduced a new currency, the syli, in 1971, reverting to the CFA franc zone in 1984 (Pick[9] lists a large issue of franc notes in 1985 in the name of Guinea's own central bank). When Mauritania seceded in 1973 it formed its own central bank and adopted a new currency unit, the ouguiya, valued at CFAF5. The most recent recruit, Guinea-Bissau, became independent of Portugal in 1974 and introduced its own currency, the peso before deciding to join the CFA franc zone.

### Central Africa (Afrique Equatoriale Française)

The Central Bank of Equatorial African States and Cameroon was reorganised in 1972–3 as the Bank of Central African States (BEAC) 'to give greater African control of its operations'. Its operations were transferred from Paris to Yaounde in 1977, and in 1978 an African governor was appointed. Its operations covered Cameroon, Central African Republic, Chad, Congo (Brazzaville) and Gabon. Equatorial Guinea, a former Spanish colony, joined in 1985. They all now belong to the Central African Monetary Area (now CAEMC), established 16 March 1994.

### Comoros

A third central bank in the CFA franc zone was originally shared between Madagascar and the small island group of Comoros (population 560,000), but Madagascar seceded in 1973, leaving Comoros as an independent African member of the CFA franc zone. When the CFA franc was devalued in 1994, the Comorian franc was only devalued to 75, losing its parity with other members of the CFA franc zone. The Malagasy franc has since fallen sharply in value.

# 51 Monetary unions in former colonies

## Introduction

The British former colonies, in Africa and elsewhere, initially retained their links with sterling, but many eventually developed independent monetary policies. In contrast, the French colonies mostly retained the link with the French franc. Following the European fashion, some groups of these smaller territories have set up, and others are considering, local monetary unions, in spite of having very different monetary histories.

## The Caribbean[1]

The Caribbean region had strong economic ties with the United States, and it made sense for the British colonies to switch from a sterling to a dollar link. The East Caribbean Currency Area can be regarded as either another, rare, example of a monetary union between otherwise independent states or as a mutual currency board. The earlier history of the region includes several 'disunions'. There are now several overlapping organisations aiming for closer economic union: if these ever move towards monetary union there seems no practical alternative to the US dollar, to which many currencies are already fixed. Others, though, use the euro or float.

### The British territories

The British Caribbean territories had typically used British coins, supplemented by banknotes issued by local branches of Canadian banks and Barclays DCO, until in the 1920s separate boards of commissioners were set up in Trinidad and Tobago, British Guiana and Barbados, the latter also serving the Leeward and Windward Islands, to issue currency.

Following a conference in 1946, the territories agreed to adopt a common currency based on the West Indian dollar, and the British Caribbean Currency Board began operations in 1950. It was a classic currency board with 100 per cent backing, maintaining a fixed exchange rate of \$4.80 to the £, or \$1 = 4s 2d in predecimal money.

In January 1965 the BCCB was replaced by the Eastern Caribbean Currency Authority, then covering Barbados, the Leeward Islands (Anguilla, Antigua and Barbuda and St Kitts-Nevis) and the Windward Islands (Dominica, Grenada, St Lucia, St Vincent and the Grenadines). The currency was renamed the East Caribbean dollar, at the same parity ($4.80), but foreign exchange cover was now only 70 per cent. The formal sterling link was retained until 1976 when a dollar link was established at EC$2.70 = US$1.00.

The East Caribbean Central Bank was established in 1983 to take over the functions of the ECCA, and acts as the bank of issue for the remaining seven members. Banknotes issued are coded to show the country in which they were issued, and imputed reserves can be calculated to allocate seigniorage profits.

Meanwhile several British or former British territories had gone their own way. The Bahamas (1966) and Bermuda (February 1970), which had not been part of the BCCB, adopted their own currencies at par with the US dollar, both having previously been on a legally sterling, but unofficially substantially dollarised, basis.

Trinidad and Tobago left the BCCB in 1962 after independence, and set up its own central bank in 1965. Its dollar was devalued in 1985 and 1988, since when it has been stable.

Jamaica issued government notes as early as 1904, but mainly used banknotes, and had had its own 'English' coins until introducing a decimal coinage based on the US dollar after the sterling devaluation in September 1969. Jamaica floated with the pound in 1972, devalued in 1973 and subsequently had a series of devaluations and periods of floating before, in 1991, abolishing exchange control, freeing up financial markets generally and adopting a free float.

Barbados[2] formed its own central bank in 1972, fixing its rate at B$2 = US$1: this round figure seems to have been a fortunate accident of timing. Although there is no formal currency board type backing, the currency has remained stable. In 1991, the governor of the central bank persuaded trade unions to accept an 8 per cent pay cut as an alternative to devaluation – surely an unprecedented achievement!

### Area economic cooperation

There are now several overlapping economic groupings in the Caribbean area, including CARICOM, the Organisation of East Caribbean States, and the Caribbean Free Trade Association (CARIFTA), and there are hopes of increased cooperation. The concept of a broader monetary union was seriously discussed in 1992, and comes up from time to time, but it is hard to see how any such 'union' could take any form other than a link with the US dollar, which many already have. Some have simply adopted a currency at par with the dollar, but Cuba, Guyana, Haiti, Jamaica, Surinam, and

Trinidad and Tobago now have independent (floating) currencies, while the French islands, notably Guadaloupe and Martinique, are politically part of metropolitan France and used the French (*not* the CFA) franc, and now the euro. The Netherlands Antilles retains a link with the Dutch guilder and hence now also with the euro.

## West Africa

In spite, or perhaps because, of their diverse experiences a group of West African countries began to contemplate a monetary union, the WEAMU, but this is still work in progress rather than history. The prospective members, all members of the Economic Community of West African States (ECOWAS), include eight former French colonies now in the CFA franc (and hence the euro) zone, the four former 'sterling' countries (which now have independent currencies), two other former (Portugese and Spanish) colonies and always independent (and, until 1998, dollarised) Liberia. If it were to go ahead, the union's currency could well be linked to the euro. Meanwhile the West African Monetary Institute has been set up, working towards a more limited Second Monetary Zone of the non-euro members, with the hope that the two will eventually link.

### Postwar history

The postwar history of the four former British colonies (Nigeria, Ghana, Gambia and Sierra Leone), once served by a single currency issued by the West African Currency Board, has been discussed in Chapter 48, and the CFA franc countries were covered in Chapter 49.

*Equatorial Guinea* used locally printed peseta notes until 1975, but on becoming independent of Spain first introduced the equele, switching to the bipquele (plural epqwele) in 1980, joining the CFA franc zone in 1985.

*Cape Verde,* a former Portugese colony, independent since 1975, formally pegged its currency to the Portugese escudo in 1998. Its exchange rate is now, like the CFA franc countries, fixed against the euro.

*Liberia* is different. Having been independent since its creation, under American auspices, it issued its own (dollar) currency until 1880. British West African notes were in circulation for a time, but in 1943 the US dollar was declared legal tender and the country was effectively dollarised. In 1989 Liberian notes, 'J. J. Roberts' notes, were issued at par with the US dollar, but in August 1998 the Liberian dollar was floated, a central bank was established in November 1999, and in March 2000 new Liberian dollar bills replaced the US and Liberian 'J. J. Roberts' issues.

### From ECOWAS to monetary union?

In 1975 the Economic Community of West African States (ECOWAS) was formed to encourage economic integration between its members. It had, from the start, aimed at eventual economic and monetary union and, also in 1975 set up a West African Clearing House (WACH) to stimulate cooperation between the central banks of the region, which were typically operating exchange controls within illiberal trade regimes. Rather like the postwar European Payments Union, it stimulated trade within the region by allowing participating countries to offset balances, settling only the net surplus or deficit in hard currency. Later, when exchange was liberalised, transactions no longer needed to be settled in this way and WACH became less relevant.[3]

The ECOWAS Monetary Cooperation Programme (EMCP) began in 1991, aimed at making currencies more convertible within the region, but it was only in 1998 that it achieved one of the official aims of creating a system of regional travellers' cheques. The formation of the Union Economique et Monetaire Ouest Africaine (UEMOA) between the CFA franc members also tended to draw support away from ECOWAS.

In December 1999 the members of ECOWAS met in Lome to discuss closer integration, including monetary union. Following this the six members not effectively linked to the euro met and issued the 'Accra Declaration', committing themselves to create a monetary union by January 2003, in the hope of including the other ECOWAS countries by 2004. The 'convergence criteria' include 5 per cent inflation and enough reserves to cover six months' imports by 2003, and a commitment to limit central bank lending to government to 10 per cent of the previous year's tax receipts. Its prospects are analysed in an IMF Occasional Paper published in 2001.[4]

A West African Monetary Institute was created, with Dr Addison as a chief economist. A Convergence Council reports to a Conference of Heads of State, and has the functions we might expect. At the end of 2001, Gambia was held to have met all four convergence criteria, Nigeria three, Guinea and Sierra Leone one, and Ghana none.[5]

## East Africa

The East African Currency Board was originally set up for Kenya and Uganda, but Zanzibar joined in 1936. During the Second World War the board took over responsibility for Italian Somaliland, Eritrea and Ethiopia when the Italians retreated, and its notes and coins also began to circulate, alongside rupees, in British Somaliland and Aden. At the end of the war Ethiopia established its own central bank. Somalia reverted to Italian administration in 1950, with its own currency board, but established a central bank on becoming independent in 1960.

Four former British colonies, Kenya, Uganda, Tanganyika and Zanzibar, pursued their own currency policies after independence, and the last two have now merged to form Tanzania. In 1999 a treaty to create an East

African Community was signed, and after ratification in the three countries began operations on 15 January 2001, with the hope of creating a common currency.

## Southern Africa

Southern Africa has also been exploring monetary and economic union. The largest country, the Republic of South Africa, has had a turbulent transition from white domination to majority rule, and this is reflected in the economics. There has long been a highly sophisticated banking and financial system, coupled with considerable poverty and a weak and volatile currency unsuccessfully protected by exchange controls. South Africa leads a Common Monetary Area, based on the rand, with Lesotho, Namibia and Swaziland. These four countries, together with Botswana, also constitute the South African Customs Union (SACU).

Botswana is an underpopulated country with a prosperous economy based on diamonds. As Bechuanaland, its currency was the pound sterling and after independence in 1966 it became part of the rand zone. In 1974–5 it left the rand zone, formed its own central bank, and in 1976 introduced the pula, initially at par with the South African rand. It is now linked to a basket of currencies.

A Southern African free trade zone was established in September 2000, building on the long-established Southern African Development Community (SADC) and including the SACU five, plus Lesotho, Malawi, Mauritius, Mozambique, Tanzania and Zimbabwe. Zambia may join, and monetary union is on the longer-term agenda.

# 52  Two monetary unions that did not happen

## US/Canada and ANZAC

### General introduction

This chapter deals with two monetary unions that might have happened, but didn't, between Canada and the United States (possibly including Mexico), and between Australia and New Zealand. In both cases, their currencies had been at par with each other during much of their early history. The Canadian dollar floated from 1950 to 1962 (the appendix below summarises some earlier Canadian history) and again from 1970: the Australian and New Zealand dollars have floated independently since 1985. There were occasional proposals for a return to fixed rates, the most recent being launched at about the time that EMU became a reality, and (not surprisingly) from the smaller of the two countries in each case.

### The US and its neighbours

Canada has a long land frontier and close trading links with the United States, with which it shares one of its two languages. The two countries might seem an obvious case for a monetary union, but the main argument against is of course political: it is unlikely that the Canadians would be able to negotiate more than a token say in American monetary policy, at best being treated as another 'Federal Reserve District'. No 'union' would be on offer, and the Canadians have always been free independently to dollarise or adopt a convincing policy of shadowing the US currency.

Following the development of the North American Free Trade Area (NAFTA), the idea of union has been given an airing in two papers. Herbert Grubel[1] claims that 'Canada's flexible exchange rates have contributed to poor economic performance ... [and] brought high currency-exchange cost and a significant risk premium on Canadian interest rates'. He proposed that Canada, the United States and Mexico should replace their currencies with the 'Amero' and that their central banks should be replaced by a North American Central Bank, with the three countries represented on its board of governors. The Amero would be exchanged for the US dollar at par: the other initial exchange rates would be fixed to 'leave unchanged their nations' competitiveness and wealth' – which begs not a few questions. There would be provisions to ensure that members did not incur persistent budget deficits.

This view was criticised by David Laidler and Finn Poschmann,[2] who point out that:

> There is no interest in the United States giving up the US dollar or sharing the US electorate's exclusive authority over monetary policy. ... The only common currency arrangement available to Canada is the unilateral adoption of the US dollar.

Grubel discusses the alternatives, including a 'soft fix' (rejected), currency boards and dollarisation, simply adopting the US dollar as Canada's currency (this would result in the loss of seigniorage, a sum he puts at $2.5 billion per annum, or 1.5 per cent of Canadian federal tax revenue). He mentions the work of Richard Harris and Tom Courchene, who have advocated fixing the rate of the Canadian dollar to the US unit, and who believe that the 'Amero' would not be acceptable to Canadian nationalists.

Harris[3] in one paper does specifically propose a North American Monetary Union (NAMU) on the basis that the Canadians and Mexicans would join the twelve Federal Reserve Banks. He also discusses dollarisation, and expresses a low opinion of the history of exchange rate management, and of floating rates, in Canada. He produces more statistics than Grubel about trends in inter-provincial versus cross-frontier trade, discusses the adjustment mechanism, and states categorically that monetary union (or dollarisation) will not require tax harmonisation (a view shared by many tax economists, including myself, in the European Union but not, it seems, by the Commission).

Grubel argues that a mere 'commitment to fixed rates is too easily reversed' and, correctly, prefers a 'hard' form of unified rates which, he argues, would have the disadvantage of a loss of monetary sovereignty (but surely no more than his proposals envisage) but the great advantage of not requiring any international agreement.

Laidler and Poschmann suggest that one motive for the proposal has been the fear of informal dollarisation, which supporters say would produce domestic monetary instability, going on to argue that it is better to 'adopt, in a conscious and orderly fashion, some coherent monetary system based on the US dollar'. They themselves say that there is little evidence of 'real' dollarisation of domestic transactions although Canada, like any country doing business with a much larger neighbour, handles much of its international trade and financial transactions in the currency of that neighbour.

Laidler and Poschmann fear the loss of monetary sovereignty, given the structure of Canadian labour markets, and of 'lender of last resort' facilities, and are particularly concerned with the dangers of finishing up with a 'half baked' and unconvincing fixed rate. 'Asymmetric shocks' between different parts of the United States are common enough, but are dealt with by high labour mobility and substantial transfers of federal funds. Neither benefit would be available to Canada. Generally they favour retaining the status quo.

The other member of the North American Free Trade Area (NAFTA), Mexico, although a less likely candidate to gain such a currency area, actually did have a fixed exchange rate with the US dollar for many years.

## An ANZAC dollar? Australia and New Zealand as a monetary union?

Australia and New Zealand are both now independent English-speaking dominions within the British Commonwealth, and for much of their existence shared a common currency as fellow members of the sterling area. They might therefore seem an obvious candidate for monetary union, and indeed such a union has been discussed. The distances, though, are deceptively large: it is over 2,000 kilometres across the Tasman Sea from Auckland to Sydney, about the same as from London to Kiev.

### Early history

As explained in Chapter 18, these British territories originally came within UK monetary law and practice. The Australian colonies were united as the Commonwealth of Australia in 1901, and the new country adopted its own coinage legislation in 1909. Although Australia was then technically free to pursue an independent monetary policy, it continued to link to British sterling and became affiliated to the sterling area after the UK left the gold standard. After the war the two Dominions remained part of the sterling area, but imposed exchange controls on transactions with other sterling countries, including each other. Residual exchange controls persisted after the UK abolition in 1979, finally disappearing only in 1985.

The Commonwealth Bank of Australia was formed in 1911,[4] taking on a number of central bank functions over the years, but only taking on the full role when relaunched as the Reserve Bank in 1960. New Zealand became a dominion in 1907 and the Reserve Bank of New Zealand was formed in 1934. In the 1930s both currencies were devalued, making £1.25 (Australian or NZ) worth £1 sterling. New Zealand reverted to parity in August 1948, but otherwise both retained the sterling peg until the 1967 devaluation. When the currencies went their separate ways, the New Zealand dollar was successively pegged to the US dollar, to a basket of currencies, and followed a 'crawling peg'. It was floated in May 1985 in accordance with the then current fashion, and as part of the more far-reaching market reforms initiated by Roger Douglas.

The worldwide currency turmoils of the 1980s were followed by comparative stability in the 1990s, during which exchange rates and interest rates tended to converge on each other and to a lesser extent on the US dollar. There was a rather cautious Free Trade Agreement between the two countries in 1964, followed by the Closer Economic Relations Agreement of 1983, which achieved virtual free trade by 1990. In 1990 there was a tentative discussion of monetary union, but the New Zealand Reserve Bank was just beginning its new regime under Don Brash, which was specifically designed to promote low inflation and stability, and it seemed better not to disturb the arrangement.

### The 1999 discussions

From then until September 1999, the question of monetary union then seems to have been little discussed, but the Australia New Zealand Business Council then commissioned the Institute of Policy Studies to consider 'whether it would be desirable and practicable for New Zealand to establish a currency union with Australia'.

The Director of the Institute of Policy Studies, Dr Arthur Grimes, collaborated with Sir Frank Holmes and Professor Roger Bowden in producing a report,[5] which in turn drew on reports by the New Zealand Treasury[6] and Reserve Bank.[7] It asks the question: 'Should New Zealand remain the smallest industrialised country to run an independent monetary policy?', and considers the alternatives of simply adopting the Australian dollar or attempting to negotiate an agreement with Australia to create an ANZAC dollar.

The Governor of the Reserve Bank, Don Brash, commented on the report in a speech in Auckland on 22 May 2000,[8] assuring his listeners 'that neither the Reserve Bank nor Don Brash is opposed to currency union', even though 'Don Brash would lose his job' (given his record it would hardly be difficult for him to find another one!). He gives a balanced, if mildly sceptical, account of the issues but we can take issue with him on two points.

First, he says that the issue is 'a major foreign policy decision and thus a matter for elected politicians' on which he, as a central banker, should not express an overall opinion. Surely, though, if the histories set out in this book have one lesson, it is that where monetary changes derive from political initiatives rather than competent technical analysis, disaster follows. Second, he appears to assume that 'dollarisation' will necessarily involve a loss of seigniorage income. This could be avoided by negotiation, and if that failed New Zealand could capture the seigniorage by setting up a currency board.

### The Holmes/Grimes report

Turning to the report itself, obviously an agreement with Australia would be more politically acceptable than simply 'dollarising' on the Australian unit, and would involve negotiating the creation of a joint central bank where both countries will be represented. The other alternative considered is simply to adopt the US dollar, but this is felt to be unattractive unless the Australians do the same. There was no evidence that they were interested, and there was also a rather optimistic and tentative suggestion that there could be a fully fledged monetary union with the United States:

> there is a reasonable chance that Australia will accept the concept of a joint trans-Tasman Central Bank and common currency with some New Zealand input into monetary and exchange rate policy. In a currency union with the United States New Zealand would have no such input.
>
> (Grimes and Holmes 2000, 26)

However, such an exercise would amount to dollarisation. There is perhaps a very slight possibility that if Canada as well as some Latin American countries were effectively to dollarise, some token representation might be available on the Federal Reserve Board and some agreement might be reached for the division of seigniorage, if dollarisation rather than the currency board were to be adopted.

The first two chapters of the report deal with the general issues of monetary union and, more specifically, how they have been debated in New Zealand. It was claimed (14) that currency union would not prevent the government pursuing different taxation and social welfare policies: a major issue within the EU. The authors are on safer ground when they say that union would not 'diminish the intensity of sporting rivalry between the two countries': Scotland and England have had a common currency since 1605, but 'sporting rivalry' continues unabated!

The economic arguments put forward are inevitably drawn from the general literature. The authors implicitly accept that in modern conditions a small economy must essentially choose between a floating exchange rate and a really credible fixed rate in the form of a currency board, dollarisation, or monetary union. There was a discussion of the 1990 debate (45–6) which gave less prominence to more recent discussions on the way in which capital account movements could destabilise exchange rates, and the effective prices enjoyed by producers. Inflation and interest rate differentials, more serious then than now, were discussed, and at that time the prospects for European Monetary Union looked less encouraging than subsequent events have suggested.

The other issue that is inevitably given a good airing is the optimum currency area analysis (an ANZAC area scores better than a relationship with the US dollar), the mechanism for dealing with asymmetric shocks (trade shocks have been more important in Australia, and the housing price cycle in New Zealand) and the benefit of integrated capital markets.

Seigniorage, and the problem of setting the initial conversion rate (page 23) are discussed together with the mechanics of implementation, transaction costs (the benefits here of a simple ANZAC union are reckoned to be small) and the dangers of this fiscal federalism. 'The regional agricultural and other policies of the EU already provide for much larger transfers of income within the EU than exist between Australia and New Zealand' (page 21) but of course much less than in the United States (page 21). The comment that the union would 'strengthen the case for greater harmonisation of fiscal policies between the two countries' seems to contradict what was on their page 14.

The report's chapter 3 looks at the economic data, and chapter 4 analyses the question of whether the exchange rate is a buffer against external shocks. Chapter 5 gives the result of a survey of New Zealand businessmen. Of these, 58 per cent were in favour of adopting the Australian dollar, 28 per cent were neutral and 14 per cent opposed.

### Australian views

At first there were no serious comments from the other side of the Tasman, but the Reserve Bank of Australia organised a conference on 24 July 2001. At this, Andrew Coleman of the University of Michigan (the author of an earlier paper for the New Zealand Treasury) gave a paper[9] at which he said that a 'monetary union' would in practice mean New Zealand simply 'dollarising' on the Australian dollar without having any influence on the management of the currency, and went on to ask four questions:

(a)  Why should Australia care?
(b)  What makes New Zealand different to Queensland?
(c)  Why should a currency go quietly?
(d)  Can New Zealand have its cake and eat it?

His arguments (inevitably) follow the optimum currency area issues discussed in the general literature, but his 'Queensland' comparison is interesting. The macroeconomic issues are, he argues, similar, but New Zealand, unlike Queensland, can exercise the political power to issue legal tender to raise funds. It is also 'financially and psychologically more expensive to cross the Tasman than to slop by Point Danger'. He draws on experience from Canada and from commodity markets, and has some useful comments about the influence of the shape of the yield curve which, he says, more or less defines an independent currency.

Why should Australia care? He argues that a currency union could create a big expansion (possibly a doubling) of trade across the Tasman which, although there will be winners and losers, will raise income in both countries, while even a modest increase in the liquidity of the financial markets should be welcome. Although (if there is a balance of advantage) New Zealand would enjoy a larger relative improvement, 'an increase in income is good for Australia, even if the increase is only modest: a richer New Zealand should also be good for Australia'.

He has an intriguing answer to his last question, based on an 1887 proposal by Alfred Marshall. New Zealand can, he suggests, 'have its cake and eat it' by adopting the Australian dollar and at the same time introducing a 'new indexed unit of account', whether in terms of nominal GDP, the CPI index or of house prices. 'Such a policy ... would provide the benefits of greater integration with the Australian economy as well as a means for New Zealanders to insure against shocks peculiar to New Zealand'. Coleman discusses the success of the Chilean Unidad de Fomento as a basis for believing that 'Marshall's dream' might be implemented.

## Appendix

### *The earlier history of money in Canada*

In the early days of the Canadian colonies, the pound sterling was the unit of account, but the Spanish dollar was the most widely used currency. Several units were used in different parts of Canada, the Halifax dollar, for instance, being at a premium of one ninth over the Spanish dollar. The colonies were united in the Dominion of Canada by the British North America Act of 1867, when the United States was still on an inconvertible paper standard following the Civil War. Neither 'greenbacks' nor United States private banknotes were treated with much confidence outside their place of origin.

The new Dominion formally adopted the gold standard on the UK model. The Canadian dollar was defined in terms of gold, at the pre-Civil War US standard of 232 grains of fine gold to the eagle of $10.) Gold sovereigns (at $4.867), US eagles (at par) and Dominion banknotes were all legal tender. Few gold coins circulated, and no gold coins were minted in Canada until 1908, when a branch of the UK mint started minting sovereigns, adding Canadian gold dollar coins in 1912. The Dominion government had a monopoly on the issue of smaller notes (less than $5) and also issued subsidiary silver and copper coins.

The Canadian dollar was at par with the US from 1879, when the US resumed specie payments at the prewar parity, until 1913, but this was on 'gold standard' terms. Georg Rich[10] discusses the business cycle aspects and the problems arising from having a common currency with such a powerful neighbour.

Canada was spared its large neighbour's 'Bank Wars', and the problems arising from the monetary provisions in the American Constitution which had been drawn up before it was realised that banks could create money, and which was seriously to impede the development of a national banking system in the United States. In contrast the new Dominion developed a sophisicated nationwide banking system with no artificial impediments to inter-province activities. Canadian chartered banks issued banknotes for $5 and more. These were not legal tender but were redeemable in specie or in

Dominion notes, the latter having little circulation outside the banking system, being mainly used as a reserve asset. There was little formal regulation, but Rich says (33) that 'despite the relaxed regulatory environment' the system was 'remarkably resistant to financial crises'. (He adds in a footnote that Hayek would substitute 'because of' for 'despite'.) Indeed, the panics of 1893 and 1907 did not, in Canada, result in bank failures or the suspension of specie payments, although in the latter case 'a liquidity squeeze ... prompted the government to act informally as a lender of last resort'.

On the outbreak of the First World War Canada abandoned convertibility and imposed exchange controls. Paul Wonnacott[11] gives a chart showing the fluctuations of the Canadian dollar from 1919–50. It fell below 90 cents in the period immediately following the First World War but quickly recovered to around par. Canada returned to the gold standard in 1926, but following a large outflow of gold in 1928 there was a *de facto* suspension early in 1929. The currency then again dipped below 90 cents but recovered by 1934, and indeed remained at a premium over the US dollar until the outbreak of war.

Canada did not have a central bank until 1935, when one was formed following Montagu Norman's crusade to ensure that every country had one. Indeed, Norman despatched the Bank of England's Secretary, Osborne, to be its first deputy Governor. There was a Royal Commission on Banking and Currency in 1933, but it deals almost entirely with domestic banking, with barely a mention of foreign exchange.[12]

### The Second World War and after

On the outbreak of war in 1939 the previously floating exchange rate of the British pound was fixed at $4.03, substantially below the rate that had been ruling in the late 1930s. This effective devaluation of the currency of its second main trading partner brought Canada's dollar under pressure, and the value was officially fixed at US$0.909. A Foreign Exchange Control Board was set up, bringing into force the Exchange Fund Act of 1935, mainly to prevent a flight of capital from Canada to the United States (this Act was superseded by the Foreign Exchange Control Act 1947, renewed in 1949 and 1951). There was nevertheless a sharp fall in Canadian official reserves, and new restrictive measures were introduced on 18 November 1947. The associated legislation did not pass until four months later, and there were bitter attacks by the opposition on such arbitrary action and a 'complete outright and a deliberate breach of faith with Parliament' (Wonnacott 1965, 52 and n16). The question of whether exchange control could have been avoided by devaluation was widely discussed: the currency had been revalued to par with the US dollar in 1946. Differential consumption taxes were applied to discourage imports, supplemented by controls of imports, largely removed after 1948.

The Canadian dollar was formally devalued to 92.5 cents shortly after the corresponding devaluation of sterling in 1949. In 1950 Canada, the nearest neighbour of the United States, whose dollar was beyond doubt the anchor currency of the period, was perhaps surprisingly the first to make a break with Britain in wanting to float its currency. The Canadian dollar immediately rose to over 95 cents, and indeed after 1952 was consistently at a modest premium over its US counterpart. The currency was again fixed at 108 cents in 1962, but floated again in 1970. Again, it initially went to a premium, about 104 cents in 1974, before falling sharply to 79 cents by 1986, recovering to 89 cents in 1991, but trading in the 64–9 cent range for most of the 1990s.

# Part X

# Postwar Latin America and the Far East

# 53  Postwar Latin America

## Introduction

Latin America is an area generally notorious for currency instability, but even after the collapse of the Bretton Woods system in 1973, many countries still continued to fix their exchange rates to the US dollar. The monetary experiences of the area include currency boards and dollarisation as well as hyper-inflationary collapses, but with little interest in regional monetary unions. There seems to be no comparative monetary history of Latin America, and this chapter does not aspire to fill the gap, dealing selectively only with a few topics relevant to the theme of the book, with a little more detail on Argentina, Brazil and Chile. Those who believe that 'floating' means 'sinking' will find many examples to support their views – but so will those who argue that fixed rates will sooner or later end in tears.

## Latin America between the wars

To pick up the story from Chapter 16, before the First World War many, but not all, Latin American countries had adopted a gold standard. Some – Cuba, the Dominican Republic, Haiti, Nicaragua and Panama – were effectively dollarised and maintained fairly stable exchange rates through and immediately after the war. In the 1920s some of the others joined the gold standard, but the laggards, Argentina, Bolivia, Brazil, Ecuador and Peru, only stabilised their currencies in around 1928,[1] and were then soon to suffer from the UK's suspension of the gold standard on 21 September 1931. Colombia tried to maintain the standard, but abandoned the attempt when international reserves declined by 65 per cent in four days. Argentina, Mexico and Uruguay had already suspended the gold standard and most countries (except the 'dollarised' ones) introduced exchange controls.

Argentina, Bolivia, Paraguay and Uruguay had effectively been on a sterling exchange standard, and their currencies fell sharply against the US dollar in 1931, but appreciated in April 1933 when the Americans in turn abandoned the gold standard. As with the collapse of bimetallism, these currency movements resulting from far away and irrelevant events seriously disrupted their own economies. The five originally dollarised countries, plus

Honduras, then pegged their currencies to the US dollar, but Costa Rica, El Salvador and Nicaragua, having tried and failed to follow their examples, were forced to devalue. The Venezuelan Bolivar was floated, actually rising 50 per cent against the US dollar between end 1932 and end 1937, while some other countries adopted a dual exchange system.[2]

## Post 1945: a general outline

After the war, international finance and trade was limited by exchange controls. Bolivia, Chile and Paraguay had high rates of inflation during 1950–5, as did Argentina, Brazil and Uruguay during the next fifteen years. In spite of this, as late as 1979, thirteen countries still continued to fix their exchange rates to the US dollar, although of these, all but Panama, Haiti and the Dominican Republic had left by 1990.[3] Kiguel and Liviatan[4] discuss hyper-inflations in Argentina, Brazil and Peru and contrast them with those of the 1920s, commenting that Bolivia (1982) follows the classic pattern: inflation of 'only' 25 per cent in 1981 jumped to 300 per cent in 1982, and 8,000 per cent by 1985. They describe Peru as 'unique' in that an inflation rate of 30–40 per cent per month (just short of the 50 per cent classic hyper-inflation definition which usually signals the imminent destruction of a currency) persisted for years.

Wise and Roett (2000)[5] deal almost entirely with the 1990s, and include an interesting chapter by Max Corden on the merits of fixed and floating regimes. Carol Wise (2000, 94) points out that in 1975 countries with fixed regimes accounted for 75 per cent of world trade: by 1996 the figure was down to 2 per cent.

When 'fixed' systems began to break down, some countries adopted 'crawling peg' and 'band' systems. Mexico used exchange rate bands, hoping to provide flexibility while holding on to an anchor. Managed floats were used by Bolivia (1985) and Peru (1990) in attempts to stabilise, and by Mexico (1994) and Brazil (1999) to recover from a crisis. Venezuela established fixed rates in 1994 but had to abandon them in 1996. Peru had flexible rates and low inflation from 1992 to 1994. As in Chile, which also had low inflation, there was substantial effective *de facto* wage indexation. The monetary crises in Brazil (1997) and Argentina (2001) are too recent and complex for a dispassionate analysis, but already have some interesting lessons.

## Argentina

Argentina at first suffered from chronic inflation, but in 1967 had a mildly successful stabilisation programme based on price controls and cuts in government expenditure in 1967. This broke down with a devaluation and renewed inflation in 1970, and a new government imposed a price freeze in June 1973. This was followed by a military coup in March 1976. A policy of using the exchange rate with a schedule ('tablita') of pre-determined valuations, was abandoned in March 1981 because of major problems with foreign debt.

### The Austral Plan

Following the Falklands conflict there were further devaluations and a run on the peso. In June 1983 the 'peso Argentino' replaced the peso, dropping four noughts, and inflation accelerated. The Austral Plan was introduced in June 1985, with a more formal system of indexation and a new currency, the austral, worth a thousand peso Argentino (10 million old pesos) was pegged at 0.8 to the dollar. Inflation initially fell, but certain provinces began issuing their own bonds which served as money to meet their expenditure. Inflation rose again in 1987: the austral was devalued and replaced with a crawling peg. In October 1987 there was a further devaluation and a two-tier exchange rate system, while in August 1988 the commercial rate fell to 12 and the financial rate to 14.4 per dollar.

A paper by Pedro Pow,[6] Governor of the Central Bank, gives a brief mention of the aftermath of the austral plan when he says the first debt crisis was in full swing. Growth of real output stagnated, financial markets collapsed, prices rose as the currency steadily depreciated and capital fled the country in pursuit of safer havens. Most public enterprises were running large deficits and the external debt kept mounting. The government, unable to collect sufficient taxes, turned on the printing presses, inflation reached 'average annual rates' of 2,600 per cent in 1989 and 1990, and the banking system virtually collapsed.

### The convertibility plan

President Carlos Menem introduced the Convertibility Plan in April 1991, the law providing that the Central Bank could print pesos only to the level of its gold and foreign exchange reserves. Although it was effectively operating as a currency board, it was not subject to the same 'hard' disciplines and could include dollar (or gold) denominated government bonds (at market price) as part of the reserves. The bank continued to carry on 'lender of last resort' functions (using reserves surplus to those required as currency backing) and retained power to control reserve requirements and to increase deposit insurance premiums. In common with true currency boards, it only purported to guarantee banknotes, and not the substantial deposits built on the monetary base.

The Convertibility Law prohibited indexation but provided that contracts denominated in foreign currencies could be made and enforced. The country in fact became substantially dollarised, and specifically many domestic mortgage loans were in US dollars.

A currency reform as such is not of itself sufficient for economic stability, and the 1991 package included improvements in tax collection and checks in public expenditure. However, the lack of a hard budget constraint made it possible for the government to overspend, and the problem was compounded by the lack of any effective central control on expenditure by the individual states, which had substantial *de facto* fiscal independence.

The currency regime survived the effects of the Mexican crisis of 1995, but bank deposits declined by 18 per cent over five months, causing a liquidity squeeze. Substantial government support was given to the banking system, and the Central Bank set up a mandatory private deposit insurance in April 1995 up to $20,000 (later $30,000) per depositor. Subsequent events in South-East Asia (1997) and Russia (1998) seem to have had relatively little effect.

### Monetary union with Brazil?

There was talk at that time of dollarisation and also of monetary union. Calvo[7] discusses the advantages of dollarisation. His proposals involved negotiating with the US government to receive a gift of the seigniorage of $750 million lost. This (he says) would enable the Argentinian government to borrow over $10 billion at essentially the risk free rate, but this would eliminate currency crises and (he claims) help create bank liquidity but this seems optimistic.

In June 1999 there were reports that Argentina and Brazil were meeting to discuss a monetary union, intending to create a Maastricht-type programme. This might well have been disastrous for both countries.

### The collapse of the convertibility plan

The growth in public expenditure put the system under considerable strain in 2001, and the government first took action to block bank deposits. This naturally proved unpopular and there have been variants. Attempts were made to impose differential rules on assets and liabilities. Mortgages might be redenominated in pesos while dollar deposits would (eventually) be made in dollars, which could put a serious squeeze on the banks. There was also an asymmetric treatment of the tax effects of foreign currency movements: profits on foreign exchange assets or liabilities would be taxed in the normal way but loses would have to be spread over a five-year period. There were the usual distortions of renewed inflation on tax computations. The story continues.

Many commentators had argued (Steve Hanke being an exception) that the country needed a real depreciation in its currency to bring down dollar wages and generally to mop up surplus purchasing power. 'Devaluation' of perhaps 20 per cent was needed, but this was difficult to engineer. Interestingly, both in Russia and elsewhere devaluations during the past twenty years have typically worked, activating a lasting fall in real exchange rates and discrediting the belief, widely held in the 1970s and sometimes put forward years later, that devaluation 'didn't work' as it automatically led to correspondingly rising prices.

## Brazil

Brazil has renamed its currency many times, but without the predecessor currency ever being completely destroyed: the typical operation has involved simply dropping three noughts. The cumulative effect, though, has resulted in the 'real', introduced in July 1994, being worth 2,750 million million million of the early postwar cruzieros!

### *Monetary correction*

After the revolution of March 31, 1964, Roberto Campos introduced a policy of price correction with two new classes of indexed government security (ORTNs and LTNs), designed to give a real return on savings and to allow the creation of credit without letting inflation get out of hand. These continued to be issued until 1986. In 1966 a more comprehensive policy of 'monetary correction' was introduced, going far beyond 'indexation' as normally understood and covering most types of financial transaction. In 1967, as a mark of confidence, the new cruziero was issued equal to 1,000 of the cruziero which had been current since 1942 (in 1970 'new' was dropped from the name). Inflation fell at first, but increased after 1979.

The oil crisis and the overexpanding money supply ruined Delfim's plans, and he was replaced as minister by Mario Simonsen, who introduced the National Development Plan, involving more international borrowing, which financed profitable investment until upset by the Second Oil Shock.

### *The Cruzado Plan*

In 1984 Jose Sarney took over from an unpopular military government. Inflation rose and the currency collapsed. He continued the high-growth strategy but the falling currency and high government spending caused inflation to rocket to 225 per cent in 1985. The central bank reckoned that price increases could reach 800 per cent by the end of 1986, and the Cruzado Plan was born. Another three noughts were dropped, the cruzado being worth 1,000 1967 cruziero novo.

The Cruzado Plan had as its objective the elimination of inflation and the maintenance of the purchasing power of the currency. Although the news of de-indexing was welcome to the Brazilian population, it was not expected, so the impact of the short sharp shock was all the greater. It had several elements.

The indexed ORTN was replaced by the National Treasury Bond (OTN). Monetary correction was abolished, but agreements with a term of more than one year may be indexed to the par value of OTN. Certain savings accounts, employees' severance indemnity funds (FGTS) and certain welfare programme funds remained subject to limited indexation. Wages and salaries were converted from cruzeiros to cruzados by a formula.

Depreciation then resumed, and on two occasions three more noughts were dropped. In January 1989 the cruzado novo (Cz$1,000) was created, replaced by the cruziero (Cr$1 = Cz1,000) which was in turn superseded by the cruziero real (CR$1 = Cr$1,000) in August 1993.

### The Real Plan

This was followed by a more successful reform, the Real Plan, implemented on 1 July 1994, the 'real' (plural reais) being equal to £CR2750 or 2.75 billion of the 1984 cruzados. The first stage was to convert salaries and certain other prices into URVs (real value units) linked to the US dollar, and these were eventually converted into reais. The plan did not depend on a price and wage freeze, and effectively involved de-indexing the economy. Unlike Argentina, Brazil did not make a commitment to stabilise the currency. Initially the real actually appreciated against the US dollar, and inflation fell from over 400 per cent per annum to 23 per cent (1995), 11 per cent (1996), 5.3 per cent (1997) and 2 per cent (1998). The value of the real fell by only 20 per cent against the dollar in four and a half years.

A 'crisis' hit in January 1999 when, following the events in South-East Asia and Russia, there was a 'dramatic collapse' of the real – by 19 per cent, followed by a free float. The currency lost half of its value over the next two years, and two-thirds by the end of 2001, by which time the Argentinian crisis had hit.

It is too early to discuss the very interesting contrast between various Latin American countries, but the performance of the Real Plan during the first seven years compares favourably with the performance of the previous half century: the real on its introduction was worth 2,750,000,000,000,000, 000,000 immediate postwar cruzerios!

## Chile

This is a contrasting case study. In September 1973, General Pinochet 'inherited a battered economy and an inflation of more than 500 per cent per year',[8] and in 1978 adopted an exchange rate based policy, 'tablita', setting targeted rates of devaluation at below the rate of inflation.[9] This was designed to force price discipline and change expectations, but wage indexation was retained. In June 1979 the peso was pegged at 39 to the US dollar, even though annual inflation was still 34 per cent and, contrary to expectations continued high, forcing a real appreciation and a deep recession. First results were good: inflation fell to 29 per cent in 1980 and 12 per cent in 1981; there was a sharp recovery and an inflow of foreign capital. Unfortunately, though, the US was about to adopt a tight money policy, leading to a sharp recession and an appreciation in the value of the dollar.

Chile was forced by its monetary regime to shadow this inappropriate policy, the fixed parity was abandoned in 1982, and in 1985 a 'crawling peg' regime was introduced. Edwards analyses the figures, which suggest that in this case the exchange rate anchor failed to change inflationary expectations, perhaps because of the indexation provisions. At the end of 2001, inflation was still low and the currency was stable.

# 54 Hong Kong and the Far East post-1945

## Introduction

Since 1945 the Far East has been the scene of great economic triumphs – and disasters. Japan's economy grew to be second in size only to the United States, with a booming stock exchange and property prices, but the bubble burst and by the end of the century the Japanese banking system was probably insolvent. The 'Asian Tigers' such as South Korea, Malaysia, and Thailand, became major industrial powers – but had their own problems in 1997. Hong Kong and Singapore became major international financial centres, and China, while remaining communist, seemed to adopt capitalism more smoothly than the Russians.

Japan is, from many points of view, the most interesting country. Making a rapid postwar economic recovery, it put its exchange control into reverse in 1968 to stop hot money coming in. After the collapse of Bretton Woods it was the second currency, after the deutschmark, to float – upwards. The Japanese economy grew to be second only to that of the United States, the yen became a major world currency and, with the Tokyo stock market, a favourite of investors.

Perhaps surprisingly though, there was little interest in regional monetary unions, and the yen neither became a reserve currency nor took on a regional role. Neither the Japanese nor their neighbours seemed to want this, and much international trade, even with Japan, was conducted in dollars.

The eventual collapse was equally dramatic, and by the end of the century the economy was still in a long recession with little evidence of any political will to do anything about it. Although Japan's history is an important backdrop to a broader discussion of the economy of the region, the yen never formed the basis for any actual or seriously projected monetary area, and a detailed discussion is outside the scope of this book.

## Hong Kong to 1997

Hong Kong has had a particularly interesting history, with successive links with silver, sterling, the US dollar and China. Following the US Silver

Purchase Act of 1934,[1] Hong Kong moved from a silver standard to a sterling-based currency board system in December 1935. The Exchange Fund effectively acted as a currency board, maintaining a fixed rate of 16 HK$ per pound sterling. Legal tender notes were issued, not by the Exchange Fund itself but by the banks against its certificates of indebtedness.

In July 1972 the relationship ended following the sterling float, and the Hong Kong dollar was briefly pegged to the US dollar, but in 1974 this was in turn abandoned following the effective devaluation of the dollar. From then until 1983 the HK$ floated, but the issuing banks still had to buy (now HK$-denominated) CIs against note issues. The HK$ remained strong until 1977, but from May 1979 these banks were required to maintain 100 per cent reserves, and in 1982 there were financial crises, a run on the banks and a sharp depreciation in the HK$, occasioned partly by the start of Sino-British negotiation over the future of the territory.[2]

On 17 October 1983 the HK$ was again pegged, but this time against the US dollar at HK$ 7.8 = US$1. In 1988 the Exchange Fund was permitted to conduct open market operations, and in December 1992 its functions, together with those of the Commissioner of Banking, were transferred to the Hong Kong Monetary Authority.

The system is a modified currency board requiring the two note-issuing banks (HSBC and Chartered) to hold 100 per cent backing in certificates of indebtedness issued by the Hong Kong Monetary Authority (previously the Exchange Fund) which are themselves backed by foreign assets. HSBC acts as the *de facto* lender of last resort. In January 1988 there were capital inflows expecting revaluation, and in January 1995 the HK$ came under pressure in the wake of the Mexican crisis. Alan Walters[3] (discussing the contrasting experiences of a number of countries with different monetary arrangements) points out that Hong Kong's fixed exchange rate meant that, given free markets, the interest rate structure in Hong Kong was determined by US policy and could not be adjusted to meet the specific requirements of Hong Kong. Inflation rates would be higher if productivity growth were greater.

## China

China had benefited from its silver standard in the early years of the Depression, but later there was a large outflow of silver,[4] a currency reform on 3 November 1935, a major inflation after 1937, and a 'Cagan' hyperinflation in 1949 when the nationalists lost power to the communists.

Pyle[5] gives a succinct outline of China's economy from 1800 through the communist victory of 1949, the 'Great Leap Forward' of 1958–66 and the horrors of Mao's Cultural Revolution during the next ten years. He goes on to discuss[6] the problems and defects of money, banking and fiscal reform, but says 'compared with the countries of Eastern Europe, China's path to economic transition has been remarkably smooth'. To him the real puzzle was how China achieved relative price level stability, but this 'success' surely reflects the failure to create proper price signals: the Soviet Union had very stable prices and exchange rates until the system of administered prices was abolished. The reforms have on the whole been more successful than those of Eastern Europe in delivering rising living standards,[7] but there are no simple answers, and Pyle concludes, 'The future of China, like its past, looks exciting, unpredictable and fraught with danger.'

## The Asian Tigers

Growth and prosperity in the so-called 'Asian Tigers' had seemed unstoppable, but there was a collapse of financial markets, beginning with the devaluation of the Thai baht, in June 1997. This was quickly followed in Indonesia, Korea, Malaysia and, less dramatically, in the Philippines, Singapore and Taiwan. Hong Kong came under attack, but held its parity thanks to its substantially over-reserved currency board. Since then most of the countries (Indonesia being the exception) have recovered part of the exchange loss and enjoyed a fairly general economic recovery.

What went wrong? The currencies of the countries concerned had all been, more or less, and generally informally, shadowing the US dollar, only Hong Kong having a formal peg. This might seem odd, given that Japan is the largest trading nation in the region, but that does not in fact seem to have been the problem, and Japan still actually invoices more of its exports in dollars than it does in yen. The weakness of the Japanese economy and the large fluctuations of the yen against the dollar, were a contributory, if not a key, factor.

The main problem seems to have been very substantial unhedged foreign currency borrowing (based on a belief that the exchange rates would hold) to take advantage of profitable interest rate differentials. (Even after this experience the banks made very similar mistakes in Russia, Argentina and Turkey!) This was encouraged by what is politely referred to as 'moral hazard'. A solvent commercial organisation will take calculated risks in managing its finances, balancing the immediate benefit of interest rate differentials with the risk of adverse foreign exchange rate movements, on the basis that the calculated odds are in its favour and that the 'worst case' outcome will not threaten the survival of the business. A solvent and well conducted bank will be even more cautious: the gains of guessing right are only money, but the penalty of being seen to guess wrong can damage reputation.

It is very different for a bank (or other organisation) where the management knows, but lenders and depositors do not, that its solvency is threatened. A high-risk strategy may then, if it works out, save the situation and at worst stave off the evil day. From the point of view of management it does not matter whether the bank closes down quietly, paying 90 cents in the dollar to its depositors, or collapses disastrously. Either way they will lose their jobs, a risk many of them regard more serious than the much larger losses borne by mere depositors. (In the Barings and other similar cases generally irrelevant to our history, 'rogue traders' bet, and lost, the value of the bank simply in the hope of preserving their bonuses.) In Asia enthusiastic and ill-informed foreign investors rushed to take advantage of higher returns, not realising that, thanks to 'crony capitalism', any profits are extracted by insiders while risks are left with investors and depositors. As with Russia a year later, unwise borrowing, and lending, was the key to the crisis.

The IMF moved in quickly to give assistance, and although there is more than one school of thought about how effective this was, a paper by Stanley Fischer[8] argues, almost convincingly and with the help of an accompanying chart, that the crisis was in fact contained.

## Hong Kong's reversion to China in 1997

The Sino-British Joint Declaration of 1985 stated that Hong Kong would retain its system for fifty years, and the Basic Law provides that Hong Kong will maintain its own currency and independent monetary policy. Anna Schwartz, writing in 1992, was not convinced, and commented on the 'slippery slope' away from a rule-based system.[9]

A 1996 conference looked at the possible economic consequence of the then imminent union of Hong Kong with China.[10] Two contributors discussed, from different standpoints, the future of the Hong Kong currency. As explained above, the Hong Kong dollar had been pegged at the US dollar since 1980, backed by what amounts to a currency board. The Basic Law provides that the Hong Kong dollar should be freely convertible and backed by a 100 per cent reserve fund, but although it was generally assumed that China would defend the peg there is no formal mention in the documents. Would there indeed be 'one country, two currencies', with free markets between the rembinini and the Hong Kong dollar?[11] The official line was that 'the Hong Kong dollar and the rembinini will circulate as legal tender in Hong Kong and the mainland respectively. The HK dollar will be treated as a foreign currency in the mainland. Likewise the rembinini will be treated as a foreign currency in Hong Kong.'

Milton Friedman was quoted as predicting that the currencies would be merged in a couple of years, and Hong Kong's reserves taken over by China. If the Chinese currency were to become fully convertible this would create no problems, and the US dollar could then, if necessary, become the *de facto* currency of international business in Hong Kong, but if the convertible Hong Kong dollar was tied to an inconvertible Chinese currency, this would create the interesting problems and opportunities we had in the days of UK exchange control and 'external sterling'.

Bowring commented that

> it is perhaps curious that while the Hong Kong premium ... is only 50–60 basis points the premium for the Thai Baht which has *a better*

*history of stability than the Hong Kong dollar and no fundamental polit-*
*ical problems* is around 350 basis points.

(emphasis added)[12]

Soon afterwards the baht collapsed, but although there was a huge spike in
the Hong Kong interest premium, the currency itself held firm.

It is possible to conceive of two currencies remaining legal tender, at least
in certain areas. This is rare: 'a few countries or territories have opted to use
as legal tender another country's currency (for example Panama) however
none has yet opted for more than one legal tender'. Maybe, in this century,
but the range of possibilities is more than adequately discussed in the
history of bimetallism.

If there was a crisis of confidence, and Hong Kong residents tried to
convert their Hong Kong dollar deposits into US dollars, they could, in the
last resort, do so only by first converting their bank deposits into Hong
Kong dollar bills, and this would probably break the banks. The Hong Kong
Monetary Authority would either have to accept this (as in rather different
circumstances did the Estonians) or be prepared to break the link, subject to
the (presumably) inalienable right of actual holders of banknotes to convert
these into US dollars.

The handover of Hong Kong was completed without serious hitches, and
in September 1997 the Chinese president announced what sounded like a
far-reaching reform of the state sector. China and Hong Kong have (so far)
avoided the major financial meltdown suffered in the area, although a study
by the Peregrine Group (brokers) suggested that China's banks had 'non-
performing loans' of some $270 billion or 30 per cent of total loans, a
proportion comparable with Korea and Thailand (the figure given for Hong
Kong was just 1 per cent). China may have been saved by its more protec-
tionist and controlled policies, its weaker currency and substantial reserves,
which raises a very interesting question. While China's rulers react to the
shock by continuing to insulate the economy from the outside world, will
such polices simply delay the crisis, or will they find themselves in a position
of strength from which to make a less painful transition to liberalisation?

## Singapore

The Malayan Currency Board was replaced in June 1967 by the Singapore
Board of Commissioners of Currency, issuing notes and coin fully backed
by sterling, and the Bank Negara Malaysia, established 1958, began to issue
gold backed ringgits. Following the floating of the pound in 1972, both
pegged to the US dollar with an IMF-approved wide band of 4.43 per cent.
In February 1973, when the US dollar devalued against gold, both reverted
to a gold parity, but in June 1973 both currencies floated and ceased to be
interchangeable. The currencies initally strengthened. There is a chart in
IMF 1997.[13]

## East Timor and Indonesia: a 'disunion'

East Timor was a Portugese colony, and part of the escudo zone, until 1975 when the country was invaded by Indonesia (formerly a Dutch colony), which introduced the rupiah and established a branch of the Indonesian Central Bank to handle currency matters. In October 1999 East Timor voted for independence under United Nations supervision, but the transition was not peaceful. A newly independent country needed a currency, and the rupiah was hardly an ideal candidate.

Fernando DePeralto, a former deputy Governor of the Jamaican Central Bank, was appointed head of a Central Payments Office with, in effect, the task of creating a new monetary system. He considered a number of currencies, including the Australian dollar, rejected the euro as not then being a fully operational currency, and finally opted for the US dollar. The UN Transitional Administration has been active in repatriating rupiahs, and in April 2002 the dollar became the official currency.

# Notes

## 1 General introduction

1  Chown, John, *A History of Money*, Routledge: London, 1994, paperback edn 1996.

## 2 The gold standard

1  Chown, John, *A History of Money*, Routledge: London, 1994, paperback edn 1996.
2  Panic, Mica, *European Monetary Union: Lessons from the Classical Gold Standard*, Macmillan: London, 1992.
3  Triffin, Robert, *Money and Banking in Colombia Federal Reserve System*, Washington DC, June 1944.
4  Edwin W. Kemmerer, *Gold and the Gold Standard*, McGraw Hill: New York and London, 1944, 98.

## 3 Fixed versus floating exchange rates

1  Wyplosz, Charles, 'A Monetary Union in Asia? Some European Lessons', paper to conference organised by Reserve Bank of Australia, 24 July 2001. Further reference is also to this work.
2  This comment appeared in my 1994 book. More recently George Soros has put the same point rather better: 'I often compare currency arrangements with matrimonial arrangements: whatever regime prevails, its opposite looks more attractive'.
3  Barry Eichengreen, *International Monetary Arrangements for the 21st Century*, Brookings Institution: Washington DC, 1995.

## 4 Types of 'fixed' monetary arrangement

1  Hayek, F. A., 'Choice in Currency: A Way to Stop Inflation', Institute of Economic Affairs, London, 1976.
2  Schwartz, Anna, 'Do Currency Boards Have a Future?', IEA Occasional Paper 88, November 1992.
3  See e.g. his contribution on currency boards in *The New Palgrave*, Macmillan: London, 1987.
4  A bibliography and some recent contributions can be found at http:///www.erols.com/currency/index.html.
5  Tomas, J. T. and Charles Enoch Balino, 'Currency Board Arrangements, Issues and Experience', IMF Occasional Paper: Washington DC, August 1997. See also Charles Enoch and Anne Marie Guile, 'Making a Currency Board Operational', IMF Occasional Paper: Washington DC, October 1997.

6 'Proceedings of a Conference on Currency Substitution and Currency Boards', ed. Nissan Liviatan, World Bank Discussion Paper 207, October 1993.
7 Kurt Schuler, 'So You Want to Dollarise?', May 1998, Available at http://www.erols.com/kurrency.
8 Hanke, Steve H., Lars Jonung and Kurt Schuler, *Russian Currency and Finance: A Currency Board Approach to Reform*, London: Routledge, 1993.
9 *Palgrave's Dictionary*, 1926 edn.
10 Friedman, Milton, *Money Mischief*, Harcourt Brace: New York, 1992, ch. 9.
11 Tomas, J. T. and Charles Enoch Balino, 'Currency Board Arrangements, Issues and Experience', IMF Occasional Paper 151: Washington DC, August 1997.
12 *Ibid.* cites Virgil Salera, *Exchange Control and the Argentine Market*, Columbia University Press: New York, 1941, 18–51.
13 Chown, John, *A History of Money*, Routledge: London, 1994, paperback edn 1996, particulary ch. 2.
14 Neumann's definition of monetary seigniorage is 'obtained by simply measuring the change in base money, deflated by some price index. The Central Bank issues base money in return for some non-money asset. The real value of that asset is seigniorage.' While 'opportunity cost seigniorage', more relevant to a studies of optimal inflation rates can be measured as 'the product of the nominal rate of interest and of the holdings of real base money'. There is a table on page 75 giving some key statistics for a number of CIS countries and quoting an OECD source (Manfred J. M. Neumann, 'Seigniorage in the United States: How much Does the US Government Make from Money Production?', Federal Reserve Bank of St Louis, March/April 1992).
15 Despres, Emile, Charles P. Kindleberger and Walter S. Salant, 'The Dollar and World Liquidity: A Minority View', *Economist*, 5 February 1966.

## 5  Monetary unions

1 Mundell, Robert A., 'Theory of Optimal Currency Areas', *American Economic Review*, 51, 1961.
2 Frankel, Jeffrey A. and Andrew K. Rose, 'Estimating the Effect of Currency Unions on Trade and Output', Working Paper 7857, National Bureau of Economic Research, Cambridge MA, August 2000.
3 Chown, John, 'Monetary Union and Tax Harmonisation', in Lindencrona, Lodin and Wiman (eds) *International Studies in Taxation: Law and Economics. Liber Amicorum Leif Muten*, Kluwer Law International: London, The Hague and Washington, 1999. An updated version of this paper was published in *Intertax*, vol. 23, no. 3, 2000.
4 Chadha, Jagjit S. and Suzanne L. Hudson, 'A Short Survey of Monetary Unions', Monetary Analysis, Bank of England 1997 (Copies available from Publications Group, Bank of England, London EC2R 8AH, tel. 020 7601 4030).
5 Panic, Mica, *European Monetary Union: Lessons from the Classical Gold Standard*, Macmillan: London, 1992.

## 6  Exchange control and currency reconstructions

1 Ellis, Howard S., 'Exchange Control in Central Europe', *Harvard Economic Studies*, vol. 69, 1941.

## 7  Some early history

1 Brooke, G. C., *English Coins*, Methuen: London, 1932.

2  A fairly comprehensive range of these imitations is described and illustrated in the catalogue of the 'Viking' collection sale by Spink, London, 14 March 2001.
3  Chown, John, *A History of Money*, Routledge: London, 1994, paperback edn 1996.
4  Clapham, John, *The Bank of England: A History*, Cambridge University Press: Cambridge, 1970, vol. I, 60.
5  Meadows, Andrew, 'Earlier Monetary Unions', paper given to American Numismatic Society, 1999. Since published as 'Le unione monetarie e la sfida del nazionalismo', in L. Sommo and G. Campani (eds) *L'Euro. Scenari Economici e Dimensione Simbolica*, Milan, 2001.
6  Davies, Glyn, *A History of Money From Ancient Times to the Present Day*, University of Wales Press: Cardiff, 1994.
7  Burns, A. R., *Monery and Monetary Policy in Early Times*, Kegan Paul: London, 1927, 20.

## 8  The Napoleonic Wars and after: bimetallism

1  *Palgrave's Dictionary*, 1926 edn.
2  Chown, John, *A History of Money*, Routledge: London, 1994
3  Redish, Angela, *Bimetallism: An Economic and Historial Analysis*, Cambridge University Press: Cambridge, 2000.
4  Chown, John, *A History of Money*, Routledge: London, 1994, ch. 23. See also Murphy, Antoin E., *John Law: Economist, Theorist and Policy Maker*, Clarendon Press: Oxford, 1997.
5  Chown, *ibid.*, ch. 7.
6  Clapham, John, *The Bank of England: A History*, Cambridge University Press: Cambridge, 1970.

## 9  Monetary union in Germany, Italy and Switzerland

1  Kindleberger, Charles H., *Financial History of Western Europe*, George Allen & Unwin: London, 1984.
2  According to A. Del Mar (in A History of Monetary Systems, Effingham Wilson, London, 1895), from 1 January 1841 the thaler was legal tender in the Prussian states, Saxe-Royal Electorial Hesse, Saxony, Saxe-Altenburg, Saxe-Coburg Gotha, Saxe-Anhalt-Bemburg, Schwartzburg-Sondenhausen, Schwartzburg-Rudolstadt, and the Reuss States, while the florin had this status in Bavaria, Wurtemburg, Baden, Ducal Hesse, Saxe-Meininngen, Ducal Saxe-Coburg Gotha, Nassau, Schwartzburg-Rudolstadt, and the City of Frankfurt.
3  *United States National Monetary Commission 1909*, vol. X, 11.
4  I am indebted to Professor David Speiser, whose wife and mine are cousins, for additional information on his ancestor.
5  Preliminary Report of the Decimal Coinage Commissioners, London, 1857.
6  *Ibid.*, 292.
7  Julius Landmann, 'The Swiss Banking Law' in *United States National Monetary Commission 1909*, vol. XVII.
8  *Ibid.*, 12–13.
9  Chown, John, *A History of Money*, Routledge: London, 1994.
10  Julius Landmann, 'The Swiss Banking Law' in *United States National Monetary Commission 1909*, vol. XVII, 69–70.

## 10  The Austro-Hungarian empire as a monetary union: history to 1914

1  *National Monetary Commission*, vol. 18, 'Banking in Italy, Russia, Austro-Hungary and Japan', The Austro-Hungarian Bank. Professor Zuckerkandl, Washington DC, 1911,pp. 57 ff.

2 *Ibid.*, 61.

3 *Ibid.*, 75.

4 Del Mar: he lists ten systems in existence in Germany. He refers to his 'Money and Civilisation' at 339 and to 'United States Commercial Relations' 1867, at 447.

5 Dornbusch, Rudiger, *Monetary Problems of Post-Communism: Lessons from the End of the Austro-Hungarian Empire*. Archiv: Review of World Economics. (Journal of the Kiel Institute of World Economics Tubingen. Band 128 Heft 3 1992, 391 ff.

6 Krause, Chester L. and Clifford Mischler, *Standard Catalog of World Coins*, Krause Publications: Iola WI.

7 Flandreau, Marc, 'The Bank the States and the Market: An Austro Hungarian Tale for EMU 1867–1914', paper to City University Monetary Unions Conference, May 1999. He cites Simon Aberdam, 'La banque d'emission hongroise', *Journal des Economistes*, May 1910, vol. VI, no. XXVI, 223–31.

8 'By contrast to the common accounts they were not bound to be in equilibrium. This was the expression of each country's sovereignty and an essential building block of dualism' (Flandreau 1999, 6).

9 *National Monetary Commission*, vol. 18, 'Banking in Italy, Russia, Austro-Hungary and Japan', The Austro-Hungarian Bank. Professor Zuckerkandl, Washington DC, 1911, 100.

10 G. F. Knapp, author of *The State Theory of Money*. The English translation by H. M. Lucas and J. Bonar (Macmillan, 1924) omits the historical country analyses.

11 Young, John Parke, *Commission of Gold and Silver Inquiry, United States Senate. Foreign Currency and Exchange Investigation*, GPO: Washington DC, 1925, Serial 9, vol. II, 10.

12 Garber, Peter N. and Michael G. Spencer, *The Dissolution of the Austro-Hungarian Empire: Lessons for Currency Reform*, Princeton Essays in International Finance, no. 191, February 1994, 4.

13 *Ibid.*, 32.

## 11 The Latin Monetary Union

1 Redish, Angela, *Bimetallism: An Economic and Historial Analysis*, Cambridge University Press: Cambridge, 2000.

2 For English translation of the text see J. Laurence Laughlin, *The History of Bimetallism in the United States*, 2nd edn, Appleton and Company: New York, 1892, appendix IIID.

3 Russell, Henry B., *International Monetary Conferences*, Harper Brothers: New York and London, 1898, 28.

4 Since this chapter was drafted, Luca L. Einaudi (*Economic History Review*, vol. LIII, no. 2, May 2000, 284–308) has published an article 'From the Franc to the "Euro": Latin Monetary Union into a European Monetary Union 1865–1873', with some valuable insights into the diplomatic process.

5 *Report of the Royal Commission on International Coinage*, London, 1868.

6 Groseclose, Elgin, *Money: The Human Conflict*, University of Oklahoma Press: Norman, OK, 1934, 164–6.

## 12 The collapse of bimetallism

1 Stern, Fritz, *Gold and Iron: Bismarck, Bleichroder and the Building of the German Empire*, Knopf: New York, 1977, 180–1.

2 Rockoff, H., '*The Wizard of Oz* as a Monetary Allegory', *Journal of Political Economy*, August 1990, 739–60.

3 Bagehot, Walter, *Some Articles on the Depreciation of Silver*, reprinted from the *Economist*, Henry S. King and Co.: London, 1877.

4 Redish, Angela, *Bimetallism: An Economic and Historial Analysis*, Cambridge University Press: Cambridge, 2000.

## 13  The United States in the nineteenth century

1 Rockoff, Hugh, 'How long Did It Take for the United States to Become an Optimum Currency Area?', paper presented at a monetary unions conference, City University, London, 14 May 1999.

2 Michael Kouparitsas, letter, October 1999. Federal Reserve Bank of Chicago.

3 Chown, John, *A History of Money*, Routledge: London, 1994.

4 *Early Origins of American Banking*, reprints of key documents originally published 1832–42, with an introduction by John Chown. 7 vols, Routledge/Thoemmes Press: London, 1996.

5 Friedman, Milton and Anna Schwartz, *A Monetary History of the United States, 1867–1960*, National Bureau of Economic Research, Princeton University Press: Princeton, 1963.

6 Kross, Herman F. (ed.) *Documentary History of Banking and Currency in the United States*, 4 vols, introduction by Paul A. Samuelson, Chelsea House Publishers: New York, 1969–83. Gives full text of many key documents. Vol. I, 133.

7 *Ibid.*, 261–304.

8 *Ibid.*, II, 99–111

9 *Ibid.*, 112–5

10 Laughlin, J. Laurence, *The History of Bimetallism in the United States*, 4th edn, Appleton and Company: New York, 1900, 64.

11 *Documentary History of Banking and Currency in the United States*, II: 119–20.

12 *Ibid.*, 233–4.

13 Russell, S., *The US Currency System: A Historical Perspective.* Federal Reserve Bank of St Louis Review, Sept/Oct 1991.

14 Chaddock, Robert E., 'The Safety Fund Banking System in New York 1829–1866', in *National Monetary Commission*, Washington DC, 1910.

15 See White, L. H. and G. A. Seglin, 'The Evolution of a Free Banking System', in L. H. White (ed.) *Competition and Currency*, New York University Press: New York, 1989.

16 Myers, Margaret, *A Financial History of the United States*, Columbia University Press: New York, 1970, 204–6.

17 *Ibid.*, 199.

18 Laughlin, J. Laurence, *The History of Bimetallism in the United States*, Appleton and Company: New York, 1890.

19 De St Phalle, Thibaut, *The Federal Reserve: An Intentional Mystery*, Praeger: New York, 1985.

20 Warburg, P. M., *The Federal Reserve System: Its Origins and Growth*, 2 vols, Macmillan: New York, 1930.

## 14  The collapse of bimetallism in the Eastern silver countries: a monetary disunion

1 Davies, Glyn, *A History of Money From Ancient Times to the Present Day*, University of Wales Press: Cardiff, 1994, 622.

2 Kann, Edward, *The Currencies of China*, Kelly & Walsh: Singapore, 1927, 361.

3 Spalding, W. F., *Eastern Exchange Currency and Finance*, 6th edn, 1924 (1st edn 1917) Macmillan: London.

4 'The Currency of the British Colonies', no author. HMSO: London, 1848.

5 Royal Mint, 'Statutes and Statutory Rules and Orders, relating to Coinage &C, in force on December 31, 1914', HMSO: London, 1915.

6 Stewart Lockhart, J. H., 'The Currency of the Farther East', Noronha & Co.: Hong Kong, 1895.

7 Wicks, Robert S., 'Money, Markets, and Trade in Early South East Asia: The Development of Indigenous Monetary Systems to AD 1400', Southeast Asia Program, Cornell University: Ithaca NY, 1992.

8 *Report of the Committee Appointed to Inquire into the Indian Currency* (the Herschell Report). HMSO London, 1892. This copy is a reprint by the Government Printing Office Washington DC 1893.

9 Fisher, Irving, *The Purchasing Power of Money*, Macmillan: New York, 1920.

10 Rothwell, W. T., *Bimetallism Explained*, Chapman and Hall: London, 1897.

11 Keynes, J. M., *Indian Currency and Finance* (1st edn 1913), Macmillan for the Royal Economic Society: London, 1971, 4–5.

12 Kemmerer, E. W., *Modern Currency Reforms*, Macmillan: New York, 1916.

13 Jevons, H. Stanley, *The Future of Exchange and The Indian Currency*, Oxford University Press: Oxford, 1922.

14 Spalding, W. F., *Eastern Exchange Currency and Finance*, 6th edn, 1924 (1st edn 1917) Macmillan: London, 235–6.

15 Kemmerer, E. W., *Modern Currency Reforms*, Macmillan: New York, 1916, 392.

16 *Ibid.*, 393.

17 Kann, Edward, *The Currencies of China*, Kelly & Walsh: Singapore, 1927, 361.

18 Wen Pin Wei, *The Currency Problem in Modern China*, Columbia University Press: New York, 1914, reprinted Taipei, 1971, 30.

19 Kann, Edward, *The Currencies of China*, Kelly & Walsh: Singapore, 1927, ch. XV.

20 Vissering, G., 'On Chinese Currency', preliminary remarks about the monetary reform in China with the cooperation of Dr W. A. Roest, J. H. de Bussy: Amsterdam, 1912. (Dr G. Vissering was the younger brother of Dr W. Vissering, author of *On Chinese Currency*, published in 1877. Their father, Dr S. Vissering, was at one time Dutch Minister of Finance.)

21 King, Frank H. H., *Money and Monetary Policy in China 1845–1895*, Harvard University Press: Cambridge MA, 1965.

22 Anonymous, *A History of Chinese Currency, 16th Century, BC–20th Century AD*, Xinhua (New China) Publishing House and NCN Limited, English Language edn 1983. Copiously illustrated with tables of dates but little economic analysis.

23 Kann, Edward, *The Currencies of China*, Kelly & Walsh: Singapore, 1927, 357.

24 *Ibid.*, 360.

25 *A History of Chinese Currency, 16th Century, BC–20th Century AD*, Xinhua (New China) Publishing House and NCN Limited, English Language edn 1983. Mainly an illustrated numismatic work: there is more on the earlier period in Spalding (see above note 26).

26 Davies, Glyn, *A History of Money From Ancient Times to the Present Day*, University of Wales Press: Cardiff, 1994, 626. Davies refers to Lee and Jao, *Financial Structures and Monetary Policies in South East Asia*, London, 1982 – not consulted.

27 Spalding, W. F., *Eastern Exchange Currency and Finance*, 6th edn, 1924 (1st edn 1917), Macmillan: London, 373.

28 Muhleman, Maurice L., *Monetary and Banking Systems,* New York, 1908.

29 Spalding, W. F., *Eastern Exchange Currency and Finance*, 6th edn, 1924 (1st edn 1917), Macmillan: London, 373.

## 15  Japan and Korea

1  Munro, Neil Gordon, *Coins of Japan*, Box of Curios Publishing Company: Yokohama, 1904

2  Tamaki, Noro, *Japanese Banking: A History 1859–1959*, Cambridge University Press, 1996.

3  *Ibid.*, xiii.

4  Tamaki gives a reference to Peter Frost (*The Bakumatsu Currency Criss*, Massachusetts, 1970), for a fuller account.

5  Jevons, W. Stanley, *Investigations in Currency and Finance*, 2nd edn, Macmillan: London, 1909, 84. The story is also told by Walker 1888: 230. He uses the charming spelling of 'Itzi Boo' for the silver coin.

6  Chester L. Krause and Clifford Mishler, *Standard Catalog of World Coins*, Krause Publications: Iola WI.

7  J. H. Stewart Lockhart, *Currency of the Farther East*, Noronha & Co.: Hong Kong, vols I and II 1895, vol. III 1898.

8  Munro, Neil Gordon, *Coins of Japan*, Box of Curios Printing and Publishing Company: Yokohama, 1904.

9  Goodhart, Charles, *The Evolution of Central Banks*, MIT Press: Cambridge MA, 1988, 144, 150.

10  Tamaki, Noro, *Japanese Banking: A History 1859–1959*, Cambridge University Press, 1996, xv. Sir Paul Newall has some brief, relevant comments in *Japan and the City of London*, Athlone Press, London, 1996, including the key role of Prince Matsukata Masayoya, who as finance minister visited London in 1902 and was appointed KCMG. He refers to Norio Tamaki, *Japan's Adoption of the Gold Standard and the London Money Market 1881–1903*, to which I should refer (in Ian Nish, (ed.) *Britain and Japan*, Japan Library, 1994.) As Prime Minister, Matsukata was responsible for seeing the gold standard legislation through the Diet.

11  *Report on Currency Adjustment in Korea* (translation), no date, no author, no publisher, but letter of transmittal dated November 1909 from Baron Eiichi Shibusawa, President of Dai Ichi Ginko, to Mr Ko Yung Heui, Korean minister of finance.

12  Early history is given in *ibid.*, ch. 1. This is a Japanese source which may not be sympathetic to Korean culture and history.

## 16  Latin America in the nineteenth century

1  Lang, James, *Conquest and Commerce: Spain and England in the Americas*, Academic Press: New York, 1975, 99.

2  Young, John Parke, *Central American Currency and Finance*, Princeton University Press: Princeton, 1925.

3  Deane, Marjorie, and Robert Pringle, *The Central Banks*, Hamish Hamilton: London, 1994.

4  Subercaseaux, Guillermo, *Essai sur la Nature de Papier Monnaie*, Paris, 1909.

5  Del Mar, A., *History of Monetary Systems*, Effingham Wilson: London, 1895, has a comprehensive chapter on Argentina, going back to the early monetary history of that country, and making some contribution to the then still smouldering debate on bimetallism.

6  *Ibid.*, 457.

7  Deaver, J. V. 'The Chilean Inflation and the Demand for Money', in D. Meiselman (ed.) *Varieties of Monetary Experience*, University of Chicago Press: Chicago, 1970.

8 Triffin, Robert, *Money and Banking in Colombia's Federal Reserve System*, Federal Reserve System: Washington DC, June 1944.

9 Kemmerer, E. W. *Modern Currency Reforms Part V*, Macmillan: New York, 1916.

10 Commission on International Exchange 1903 and Report on the Introduction of Gold Exchange Standard into China, the Philippine Islands, Panama and the silver using countries.

### 17 Money in Russia before the Revolution

1 Hingley, Ronald, *Russia: A Concise History*, revised edn 1991, Thames & Hudson: London, 1972, 26.

2 Spassky, I. G., *The Russian Monetary System: A Historico-Numismatic Survey*, trans. from the Russian by Z. I. Gorishina and revised by L. S. Forrer, Jacques Schulman: Amsterdam, 1967, 69.

3 Pushkin's play, and Mussorgsky's opera on which it is based, tell a version of the story.

4 There is numismatic information in Elvira Clain-Stefanelli, *Monnaies européennes,* Office du Livre: Fribourg Suisse, 1978. Figures 230 and 233 illustrate fifteenth-century dengas weighing 0.76gm. There are further illustrations and comment at 103, 104, 195, 198 and 204–6.

5 Zander, Randolph, *The Silver Rubles and Yefimoks of Romanov Russia, 1654–1915*, Russian Numismatic Society: Bellingham WA, 1996.

6 At the end of the twentieth century, Russian hotels and restaurants published prices in 'units' (*de facto* dollars) but accepted cash payment only in roubles calculated at a rate posted daily and which differed from the rate available for converting actual dollars. The well advised used credit cards.

7 Zander, Randolph, *The Silver Rubles and Yefimoks of Romanov Russia, 1654–1915*, Russian Numismatic Society: Bellingham WA, 1996, 19.

8 Porteous, John, *Coins in History*, Weidenfeld and Nicolson: London, 1969, 216.

9 Zander, Randolph, *The Silver Rubles and Yefimoks of Romanov Russia, 1654–1915*, Russian Numismatic Society: Bellingham WA, 1996, 65 and 70.

10 Seligman, Edwin R. A., *Currency, Inflation and Public Debts*, New York, 1921, 31.

11 Clain-Stefanelli, Elvira, *Monnaies européennes,* Office du Livre: Fribourg Suisse, 1978, 317: no supporting evidence in Krause catalogue.

12 The (UK) *Royal Commission on Decimal Currency* (Appendix, 320) gives a detailed description of the Russian coinage system as it was in 1857 (*Preliminary Report of the Decimal Coinage Commissioners*, Eyre and Spottiswoode for HMSO: London, 1857); and the 1868 Royal Commission on International Coinage (*Report from the Royal Commission on International Coinage together with Minutes of Evidence and Appendix*, Eyre and Spottiswoode for HMSO: London, 1868, 265) gives details of mint practice.

13 Shishavov, Valery, 'The Assignats of 1802–1803', *Journal of the Russian Numismatic Society*, Santa Rosa CA, no. 68, summer 1999, 58–67.

### 18 The British empire and the sterling area: an accidental monetary union

1 *The Currency of the British Colonies*, W. Clowes for Her Majesty's Stationery Office: London, 1848, 184, 198. This reproduces the text of the documents.

2 Chown, John, *A History of Money*, Routledge: London, 1994, ch. 7, 185.

3 'Papers relative to the affairs of New Zealand (Mr Somes). Return to an ADDRESS of the Honourable G. W. Hope, the House of Commons, dated 11 March 1845. Colonial Office, Downing Street, 14 March 1845). Ordered by the House of Commons to Be Printed 14th March 1845'.

4 Royal Mint, *Statutes ... Relating to Coinage in Force on December 31 1914 and ...
Legislation Relating to Coinage etc of Colonies*, HMSO: London, 1915, 16.
5 *Ibid.*, 103.
6 *Ibid.*, 114.
7 Eyo, Ekpo, *Nigeria and the Evolution of Money*, Central Bank of Nigeria: Lagos,
1979, 94–5.
8 Royal Mint, *Statutes ... Relating to Coinage in Force on December 31 1914 and ...
Legislation Relating to Coinage etc of Colonies*, HMSO: London, 1915, 131.
9 Pick, Albert, *Standard Catalog of World Paper Money*, Krause Publications: Iola
WI, published annually.
10 'West Africa Departmental Committee Appointed to Enquire into Matters
Affecting the Currency of the British West African Colonies and Protectorates.
Minutes of Evidence', HMSO Cd. 6247; London, October 1912 (the report is
Cd. 6246).
11 Muhleman, Maurice L., *Monetary and Banking Systems*, Monetary Publishing
Co.: New York 1908.
12 Anon., *International Currency Experience: Lessons of the Inter-War Period*,
League of Nations: Geneva, 1944.

## 19 Introduction to the early twentieth century

1 Laughlin, J. Laurence, *The History of Bimetallism in the United States*, Appleton
and Company: New York, 1890.
2 Kross, Herman F. (ed.) *Documentary History of Banking and Currency in the
United States*, 4 vols, introduction by Paul A. Samuelson, Chelsea House
Publishers: New York, 1969–83, vol. 3, 19.
3 National Monetary Commission, Washington DC. This is a series of volumes
published by a commission set up by the government, and a major source of
information.
4 Feavearyear, A. T., *The Pound Sterling*, Oxford University Press: Oxford, 1931.

## 20 The Great War and its aftermath

1 Sayers, R. S., *The Bank of England 1891–1944*, vol. 1, Cambridge University
Press: Cambridge, 1976, 74.
2 Deane, Marjorie and Robert Pringle, *The Central Banks*, Hamish Hamilton:
London 1994, 202.
3 Feavearyear, Albert, *The Pound Sterling*, 2nd edn, revised by E. Victor Morgan,
Clarendon Press: Oxford, 1963, 318–19.
4 Robertson, D. H., *Money*, Cambridge University Press: Cambridge, 1922, revised
edn 1948, 124.
5 *Ibid.*
6 *Ibid.*

## 21 Germany and the great inflation

1 Philip Cagan, 'The Monetary Dynamics of Hyperinflation', in Milton Friedman
(ed.) *Studies in the Quantity Theory of Money*, University of Chicago Press:
Chicago, 1956. Also reprinted in Capie, Forrest H. (ed.) *Major Inflations in
History*, Edward Elgar: Aldershot, 1991.
2 Young, John Parke (ed.), *European Currency and Finance*, Commission of Gold
and Silver Enquiry, United States Senate Foreign Currency and Exchange
Investigation, 1925, Serial 9.

3  Schacht, Hjalmar, *The New German Currency*, trans. M. L. Jacobson, in *ibid.*, vol. I, 199–204.

4  Chernow, Ron, *The Warburgs: A Family Saga*, Chatto & Windus: London, 1993, 231.

5  Costantino Bresciani-Turroni, *The National Finances, the Inflation and the Depreciation of the Mark Economia 1924*, trans. M. E. Sayers, Allen & Unwin: London, 1937. Review by Joan Robinson, *Economic Journal*, 1938. Both reprinted in Capie, Forrest H. (ed.) *Major Inflations in History*, Edward Elgar: Aldershot, 1991. Page references are to Capie.

6  *Borsen-Courier*, 4 April 1922, quoted in *ibid.*: the date doesn't tie up.

7  A long footnote to page 444 lists the various laws passed in 1923.

8  Shades of Asgill, Chamberlain and John Law: see John Chown, *A History of Money*, Routledge: London, 1994, ch. 23.

9  Davies, Glyn, *A History of Money From Ancient Times to the Present Day*, University of Wales Press: Cardiff, 1994, 574.

10  Chernow. Ron, *The Warburgs: A Family Saga*, Chatto & Windus: London, 1993.

11  J. M. Keynes, 'Melchior, A Defeated Enemy', in *Two Memoirs,* RES edition, London, 1972, vol. X, 389.

## 22  The temporary return to gold and the Great Depression

1  Ricardo, Royal Economic Society edition, Macmillan: London, 1951, vol. iv, 49–142

2  Kindleberger, Charles H., *Financial History of Western Europe*, George Allen & Unwin: London, 1984, 339. Feavearyear, Albert, *The Pound Sterling*, 2nd edn, revised by E. Victor Morgan, Clarendon Press: Oxford, 1963, 360.

3  Robertson, D. H., *Money*, Cambridge University Press: Cambridge, 1922, revised edn 1948, 127.

4  *Documentary History of Banking and Currency in the United States*, 4 vols, introduction by Paul A. Samuelson, ed. Herman F. Kross, Chelsea House Publishers: New York, 1969–83, vol. IV, 240.

5  *Ibid.*, 256–61.

6  Friedman, Milton, 'FDR, Silver, and China', in *Money Mischief*, Harcourt Brace: New York, 1992.

## 23  The Russian Revolution and after

1  Young, John Parke (ed.), *European Currency and Finance*, Commission of Gold and Silver Enquiry, United States Senate Foreign Currency and Exchange Investigation, 1925, Serial 9.

2  Laurila, Pentii, *Soviet Paper Money and Bonds Used as Currency, 1895–1990*, Neuvosoliiton Paperirahay: Tornio, Finland, 1990, 39.

3  *Ibid.*, 60.

4  Hanke, Steve H. and Kurt Schuler, 'Ruble Reform: A Lesson from Keynes', *Cato Journal*, vol. 10, no. 3, winter 1991.

5  Young, John Parke (ed.), *European Currency and Finance*, Commission of Gold and Silver Enquiry, United States Senate Foreign Currency and Exchange Investigation, 1925, Serial 9.

6  Krause, Chester L. and Clifford Mishler, *Standard Catalog of World Coins*, Krause Publications: Iola WI. Laurila mixes up his figures.

7  Laurila, Pentii, *Soviet Paper Money and Bonds Used as Currency, 1895–1990*, Neuvosoliiton Paperirahay: Tornio, Finland, 1990, 90.

8  Spassky, I. G., *The Russian Monetary Systems: A Historico-Numismatic Survey*, trans. Z. I. Gorishine and revised by L. S. Forrer, Jacques Schulman: Amsterdam, 1967, 244–6.
9  Woodruff, David, *Money Unmade: Barter and the Fate of Russian Capitalism*, Cornell University Press: Ithaca NY, 1999, ch. 1.

## 24  The monetary consequences of the break-up of the Austro-Hungarian empire

1  Young, John Parke (ed.), *European Currency and Finance*, Commission of Gold and Silver Enquiry, United States Senate Foreign Currency and Exchange Investigation, 1925, Serial 9, vol. II, 11.
2  E. V. D. Wight in *ibid.*, 15–17.
3  For Austrian exchange control in the 1930s see Chapter 3.
4  Garber, Peter N. and Michael G. Spencer, *The Dissolution of the Austro-Hungarian Empire: Lessons for Currency Reform*, Princeton Essays in International Finance, no. 191, February 1994, 3–4.
5  Young, John Parke (ed.), *European Currency and Finance*, Commission of Gold and Silver Enquiry, United States Senate Foreign Currency and Exchange Investigation, 1925, Serial 9, vol. II, 12.
6  Garber, Peter N. and Michael G. Spencer, *The Dissolution of the Austro-Hungarian Empire: Lessons for Currency Reform*, Princeton Essays in International Finance, no. 191, February 1994, 19, citing Notel 1986, 176.
7  *Ibid.*, 20ff.

## 25  Austria after the break-up of the Austro-Hungarian empire

1  Pick, Albert, 'Austria', *Standard Catalog of World Paper Money*, Krause Publications: Iola WI, 49–66.
2  1883–1950. Later author of *Capitalism, Socialism and Democracy*, and *History of Economic Analysis*, the latter being an essential reference for writers on economic history.
3  Stolper, Wolfgang F., *Joseph Alois Schumpeter: The Public Life of a Private Man*, Princeton University Press: Princeton, 1994.
4  Allen, Robert Loring, *Opening Doors: The Life and Work of Joseph Schumpeter, Volume One: Europe*, Transaction Publishers: New Brunswick NJ and London, 1991.
5  März, Eduard, *Joseph Schumpeter: Scholar, Teacher and Politician*, Yale University Press: New Haven and London, 1991. The book was first published in German in 1983, but the relevant chapter 9 had first appeared, in English, in Helmut Frisch (ed.) *Schumpeterian Economics*, New York, 1982. Allen contrasts this essay with Haberler, *Economie Appliquee 3* (1950).
6  Stolper, Wolfgang F., *Joseph Alois Schumpeter: The Public Life of a Private Man*, Princeton University Press: Princeton, 1994, 217.
7  Allen, Robert Loring, *Opening Doors: The Life and Work of Joseph Schumpeter, Volume One: Europe*, Transaction Publishers: New Brunswick NJ and London, 1991, 166.
8  'Die Krise der Steuerstaates', Graz and Leipzig, 1918. Trans. Wolfgang Stolper and R. A. Musgrave, *International Economic Papers*, vol. 4 (1954) 5–38.
9  Allen, Robert Loring, *Opening Doors: The Life and Work of Joseph Schumpeter, Volume One: Europe*, Transaction Publishers: New Brunswick NJ and London, 1991, 168.
10  *Ibid.*, 170.

11  Young, John Parke (ed.), *European Currency and Finance*, Commission of Gold and Silver Enquiry, United States Senate Foreign Currency and Exchange Investigation, 1925, Serial 9, vol. I, 225–31.

12  Allen, Robert Loring, *Opening Doors: The Life and Work of Joseph Schumpeter, Volume One: Europe*, Transaction Publishers: New Brunswick NJ and London, 1991, 176.

13  *Ibid.*, 178.

14  Private letter, December 1919, quoted (at more length) in *ibid.*, 180. Gustav was the father of Wolfgang Stolper.

15  Young, John Parke (ed.), *European Currency and Finance*, Commission of Gold and Silver Enquiry, United States Senate Foreign Currency and Exchange Investigation, 1925, Serial 9, vol. II, 18ff.

16  Sargent, Thomas J., 'The Ends of Four Big Inflations', in R. H. Hall (ed.) *Inflation: Causes and Effects*, University of Chicago Press: Chicago, 1982, 49.

17  *Ibid.*, 49, citing Keynes' *Tract on Monetary Reform*.

18  Young, John Parke (ed.), *European Currency and Finance*, Commission of Gold and Silver Enquiry, United States Senate Foreign Currency and Exchange Investigation, 1925, Serial 9, vol. II, 18.

19  Sargent, Thomas J., *The Ends of Four Big Inflations*, 1982, 53.

20  *Ibid.*.

21  The 1924 schilling weighed 7.0000g .800 fine, .1800oz ASW but from 1925 the standard was reduced to 6.0000g .640 fine, .125 ASW. A very few gold 25- (and 100-) schilling coins were struck to the exact standard.

22  E. V. D. Wight in Young, John Parke (ed.), *European Currency and Finance*, Commission of Gold and Silver Enquiry, United States Senate Foreign Currency and Exchange Investigation, 1925, Serial 9, vol. II, 25.

## 26  Other former members of the Austro-Hungarian empire

1  Young, John Parke (ed.), *European Currency and Finance*, Commission of Gold and Silver Enquiry, United States Senate Foreign Currency and Exchange Investigation, 1925, Serial 9, vol. II, 106–7 (The Hungarian chapters were written by Young). See also Alexander Popovics in *ibid.*, vol. I, 232–42; in Sargent, Thomas J., *The Ends of Four Big Inflations*, 1982, 56–7/165–6; and in Costantino Bresciani-Turroni, *The National Finances, the Inflation and the Depreciation of the Mark Economia 1924*, trans. M. E. Sayers, Allen & Unwin: London, 1937, 171ff.

2  Garber, Peter N. and Michael G. Spencer, *The Dissolution of the Austro-Hungarian Empire: Lessons for Currency Reform*, Princeton Essays in International Finance, no. 191, February 1994, 17.

3  Dornbusch, Rudiger, *Monetary Problems of Post-Communism: Lessons from the End of the Austro-Hungarian Empire*. Archiv: Review of World Economics. (Journal of the Kiel Institute of World Economics Tubingen. Band 128 Heft 3 1992, 391 ff.

4  Sargent, Thomas J., *The Ends of Four Big Inflations*, 1982, 61.

5  Costantino Bresciani-Turroni, *The National Finances, the Inflation and the Depreciation of the Mark Economia 1924*, trans. M. E. Sayers, Allen & Unwin: London, 1937, 172, mentions opposition by the little entente of Czechoslovakia, Yugoslavia and Rumania.

6  Young, John Parke (ed.), *European Currency and Finance*, Commission of Gold and Silver Enquiry, United States Senate Foreign Currency and Exchange Investigation, 1925, Serial 9, vol. II, 119.

7  *Ibid.*, 120.

8  *Ibid.*, 121.

9 Sargent, Thomas J., *The Ends of Four Big Inflations*, 1982, 174. He gives detailed tables.

10 Young, John Parke (ed.), *European Currency and Finance*, Commission of Gold and Silver Enquiry, United States Senate Foreign Currency and Exchange Investigation, 1925, Serial 9, vol. II, 163ff. The Polish chapters were written by Young.

11 *Ibid.*, 55–77.

12 Sargent, Thomas J., *The Ends of Four Big Inflations*, 1982, 194.

13 For details see Young, John Parke (ed.), *European Currency and Finance*, Commission of Gold and Silver Enquiry, United States Senate Foreign Currency and Exchange Investigation, 1925, Serial 9, vol. II, 58.

14 Kisch, C. H. and W. A. Elkin, *Central Banks*, Macmillan: London, 1928, appendix I, give a summary of the provisions of various central bank rules including the countries mentioned in this chapter.

15 Garber, Peter N. and Michael G. Spencer, *The Dissolution of the Austro-Hungarian Empire: Lessons for Currency Reform*, Princeton Essays in International Finance, no. 191, February 1994. The authors refer to Lampe and Jackson 1982 and Steiner 1921, translated in Walre de Bordes, *The Austrian Crown*, P. S. King: London, 1924.

16 Garber and Spencer 1994, 10, quoting Leo Pasvolsky, *Economic Nationalism of the Danubian States*, Macmillan: New York, 1928.

17 Garber and Spencer 1994, 15–16.

18 Staff of the Banca Nationala a Romanei, *130 years since the Establishment of the Modern Romanian Monetary System*, English translation, Editura Enciclopedica: Bucharest, 1997, 349–55.

19 Russell, Henry B., *International Monetary Conferences*, Harper & Brothers: New York and London, 1898, 40.

20 See *ibid.*, 360; see also 376 and 403 on Romania's contribution to the 1892 conference.

21 Barbara Jelavich, *History of the Balkans: Volume 2 – the Twentieth Century*, Cambridge University Press: Cambridge, 1984, 157.

## 27 Germany and Austria in the 1930s

1 Ellis, Howard S., 'Exchange Control in Central Europe', *Harvard Economic Studies*, vol. 69, 1941.

2 Schubert, Auriel, *The Credit-Anstalt Crises of 1931*, Cambridge University Press: Cambridge, 1991.

3 Chernow, Ron, *The Warburgs: A Family Saga*, Chatto & Windus: London, 1993.

4 *Haavara* = 'transfer' in Hebrew.

5 Skidelsky, Robert, *John Maynard Keynes, vol. III, Fighting for Britain 1937–46*, Macmillan: London, 2000, 195.

6 Ellis, Howard S., 'Exchange Control in Central Europe', *Harvard Economic Studies*, vol. 69, 1941.

7 *Ibid.*, 40.

## 28 Scandinavia and the Baltic states: the Nordic Monetary Union

1 Eagly, Robert V., *The Swedish Bullionist Controversy*, trans. with introduction on P. N. Christiernin's 1761 *Lectures on the High Price of Foreign Exchange in Sweden*, American Philosophical Society: Philadelphia, 1971.

2 Talvio, Tuukka, *The Coins and Banknotes of Finland*, Bank of Finland: Helsinki, 1987, 12–14. The source goes on to discuss the actual currency in some detail.

3 *Ibid.*, 20.

4 *Ibid.*, 24ff.
5 Young, John Parke (ed.), *European Currency and Finance. Commission of Gold and Silver Enquiry*, United States Senate Foreign Currency and Exchange Investigation Serial 9, Government Printing Office: Washington, 1925, vol. II, 245.
6 Young, *ibid.*, vol. II, gives a detailed description of the period to 1925 for these and other countries, including prices, exchange rates money supply and purchasing power parities.
7 Lester, Richard A. 'The Gold Exclusion Policy in Sweden, 1916–1919', ch. viii in *Monetary Experiments: Early American and Recent Scandinavian*, Princeton University Press: Princeton, 1939.
8 *Ibid.*, 178.
9 *Ibid.*, 182.
10 Young, John Parke (ed.), *European Currency and Finance. Commission of Gold and Silver Enquiry*, United States Senate Foreign Currency and Exchange Investigation Serial 9, Government Printing Office: Washington, 1925, vol. II, 248.
11 *Ibid.* The source gives tables and charts.
12 Kindleberger, C. P., *A Financial History of Western Europe*, George Allen & Unwin: London, 1984, 297.
13 See table in Young, John Parke (ed.), *European Currency and Finance. Commission of Gold and Silver Enquiry*, United States Senate Foreign Currency and Exchange Investigation Serial 9, Government Printing Office: Washington, 1925, vol. II, 385.
14 Richard A. Lester, 'The Gold-parity Depression in Norway and Denmark, 1925–1928, and Devaluation in Finland 1925', ch. ix in *Monetary Experiments: Early American and Recent Scandinavian*, Princeton University Press: Princeton, 1939.
15 Rydbeck, Oscar, President of Skandinaviska Kredit AB Stockholm, quoted in John Parke Young (ed.), *European Currency and Finance. Commission of Gold and Silver Enquiry*, United States Senate Foreign Currency and Exchange Investigation Serial 9, Government Printing Office: Washington, 1925, vol. I, 207.
16 *Ibid.*, 209.
17 Young, John Parke (ed.), *European Currency and Finance. Commission of Gold and Silver Enquiry*, United States Senate Foreign Currency and Exchange Investigation Serial 9, Government Printing Office: Washington, 1925, vol. II, 191.
18 *The Currency of Iceland 1778–1997*, Myntsafn Sedlabank og Pjodminjasafns: Reykjavik, 1997.
19 Lester, Richard A., 'The Gold-parity Depression in Norway and Denmark, 1925–1928, and Devaluation in Finland 1925', ch. ix in *Monetary Experiments: Early American and Recent Scandinavian*, Princeton University Press: Princeton, 1939.
20 *Ibid.*, 211, and see his purchasing power parity Table 19.
21 'Professor Heckscher's Scheme for Monetary Reform in Finland', *Bank of Finland Monthly Bulletin*, December 1923.
22 Lester, Richard A., 'The Gold-parity Depression in Norway and Denmark, 1925–1928, and Devaluation in Finland 1925', ch. ix in *Monetary Experiments: Early American and Recent Scandinavian*, Princeton University Press: Princeton, 1939, 219.
23 Talvio, Tuukka, *The Coins and Banknotes of Finland*, Bank of Finland: Helsinki, 1987, 65.

24  Karys, Jonas K., *Currency of the Independent Lithuania*, New York, 1953 (in Lithuanian with a short English summary). The experience of other countries was broadly similar.
25  *Ibid.*, 240.
26  *Ibid.*, 241 discusses this period: probably not relevant.
27  This interesting period gets a frustratingly brief coverage in the Karys' English summary.
28  Leimus, Ivar, *Eesti Vabariigi rahad 1918–1992 (Coins and Banknotes of the Republic of Estonia)*, Olion Tallinn, 1993 (in Estonian with a rather longer English [and Russian] summary).
29  *Ibid.*, 76.
30  Young 1925, 360 (see note 58 above) gives figures.

## 30  Bretton Woods and the IMF

1  There is a wealth of analytical material in *A Retrospective on the Bretton Woods System Lessons for International Monetary Reform*, eds Michael D. Bordo and Barry Eichengreen, University of Chicago Press for NBER: Chicago, 1993.
2  Gardner, Richard N., *Sterling-Dollar Diplomacy. Anglo-American Collaboration in the Reconstruction of Multilateral Trade*, Oxford University Press: Oxford, 1956; for the Keynes/White issue see chapter V.
3  Skidelsky, Robert, *John Maynard Keynes Volume III: Fighting for Britain 1937–1946*, Macmillan: London, 2000.
4  Proposals for an International Clearing Union, April 1943.
5  E.g. 'A Tract on Monetary Reform', in *The Collected Works of John Maynard Keynes*, Macmillan for the Royal Economic Society, 1971, chapter IV, originally published 1923, but he had modified his views by 'Essays in Persuasion', 1933, in *ibid.*, 362.
6  Gardner, Richard N., *Sterling-Dollar Diplomacy. Anglo-American Collaboration in the Reconstruction of Multilateral Trade*, Oxford University Press: Oxford, 1956, 79–80.
7  'Suggested Plan for a United Nations Stabilisation Fund and a Bank for Reconstruction of the United and Associated Nations'.
8  Edwards, Sebastian and Julio A. Santaella, 'Devaluation Controversies in the Developing Countries: Lessons from the Bretton Woods Era', in Michael D. Bordo and Barry Eichengreen (eds) *A Retrospective on the Bretton Woods System: Lessons for International Monetary Reform*, University of Chicago Press for NBER: Chicago, 1993, 405ff.

## 31  Postwar monetary reconstructions

1  The major papers on this subject are conveniently found in Forrest H. Capie (ed.) *Major Inflations in History*, Edward Elgar: Aldershot, 1991.
2  Metzler, Lloyd A., 'The Colm-Dodge-Goldsmith Plan Appendix O: Recent Experience with Monetary and Financial Reform', *Zeitscrift für die Gesamte Staatswissenschaft*, J. C. B. Mohr (Paul Siebeck): Tübingen, 1979.
3  Gerhard Colm, Joseph M. Dodge and Raymond W. Goldsmith, 'A Plan for the Liquidation of War Finance and the Financial Rehabilitation of Germany'. Published in *Zeitscrift für die Gesamte Staatswissenschaft,* J. C. B. Mohr (Paul Siebeck): Tübingen, 1955.
4  See note 2 above.
5  Lutz, F. A., 'The German Currency Reform', *Economica*, May 1949.
6  Kindleberger, Charles H., *Financial History of Western Europe*, George Allen & Unwin: London, 1984.

7 Bomberger, William A. and Gail E. Makinen, 'The Hungarian Hyperinflation and Stabilisation of 1945–1946', *Journal of Political Economy*, vol. 91, no. 5, 1983. Reprinted in Forrest H. Capie (ed.) *Major Inflations in History*, Edward Elgar: Aldershot, 1991.

8 Makinen, Gail E. 'The Greek Hyperinflation and Stabilisation of 1943–46', *Journal of Economic History*, vol. XLVI, no. 3 (September 1986).

## 32 The UK 1945–51

1 Dell, Edmund, *The Chancellors: A History of the Chancellors of the Exchequer, 1945–1990*, Harper Collins: London, 1996, 34.

2 Kindleberger, Charles H., *Financial History of Western Europe*, George Allen & Unwin: London, 1984, 430. He suggests that the US abolition of price controls in 1946 made the sum inadequate.

3 Dell, Edmund, *The Chancellors: A History of the Chancellors of the Exchequer, 1945–1990*, Harper Collins: London, 1996, 51.

4 Skidelsky, Robert, *John Maynard Keynes Vol. II: The Economist as Saviour*, Macmillan: London, 1992.

5 Newton, C. C. S. 'The Sterling Crisis of 1947 and the British Response to the Marshall Plan', *Economic History Review*, vol. XXXVII, 3 August 1984, 391–408.

6 *Ibid.*, 399.

7 Dell, Edmund, *The Chancellors: A History of the Chancellors of the Exchequer, 1945–1990*, Harper Collins: London, 1996, 41.

8 Newton, C. C. S. 'The Sterling Crisis of 1947 and the British Response to the Marshall Plan', *Economic History Review*, vol. XXXVII, 3 August 1984, 397–8.

9 Exchange of letters, quoted in Feavearyear, Albert, *The Pound Sterling*, 2nd edn, revised by E. Victor Morgan, Clarendon Press: Oxford, 1963, 416.

10 Pimlott, Ben, *Hugh Dalton*, Jonathan Cape: London, 1985, 540.

11 Dell, Edmund, *The Chancellors: A History of the Chancellors of the Exchequer, 1945–1990*, Harper Collins: London, 1996, 104.

12 Dell, *ibid.*, 113–129, gives a really excellent account of the politics.

## 33 Europe 1945–58: bilateral

1 Tew, Brian, *The Evolution of the International Monetary System 1945–77*, Hutchinson: London, 1977.

2 Scammell, W. M., *International Monetary Policy*, London: Macmillan, 1957, 265.

3 Bordo, Michael D. and Barry Eichengreen (eds), *A Retrospective on the Bretton Woods System: Lessons for International Monetary Reform*, University of Chicago Press for NBER: Chicago, 1993, 46.

4 Kindleberger, Charles H., *Financial History of Western Europe*, George Allen & Unwin: London, 1984, 436. Here Kindleberger quotes Roy Harrod, *Are These Hardships Necessary?*, Rupert Hart-Davis: London, 1947.

5 Vanthoor, Wim F. D., *European Monetary Union since 1848: A Political and Historical Analysis*, Edward Elgar: Aldershot, 1996, 66.

## 34 The UK 1951–79

1 A sinecure title brought into use from time to time for ministers without portfolio, often, as in this case, gurus without departmental responsibility.

2 The name may have been derived from its three advocates, Sir Leslie **RO**wan, Sir George **B**olton and **OT**to Clarke – see Dell, Edmund, *The Chancellors: A History of the Chancellors of the Exchequer, 1945–1990*, Harper Collins: London, 1996,

166. Otto Clarke's son Charles is, late 2001, being spoken of as a future leader of the UK Labour Party.

3  *Ibid.*, 167.

4  25 January 1952, quoted in *ibid.*, 171, citing John Fforde, *The Bank of England and Public Policy, 1941–1958*, Cambridge University Press: Cambridge, 1992.

5  Brittan, Samuel, *The Treasury under the Tories 1951–1964*, Secker & Warburg and Pelican: London, 1969, 173.

6  Tew, Brian, *The Evolution of the International Monetary System 1945–77*, Hutchinson: London, 1977, 41; Scammell, W. M., *International Monetary Policy*, London: Macmillan, 1957, 246; etc.

7  Dell, Edmund, *The Chancellors: A History of the Chancellors of the Exchequer, 1945–1990*, Harper Collins: London, 1996, 196.

8  *Ibid.*, 229.

9  Brittan, Samuel, 'Steering the Economy', in *The Treasury under the Tories 1951–1964*, Secker & Warburg and Pelican: London, 1969, 133.

10  Dell, Edmund, *The Chancellors: A History of the Chancellors of the Exchequer, 1945–1990*, Harper Collins: London, 1996, 246–9.

11  For a fuller discussion see Brittan, Samuel, 'Steering the Economy', in *The Treasury under the Tories 1951–1964*, Secker & Warburg and Pelican: London, 1969, 157–65.

12  Dell, Edmund, *The Chancellors: A History of the Chancellors of the Exchequer, 1945–1990*, Harper Collins: London, 1996, 312.

13  *Ibid.*, 326.

14  *Ibid.*, 336, citing Wilson's diary.

15  Dell, *ibid.*, cites Wilson, J. Harold, *The Labour Government 1964–1970: A Personal Memoir*, Weidenfeld & Nicolson/ Michael Joseph: London, 1971, 448; and Crossman, R. H. S., *The Diaries of a Cabinet Minister*, vol. 2, Hamish Hamilton and Jonathan Cape: London, 1976, 567.

16  Dell, Edmund, *The Chancellors: A History of the Chancellors of the Exchequer, 1945–1990*, Harper Collins: London, 1996, 344.

17  Dell, *ibid.*, cites Jenkins, Roy, *A Life at the Centre*, Macmillan: London, 1991, 282; and refers to Wilson 1971, 455–6.

18  Dell 1996, 358. Dell was by this time a junior member of the Government but, unlike Julius Caesar, does not mention his own role.

19  Dell, Edmund, *The Chancellors: A History of the Chancellors of the Exchequer, 1945–1990*, Harper Collins: London, 1996, 366.

20  *Ibid.*, 389.

21  *Ibid.*, 463–4.

22  Lawson, Nigel, *The View from No. 11: Memoirs of a Tory Radical*, Bantam Press: London, 1992, 38–43.

23  A few non-ministers close to policy matters were given a little more warning!

24  Howe, Geoffrey, *Conflict of Loyalty*, Macmillan: London, 1994, 140–3. The pamphlet is Robert Mille and John B. Wood, 'Exchange Control for Ever?', Institute of Economic Affairs: London, 1979.

25  Chown, John, 'Exchange Control for Ever?', *The Banker*, May 1979, 19.

## 35  The collapse of Bretton Woods

1  Garber, Peter, 'The Collapse of the the Bretton Woods Fixed Exchange Rate System', in Michael D. Bordo and Barry Eichengreen (eds) *A Retrospective on the Bretton Woods System: Lessons for International Monetary Reform*, University of Chicago Press for NBER: Chicago, 1993.

2  Hawtrey, R. G., *Bretton Woods for Better or Worse*, Longmans Green: London, 1946.

3 Harris, Seymour E. (ed.) *The Dollar in Crisis*, Harcourt Brace/World: New York and Burlinghame, 1961.

4 Edwards, Sebastian and Julio A. Santaella, 'Devaluation Controversies in the Developing Countries: Lessons from the Bretton Woods Era', in Michael D. Bordo and Barry Eichengreen (eds) *A Retrospective on the Bretton Woods System: Lessons for International Monetary Reform*, University of Chicago Press for NBER: Chicago, 1993, 405ff.

5 Cottarelli, Carlo and Curzio Giannini, 'Credibility without Rules? Monetary Frameworks in the post Bretton Woods Era', IMF Occasional Paper 154: Washington DC, December 1997.

6 Cottarelli and Giannini (*ibid.*) cite Lindberg and Maier (1985) and Bruno and Sachs (1985).

7 Giovannini, Alberto, *Bretton Woods and Its Precursors*, in Michael D. Bordo and Barry Eichengreen (eds), *A Retrospective on the Bretton Woods System: Lessons for International Monetary Reform*, University of Chicago Press for NBER: Chicago, 1993, 109.

## 36 Early moves towards European Monetary Union

1 Vanthoor, Wim F. D., *European Monetary Union since 1848: A Political and Historical Analysis*, Edward Elgar: Aldershot, 1996, 75.

2 'Report to the Council and the Commission on the realisation by Stages of Economic and Monetary Union in the Community. Supplement to Bulletin 11–70 of the Communities' – the 'Werner Report', European Commission: Luxembourg.

3 Vanthoor, Wim F. D., *A Chronological History of the European Union 1946–1998*, Edward Elgar: Cheltenham, 1999, 43.

4 *Ibid.*, 77.

5 *Ibid.*, 78.

6 Deane, Marjorie and Robert Pringle, *The Central Banks*, Hamish Hamilton: London 1994, 202.

7 Vanthoor, Wim F. D., *A Chronological History of the European Union 1946–1998*, Edward Elgar: Cheltenham, 1999, 82.

8 *Ibid.*, 84.

9 'Intervention Arrangements in the European Monetary System', *The Bank of England Quarterly Bulletin*, June 1979, 190–4.

10 'Intervention Arrangements in the European Monetary System', *ibid.*.

11 Barrell, Ray, Andrew Britton and Nigel Pain, 'When the Time Was Right? The UK Experience of the ERM', ms, 17 December 1993.

12 Dell, Edmund, *The Chancellors: A History of the Chancellors of the Exchequer, 1945–1990*, Harper Collins: London, 1996, 440.

13 Chown, John and Geoffrey Wood, 'The Right Road to Monetary Union', IEA Inquiry No. 11, published by Institute of Economic Affairs, 2 October 1989. Also published in *Economic Affairs*, February/March 1990; and reprinted in Russell Lewis (ed.) *Recent Controversies in Political Economy*, Routledge: London, 1992; and 'The Road to Monetary Union', 1991, Institute of Directors discussion paper; and (with Massimo Beber) 'The Road to Monetary Union Revisited', *Institute of Economic Affairs, Current Controversies*, no. 8, 1994.

14 Dell, Edmund, *The Chancellors: A History of the Chancellors of the Exchequer, 1945–1990*, Harper Collins: London, 1996, 543.

## 37 The reunification of Germany and the collapse of the EMS

1 Howe, Geoffrey, *Conflict of Loyalty*, Macmillan: London, 687–90.

2   Philip Stephens, *Politics and the Pound: The Conservatives' Struggle with Sterling*, Macmillan: London, 1996. Reviewed by Robert Pringle, *Central Banking*, vol. VI, no. 4, spring 1996. Stephens puts the loss at £3–4 billion, while Robert Pringle in his review has now raised his earlier estimate of £4.7 billion (which included some double counting to about £6 billion. Chapter 10, 'Humiliation', gives a very full account of the events surrounding 26 August, which confirms this impression, but we cannot find the point made explicitly in Stephens' book.

3   Siedentop, Larry, *Democracy in Europe*, Penguin Books: London, 2001.

## 38  European Monetary Union: 1988–99

1   'Report by the Committee for Studying European Monetary Union', *Bulletin of the European Communities*, 1989, no. 4.

2   Bilepsky, Dan and Ben Hall, with Lionel Barber, *The Birth of the Euro: The Financial Times Guide to Emu*, Penguin Books/FT, London, 1998.

3   Vanthoor, Wim F. D., *A Chronological History of the European Union 1946–1998*, Edward Elgar: Cheltenham, 1999, 97.

4   Peter Norman in Dan Bilepsky and Ben Hall, with Lionel Barber, *The Birth of the Euro: The Financial Times Guide to Emu*, Penguin Books/FT, London, 1998, 50.

5   *The Delors Committee Report with Evidence*, House of Lords (HL Paper 3–II) 22 November 1989, HMSO: London.

6   Philip Stephens, *Politics and the Pound*, Macmillan: London, 1996, 114–15.

7   Vanthoor, Wim F. D., *A Chronological History of the European Union 1946–1998*, Edward Elgar: Cheltenham, 1999, 99.

8   David Buchan, in Bilepsky, Dan and Ben Hall, with Lionel Barber, *The Birth of the Euro: The Financial Times Guide to Emu*, Penguin Books/FT, London, 1998, 56–57.

9   Lionel Barber in *ibid.*, 77.

## 39  European Monetary Union: policy issues

1   'Green Paper on the Practical Arrangements for the Introduction of a Single Currency', Commission of the European Union: Brussels, 31 May 1995.

2   *Ibid.*, para. 14.

3   Pedro Schwarz, 'Back from the Brink: An Appeal to Fellow Europeans Over Monetary Union', Occasional Paper 101, Institute of Economic Affairs: London, 1997; Robert Mundell, 'A Theory of Optimum Currency Areas', *American Economic Review*, 1961; Milton Friedman, in *The Times*, 19 November 1997.

4   'A Reconstruction of the Optimum Currency Area Approach', *National Institute Economic Review*, no. 158, 108–17.

5   'Moving Towards Emu: The Challenges Ahead', *National Institute Economic Review*, no. 158, 64–90: see 85.

6   Jacquet, Pierre, 'EMU: A Worthwhile Gamble', *International Affairs*, vol. 74, no. 1, January 1998, 55–71.

7   Wyplosz, Charles, 'EMU: Why and How It Might Happen', *Journal of Economic Perspectives*, vol. 11, no. 4, fall 1997, 3–22.

8   Feldstein, Martin, 'The Political Economy of the European Economic and Monetary Union: Political Sources of an Economic Liability', *Journal of Economic Perspectives*, vol. 11, no. 4, fall 1997, 23–42.

9   Siedentop, Larry, *Democracy in Europe*, Penguin Books: London, 2001.

## 40 Parallel currency proposals

1 Russell, Henry B., *International Monetary Conferences*, Harper Brothers: New York and London, 1898, 403.
2 I have been unable to find any other reference to this initiative.
3 Marshall, Alfred, *Official Papers*, ed. J. M. Keynes, Macmillan for Royal Economic Society, London, 1926.
4 Coleman, Andrew, 'Three Perspectives on an Australasian Monetary Union', paper to conference on 'Future Directions for Monetary Policies in East Asia', H. C. Coombs Centre for Financial Studies, Kirribilli (Sydney) NSW, 24 July 2001.
5 Giorgio Basevi, Italy; Michele Fratanni and Theo Peeters, Belgium; Herbert Giersch, Germany; Pieter Korteweg, Netherlands; David O'Mahony, Ireland; Michael Parkin, UK; Pascal Salin, France; and Niels Thygesen, Denmark.
6 This parallels the arguments in Chown and Wood (1989) (see note 13 above) which came down in favour of the basket Ecu (which could be introduced without formal agreements) over the 'hard Ecu' (which was otherwise much more attractive in giving better protection against inflation).
7 Kindleberger, Charles H., *Financial History of Western Europe*, George Allen & Unwin: London, 1984, 458–9.
8 Federal Trust for Education and Research, 'Report on European Monetary Integration', reprinted as appendix to G. Magnifico, *European Monetary Unification*, Wiley: New York, 1973, 199–222.
9 Meade, J. E. (1990) 'A Blueprint for a European Central Bank', Open Forum Pamphlet no. 7, Hebden Royale Publications, Hebden Bridge, 1990.
10 Giersch, Herbert, 'Hardening the Euro', *Central Banking*, vol. VIII, no. 4, spring 1998.
11 Chown, John and Geoffrey Wood, 'The Right Road to Monetary Union', Institute of Economic Affairs: London, 2 October 1989 (IEA Inquiry no. 11). Also published in *Economic Affairs*, February/March 1990; and reprinted in Russell Lewis (ed.) *Recent Controversies in Political Economy*, Routledge: London, 1992.
12 Johnson, Christopher, *In with the Euro Out with the Pound*, Penguin: London, 1996, 43, 151, table 18.
13 Our proposals were sometimes confused with the 'hard Ecu' ones discussed below. These were technically different approaches, with the same objective.
14 British Invisible Exports Council, 'The Next Stage in an Evolutionary Approach to Monetary Union', BIEC: London, March 1990.
15 Governor of the Bank of England, 11 July 1990.
16 *Ibid.*
17 *Ibid.*
18 Fry, Maxwell J., 'The Hard Ecu and Alternative Paths to European Monetary Union', IFGWP (International Financial Group, University of Birmingham Working Paper) no. 28, 1990, 90–3.
19 Vanthoor, Wim F. D., *A Chronological History of the European Union 1946–1998*, Edward Elgar: Cheltenham, 1999, 120.
20 *Ibid.*, 122.

## 41 Exchange control

1 Mann, F. A. *The Legal Aspect of Money*, 4th edn, Clarendon Press: Oxford, 1982, 355–6.

2 Text from Gold, Joseph, 'Article VIII 2 (b) of the IMF Articles in Its International Setting', *Studies in Transnational Economic Law*, vol. 6, Boston MA, 1989.

3 *Ibid.*, 105.

4 Evitt, H. E., *Exchange and Trade Control in Theory and Practice*, Pitman: London, 1945, 43–8.

5 Tew, Brian, *The Evolution of the International Monetary System 1945–77*, Hutchinson: London, 1977, 41; Scammell, W. M., *International Monetary Policy*, London: Macmillan, 1957, 246.

6 Chown, John, *The Taxation of Multinational Enterprise*, Longman: London, 1974, gives a fuller account of exchange control practices at that time.

## 42 The collapse of the Soviet Union

1 Service, Robert, *A History of Twentieth Century Russia*, Penguin: London, 1997, chs 23–5, gives a more general account of these events.

2 Gaidar, Yegor, *Days of Defeat and Victory*, original edn 1996, trans. Jane Ann Miller, University of Washington Press: Seattle and London, 1999.

3 Service, Robert, *A History of Twentieth Century Russia*, Penguin: London, 1997, 490.

4 Layard, Richard and John Parker, *The Coming Russian Boom*, The Free Press: New York, 1996, 50.

5 Service, Robert, *A History of Twentieth Century Russia*, Penguin: London, 1997, 492.

## 43 The end of the rouble zone

1 Conway, Patrick, 'Currency Proliferation: The Monetary Legacy of the Soviet Union', *Princeton Essays in International Finance*, no. 197, June 1995, 1.

2 Gaidar, Yegor, *Days of Defeat and Victory*, original edn 1996, trans. Jane Ann Miller, University of Washington Press: Seattle and London, 1999, 66.

3 Shleifer, Andrei and Daniel Trieisman, *Without a Map: Political Tactics and Economic Reform in Russia*, MIT Press: Cambridge MA, 2000.

4 Gaidar, Yegor, *Days of Defeat and Victory*, original edn 1996, trans. Jane Ann Miller, University of Washington Press: Seattle and London, 1999, 78–9.

5 Aslund, Anders, *How Russia Became a Market Economy*, Brookings Institution: Washington DC, 1995, ch. 4.

6 Granville, Brigitte, 'The Problem of Monetary Stanbilisation', in Brigitte Granville and Peter M. Oppenheimer (eds) *Russia's Post Communist Economy*, Oxford University Press: Oxford, 2001.

7 Skidelsky, Robert and Liam Halligan, *Macroeconomic Stabilisation in Russia: Lessons of Reform 1992–1995*, Social Market Foundation: London, 1996, 17.

8 Gaidar, Yegor, *Days of Defeat and Victory*, original edn 1996, trans. Jane Ann Miller, University of Washington Press: Seattle and London, 1999, 82–83.

9 Gaidar, Yegor, Robbins Lectures, 4–6 May 1993, quoted in Skidelsky and Halligan 1996.

10 Goldberg, Linda, Barry Ickes and Randi Ryterman, 'Departures from the Ruble Zone: The Implications of Adopting Independent Currencies', *The World Economy*, 1994/5, 303–4.

11 Conway, Patrick, 'Currency Proliferation: The Monetary Legacy of the Soviet Union', Princeton Essays in International Finance no. 197, June 1995, 39.

12 Aslund, Anders, *How Russia Became a Market Economy*, Brookings Institution: Washington DC, 1995, 112.

13 Shagalov, George, Urpo Kivikari and Eric Brunat, 'The Euro as an Instrument for Promoting Russian-CIS Trade and Economic Growth', *Russian Economic Trends*, 2001.

14 Conway, Patrick, 'Currency Proliferation: The Monetary Legacy of the Soviet Union', Princeton Essays in International Finance no. 197, June 1995, 38.

15 Goldberg, Linda, Barry Ickes and Randi Ryterman, 'Departures from the Ruble Zone: The Implications of Adopting Independent Currencies', *The World Economy*, 1994/5, 318.

16 Aslund, Anders, *How Russia Became a Market Economy*, Brookings Institution: Washington DC, 1995, 218.

17 Layard, Richard and John Parker, *The Coming Russian Boom*, The Free Press: New York, 1996.

## 44 The twelve CIS countries following monetary disunion

1 Chown, John and Geoffrey Wood, 'Russia's Currency – How the West can Help', *Central Banking*, vol. 3, no. 3, winter 1992–3, 39–46.

2 Hanke, Steve H., Lars Jonung and Kurt Schuler, *Russian Currency and Finance: A Currency Board Approach to Reform*, Routledge: London, 1993.

3 Auerbach, P., G. Davidson and J. Rostowski, 'Secondary Currencies and High Inflation: Implications for Monetary Theory and Policy' LSE Centre for Economic Performance Discussion Paper no. 58: London.

4 'The Remonetisation of the Commonwealth of Independent States in The Road back from Serfdom: A Tribute to Friedrich A. Hayek', *American Economic Review*, May 1992.

5 There were other contributions to the discussion. For instance P. Auerbach, G. Davidson and J. Rostowski ('Secondary Currencies and High Inflation: Implications for Monetary Theory and Policy', LSE Centre for Economic Performance Discussion Paper no. 58) also reached similar conclusions using a different analytical approach; while Samantha Carrington ('The Remonetisation of the Commonwealth of Independent States', in 'The Road back from Serfdom: A Tribute to Friedrich A. Hayek', *American Economic Review*, May 1992) envisaged the creation of 'new rubles', with the United States guaranteeing 'to convert the fixed number of new rubles that are going to be created into US dollars on a one-to-one basis in perpetuity'.

6 *Central Banking*, Autumn 1996, 133–38.

7 Granville, Brigitte, 'The Problem of Monetary Stabilisation', in Brigitte Granville and Oppenheimer (eds) *Russia's Post Communist Economy*, Oxford University Press: Oxford, 2001,110.

8 *Russian Economic Trends 1998*, 14.

9 In my day job as an international tax and financial market specialist, we had been studying ways through the maze, as we had done with Brazil some years earlier. We maintained a spreadsheet, updated weekly, of the corrected returns for individual securities.

10 Giedroyc, Richard, 'Belarus Has Short Stormy Numismatic History', *Newsletter of the Russian Numismatic Society*, spring 2001.

11 Nell, Jacob, 'Stabilising the Lari', *Central Banking*, Autumn 1995.

12 Kakukia, Merab and Nana Aslamazishvili, 'Dollarisation in Georgia: Size of Problem, Factors and the Ways of Solution'.

13 Kaser, Michael, 'Stabilisation and Reform: Experience of Five Central Asian States', conference paper (where and when?) 'Session IV'.

**45 The Baltic states from 1991: successful monetary reform**

1   Leimus, Ivar, *Eesti Vabariigi Rahad 1918–1992*, in Estonian with English and Russian summaries, copiously illustrated, including a catalogue of notes and coins, Olion: Tallinn, 1993.
2   Giedroyc, Richard, 'Estonia's Currency System Well Planned', *Journal of the Russian Numismatic Society*, no. 71, winter 2001.
3   Tomas, J. T. and Charles Enoch Balino, 'Currency Board Arrangements, Issues and Experience', IMF Occasional Paper: Washington DC, August 1997, 43.
4   Bennett, Adam G. G., 'The Operation of the Estonian Currency Board', IMF Staff Papers, vol. 40, no. 2, June 1993.
5   Hanke, Steve H., Lars Jonung and Kurt Schuler, *Monetary Reform for a Free Estonia: A Currency Board Solution*, 1992.
6   Viksnins, George J. and Ilmars Rimshevitchs, 'The Latvian Monetary Reform', in Thomas D. Willett, Richard C. K. Burdekin, Richard J. Sweeney and Clas Wihlborg (eds) *Establishing Monetary Stability in Emerging Market Economies*, Westview Press: Boulder, 1995.
7   Private conversation with Helmuts Ancans of the Bank of Latvia, May 1999.
8   'Currency Board Arrangements', IMF 1997, 43.
9   Reedik, Reet, 'Real Exchange Rate Indices Measures of Competitivenes. The Case of Central and Eastern Europe', University of Tartu.http://www.CEP. Yale.edu/projects/studcon/papers/97/redik.html/.


**46 The break-up of Yugoslavia**

1   'Croatia Stablises the Kuna', *Central Banking*, vol. VI, no. 3, 46.
2   'What About a Currency Board?', *Central Banking*, vol. X, no. 3, February 2000, 50–5.
3   Trpeski, Ljube, 'Ten Years from the Monetary Independence of the Republic of Macedonia', 2001. National Bank of the Republic of Macedonia's website at http://www.nbrm.gov.mk. website).
4   Nicholl, Peter, 'Report from Bosnia and Herzegovina', *Central Banking*, vol. IX, no. 4, May 1999.
5   Nicholl, Peter, 'Euro Benefits in the Balkans', *Central Banking*, vol. XII, no. 4, May 2002.


**48 The end of the sterling area**

1   Bell, Philip W., *The Sterling Area in the Postwar World 1946–52*, Oxford University Press: Oxford, 1956.
2   Davies, Glyn, *A History of Money From Ancient Times to the Present Day*, University of Wales Press: Cardiff, 1994, 609, citing Ajayi, S. I. and O. O. Ojo, *Money and Banking in the Nigerian Context*, n.p.: London, 1981; Nwanko, G. O., *The Nigerian Financial System*, n.p.: London, 1980.
3   Eyo, Ekpo, *Nigeria and the Evolution of Money*, Central Bank of Nigeria, 1979, 100.


**49 The Irish pound**

1   Honohan, Patrick, 'Currency Board or Central Bank? Lessons from the Irish Pound's Link with Sterling 1928–79', CEPR Discussion Paper Series no. 1040, October 1994, CEPR: London.
2   *Ibid.*

3 Tomas, J. T. and Charles Enoch Balino, 'Currency Board Arrangements, Issues and Experience', IMF Occasional Paper 151: Washington DC, August 1997.
4 Donald J. Mathieson and Liliana Rojus Suarez, 'The Liberalisation of the Capital Account: Experience and Issues', IMF Occasional Paper 103: Washington DC, March 1993, 10–11.
5 Browne, F. X. and Paul D. McNelis, 'Exchange Controls and Interest Rate Determination with Traded and Nontraded Assets: The Irish-United Kingdom Experience', *Journal of Money and Finance*, March 1990, 41–59.
6 Honohan, Patrick, *Costing the Delay in Devaluing 1992–93*, The Irish Banking Review, Dublin, spring 1994.

## 50 The former French colonies: the CFA franc zone

1 Fielding, David, *The Macroeconomics of Monetary Union: An Analysis of the CFA Franc Zone*, Routledge: London, 2002.
2 *Ibid.*, 190.
3 *Ibid.*, 5.
4 *Ibid.*, 187.
5 Clement, Jean A. P. 'Aftermath of the CFA Franc Devaluation', IMF Occasional Paper: Washington DC, May 1996, 1–3.
6 *Ibid.*, 3.
7 Addison, Ernest, 'Towards a Common Currency for West Africa', *Central Banking*, vol. XII, no. 3, February 2002, 49–58.
8 Hadjimichael, Michael T. and Michel Galy, 'The CFA Franc Zone and the EMU', IMF Occasional Paper: Washington DC November 1997.
9 Pick, Albert, *Standard Catalog of World Paper Money*, Krause Publications: Iola WI, various edns.

## 51 Monetary unions in former colonies

1 Van Beek, Frits, Jose Roberto Rosales, Mayra Zermeno, Ruby Randall and Jorge Shepherd, 'The Eastern Caribbean Currency Union: Institutions, Performance and Policy Issues', IMF Occasional Paper 195: Washington DC, July 2000.
2 See Marion V. Williams, *Liberalising a Regulated Banking System: The Caribbean Case*, Avebury: Aldershot, 1996, for other aspects of the banking system.
3 Addison, Ernest, 'Towards a Common Currency for West Africa', *Central Banking*, vol. XII, no. 3, February 2002, 49–58.
4 Masson, Paul and Catherine Pattillo, 'Monetary Union in West Africa (ECOWAS): Is It Desirable and Could It Be Achieved?', IMF Occasional Paper 204: Washington DC, 2001.
5 Addison, Ernest, 'Towards a Common Currency for West Africa', *Central Banking*, vol. XII, no. 3, February 2002, 54.

## 52 Two monetary unions that didn't happen: US/Canada and ANZAC

1 Grubel, Herbert, *The case for the Amero: the Economics and Politics of a North American Monetary Union*, Fraser Institute: Vancouver, 1999.
2 Laidler, David and Finn Poschmann, 'Leaving Well Enough Alone: Canada's Monetary Order in a Changing International Environment', C. D. Howe Institute: Toronto, May 2000.

3   Harris, Richard G., 'The Case for North American Monetary Union', *ISUMA*, vol. 11, no. 1, spring 2000, ISSN 11492–062X, http:/www.isuma.net/v01n01/harris/harris.htm.
4   Sayers, R. S., *The Bank of England 1891–1944*, vol. 1, Cambridge University Press: Cambridge, 1976, 204.
5   Grimes, Arthur and Frank Holmes with Roger Bowden, *An Anzac Dollar? Currency Union and Business Development*, Institute of Policy Studies, Victoria University of Wellington: Wellington, 2000.
 6   Coleman, Andrew, 'Economic Integration and Monetary Union', New Zealand Treasury Working Paper 99/6: Wellington, 1999.
 7   Hargreaves, David and John McDermott, *Issues relating to Optimum Currency Areas: Theory and Implications for New Zealand*. Reserve Bank of New Zealand Bulletin, 62, 16-29.
 8   Brash, Don, 'The Pros and Cons of Currency Union: A Reserve Bank Perspective', address to the Auckland Rotary Club, 22 May 2000. Available on RBNZ website.
 9   Coleman, Andrew, 'Three Perspectives on an Australasian Monetary Union', paper to conference on 'Future Directions for Monetary Policies in East Asia', H. C. Coombs Centre for Financial Studies, Kirribilli (Sydney) NSW, 24 July 2001.
10   Rich, Georg, *The Cross of Gold: Money and the Canadian Business Cycle 1867–1913*, Carleton University Press: Ottawa, 1988.
11   Wonnacott, Paul, *The Canadian Dollar, 1948–1962*, University of Toronto Press: Toronto, 1965.
12   *Report of the Royal Commission on Banking and Currency in Canada*, J. Paternaude: Ottawa, 1933.

## 53  Postwar Latin America

 1   Bulmer-Thomas, Victor, *The Economic History of Latin America since Independence*, Cambridge University Press: Cambridge, 1994, 177–9.
 2   *Ibid.*, 202–4.
 3   Edwards, Sebastian, 'Exchange Rates, Inflation and Disinflation: Latin American Experiences', ch. 12 in *Capital Controls, Exchange Rates and Monetary Policy in the World Economy*, Cambridge University Press: Cambridge, 1993.
 4   Kiguel, Miguel A. and Nissan Liviatan, 'Stopping three Big Inflations: Argentina Brazil and Peru', in Rudiger Dornbusch and Sebastian Edwards (eds) *Reform, Recovery and Growth: Latin America and Middle East*, University of Chicago Press: Chicago, 1993(?).
 5   Wise, Carol and Riordan Roett (eds), *Exchange Rate Politics in Latin America*, Brookings Institution: Washington DC, 2000.
 6   Pow, Pedro, 'Argentina's Structional Reforms of the 1990s', *Finance and Development* (IMF) March 2000.
 7   Calvo, Guillermo A., 'Argentina's Dollarisation Project: A Primer', photocopy, Argentina, 18 February 1999.
 8   Friedman, Milton, 'Chile and Israel: Identical Policies, Opposite Outcomes', in *Money Mischief*, Harcourt Brace: New York, 1992.
 9   Edwards, Sebastian, *Capital Controls, Exchange Rates and Monetary Policy in the World Economy*, Cambridge University Press: Cambridge, 1993, 327.

## 54  Hong Kong and the Far East post-1945

 1   Text in *Documentary History of Banking and Currency in the United States*, 4 vols, introduction by Paul A. Samuelson, ed. Herman F. Kross, Chelsea House Publishers: New York, 1969–83, vol. IV, 256–61.

2 Yum K. Kwan and Francis Lui, 'Hong Kong's Currency Board and Changing Monetary Regimes', National Bureau of Economic Research, Cambridge MA, Working Paper 5723, August 1996.

3 Alan Walters, *AIG World Market Advisory*, privately circulated newsletter, American Insurance Group, May 1994.

4 Friedman, Milton, 'FDR, Silver, and China', in *Money Mischief*, Harcourt Brace: New York, 1992.

5 Pyle, David J., *China's Economy: From Revolution to Reform*, Macmillan: London 1997.

6 *Ibid.*, 137–49.

7 *Ibid.*, 154.

8 Fischer, Stanley, 'The Asian Crisis: The Return of Growth', International Monetary Fund, 17 June 1999. Obtained from IMF website at http://www.imf.org/external/np/speeches/1999/061799.HTM.

9 Schwartz, Anna, 'Do Currency Boards Have a Future?', IEA Occasional Paper 88, November 1992.

10 Cohen, Warren I. and Li Zhao (eds), *Hong Kong under Chinese Rule: The Economic and Political Implications of Reversion*, Cambridge University Press: Cambridge.

11 *Ibid.*, 143–7.

12 *Ibid.*, 18.

13 Tomas, J. T. and Charles Enoch Balino, 'Currency Board Arrangements, Issues and Experience', IMF Occasional Paper: Washington DC, August 1997, 27.

# Index